JEWS AND GREEKS IN ANCIENT CYRENE

BY

SHIM'ON APPLEBAUM

LEIDEN
E. J. BRILL
1979

To my Parents,
who worked for the brotherhood of man,

and

to Courtney Edward Stevens,
my teacher.

εὐάρματον

πόλιν ἐν ἀργεννόεντι μαστῷ . . .

Ἀλλὰ ἐπιστήσει τὲ κακῶν αἰῶνι τρόπαια.

CONTENTS

PREFACE

The origin of this book can be traced to my somewhat drastic translation from the GHQ Press, Cairo, in the year 1943, to an undefined posting which turned out to be the care of the Antiquities of Cyrenaica for the British Military Administration of that territory.

The task was not an easy one, and some of its problems had to be faced alone and unassisted, while the rank of sergeant that went with it was not always commensurate with what was demanded of me. I also had to tackle the job with a minimum of literature and experience of Greek antiquities. Not all the archaeologists who devoted themselves to the territory after my release seem to have appreciated the difficlut conditions in which I had to work. But it was an invaluable training in epigraphy, in field archaeology, in the study and conservation of excavated urban sites and in the surveying of their rural background. Above all, by virtually living for eighteen months in an ancient Greek city I was able greatly to enlarge my understanding of the hellenic religion.

But I also encountered an unanticipated facet of the country's history. My daily work in Cyrene revealed to me slowly but ever more clearly the historical episode known to Jews as "the revolt of the Diaspora" and to the Roman authorities of that time as the *tumultus Iudaicus*. In Egypt this rebellion is reflected chiefly in the papyri; in Cyrenaica it presents itself to view in inscriptions, in the destruction of inhabited centres and in the restoration of buildings. All this awoke in me the desire to explore the roots and character of the revolt in relation to the country's nature and history.

Much new work has been carried out in the realm of Cyrenaican studies both by historians and archaeologists since the present book appeared in Hebrew in 1969. This has involved much reading of new material and a considerable revision of the original text. The principal thesis of the work nevertheless remains as it was.

My first thanks must go to Professor Alexander Fuks, whose influence in no small measure enabled the publication of this book

in Hebrew. It has been to the enthusiasm of Professor J. Neusner
and of Messrs Brill that I owe the printing of the English version. I
can only mention a few of those who have assisted me in the scholarly field: such were Professor A. Schalit, Peter Fraser, Miss
Joyce Reynolds, Professor P. Romanelli, Dr. Ruth Neuberger,
Dr. A. Kasher and Professor David Asheri.

Among those who encouraged and aided me, and are no longer
able to read of my appreciation, were Sir John Myres, who en-
couraged me to continue the work, my teacher and friend C. E.
Stevens, who read and criticized the first text, Professor Sir E.
Evans-Pritchard, whose understanding of the physiography of
Cyrenaica gave me the key to its history, Dr. Irene Garbel, Sir
Ian Richmond, Professor V. Tcherikover, R. G. Goodchild and
Professor Ḥ. Z. Hirschberg. It was the late Professor M. Avi-
Yonah who first drew my attention, in one of his articles, to the
historical importance of the *ager publicus* in the Roman history of
the territory. I also learned much from Dr. Frederick Wilson, who
was then serving in Cyrenaica.*

I was able to carry out the present translation and revision of
the Hebrew version of this book in the year 1972-3 while enjoying
the generous hospitality of All Souls College, Oxford. In the revision
of the text from recent studies I am greatly indebted to the biblio-
graphical guidance of Michael Vickers. I also received the assistance
of the Deutsche Archäologische Institut and of the Istituto
Italiano di Cultura in Israel, in the person of Professor A. Gerline,
in the obtaining of illustrations; and of the Royal Botanical
Gardens, Kew, for botanical advice. Thanks are due to the Faculty
of Arts of Tel Aviv University for a grant towards the preparation of the maps.

Finally I recall with appreciation the support of Brigadier
General Sir Duncan Cumming, Chief Administrator of Cyrenaica
during my service there, no less the assistance and encouragement
of Major M. Hyslop, then antiquities officer of Tripolitania and
Cyrenaica, during his visits to the latter territory.

---

* Since the above was written, Professor Fuks has, to my great sorrow,
joined those who can no longer read these lines.

Last but not least, I would remember the aid of many Libyan friends, whom I would be glad to meet again over a pot of tea and mint-leaves.

Tel Aviv University, Dept. of Jewish History
April, 1977

We here record our thanks to the Chaim Rosenberg School of Jewish Studies of Tel Aviv University, who have borne the expense of the author's corrections incurred during the printing of this book.

ABBREVIATIONS

AA   *Archäologischer Anzeiger—Beiblatt zum Jahrbuch des Deutschen Archäologischen Instituts.* 1885-

ABA   *Abhandlungen der Berliner Akademie, Philologisch-Historische Klasse.*

ABP   F. Heichelheim, *Die Auswärtige Bevölkerung des Ptolemäerreiches* — Klio Beiheft, XVIII. 1925.

AC   *Agricoltura Coloniale.* 1922-

AE   *L'année épigraphique* — *Supplément de Revue archéologique.* 1888-

AI   *Africa Italiana.* I-1927; II-1928-9; III-1930; IV-1931; V-1933; VI-1935; VII-1940.

AJA   *American Journal of Archaeology.* 2nd series, 1897-

Antiq   *Antiquity.* 1927-

AP   *Archiv für Papyrusforschung.* 1900-

APM   H. A. Musurillo, *The Acts of the Pagan Martyrs.* 1954.

ASAA   *Annuario della Scuola archeologica di Atene.* 1914-

BASOR   *Bulletin of the American Schools of Oriental Research.* 1919.

BCH   *Bulletin de correspondence hellénique.* 1876-

BGU   *Ägyptische Urkunden aus dem staatlichen Museum zu Berlin: Griechische Urkunden.* 1895-

BIDR   *Bolletino del Istituto di diritto romano.* 1888-

BIES   *Bulletin of the Israel Exploration Society.* 1950-

BJ   *Bonner Jahrbücher.* 1895-

BMA   *British Military Administration Handbooks for Cyrenaica.* 1943.

BMC   E. S. G. Robinson, *Catalogue of Greek Coins in the British Museum: Cyrenaica.* 1927.

BSA   *Annual of the British School at Athens.* 1900-

BSAA   *Bulletin de la société royale d'archéologie d'Alexandrie.* 1904-

CAH   *Cambridge Ancient History.* 1924-39.

CERP   A. H. M. Jones, *Cities of the Eastern Roman Provinces.* 1938.

CIG   A. Boeckh, *Corpus Inscriptionum Graecarum.* 1825-77.

CIJ   J. B. Frey, *Corpus Inscriptionum Judaicarum*, I, 1936; II, 1952.

CIL   Mommsen, Hübner et al., *Corpus Inscriptionum Latinarum.* 1863-

CIC   T. Mommsen, *Corpus Iuris Civilis*, 1911.

CMB   F. Chamoux, *Cyrène sous la monarchie des Battiades.* 1953.

CPJ   F. Tcherikover, A. Fuks, *Corpus Papyrorum Judaicarum.* I-III. 1957-64.

CR   P. Romanelli, *La Cirenaica romana.* 1943.

CRAI   *Contes-rendues de l'Académie des Inscriptions et Belles-Lettres.* 1865-

DO   H. W. Parke, D. E. W. Wormell, *The Delphic Oracle.* I, II, 1956.

DAI   *Documenti antichi dell' Africa Italiana*: I, Cirenaica, i, 1932; I, Cirenaica, ii, 1933; II, Cirenaica, i, 1933; II, Cirenaica, ii, 1936.

DS   C. Daremberg, E. Saglio, *Dictionnaire des antiquités grecques et romaines.* 1877-1919.

EI	*Enciclopedia Italiana.* 1929-1939.
EL	O. Bates, *The Eastern Libyans.* 1914.
ESAR	Tenney Frank (ed.), *An Economic Survey of Ancient Rome.* I-V, 1933-40.
FA	*Fasti Archaeologici.* 1946-
FGH	F. Jacoby, *Die Fragmente der griechischen Historiker.* 1926.
FHG	C. Müller, *Fragmenta Historicorum Graecorum.* 1841-70.
GJ	*The Geographical Journal.* 1893-
GJV	E. Schürer, *Geschichte des jüdischen Volkes im Zeitalter Jesu Christi.* I-III, 1909.
GS	G. Busolt, *Griechische Staatskunde.* I, II, 1920, 1926.
GSAI	*Giornale della societa asiatica Italiana.* 1887-
Ha	*Historia.* 1950-
HC	W. W. Tarn, G. T. Griffith, *Hellenistic Civilization.* 1952.
HCJ	V. Tcherikòver, *Hellenistic Civilization and the Jews.* 1959.
IEJ	*Israel Exploration Journal.* 1950-
IG	A. Boeck et al., *Inscriptiones Graecae.* 1873-
IGR	R. Cagnat, G. Lafaye, *Inscriptiones Graecae ad res Romanas pertinentes.* 1911-27.
ILCV	E. Diehl, *Inscriptiones Latinae Christianae Veteres.* I-III, 1925-31.
ILS	H. Dessau, *Inscriptiones Latinae Selectae.* I-III, 1892-1916.
JEA	*Journal of Egyptian Archaeology.* 1914-
JHS	*Journal of Hellenic Studies.* 1880-
JSS	*Journal of Jewish Studies.* 1948/9-
JPCI	S. Klein, *Jüdische-palästinensisches Corpus Inscriptionum.* 1920.
JPOS	*Journal of the Palestine Oriental Society.* 1920/1-
JQR	*Jewish Quarterly Review.* 1889-
JRS	*Journal of Roman Studies.* 1910-
MGH	*Monumenta Germanica Historica (Auctorum antiquissimorum).* 1877-
MUC	A. Rowe, D. Buttle, J. Gray. *The Cyrenaican Expedition of the University of Manchester,* 1952. 1956.
NAMC	*Notizie archeologice del Ministerio dei Colonie:* I-1915; II-1916; III-1922; IV-1927.
NC	*Numismatic Chronicle.* 1860-
NMA	F. Preisigke, *Namenbuch enthaltend alle Menschennamen soweit sie in griechischen Urkunden Ägyptens sich vorfinden.* 1922.
NV	M. Norsa, G. Vitelli, *Studi e testi: Il papiro greco Vaticano* 11. 1931.
OGIS	W. Dittenberger, *Orientis Graecae Inscriptiones Selectae.* 1903-05.
PBSR	*Papers of the British School at Rome.* 1895-
PEQ	*Palestine Exploration Quarterly.* 1937-
PG	Migne: *Cursus Patrologiae, Series Graeca.* 1886.
PL	Migne: *Cursus Patrologiae, Series Latina.* 1844.
PO	R. Graffin, F. Nau, *Patrologia Orientalis.*
PP	*Le Parola del Passato.* 1946-
PW	A. Pauly, G. Wissowa, W. Kroll, *Realenzyklopädie der Classischen Altertumswissenschaft.* 1893-
QAL	*Quaderni del archeologia della Libia.* 1950-
QDAP	*Quarterly of the Department of Antiquities of Palestine.* 1932-1949.

RA   *Revue archéologique.* 1844-
RAL   *Rendiconti della Reale Accademia dei Lincei.* 1884-
RC   J. Thrige, *Res Cyrenensium* (1825), ed. S. Ferri. 1943.
REA   *Revue des études anciennes.* 1898-
REC   *Rassegna economica dei colonie italiane.* 1926-
REG   *Revue des études grecques.* 1888-
R ét J   *Revue des études juives.* 1880-
RFC   *Rivista di Filologia Classica.* 1922-
RH   *Revue historique.* 1876-
RIC   E. Pantanelli, *Le Risorse idriche della Cirenaica.* 1940.
RL   *Rendiconti della reale Accademia dei Lincei.* 1884-
RM   *Rheinisches Museum für Philologie.* 1827-
SB   F. Preisigke, F. Bilabel, *Sammelbuch griechischer Urkunden aus Ägypten.* 1915-
SCC   G. Narducci, *Storia della colonizzazione della Cirenaica.* 1942.
SEG   *Supplementum Epigraphicum Graecum:* IX-1938; XVI-1959; XVII-1960; XX-1964.
SEHHW   M. Rostovtzeff, *A Social and Economic History of the Hellenistic World.* I-III, 1941.
SEHRE   M. Rostovtzeff, *A Social and Economic History of the Roman Empire.* I-II, 1957.
SGDI   H. Collitz, F. Bechtel, *Sammlung der griechischen Dialekt-Inschriften.* 1884-1915.
SH   *Scripta Hierosolymitana.* 1954-
SHA   *Scriptores Historiae Augustae.*
SIG   W. Dittenberger, *Sylloge Inscriptionum Graecarum.* 1915-24.
SP   R. M. Smith, E. A. Porcher, *A History of the Discoveries at Cyrene.* 1864.
SRHJ   S. W. Baron, *A Social and Religious History of the Jews.* 1952-
TA   L. Pernier, *Il Tempio e altare di Apollo a Cirene.* 1935.
TRJ   T. Reinach, *Textes d'auteurs grecs et romains relatifs au Judaïsme* 1895.
WGA   F. Heichelheim, *Wirtschaftsgeschichte des Altertums.* I, II, 1938.
WGE   G. Papé, G. Benseler, *Wörterbuch der griechischen Eigennamen.* 1911. 2nd ed. 1959.
ZDPV   *Zeitschrift des Deutschen Palästinavereins.* 1878-
ZNTW   *Zeitschrift für Neutestamentliche Wissenschaft.* 1900-

CHAPTER ONE

THE LAND OF THE CYRENES

The peculiar geographical characteristic of Cyrenaica is its relative isolation from other centres of ancient culture: it is in effect a desert oasis cut off on the east and south by desert tracts, and on the north and west, by the sea.[1] The country differs geologically from the surrounding areas, resembling as it does mainland Greece in its landscape and character. Because of its geographical situation, Cyrene's entry into the sphere of ancient culture depended on the development of sea-routes, yet even this development did not lead immediately to settlement, since the Phoenicians, did not lead immediately to settlement, since the Phoenicians, for example, in their quest for lands with abundant natural resources, Greeks reached Libya comparatively late in their period of overseas colonization, evidently on account of population growth in their home-country, and settled Cyrene because the coasts to east and west had been long occupied by other peoples, or were hardly worth settling. Unlike the Phoenicians, the Greeks settled in their new country primarily to earn their living by agriculture, and turned to commerce only subsequently.[2]

Cyrene's isolation from the continent, and the prevailing Mediterranean winds, destined her to be a *point d'appuie* for European civilization in Africa, although the same isolation impressed upon her certain cultural features of her own and determined her distinctive development. Thus, for a long time the country was more

---

[1] On the geography of Cyrenaica, G. Narducci, *SCC*, 1942; R. Horn, *Die Antike*, 19, 1943, pp. 163 sqq.; E. Evans Pritchard, *BMA* 7, 1943, Cyrenaican Tribes = idem, *The Sanusi of Cyrenaica*, 1949, pp. 29 sqq.; H. W. Ahlmann, *La Libia Settentrionale*, 1930; *EI* 10, 1931, pp. 417 sqq. sv. Cirenaica; M. Cary, *The Geographic Background of Greek and Roman History*, 1949; F. Chamoux, *CMB*, 1953, Introduction, pp. 11-17; R. G. Goodchild, *Tabula Imperii Romani, Cyrene*, 1954; C. B. M. Burney, R. W. Hey, *Prehistory and Pleistocene Geology in Cyrenaican Libya*, 1955, pp. 5 sqq.; W. B. Fisher, *The Middle East*, 1956, pp. 485 sqq. For bibliography till 1959, R. W. Hill, *A Bibliography of Libya*, Univ. of Durham, 1959.
[2] Cf. E. Kirsten, *Die griechische Polis als historisch-geographisches Problem des Mittelmeeres*, 1956, pp. 70 sqq.; H. Bengtson, *Griechische Geschichte*, I, 1960, pp. 86 sqq.

closely connected with Crete and Greece than with the remaining
regions of Africa, and her links with Egypt, made permanent by
the conquests of Alexander the Great, only became really stable
under Roman rule. Rome recognized the situation for what it was
when she united Cyrene administratively, not with Tripolitania or
with Egypt, but with Crete, a striking testimony to Cyrene's
position on the part of a power so skilled in the creation and maintenance of communications. Only under Diocletian was Cyrene
attached to Egypt.[3]

The difficulties facing Cyrene's links with Europe, nevertheless,
should not be exaggerated. Till recently the country was thought to
lack good harbours, since her coast is rocky but not strongly in-
dented. The scarp of the Jebel al-Aḥdar, indeed, closes upon the
shore and renders difficult access to the interior, and the only
large port on the west, Bengazi, is exposed to the northern gales.
Recent surveys, however,[4] have shown that the central sector of
the coast possesses several small but viable bays suitable for the
light vessels of ancient times (Phycus, Ausigda, and Naustathmos)
in addition to the more important harbours of Ptolemais and
Apollonia. The Greek colonists settled near the coast, and there
generally remained; their two most ancient and notable inland
settlements, Cyrene and Barka, ultimately lost their importance,
which passed to their daughter-harbours, Apollonia and Ptolemais.
This was caused, not only by the Greek reluctance to live far from
the sea, but also by the country's dependance on maritime communications and by the growing pressure of the native nomadic
tribes. Even more decisive was the climatic factor, since only near
the coast was rainfall sufficient for permanent agriculture without
the use of water stored by means of dams and cisterns. Thus a
certain contradiction was produced by a shortage of natural harbours and the necessity of sea communications, and this may
explain why Cyrene never became a seapower comparable to Athens,
Carthage or Rome.

The country can be divided into three zones, differing from one

---

[3] But in the second century of the current era, after the Jewish rebellion,
part of the country's eastern territory was transferred to Egypt, apparently
for economic reasons.

[4] G. D. B. Jones, J. H. Little, *JRS* 61, 1971, pp. 64 sqq., Coastal settlements of Cyrenaica.

another in soil, climate and natural features. These are the plateau
on the north (the Jebel al-Aḥdar), the steppe, and, southernmost,
the stony wastes that fade into the Sahara desert. The Jebel, the
most prominent feature of the country, is a karst massif of miocene
limestone, occupying the centre and greater part of the country,
bordering closely with the coast, and falling gradually on the south
through the steppe to the desert. It ends abruptly on the north,
where it is highest, and falls seaward by three scarps which create
two parallel terraces. The first and lowest, is a narrow strip not
exceeding eight kilometres in width as far as Teucheira (Tocra)
on the west; it is known as es-Sahal. It stretches from Bomba on
the east to the Gulf of Syrtis on the west. On the west the escarpment swings away from the coast, forming the plains of Tocra and
Bengazi between itself and the shore. The second terrace, known as
al-Lusaita ("the middle") is broader, narrowing as it goes eastward, but continuing broad to westward to become the fertile
Plain of Barka, today the granary of Cyrenaica. The western
Lusaita terrace curves south parallel with the Syrtic shore and
disappears near es-Sulidema. Its eastern termination is at the cape
of Ras-al-Tin. The Lusaita is cut by wadis, broken by bosses, and
covered by red soil washed from the stream beds. Along it runs the
Tariq al-Arqub, which may be compared with the ridgeways of the
south of England, and constituted without a doubt the most
ancient and fundamental route in the country. The third and
uppermost terrace occupies the plateau summit, the Sidi el-Hamrin,
the Jebel's broadest massif, that falls gradually towards the south;
its highest point is 800 m. above sea-level, and its scarp stretches
from Derna on the east to Barka on the west, though not continuous throughout the central Jebel. The central plateau is rocky and
cut by stream beds; part is undulating plainland, and there are
also enclosed dales of limited size. Near Cyrene, Messa, Barka and
al-Abbiar, there stretch considerable areas of fertile plainland. The
plateau is further penetrated from the south by numerous narrow
ravines, the most important being Wadi al-Kuf, which enters from
the south-west and ends in the heart of the Jebel to west of Messa.
This long deep ravine constitutes a hidden corridor of penetration
into the country's vitals, creating a grave problem in ancient times
for the defence of permanent settlement against the raids of desert-
dwellers.

Southward the green plateau fades into steppe, and on its desert fringe shallow depressions filled with eroded silt (Arabic:baltet) are to be found, divided from one another by low ridges. Finally the landscape becomes completely desert, with stretches of flint "ḥamadah" that form the approaches of the Saharah.

Cyrenaica is composed chiefly of Eocene and Oligocene limestones of marine origin;[5] the surface is covered chiefly by rocks of the Middle Miocene phase, permeable, fragmentated and honeycombed with numerous caves; the mountains of the Jebel are thus characterized by those features known geologically as Karst. It is these that determine the country's water supply, which will be discussed at a later stage. In the western coastal sector, between Tocra and Bengazi, much sea water penetrates inland below groundlevel, so forming saltwater lagoons which dry up in summer and furnish natural salt to the inhabitants.

The country's internal communications present no great difficulty, and run generally from east to west. The main difficulty is constituted by the ascent of the coastal terraces, and also of the plateau at its east and west ends, at Derna and Tocra respectively. The Tarik el-Arkub and routes along the upper ridge of the Plateau serve east-west traffic, while the southern foot of the Jebel is skirted from east to west by the ancient Tarik al-'Azizah, which links Bengazi with Derna. Despite the penetration of convenient stream beds into the Jebel from the south, there appears to be no evidence that Cyrene was directly linked in ancient times with any route traversing the Saharah from north to south; these southern approaches, indeed were barred by the Calanshu Sand Sea and by the wastes of the Jebel Zelten.[6]

The climate of Cyrenaica, which is subject to the influence both of the Mediterranean and the desert, resembles in many ways that of the south of Israel, but is rather cooler. From January to March temperatures of 12-14 degrees are usual, while in July and August 28-29 degrees are reached on the plateau. The fluctuations in the coastal belt are less extreme, and at the highest point of the Jebel and along its watershed there are sharp differences between day and night temperatures caused by the proximity of the desert. Winter rains mixed with sleet sometimes fall on the plateau, which occasionally also experiences frost. The Plateau summer tempera-

---

[5] For the geology of Cyrenaica, F. Mühlhofer, *Speleologica Cirenaica*, 1928; E. Pantanelli, *RIC*, 1940; Burney, Hey, n. 1.

[6] Burney, Hey, *op. cit.*, pp. 7-8.

tures are generally lower than those of the lower areas to west and south, but a hot wind, the Jibli, blows from the south in the autumn and spring and is apt to parch the field crops in their period of vital growth.

The country's precipitation is restricted to the winter, between October and May, and varies in quantity from area to area. The highest rainfall is about Cyrene near the summit of the Jebel, where the annual average is 600 mm, but may reach 1000 mm in good years. On the desert fringes and on the southern slopes of the Jebel, on the other hand, precipitation averages only 100 mm. Rainfall decreases from west to east and from north to south, averaging 200-300 mm at Bengazi, 400 mm along the north coast. The west coast, south of Bengazi, however, receives no more than 150-200 mm., and the same applies to the country's coast east of Martuba. But against these averages must be set the common view of the inhabitants, that drought is apt to recur every fourth year.

The rainy season coincides with the season of maximum coolness, which restricts evaporation; but the permeable character of the country's rocks causes the loss of much water by infiltration to deep strata, in so far as the runoff does not flow to waste in the wadis. On the other hand the Jebel's relatively high rainfall has caused the formation over certain areas of layers of terra rossa, the residues of limestones in dissolution; this is a fertile water-retaining soil which possesses most of the elements required for the successful growing of cereals. These soils are distributed along the plateau between al-Gubba on the east and al-Abbiar on the west. The Plateau further possesses scattered tracts of loam, sand and chalk.

Permanently-flowing streams are rare in the country owing to the permeable character of its rock. Such, nevertheless, are Wadi Derna, which springs west of 'Ein Mara, and the Lethe near Bengazi, which flows entirely underground. Springs which break out from the rocks of the Jebel are few, as a result of the relative scarcity of water-tables formed by impermeable strata. Where such exist, they are marl strata situated principally in the eastern Jebel, the most plentiful springs being concentrated between Derna in the east and 'Ein Targuna on the west. Further westward, springs are rare, and centre in the Tecnis region. An isolated area of wells is to be found in the Martuba district, east of Derna. South of the Tecnis-Marawa-Slonta-Derna line, and east of the coastal belt south of Bengazi (Gemines, Solluk), the only available sources of water are cisterns and wells, and the southern limit of the area of cisterns is marked by the line through Sauno, Mesus and el-Mekhili.

Despite the shortage of water prevailing over a considerable part of the country, the plateau's height above sea-level over most of its area ensures a heavy dew-precipitation even in the summer months. This applies especially to the coastal belt, where summer disparities between night and day temperatures produce dew-precipitating mists.[7] Thanks to these summer dews and to winter rains, the Plateau possesses a rich plant covering, in the form of woodland and shrubs, which in the hot months become coveted pasture for the flock-owning population of the desert fringes. Thus considerable remnants of woodland survive between Messa and Mameli, chiefly cypress, while the plateau is further clothed by the juniper, lentisk, olive, ilex, arbutus, laurel, lotus and wild fig. The plateau flora also includes bushes such as poterium spinosum, the sunrose, thyme, sage, the giant fennel and the drias. Esparto grass flourishes in the Bengazi area, and along the north-western shores, between Bengazi and Tocra, the date palm. Forest ceases with the steppe, where rainfall is inadequate to support it; here low scrubs, such as wormwood, saltwort, spurge, flax, and various worts, upon which flocks can pasture, grow in the rainy season. On the steppe, springs are replaced by wells, and trees such as the thorn, lotus, and rus oxyacantha are restricted to the depressions.

Thus one of the country's most outstanding phenomena is created —the seasonal transhumance of flocks to the plateau in summer for pasture and water, and their return southward to the fringes of the plateau and to the steppe when autumn comes. With the return of summer the nomadic shepherd re-ascends the plateau and there sojourns till the autumn, sowing corn immediately after the first rains. He then reverts to the steppelands of the south to enjoy the renewed winter pastures. In harmony with this natural division between plateau and steppe, cattle and goats are at home on the Jebel, while the steppe is the home of the sheep and the camel; sheep drink little, and in the winter, hardly at all, camels at long intervals. This seasonal movement between the cultivated and steppeland areas exists in various forms in most countries of the Mediterranean and north Africa, but in few of them is the pheno-

---

[7] E. C. Semple, *The Geography of the Mediterranean Region*, 1932, p. 91; Cf. Theophrastus, *HP* IV, 3, 7; VIII, 6, 6.

menon so pronounced as in Cyrenaica, where it is such as to create an antagonism between the nomadic tribes and the settled agricultural population, when such should appear in the form of colonists from without. We shall see that this antagonism furnishes the key to an understanding of the ancient history of Cyrene.

The contrasting characteristics of the country's two main zones— the plateau and the steppe, may be summarized in the words of Professor Sir Edward Evans-Pritchard: "In Cyrenaica stand always contrasted the mountain and the plain, the forest and the steppe, the red soils and the white, the country of springs and the country of wells, the arable country and the grazing grounds, the region of goats and cows and the region of sheep and camels, settled life and nomadism . . ." [8]

---

[8] *BMA* VII, Cyrenaican Tribes, p. 7.

CHAPTER TWO

THE GREEK COLONIZATION

1. Monarchy and Democracy

Various attempts have been made by scholars to prove that the settlement of the Greeks of Thera in Libya was preceded by an older wave of Greek settlers. Allusions to this older colonization have been found in the verses of Pindar, who tells of the encounter of the settlers of Thera with the Antenorids who had come to Libya with Helen after the capture of Troy; further in the interpretation of other texts such as the Lindus Temple Chronicle and the epic writings of Eugammon. Various philologists have sought to attribute distinctive ancient elements surviving in the Cyrenean dialect, to an earlier stratum of Greek-speaking settlers in eastern Libya.[1] Schachermeier[2] has argued, that as early as the second millennium B.C., Achaeans who had reached Libya by way of Cyrene, joined the alliance of Libyan tribes to attack Egypt.

All these conjectures have encountered the insurmountable difficulty that there is no real archaeological evidence for such an early settlement. The first conclusions of Stucchi, that finds made in recent excavations at Cyrene (1959-1961), included late Minoan pottery and a Middle or Late Minoan seal[3] have been rebutted by Boardman, who dates these objects at earliest to approximately 600 B.C.[4] Pottery from excavations at Teucheira, Bengazi, and Cyrene itself, does not precede the middle of the 7th century B.C. at earliest,[5] and that at Euhesperides begins, on present evidence, in the first quarter of the 6th.[6] At Apollonia the earliest strata

---

[1] On these conjectures and their sources, *CMB*, pp. 69 sqq.

[2] *Etruskische Frühgeschichte*, 1929, p. 13; cf. H. L. Lorimer, *Homer and the Monuments*, 1950, p. 88.

[3] *QAL* 5, 1967, pp. 19 sqq.

[4] *BSA* 63, 1968, pp. 41 sqq.

[5] Stucchi, *Cirene 1957-1966*, 1967, pp. 150 sqq; Boardman, Hayes, *BSA* Supp. 4, 1966; *BSA* 61, pp. 149-150.

[6] Information from M. Vickers—*JHS Arch. Reports*, 1971-2 (1972), p. 41; Boardman, *BSA* 61, 1966, p. 152.

appear to have dated not long after the colonization of Cyrene.[7]
Libya was nevertheless known to the Homeric epic when it assumed its final form in the 8th century B.C., and the story of Korobios—as well as his rescue by a Samian vessel that touched the
Isle of Plataea (see below), suggests that the coast was not unvisited
by the Greeks before the Battiad colonization. Pre-Theran finds,
nevertheless, are at the moment confined to a Minoan lentoid
intaglio from Apollonia,[8] a Mycenaean bull-figure found in the
Temple of Apollo at Cyrene,[9] and a late Minoan lentoid gem
reported by Boardman from an archaic Greek stratum at Teucheira.[10]

The colonization of Libya by the Theran pioneers was among
the latest colonizing projects of the Greeks, and was an isolated
phenomenon. It is accordingly to be explained as arising from some
specific situation [11] created, apparently, by overpopulation on the
island of Thera (now Santorini). The initial impulse came from
Delphi, and the influence of the Oracle on Cyrene remained strong
down to the 4th century before the current era. Our chief source of
knowledge of the first colonization is the fourth book of Herodotus,
who transmits two parallel traditions, one Cyrenean and the other
Theran. His account is supplemented by the contents of a fourth-
century B.C. inscription found at Cyrene, which relates the grant
of citizen-rights to a group of Therans—perhaps residents of the
city—and preserves a part-account of the colonizing expedition.[12]
According to the Theran tradition, Grinnos, king of the island,
came to Delphi with Battus, son of Polymnestos, in his train, to
consult the Oracle, whereupon the Pythia bade him found a colony in Libya, designating Battus leader. The Therans feared to
obey because they knew nothing of Libya, but after a seven-
years' drought had afflicted their island, applied to Delphi and
received the same response. People were then sent to Crete to seek
information of the new country, and with the aid of a purple-

[7] Goodchild, *Kyrene und Apollonia*, 1971, pp. 177 sqq.; Boardman, *BSA*
1966, p. 152.

[8] O. Bates, *The Eastern Libyans*, 1914, p. 101, n. 5.

[9] *AI* I, 1927, p. 151.

[10] *BSA* 63, 1968, *loc. cit.*

[11] H. Schäfer, *RM²*, 95, 1952, pp. 142-3.

[12] *SEG* 9, 3; S. Ferri, *ABA* 1925, no. 5, pp. 19-24; A. Ferrabino, *RF*, 1928,
pp. 222 sqq.; *CMB* 105 sqq.; A. J. Graham, *JHS* 80, 1960, pp. 94 sqq.; L. H.
Jeffery, *Ha*, 10, 1961, pp. 139 sqq.

fisher, Korobios, reached the island of Plataea,[13] off the shore of
eastern Cyrenaica. They returned to Thera to announce their
success, and a group of settlers was formed, consisting of one
brother from every household with sons, under the leadership of
Battus. Two ships set out for Plataea, but Korobios, who had
remained on the island, was rescued from starvation by a Samian
vessel which had been driven off course to Plataea on her way from
Egypt.

So much for the Theran account. The Cyreneans, on the other
hand, related that Battus, who was of Cretan origin on his mother's
side, consulted Delphi on a cure for his stammer, but was bidden
by the Pythia to go to Libya as the founder of a settlement. When
a Theran delegation arrived subsequently to consult the Pythia, it
received the same order, whereupon two ships were despatched to
Libya, one under Battus. After an unsuccessful attempt, the
Therans settled on the island of Plataea. From this point, the
accounts of settlement are identical in both traditions: after a
two-years' stay on Plataea and another appeal to Delphi, the
settlers removed to the mainland and passed to Aziris,[14] somewhat
westward, remaining there six years. Finally they were led by
natives westward through the district of Irasa to Cyrene.

The Theran account evokes greater confidence than the Cyrenean
in several respects. It is known that in this period Cretan maritime
trade was flourishing, and the aid of Cretans to reconnoitre the
Libyan coast was doubtless essential. The story of Korobios the
pearl-fisher on Plataea can be understood on the analogy of the
more recent practice of sponge fishers of wintering at their fishing
grounds.[15] It is further notable that the version appearing in the
4th-century "Stele of the Founders" above referred to, is closer to
the Theran account, in that having recorded the Cyrenean people's
resolution to grant the Therans equal citizen-rights on the authority of the oath sworn by their ancestors when the first expedi-

---

[13] The place has not been identified with certainty. Till a few years ago
it was generally thought to be the island of Bomba off the east coast of
Cyrenaica; Goodchild (*Tabula Imperii Romani, Cyrene*, 1954), places it at
the island of Jeziret al-Merakhev, near 'Ein el-Gazalah, but with the addition
of a question-mark. Cf. Goodchild, *op. cit.*, p. 11.

[14] For the place's identification and its description, *The Times*, Dec. 1st,
1951, pp. 7, 10.

[15] *CMB* 102; V. Bérard, *Les Phéniciens et l'Odysée*, I, 1902-3, p. 415;
J. Myres, *Geographical History in Greek Lands*, 1953, p. 286.

tion sailed, it describes the arrangements for despatching the mission as related by the Theran tradition transmitted by Herodotus, including the main clause, viz. the selection of one son from each family possessing sons. The Cyrenean tradition, on the other hand, is closer to Herodotus in one respect only—that it makes Battus himself the recipient of Apollo's command to colonize Cyrene, but this is precisely what one would expect the Cyreneans to have told the historian.

The date of the foundation of the city has been the subject of numerous studies and discussions among scholars for many years, and we shall not become involved in this complex question. It will suffice to observe that the most recent scholar to discuss it [16] in detail in the light of old and new research alike, reaches the same conclusion as that accepted by the best scholars ever since Johannes Thrige,[17] to wit, that the Greek settlement was founded on the hill of Cyrene in 631 B.C. Yet it would seem today that the colonization was a more complex process than is reflected in Herodotus' account; this is indicated by the testimony of the Lindus Chronicle, whose thirteenth chapter [18] relates how the Lindian sons of Pankis joined Battus to sail to Cyrene, and dedicated statues of Pallas and Heracles in her temple. Herodotus' incident of the rescue of Korobios of Crete from the Isle of Plataea [19] by a ship of Samos also hints at Samian voyages along the Libyan coast in this period, the more so since the historian connects with the rescue the signing of a longstanding treaty between Cyrene and Samos. The presence of a sherd of Cameiran ware from Rhodes, dated to the late years of the 7th century,[20] in a well on the peninsula overlooking the harbour of Ptolemais (the port of Barka), where the earliest settlement may well have been established, is therefore not haphazard.[21] An Ionian sherd of the end of the 7th century comes from the area east of the Cyrenean Acropolis, while Rhodian and Cameiran wares of the second half of the same century are numerous at

---

[16] The basic problems were considered by J. Thrige, RC 1828, paras. 22-24 (ed. Ferri, 1940); for a survey and summing up of the views of various scholars, CMB, pp. 70 sqq.; 121 sqq.; cf. K. Beloch, Griechische Geschichte, I² 2, 1913., pp. 236 sq.

[17] RC, p. 101; Beloch, op. cit., pp. 236, 483, n. 3.

[18] C. Blinkenberg, Die Lindische Tempelchronik, 1915, pp. 18, 20; xvii, 109-116; Lindos, II, Inscr., I, 1941, pp. 149 sqq.

[19] Herod. IV, 152, 3.

[20] Boardman, BSA 61, 1966, p. 153, who dates c. 620 B.C.

[21] The sherd was dated by B. Shefton.

Teucheira [22] and also present at the early shrine of Opheles in the
earliest Agora of Cyrene [23] with ample Chiote ware.[24] All this
evidence points to the probability that the settlement was carried
out not by one group, but was the work of a broader movement of
colonization amongst whose initiators there were also elements
from Rhodes, Samos and Crete.[25]

Cyrene was destined by its position to be a capital city. It lies
on a defensible hill on the uppermost escarpment, commanding the
second terrace (the Lusaita) to north, and its proximity to the sea
ensured communication with mainland Greece and the islands.
The hill itself is cut off by ravines on the west and south, and on
the north by a cliff, from whose foot wells the spring of Kuré,
known as the Spring of Apollo, which flows over the pleasant
terrace that lies between the cliff of the Acropolis and the escarpment. This terrace became in a short time the Sanctuary of the city
and the site of the temples of Apollo and Artemis. The place is
fortunate not only in its abundant water supply, its defensibility
and its proximity to the sea, but in its ample rainfall, which at
this point of the plateau is the highest in the country (600-1000
mm),[26] and in its situation as the centre of a rich red-soil plain.
Those who saw Cyrene from the sea named her 'the white shining
breast' (ἀργεννόεντι μαστῷ),[27] and no title more aptly expresses
the majesty of her position and the beauty of her surroundings.

The name Cyrene (Κυράνα) belongs, as Chamoux noted,[28] to the
wide class of Greek names embodying the suffix -ηνη, which means
"place of", and is annexed chiefly to roots denoting animals,
plants and natural features. The poet Callimachus seems to have
been right when he connected the name Cyrene with the Libyan
root Κύρη, an iris,[29] the name associated with the spring that flows
from the Acropolis hill. There would appear, therefore, to be no
grounds for connecting the name with that of the nymph Cyrene,
who was a Thessalian figure already known to Hesiod before the

---

[22] Stucchi, *Cirene*, pp. 150 sqq.

[23] *Loc. cit.*

[24] *Ibid.*

[25] As noted by Parke, *DO* p. 78, the Greek cities which consulted the
Delphic oracle during the 7th century were Paros, Thera and Rhodes.

[26] Cf. Herod. IV, 158, 3.

[27] Pind., IV *Pyth.*, 14.

[28] *CMB* 126, p. 127.

[29] Dioscorides, *Materia medica*, II, 169; Callim., *Apoll.* II, 88.

city's foundation, nor does she appear among the Cyrenean deities till the end of the 4th century B.C., although Pindar in the 5th brings her from the woods of Pelion to Libya to celebrate her espousal with Apollo.[30]

It may be assumed that the small Greek settlement found its first foothold on the hill of the Acropolis,[31] and the community's weakness and isolation no doubt compelled its pioneers to find an accommodation with the Libyan natives. Marriages with Libyan women are indeed alluded to in several later sources.[32] Some scholars have believed that Battus is a Libyan word,[33] mainly since the first king of Cyrene had another name, Aristoteles[34], and Herodotus says explicitly that Battus meant 'king' in Libyan.[35] This would mean that his royal status was acquired under the influence of Libyan neighbours, and that the name itself subsequently engendered the story of his stammer (βατταρίζειν, to stammer).[36] Schäfer however thinks that the personal name, Battus, became a synonym of "king" among the Libyans, an idea finding support in the fact that Arkesilaos, the name alternating with Battus among the subsequent Battiad kings, also relates etymologically to the functions of a monarch.[37] Whatever the case, Herodotus emphasizes the mutual influence between the people of Cyrene and the neighbouring Libyan tribe, the Asbystae, who taught them to drive the four-horse chariot and themselves adopted Greek customs.[38] On the other hand various traditions, which are difficult to authenticate, point to conflicts between the Greeks and their Libyan neighbours in the city's early period.[39]

Battus I was seen by the Cyreneans as the founder of the city's cults. In this he may have been assisted by one Onymastos of Delphi,[40] whose part in the drafting of the religious law of Cyrene

---

[30] Pind., IX *Pyth*, 69.

[31] Finds of archaic pottery have been made in the area of the Acropolis; I owe this information to the late Professor Allan Wace.

[32] Pind., IX *Pyth.*, 110 (192); Callim. *ad Apoll.*, 85-7; *SEG* 9, 1, line 3.

[33] Eg. *DO* p. 74.

[34] Diod. VIII, 29; Pind. V *Pyth.*, 87; *SEG* 9, 189.

[35] Cf. the Egyptian word for the Pharaoh of Lower Egypt—"Bith" (*CMB*, p. 93).

[36] *CMB*, pp. 93 sqq. (Herod. IV, 155).

[37] *RM*², 95, 1952, pp. 150-1.

[38] *Herod*. IV, 170.

[39] The struggle of Heracles with Antaeus (Pind. *Isthm.*, II, 70) and the service of Chionis under Battus I (Paus. III, 14, 3).

[40] *SEG* 9, 72, line 23; *RFC* 1928, p. 282.

in its earliest period may reflect the great influence of the Oracle
on the cults of the new settlement. But generally it would seem
that Battus discharged the duties of king and high priest simultaneously. The steadiness of the city's cultic development, indeed,
is demonstrated by the building of the temples of Apollo and
Artemis in the middle of the 6th century,[41] and of the small shrine
of Opheles, a deity of healing, in the Agora during the last quarter
of the 7th.[42] South of the Acropolis across the Wadi bel Gadir
which defends the city on that side, the temenos of Demeter may
have existed already a generation after the first settlement.[43]

But if the Temple of Apollo was really erected as late as the
middle of the 6th century, this is contrary to the tradition that
Battus I built it, or that here there burned the fire brought from
Thera,[45] since the tumulus identified with the king's burial place
was dated in the first quarter of the same century. The Temple of
Apollo, nevertheless, appears to have been the ancient prytaneum
of the city,[44] later transferred to the Agora. The initial identity
of the prytaneum and the temple indicates the unity of the functions of government and cult characteristic of the archaic community. The building of the Temple of Apollo, which required
means and technical skill, relatively soon after the settlement's
foundation, is a measure of Cyrene's progress, of the growth of its
population and the improvement of its economic condition, and
the building's erection was accompanied by that of the Temple of
Artemis. The Temple of Apollo's plan can be paralleled in the
same period in Sicily, in Magna Graecia and in the Peloponnesus;
but the nearest parallel is that of the Temple of Hera at Olympia.[46]
The closest analogy to Artemis' shrine is to be found in the temples
of Gortyn and Prinia of Crete and in the archaic temples of Sparta.[47]

Battus I was known not only as the founder of cults, but also as
the maker of the rockcut processional way described by Pindar.[48]
It is not clear if the road leading from the Acropolis to the Agora,
where the city founder's tomb has been allegedly found,[49] is meant,

---

[41] Pind., V *Pyth.*, 120; cf. *SEG* 9, 189.
[42] Stucchi, *Cirene*, p. 50.
[43] Goodchild, *Kyr. u. Apoll.*, p. 163; Stucchi, *Cirene*, p. 28.
[44] L. Pernier, *TA*, 1935, p. 23.
[45] Callim., *Apoll.*, 77: μάλα καλόν ἀνάκτορον.
[46] *TA*, pp. 132-4.
[47] *AI* IV, 1931, pp. 178 sqq.
[48] Pind., *Pyth.*, V, 121-4 (90-93).
[49] *ASAA* 39-40, 1963, p. 661.

or whether it should rather be sought in the rockcut way descending
from the north side of the Acropolis hill to the Sanctuary of Apollo.
As Pindar, immediately after mentioning the rockcut road, continues: "And here he (Battus) lies since his death, at the end of the
Agora", scholars have inclined to the first view, and Stucchi [50]
regards the matter as settled, since the King's tomb was identified,
in his opinion, at the south-east corner of the latter. It must however be observed that the road connecting the Acropolis with the
Agora is not rockcut. Attention should in any case be directed to
the three rockcut tombs in the northern cliff face of the Acropolis
hill over the rockcut road to the Sanctuary, since according to
Pindar, Battus I was buried apart (δίχα) in the Agora, whereas
the other kings were laid to rest "before the palace" [51] (πρὸ δο-
μάτων).[52] Tombs of archaic type are also to be found in the gorge
that separates the Acropolis from the city's eastern hill, south-west
of the Acropolis over Wadi bel-Gadir, and north-eastward in the
Wadi el-Kenassiyeh near the road going down to Apollonia. This
topographical distribution may confirm the supposition that the
nucleus of the oldest settlement centred on the western hill.

Of the reign of Arkesilaos I, Battus' successor, we only know
the length—sixteen years.[53] His son Battus II, therefore, succeeded
about 599 B.C. He utilized the good offices of the Delphic Oracle to
bring new settlers to the city, under the slogan of "equal rights and
the distribution of land",[54] chiefly—to judge from the tribal
division later introduced by the reformer Demonax of Mantinea—
from Peloponnesus, Crete and the Aegean Islands. Subsequently
during the 6th century, when Cyrene's first inscribed coins appear,
they elicit the influence of Samos, Rhodes and Cyprus.[55] Excavated
pottery reveals trade contacts with Thera, Corinth, Athens, Laconia
Rhodes, Chios, Ionia and even Syria and Sardis [56] in the 7th-6th
centuries. During the 6th century the Cyrenean treasury was set up
at Olympia, and if it is the smallest of the treasuries there, it is

---

[50] *Loc. cit.* (n. 42).

[51] Pind., V *Pyth.*, 130 (97).

[52] For another view, Stucchi, *ASAA*, 39-40, p. 661.

[53] Herod. IV, 159, 1.

[54] Herod. IV, 159. The slogan finds authority, as Professor D. Asheri has
pointed out to me, in the Stele of the Founders, (*SEG* 9, 3) which promises
the settlers from Thera "citizenship, political office and ownerless land."

[55] E. S. G. Robinson, *BMC*, 1927, p. xxix.

[56] Stucchi, *op. cit.*, pp. 150 sqq.

nevertheless the oldest.[57] The earliest Cyrenean coins, known from about 560, were modelled on the famous Athenian "owls", but bore Cyrene's symbols.[58] The form of the silphium plant appears on the obverse of all of them from the first,[59] showing that it already formed a significant if not the principal, source of the city's wealth. There may also be evidence of early building activities on the city's eastern hill, where, north of the later Temple of Zeus, an archaic shrine would appear to have been found by Smith and Porcher; [60] here an archaic monolithic columnshaft, closely resembling those of the 6th-century Temple of Apollo in the Sanctuary, was observed by the writer. If this hill is the hill of Zeus Lykaeos (ὄχθος Διὸς Λυκαίου) mentioned by Herodotus,[61] it was still outside the city walls at the end of the 6th century, as the Persian army encamped on it; the connection of Zeus Lykaeos with the Peloponnesus might give reason to suppose that here an altar in the god's honour was consecrated at the time of the second wave of settlement under Battus II.

This intensification of Greek settlement led, apparently, to the expropriation of the nearby native Libyans from their lands. They therefore formed an alliance with the Egyptian Pharaoh Apries, who marched to their aid with a strong army, but in a battle near the spring of Theste in the region of Irasa, in the year 570, the Egyptians were heavily defeated,[62] perhaps because of the Pharaoh's reluctance to rely on his best troops, who were Greek mercenaries. As Herodotus, who wrote in the middle of the 5th century, records no Libyan tribes eastward as far as the Gilgamae of Marmarica,

---

[57] Paus. VI, 19, 10. But views on the building's identity have been divided: Treu, *Olympia*, III, 23; *PW* 35, 1939, cols. 124-5, sv. Olympia.

[58] *BMC*, pp. xxviii-xxix.

[59] On the plant and the problem of its identification, B. Bonacelli, Ministerio dei Colonie, *Boll. del informazione economico*, 1924; E. Strantz, *Die Silfionsfrage*, 1909; *PW²* IIIA, 1927, col. 102; *Supp.* V, 1931, cols. 972 sqq.; *BMC*, Cyrenaica, p. ccli; W. Capelle, *RM²*, 97, 1954, pp. 169 sqq.; *CMB*, pp. 246-263; C. L. G. Gemmil, *Bull. of the Hist. of Medicine*, 40, 1966, pp. 295 sqq. The silphium was a plant which grew wild in most of the country and more especially in its western part. Its sap, which was used both as a condiment and a medicine, and brought high prices in the Greek world, was tapped from the stem before the plant seeded, and this resulted in its death. Its leaves were sought hungrily by sheep. Not all the details transmitted concerning the silphium by ancient works can be reconciled with one another, and the plant's botanical identity is controversial.

[60] *SP* 1864, pp. 74-5; H. Weld-Blundell, *BSA* 1895, p. 122.

[61] Herod. IV, 203, 2.

[62] Herod. IV, 159, 5.

while in the 4th century Pseudo-Scylax [63] found Cyrene's eastern frontier beyond Cherronesoi (in the vicinity of Ras al-Tin), it has been concluded [64] that the clash was caused by the Greek occupation of the lands to the east of the city towards Derna.

Apries' successor was Amasis, a hellenizing ruler who signed a treaty with Cyrene, married a Cyrenean wife and sent statues of himself and of the goddess Athena, to Libya.[65] Signs of commerce between Cyrene and Egypt in this period are not wanting in the archaeological evidence: objects of gold and alabaster as well as scarabs, have occurred among the 6th-century dedications in the Temple of Artemis at Cyrene,[66] and Cyrenean coins form a high percentage among contemporary hoards found in Egypt.[67] A common political trend may indeed be traceable in the developments of Egypt and Cyrene in this period.

Cyrene was ruled between 560 and 544 by the son of Battus II, Arkesilaos II, known as "the hard" ($\chi\alpha\lambda\epsilon\pi\delta\varsigma$).[68] According to Herodotus, Arkesilaos fell out with his brothers, who seceded to found a joint settlement with the Libyans at Barka in the west of the country. They further incited the Libyans to revolt against the King, who suffered a severe defeat in the battle of Leukon in the east of his territory, with the loss of 7.000 hoplites. The King was also at odds with his nobles, whom he put to death or drove into exile with the aid of one Learchos, the commander (according to Plutarch) [69] of a force of mercenaries obtained from Amasis. Finally Learchos slew the king and so seized power, but himself fell a victim to the vengeance of Arkesilaos' widow Eryxo. She, aided by her brother Polyarchos, made peace with Amasis, and restored the former régime—Arkesilaos' son, Battus III, a sickly youth, acceding to the throne.

The Egyptian alliance with Cyrene, as Schäfer remarked,[70] "indicates Cyrene's entry into the Greek and oriental political world of the eastern Mediterranean basin." We may add that the

---

[63] *Perip.*, 108.

[64] *RC*, para. 31, p. 135; Wilamovitz-Moellendorf, *Cirene*, 1930, p. 13; Macan, *Herodotus*, Vol. II, Appendix xii, p. 272.

[65] Herod. II, 182, 1.

[66] *TA* 96; *AI* IV, 195.

[67] *NC* 1899, pp. 283, 287; S. P. Noe, *Bibliography of Greek Coin Hoards*,[2] 1937, nos. 322, 299, 729, 888 etc.

[68] Plut. (Barnadakis) *De Mul. virt.*, 260 sq.; Herod. IV, 160 sq.

[69] Plut., *De Mul. virt.*, 260 sq. (Eryxo).

[70] Schäfer, *RM*[2] 95, 1952, p. 159n.

second wave of Greek settlement which had been promoted by
Delphi and by Battus II, came at a time of great changes in the
Greek economy and during the floruit of the Greek tyrannies in
various Greek states. This was also the period of a prolonged
agrarian crisis in Greece and the islands, expressing itself in peasant
indebtedness and expropriation, and in a sharp struggle between
the nobility and the rising class of merchants, peasants and craftsmen. Important too, if not decisive in this period, were the introduction of coinage, and the associated intensification of trade.
These conditions, which certainly influenced the Battiads, produced
multitudes of land-hungry emigrants eager to exploit the new
allotments promised by Battus II.

Plutarch says explicitly that Arkesilaos "became a tyrant instead of a king",[71] and of Learchos, that he "conspired for the
position of tyrant".[72] Plutarch, it may be claimed, was influenced
by events then occurring in other Greek lands, but his estimate
can be shown to be accurate where contemporary Cyrenean reality
was concerned.

The internal political difficulties created by Battus III's youth
and inexperience, induced the Cyreneans to appeal once again to
Delphi for advice; the Oracle sent to Libya as arbiter and reformer
Demonax of Mantinea.[73] By his reforms, only royal properties
(τεμένεα) and the prerogatives of priesthood were left to the king,
all other affairs being handed over to popular control (τὰ ἄλλα
πάντα τὰ πρότερον εἶχον οἱ βασιλεὶς ἐς μέσον τοῦ δημῶ ἔθηκε). Demonax
further reconstituted the citizens of Cyrene as three new tribes,
the Therans and perioikoi (περίοικοι); the Peloponnesians and the
Cretans; and the islanders. It is clear, therefore, that the royal
powers were stringently curtailed, while the citizen-body was
enlarged to include new settlers and some of the native Libyans
living in the vicinity of the city (the perioikoi). Chamoux,[74] indeed,
has argued that the perioikoi were Greeks, but one can hardly
ignore the testimony of Herodotus, who himself visited Cyrene,
and makes explicit mention of the Libyan perioikoi.[75] Among the

---

[71] *De Virt. Mul.*, xxv (260).

[72] *Ibid.*; ἐπιβουλεύων τῇ τυραννίδι.

[73] Herod. IV, 161, 2.

[74] *CMB* pp. 140, 221.

[75] Herod. IV, 159, 4 (62); cf. also Jeffery, (*Ha.* 10, 1961, pp. 139 sqq.)
criticizing Chamoux's opinion. Hammond (*Hist. of Greece*, 1960, p. 123)
thinks that these were Libyans settled on the frontiers of the city territory

royal properties, one can be identified, namely, the monopoly of the silphium trade, mentioned by several sources.[76] Furthermore the famous picture on the Arkesilaos kylix,[77] hardly suits the usual interpretation that silphium is here being weighed and stored: Lane rightly commented [78] that the material is not silphium, but wool.[79] All agree that the King represented, designated "Arkesilaos" on the kylix, is the second of that name.[80] Accordingly it seems probable that the king also traded in wool and agricultural produce on a wide scale.

The paintings on the Arkesilaos kylix are certainly satirical, as Sylvia Benton noted.[81] We see the king sitting and supervising the weighing and storage of wool. The animals appearing in the painting (a stork and a lizard) indicate the action as taking place at the end of the shearing, i.e. in the spring or early summer, for the flocks in Cyrenaica have to be driven to water in April or May, when they come north to the Jebel from their winter sojourn in the southern steppe.

The satirical element of the painting lies in the fact noted by Sylvia Benton, that wool is being weighed against wool, a futile process here represented, it would seem, as a criticism of the royal wool production and export overseas. The country's sheep breeding is evidenced by various ancient sources,[82] and as the royal monopoly of silphium is known, there is no reason to deny to the royal house a decisive share in the production and marketing of wool. An analysis of the country's structure and climatic character has shown the importance of the rhythmic seasonal transmigration of flock-owners from the southern steppe to the plateau and back; it also emphasized the antagonistic ways of life of the nomadic

---

for peripheral defence, like the *perioikoi* of Sparta, who were granted secondary citizenship and a measure of internal autonomy.

[76] Schol. ad Arist., *Plut.*, 925; Hesychius sv. Battos.

[77] Illustrations of the kylix are to be found in numerous works: eg. *Corpus Vasorum Antiquorum*, I, p. 20, pl. 20, 21, no. 189; E. Pfuhl, *Masterpieces of Greek Painting and Drawing* (tr. Beazley, 1955), fig. 18; Beazley, Ashmole, *Greek Sculpture and Painting*, 1932, fig. 44 etc.

[78] Lane, *BSA*, 34, 1933-4, pp. 161-2.

[79] On the Libyan flocks, Synes., *Epp.* 148; Pind. IX *Pyth.*, 11 (8); Herod. IV, 155, 3.

[80] See particularly, H. R. W. Smith, *University of California Publications*, I, 10, 1944, pp. 272 sqq.

[81] *Archeology* 12, 1959, pp. 179 sqq.: Birds on the cup of Arkesilaus. See now Applebaum, *Doron, Katz Festschrift*, 1967, pp. 69 sqq. (Hebrew).

[82] Applebaum, *ibid.*, n. 60; on Libyan flocks, n. 58.

pastoral tribes and the settled agriculturalists and cattle-owners
concentrated on the plateau. It is further clear that the seasonal
northward transhumance of flockowners in summer plays a vital
part in the fertilizing of the agricultural areas. In much of mainland
Greece, agriculture occupies the valleys, and the flocks graze in
the hills in summer; when the livestock descends to the plains in
the winter, ploughing and sowing have already begun, restricting
the grazing areas, hence the soil suffers from shortage of organic
manure and the stock from shortage of food. The opposite is the
case in Cyrenaica, where the flocks spend the winter in the steppe,
and on passing to the plateau in summer find increasing areas of
stubble on which to feed as the harvest progresses over the Jebel
from south to north and from west to east. Hence the farmer
enjoys adequate manuring of his land, and this was a vital factor
for obtaining the country's high yields in ancient times.[83] In other
words, in Cyrenaica the fertility of the plateau's arable and the
seasonal flock transhumance were mutually complementary, and
essential for the obtaining of surplus crops in a country that suffers
quadrennial drought. The agriculture of the Plain of Barka, on the
other hand, was less dependent on the seasonal transhumance of
livestock. Its water supply is furnished by springs at Barka itself,
and its population was initially attracted by its fertile corn-
producing red soil and by the rearing of cattle and horses which
could be carried on with the help of its summer fallows.[84] It was
not by chance, therefore, that Barka remained an independent
political unit till the end of the century.[85]

The silphium-fields were situated, apparently, mainly in the
southern region. Theophrastus [86] testifies that the plant flowered
when the flocks were in the same area, i.e. in the winter, and Arrian
writes that though not cultivated, it was necessary to fence it to
protect it from the livestock.[87] Strict supervision of the seasonal
movement of the flocks was thus imperative to safeguard the
silphium as a source of income, so that if the Battiads controlled
this branch, it was essential to them to control flock-rearing as

---

[83] On the grains of Cyrene see Pind. III *Isth*. 72; Theophr. *HP* VIII, 4, 3;
CP III, 21, 2: Diod. III, 49; *SEG* 9, 2 etc.

[84] For cattle-rearing in the Plain of Barka, Polyb. V, 65-8; Soph. *Elec*. 727;
BMC p. clxvi, no. 1A.

[85] *RC*, para. 5; cf. *CERP*, pp. 354-5.

[86] *HP* IV, 3, 1.

[87] *Anab*., III, 28.

well. A careful balance was in fact needed between the two branches, since not only the wool-trade, but also the fertility of the arable areas of the north depended on the condition of the flocks.

There was, however, a limit to the development of this "symbiosis" of flock-rearing, silphium and the arable of the plateau. When settlement expanded on the plateau, and arable began to extend southward to the accompaniment of the pasturing of flocks whose origin was on the Jebel itself, fewer areas remained to the flocks of the southern nomads for summer-grazing, a situation that was apt to prejudice the Greek cultivator when he wished to send his own flock southward to graze the steppe. This situation would produce clashes between the nomads and the settled cultivators, and cause a decline in the organic content of the arable soils of the plateau.

The expansion of Greek settlement under Battus II led to an extension of the corn-growing link in the symbiosis of flock-rearing, silphium and arable, for we know from the text of the "Stele of the Founders" at Cyrene, that vacant tracts were distributed to the new settlers.[88] Whatever was the cause of the quarrel between Arkesilaos and his brothers, then, it would seem that the reason for the founding of Barka was a desire to perpetuate the squirelike cooperation of the nobility with the more permanently settled element among the Libyans (perhaps those who had suffered from the ἀναδασμὸς γῆς of Battus II) on the basis of local cattle-rearing and corn-growing in the Barka Plain. Furthermore the execution or exile of the aristocracy by Arkesilaos would have meant the confiscation of their estates and the growth of the royal lands. Even if we suppose that the King's brother Polyarchus restored the former political situation,[89] we have no means of knowing if this included the restoration of the confiscated lands to the aristocrats or to their heirs, and if this was done, the process may not have been completed, for with regard to the reforms of Demonax, Herodotus tells us,[90] that only religious functions and τεμένεα were left to Battus I, meaning that additional lands till then held by the monarchy now passed into other hands.[91]

---

[88] SEG 9, 3: πολιτηίας καὶ τιμᾶμ πεδέχ[εν] καὶ γᾶς ἀδεσπότω ἀπολάγχανεν.

[89] Plut., de mul. virt., (Eryxo), 260 sqq.

[90] Herod. IV, 161.

[91] I am grateful to Professor D. Asheri for drawing my attention to Will's study of this problem. (REA 59, 1957, pp. 11 sqq.) He interprets Battus II's

We may obtain additional information on the policy of Arkesilaos II if we assume, with other enquirers,[92] that the oracle given
by Delphi, cited by Diodorus [93] as concerning the transgressions of
one Arkesilaos, was directed to him, and this is credible, since
Arkesilaos III gained from Delphi qualified support.[94] The oracle
accused Arkesilaos II of deserting the ways of Battus II, of seizing
the revenues of the state and of diminishing the piety owed to the
gods. We can understand the second and third charges, if we
examine the economic policy of his ally and contemporary, Amasis
of Egypt. Amasis relied on a mercenary force,[95] inaugurated a
property census in order to impose taxation,[96] and confiscated
temple revenue.[97] His pro-hellenic policy was indeed closely
bound up with the development of Egypt's overseas trade,[98] and
it was in Arkesilaos' reign that the introduction of coinage into
Cyrenaica took place,[99] meaning that her external trade began to
develop more intensively, concomitantly with the royal interest in
the export of wheat, wool and silphium, and, in all probability, in
agricultural intensification (vines, olives and perfume-producing
plants). For this the King would have exploited the sequestrated
lands of the aristocracy on which to settle the mercenaries of
whom Plutarch speaks;[100] lands might also have been allocated
to the peasants whose farms had been lost owing to the negative
effects of the introduction of coinage, i.e. of the rise in the prices
of craft-products in contrast to the prices of agricultural produce,
which would have remained as before.[101] We have no decisive
proof of a royal policy of this sort, but it is probably in view of the

---

division of land as the allotment of areas recently acquired, and not as the
reassignment of soil already owned by Greeks (as opposed to the view of
G. Thompson, *Studies in Ancient Greek Society*, I, 1949, pp. 249 sqq.) Will
inclines to see the terms used in Herodotus' account of the reforms of Demonax (*loc. cit.*, n. 6; Herod. IV, 161—τὰ ἄλλα πάντα) as applying both to
the functions and estates which were taken from the king. ("L'interpréta-
tion de ce passage en termes de biens fonciers me paraît la plus immédiate").

[92] Thrige, *RC*, para. 37.
[93] VIII, 30.
[94] Herod. IV, 163.
[95] Herod. II, 154.
[96] Herod. II, 177.
[97] Herod. II, 174.
[98] Herod. II, 178.
[99] *BMC*, p. xxviii.
[100] *De mul. virt.*, 261 c.
[101] *GS* I, 176 sq.

general tyrannical trend of Amasis and Arkesilaos, who, it is important to recall, enjoyed till his death the support of the majority of the citizens of Cyrene, seven thousand of whom died for his cause at the battle of Leukon.[102] It is further necessary to explain who were the people who received the grant of citizenship from Demonax. Even if the restoration of the status quo by Polyarchos had not caused them to be deprived of their rights, Demonax would have found it necessary to create new Cyrenean tribes composed of the settlers who had responded to Battus' invitation, since the losses of Leukon had to be made good, and it is clear from the language of the "Stele of the Founders" that those newcomers who had received land—or at least the Therans amongst them,—had also, in the first place, received citizenship.

Yet Arkesilaos' situation had been difficult. On the one hand the maintenance and extension of the threefold symbiosis—flocks, silphium and arable—was rendered necessary by growing economic commercialization, and this depended on the strict safeguarding of the balance between the three branches. But the growth of the population, as a result of the settlement of mercenaries and overseas colonists, the bearers of the small intensive farm unit—led to the restriction of the pastoral areas of the plateau, and to growing hostility on the part of the nomadic elements, on whose loyalty the harvesting of the silphium depended, and on the part of the settled Libyans, whose lands were continually being diminished. The conflict between the expansion of the symbiosis and the extended colonization needed for the political strengthening and physical realization of this policy, led ultimately also to a clash with aristocratic owners of extensively farmed estates, to the battle of Leukon and to the death of Arkesilaos. Demonax found a solution to the situation by granting citizenship to the permanently settled Libyans (the περίοικοι), and by confirming or restoring the rights of the recently arrived Greek colonists. If the nobles recovered their estates at his insistence, we cannot tell; he certainly restored lands to elements whom we cannot define.

The factors disclosed by Arkesilaos' struggle are such as to make clear the sources of the conflict. Whether or not Schäfer is right in distinguishing three political elements at Cyrene, the King's brothers and their Libyan allies, the aristocracy, and the

---

[102] See p. 17.

royal family supported by the new colonists and the mercenaries,[103] the reason for the secession of the King's brothers to found a mixed settlement with the Libyans at Barka, may well have been that it was they who supported the extensive agriculture based on corn-growing, cattle-rearing and horse-rearing, carried on in conjunction with the permanently settled natives, whereas the King sought to develop a more intensified cultivation and the more efficient utilization of land.

It is easy to suppose that the settlement of newcomers by Battus II under the slogan of "the distribution of land" (ἀναδασμὸς γῆς),[104] which was not in this case a revolutionary programme, led in course of time to a demand on the part of the Cyrenean peasants for the cancellation of debts (ἀποκοπὴ χρέων), but of this we have no confirmation. The fact that Arkesilaos III, son of Battus III, in his revolt against Demonax' reforms, mobilized mercenaries from overseas by the slogan of "the distribution of land", has caused Schäfer to deduce that his action was directed against the Cyrenean peasantry whose farming had remained backward and did not utilize the full potentialities of their lands. But it is unnecessary to read into Arkesilaos III's formula more than a demagogic slogan meant to attract mercenaries, and it is preferable to distinguish between the extensive farming of the aristocracy, with which Arkesilaos was struggling, and the plight of the smallholding peasantry.[105]

Did Demonax inaugurate democracy in Cyrene? The institution of three phylae meant, no doubt, an expansion of the citizen-body in harmony with the new situation created by the rise of population under Battus II, nor need the accuracy of Herodotus be doubted when he writes that "Demonax placed all other affairs in the hands of the people." [106] But the question is, in what measure did "the people" include all the free inhabitants of the country? — and to

---

[103] Schäfer, *RM*,[2] 1952, p. 165, n. 101.

[104] Herod. IV, 159, 2-3.

[105] Cf. Chamoux's view, *op. cit.*, pp. 146 sq.; he sees the policy of Arkesilaos III as guided by characteristically tyrannical motives, and ascribes to him the aim of redividing the large estates of the Cyrenean aristocracy among the common people. I personally believe that this intention had already appeared under Arkesilaos II. H. Schäfer (*RM*[2], 1952, p. 162) attributes to the Battiads a position intermediate between the traditional monarchy and the tyrannical régime, but considers that Plutarch's account was too much influenced by the conditions of a later period.

[106] Herod. IV, 161.

this we have no answer. All that can be said is, that a sharing of citizen-rights without reference to ownership of land is hardly credible in the conditions of the period.

One event in the life of Cyrene perhaps belongs to the reign of Battus III (544-530), namely, the erection of the Temple of Zeus, the city's greatest shrine, on the eastern hill.[107] The date of the building, one of the largest temples in Greece, ranking with the Parthenon and Temple "G" at Selinus in Sicily, is a subject of controversy. Inscriptions evidence that it existed in the 5th century,[108] and its first scientific excavator, Pesce [109] dated it to that century. Dinsmoor [110] on the other hand was of the opinion that it was built shortly after 540 B.C. and Chamoux put the erection at about 520.[111] The column-contractions of the peristasis, indeed, suggest the earlier date.

The size of the project, at all events, is appropriate to the period of renascence that may well have begun with the reforms of Demonax, and perhaps symbolized the renewed harmony (ὁμόνοια) of the Cyrenean polity under the protection of Zeus, the guardian of social justice. If this suggestion is correct, the chronological limits for the Temple's construction would fall between 550 and 514. Between 550 and 525 the small shrine of Opheles (a healing deity who bestowed prosperity) was rebuilt in enlarged form; in the last quarter of the century the Agora was lengthened from east to west, and a new portico erected along its north side. By this time, apparently, the small temple of Apollo already existed at the south-western corner of the area, and the west limit of the Agora was enclosed by a new portico.

The son of Battus III, Arkesilaos III, who reigned from 530/525-514,[112] attempted to set aside the political settlement of Demonax, but faced with revolt, fled to Samos, while his mother Pheretimé found refuge with Evelthon the ruler of Salamis in Cyprus.[113]

---

[107] For various datings of the temple's erection, see Goodchild, *Kyrene und Apollonia*, p. 151.

[108] *SP*, no. 7.

[109] *BCH* 71-2, 1947, p. 347.

[110] Dinsmoor, *The Architecture of Ancient Greece*, 1950, p. 86; Cf. Rowe, Buckle, Gray, *MUE* 1952, 1956, pp. 31-2.

[111] This writer, judging by the proportions of the building's peristasis, and other details, such as the corner-triglyph contractions, concluded, after personal examination, in favour of the earlier date.

[112] Mitchell, *JHS* 86, 1966, pp. 99 sqq.

[113] Herod. IV, 162, 2-3.

Meanwhile Cambyses had gained control of Egypt and Arkesilaos, inclining like other Greek kings and absolute rulers to rely on Persian support, became his vassal. Gathering an army, after a consultation with Delphi, he reconquered his kingdom and immolated his aristocratic opponents by burning down their refuge, "the great tower of Aglomachus". Thereupon, realizing that his deed ran counter to the explicit warning of the Pythia, "not to bake the pots in the kiln, but to send them beyond the frontiers, but if you do the first, do not enter a place surrounded on two sides with water"—transferred his quarters to Barka, ruled by the Libyan Aladdeir, whose daughter he had wedded.[114] His mother Pheretimé remained at Cyrene and there exercized rule,[115] but Arkesilaos and his father-in-law were assassinated by their enemies at Barka, forcing Pheretimé to flee to Egypt. Her flight brought about the intervention of Persia (514/513); Barka was besieged and taken by the Persian general Aryandes, and its inhabitants deported to Bactria.[116] It is not clear from the existing account whether Cyrene suffered from the Persian expedition; on this Herodotus is at variance with Menecles of Barka, who wrote of a Persian occupation. Decapitated statues and damaged monuments dated in the mid-6th century B.C., found in a quarry east of the present city, may indeed be the result of Persian vandalism.[117]

From this time onward and perhaps till the end of this dynasty, the Battiads ruled Cyrene as Persian vassals, and as early as the reign of Darius son of Hystaspes (i.e. from 519 approximately) Egypt received from Cyrene, Barka, and the neighbouring regions of Libya, a tribute of 800 talents and 120,000 artabae of corn.[118]

It is only at this point that the relationships between the Cyrenean cities and Cyrene itself begin to become a little clearer. Barka was founded, as we have seen, in the reign of Arkesilaus II,[119]

---

[114] A Greek inscription apparently from Barka (*CIG* 5147) lists the descendants through seven generations of Aladdeir son of Battus, (meaning the fourth) the grandson of Arkesilaos. It may be supposed that Arkesilaos' marriage with a Libyan princess was a move in the policy of appeasement followed by Battus III in pursuance of the reforms of Demonax.

[115] Herod. IV, 165, 7.

[116] For the chronology, Mitchell, (note 112), who points out that as there is no evidence that Arkesilaos fled to Samos in Polykrates' time, his accession and flight are more probably to be dated about 525.

[117] *Libia antiqua*, 3/4, 1966, pp. 179 sqq.

[118] Herod. XII, 91, 2-3.

[119] It is difficult to accept Diodorus' statement (I, 68) that Apries' attack

but archaeological evidence shows that a settlement already existed near her harbour (the future Ptolemais, today Tolmeita) from the end of the 7th century.We further know of a Libyan king at Barka, and that the town paid its own tribute to Darius, hence it was a distinct political unit, which began to strike its own coins in the later years of the 6th century.[120] These cease, apparently, with the Persian capture and the subsequent vengeance of Pheretimé, but reappear after a short period under Battus IV; [121] by the end of the 5th century Barka is the country's principal city.[122] In 484 another Persian attack was made upon the town by the Persian general Arsamis. Several historians have seen the event as an erroneous duplication of the Persian siege after the death of Arkesilaos III,[123] but Polyaenus knew of two such attacks, and the alleged second coincided with a revolt in Egypt. Robinson, moreover, noted another cessation of Barka's coinage at this time, and that when it reappears about the year 460, it bears a resemblance to the coinage of Cyrene.[124]

The city of Euesperitae (east of the present Bengazi) had existed from the early 6th century on the evidence of pottery; in the late 5th it had been attacked (according to Herodotus)[125] by the Persians during the first campaign against Barka. One view, relying on the general similarity of the governing institutions of Euesperitae to those of Thera and Cyrene as revealed by an inscription,[126] holds that the town was founded from the latter. Her first coins appear in about 480, when according to the symbols they bear, Euesperitae was allied with Cyrene.[127] Teucheira (today Tocra), situated on the coast between the port of Barka and Euesperitae, on the other hand, shows pottery from the late 7th century. Herodotus calls her "a town of Barka",[128] but the information of the scholiast on Pindar, that this was a Cyrenean foun-

---

was directed against Barka. A settlement may already have existed there, but it would have been entirely composed of Libyans.

[120] *BMC*, p. clxvi.

[121] *Ibid.*, pp. xlv, clxv.

[122] A. H. M. Jones, *CERP*, 1937, p. 355.

[123] Eg. Beloch, *Griech. Gesch.*² I, p. 2; E. Meyer, *Gesch. Altertums*⁴, 1944, p. 151 n.

[124] *BMC*, p. clxv, n. 1.

[125] Herod. IV, 204.

[126] P. M. Fraser, *BSAA*, 39, 1951, pp. 137-8.

[127] *BMC*, pp. xliv-xlv.

[128] Herod. IV, 171.

dation,[129] would seem more correct. Her coins, extant from the first half of the 5th century, nevertheless, show an alliance with Barka,[130] and this may have been the source of Herodotus' statement.

Cyrene in this period shows signs of economic prosperity. In about 525 human figures appear on her coins,[131] which begin to elicit Athenian influence. In 500 approximately, i.e. under Battus IV, the first inscribed coins are struck. Contemporarily the façade of the Temple of Apollo was readorned with Parian marble, to judge from the Gorgon akroterion found there; [132] this figure is perhaps to be connected with the similar figure now to be seen on the city's coins.[133] Contemporary building activity in the south-east of Cyrene may be evidenced by a similar akroterion found in the area of the Agora.[134]

The country's Greek population was certainly growing at this period, if only due to the settlement of the mercenaries imported by Arkesilaos III; the head of the god Ammon, which begins to figure on Cyrenean and Barkan coins about 500,[135] hints at the drawing closer of connections with the cult of the Oasis of Ammon (Siwa) along the desert routes. Herodotus, at all events, knew of a colony of Samians settled at the Oasis of Ḥargiyeh between Ammon and Egypt in the middle of the 5th century, [136] and it is hard to explain its raison d'être except on the assumption that they were engaged in the caravan trade. In the same years Pindar dedicated to the god Ammon verses which were inscribed on stone at the Oasis, apparently in the year 442 B.C. [137]

Among the finds from the Temple of Artemis, objects dated not later than about 500 reflect trade connections with Rhodes, Crete, perhaps also with Phoenicia and Central Africa,[138] while the gold objects from the same deposit point to a sound, even a prosperous, economic situation. On the criterion of the distribution of her coin-hoards in other countries at this time, Cyrene holds eighth

---

[129] Schol. *Pyth.* IV, 26 (Drachmann).
[130] *BMC*, p. xlv.
[131] *Ibid.*, p. xxxiii.
[132] *TA*, pp. 55-56.
[133] *BMC*, pl. ii, 18.
[134] *TA*, p. 57.
[135] *BMC*, p. ccxxxiv.
[136] Herod. III, 26, 1; cf. Myres, *CAH* III, 1929, p. 668.
[137] Schol. IX *Pyth.*, 90b (Drachmann); Paus. IX, 16, 1.
[138] *TA*, p. 97; *AI* IV, 191, 200.

place after Aegina, Athens, Thasos, Chios, Corinth, Naxos and Paros, and precedes several Greek centres of no small prominence, such as Miletus, Samos and Cyprus.[139] The distribution, therefore, furnishes an indication of the importance of Cyrenean trade. Yet it is not till the second half of the 5th century (c. 450) [140] that the city began to circulate gold coins,[141] since only then, it would seem, was access obtained to a supply of this precious metal. The problem of Cyrene's trade along the desert routes will be discussed later.

The sources for Cyrene's history in the 5th century are not abundant; even the evidence for the existence of the two last Battiad kings is slight, though it need not be rejected. Nothing is known of Battus IV, unless to him can be ascribed the repair of the Temple of Apollo and the striking of the city's first inscribed coins. He appears to have died round about the year 470.[142] Arkesilaos IV, by contrast, was the subject of Pindar's verse as victor in the chariot races at Delphi in 462[143] and at Olympia in 460.[144] Some have compared his court to the magnificent courts of the Sicilian tyrants; [145] it was apparently luxurious and cultured, to judge by the royal participation in the athletics of the mainland and by the presence of the poet Pindar. The statue described by Pausanias,[146] showing Battus crowned by the nymph Cyrene, riding in a chariot driven by Libya, seems to have been set up by Arkesilaos IV, as it was the work of the sculptor Amphion of Cnossos, active between 450 and 400 approximately.[147] In the view of most scholars Arkesilaos fell out with his nobles, some of whom he exiled—this is their interpretation of Pindar's words [148]—but the view is disputed. It is known however that the King was forced to strengthen his power with the help of mercenaries brought from without, whom he settled at Euesperitai.[149] This was not the

---

[139] F. Heichelheim, *WGA*, 1938, pp. 297-8.

[140] L. Naville, *Les monnaies d'or de la Cyrénaïque*, 1951, p. 15.

[141] *BMC*, p. xlvi.

[142] *CMB*, p. 160.

[143] Pind., IV, V *Pyth*.

[144] Pind., V *Pyth.*, 124 (166).

[145] *BMC*, p. xliv.

[146] Paus. X, 15, 6.

[147] *CMB*, p. 199.

[148] IV *Pyth.*, 227, 280.

[149] Theotimus (*FHG*, IV, 517), *Lib. I de Cyrenensibus*; ap. schol. Pind., V *Pyth.*, 34 (Drachmann).

present Bengazi, which is on the site of the hellenistic city; the
original site has been identified by air photography and excavation
among the salt-lagoons near the northern shore, east of the present
city.[150] The circumstances of Arkesilaos' death are wrapped in
obscurity, but the scholiast on Pindar [151] tells us that his enemies
put and end to his life, and his son is known to have been killed at
Euesperitai.[152]

The coins of Cyrene might reveal to us at least as much as the
written records, were we able to determine the relationship between
those of the period between 480 and 435 and the two last Battiad
sovereigns. Robinson held [153] that the last of the tetradrams
datable between 480 and 450, and the first tetradrams of the period
450-435, were to be associated with the period after the end of the
monarchy, and that this applied equally to the coins of Cyrene,
Barka and Euesperitae. On this view, Arkesilaos IV reigned from
475 to 450, and his coins are the first tetradrams bearing the head
of Ammon, which reveal a complete artistic break with the past. A
remarkable tetradram published by Jenkins [154] bearing an exceptionally fine head of Ammon in the late archaic style, is dated by
Jenkins to 470-460, and thought by him to mark Cyrene's new
independent orientation after the Persian defeat at Plataea.
Pindar, indeed, gives the impression [155] that in 462 Arkesilaos
was still a young man, yet when Herodotus wrote in the middle
of the century his rule had ended, since the historian had heard
the Delphic prophecy [156] made allegedly to Arkesilaos III, that the
Battiads would reign unto the eighth generation. This can with
difficulty be reconciled with the scholiast's statement on the
Fourth Pythiad, that the dynasty ruled two hundred years (i.e.
till circa 439), but his calculation may have depended on too formal
an interpretation of the prophetic words "eight generations"
(ὀκτὼ γεννεάς). Jenkins' tetradram would indeed support an earlier
end of the Battiad dynasty. Archaeological authority for the date
of the end of Battiad rule is nevertheless found by Chamoux [157] in

---

[150] *Antiq.*, XXVI, 1952, p. 210, fig. 1.
[151] Schol. *Pind.* IV, p. 93 (Drachmann).
[152] Heraclides Ponticus, *de Repub. Cyrens.*, 8.
[153] *BMC*, p. xliii-xlv sqq.
[154] *NC*⁶ XV, 1955, p. 150, no. 25.
[155] V *Pyth.*, 109 (146).
[156] IV, 163, 2.
[157] *CMB*, p. 208.

a bronze head discovered near the Temple of Apollo, representing, he thinks, Arkesilaos IV himself, as it wears a diadem and adorned the temple before its rebuilding in the mid-4th century B.C. The style of the portrait dates it with considerable precision to 440 B.C.,[158] which would be difficult to reconcile with the coin-evidence.

It may be supposed that the two last kings of Cyrene still inclined to Persia. A Delphic response as transmitted by Diodorus Siculus [159] has been considered by several scholars [160] to belong to the time of Battus IV, since in demanding the settlement of Libya it emphasizes the royal authority of the suppliant, who appears as Battus Aristoteles. Parke therefore believes that we have here a statement meant to strengthen Battus IV in a time of political difficulty. If this is so we must interpret the resistance of Barka to the Persians in 484 as a revolt against the King. The Egyptians rose against Persia in the same year [161] and in 462, when they rose a second time, they received Libyan aid.[162] It is at least known that Arkesilaos IV planned a campaign in Egypt that year,[163] but whether to aid the rebels or the Persians, we do not know. Whatever the case, when the remnants of the Athenian expedition returned from Egypt through Cyrene in 457,[164] they were not molested, showing that by this time Persian control of Cyrene had ended. Chamoux indeed believes,[165] like Jenkins, that the new coin-types which appear in the city after 470 indicate the state's independence and its liberation from the Persian yoke.

If we attempt to summarize the little information we possess on Arkesilaos IV, we may see him as an energetic autocrat, strengthening his power with new colonization, drawing closer his ties with the desert oases, increasing the circulation of his coinage, maintaining relations with the Greek sacred centres (Delphi, Olympia, Athens), claiming rule over the other cities of Cyrenaica,[166] a patron of culture, and a breeder of thoroughbred horses. In the first

---

[158] *CMB*, pp. 209, 368.
[159] VIII, 29.
[160] *DO*, pp. 75-6; Studnicza, *Kyrene*, 1890, p. 98.
[161] *RC*, para. 44, p. 202.
[162] Diod. XI, 74, 2.
[163] Pind., IV *Pyth.*, 56 (97).
[164] Thuc. I, 110, 1.
[165] *CMB*, p. 167.
[166] 'King. . of great cities', according to Pind., V *Pyth.*, 15-16 (19-20). But his alleged relations with Athens depend on the restoration of the controversial *SEG* 2, 170.

half of the 5th century the north portico of the Agora was extended, and a heroon built over the tomb of Battus I. In the same period the nearby shrine of Opheles was replaced by a temple.[167]

How was it that the Battiad monarchy held its ground as an active political régime when monarchy had died out almost completely over most of Greece? The geographical isolation of Cyrene certainly helped to delay in some measure the state's social development, and its strong Dorian element probably displayed a conservative attitude in favour of monarchy, like its Spartan kindred. Persian influence certainly prolonged Battiad rule beyond its natural term. Social factors also had their effect; relations with the Libyans encouraged the perpetuation of a monarchy for reasons of prestige. Moreover Cyrene possessed broader areas of fertile soil for expansion than most of the states of mainland Greece, and this delayed the development of the small peasant as member of a compact aggressive group, or the crystallization of a hoplite class to claim its share of power. Cyrene further retained its economic independence in the sphere of food-supply to a greater extent than most of the Greek states, and as an exporter of agricultural produce could purchase from overseas the crafts products and luxuries which she needed. This situation was apt to delay the development of domestic crafts. Heichelheim rightly observed [168] that the tyrannies of mainland Greece could not maintain themselves for long because of the limitedness of their economic bases; the Battiads, for their part, disposed of considerable areas.

But a time came when Battiad policy contradicted itself. Trade expanded beyond the limits within which it could be conducted as a royal monopoly; colonization reached its natural bounds of development within the existent settled area and the demand of the kings for colonists who would support their rule led to the growth of a population whose economy endangered the existence of large aristocratic estates. Thus a constellation of political forces was created which hastened the end of the monarchy. When Persian support was removed, the régime collapsed, never to recover.

The written sources for Cyrenean history from the end of the Battiad dynasty to the rise of Alexander the Great are few and fragmentary. Heraclides of Pontus [169] places the death of Battus

---

[167] Stucchi, *Cirene*, pp. 47 sqq.
[168] *WGA*, p. 416.
[169] *Loc. cit.* (n. 152).

son of Arkesilaus IV "after the foundation of a democratic régime",
but there is no information on its nature or details. As a completely
democratic régime was not introduced till after 401, and was
preceded by a struggle between the aristocracy and the demos, we
must assume that a restricted democracy was in power, not participated in by all classes of the people. It is here relevant to note,
however, that some time in the second half of the 5th century,
apparently, the west portico of the Agora was replaced by a building
for public assembly.[170] The steles of the Cyrenean Demiurgi,[171]
which appear first in the middle of the 5th century, moreover,
make public the accounts of an administrative body of the state
responsible to the city and therefore reflect democratic procedure.
It may be assumed that the royal properties were now entrusted
to the city's elected officials, who included the demiurgi, for they
dispose of considerable revenues from agricultural lands which
defrayed, *inter alia*, the expenses of various cults (see below, p. 87).
It may also be supposed that the royal priestly functions now
passed into the hands of a High Priest elected by the state; such a
priest, at any rate was at a later period annually appointed and
gave his name to the year (ἱερεὺς ἐπώνυμος).[172] To what extent the
city reverted to the organization inaugurated by Demonax, it is
impossible to know, least of all because his reforms are a subject of
controversy.[173] It is difficult to solve this problem on the basis of
information on the magistracies of an earlier period, although
ephors are known to have existed in Thera and in Crete.[174] On the
other hand, the archons and council (βουλή) referred to at Barka [175]
in connection with the events of 484, might suggest the renewal of
democracy in that town.

In the middle of the 5th century the tetradrams of Cyrene,
Barka and Euesperitae manifest technical and artistic progress,[176]
perhaps indicating the end of the monarchy. These coins are imitated closely by the rulers of Lycia between about 450 and 430,[177]

---

[170] Stucchi, *Cirene*, pp. 74-5.
[171] For the functions of these magistrates, *DAI* I, Cir., ii, nos. 15, 16.
[172] See L. Robert, *Hellenica*, 11-12, 1960, pp. 542 sqq.
[173] Schäfer, for example, rejects completely the democratic character of
his reforms, thus impugning the authority of Herodotus, whose account he
regards as anachronistic.
[174] *CMB*, pp. 214-5, and references.
[175] Polyaenus, *Strateg.*, VII, 28—τοὺς ἄρχοντας . . . βουλευσαμένους.
[176] *BMC*, p. xlvi.
[177] *Ibid.*, p. xliii.

and the reason for the link may have been the Cyrenean import of silver bullion from Lycia. Before 435 Cyrene was minting gold coins, which bore the symbols both of Cyrene and Barka, thus declaring an alliance between the two states.[178] It is clear that Cyrenean trade had gained considerable impetus with the fall of the Battiads, and this was expressed in these years by her transfer from the Attic to the Asiatic monetary standard, thus strengthening Cyrene's economic ties with Egypt and the eastern Aegean, more especially with Rhodes and Samos.[179]

Arkesilaos appears to have entertained relations with Athens,[180] but after his death, on the outbreak of the Peloponnesian War, the Cyrenean cities, as Dorians, presumably inclined to Sparta, but did not intervene in the hostilities, although the Spartan Gylippus received aid from Cyrene in 413, and himself helped Euesperitae to repel a Libyan attack.[181]

Barka had manifested signs of independence under the monarchy, and had begun to pursue an independent policy from about 450; in the treaty between her and Cyrene she was the senior partner, and her decisions seem to have been decisive. Teucheira was subject to her in the middle of the century,[182] a relationship expressed in the coins of both cities.[183] Pseudo-Scylax too, writing in the mid-4th century, distinguishes between the cities subject to Cyrene and those subject to Barka,[184] and in later literature (Aeneas Tacitus, Titian, Ptolemy) the people of Barka are referred to as a separate entity. This division was doubtless rooted in geographical factors, principally in the eroded and broken waterless area separating the two cities. In the years after 435 Barka's coinage develops steadily, whereas Cyrene's is static, and her position would seem to have been one of depression and inferiority in those years. Nevertheless, as the general artistic level of the coins rose throughout the country, a growing uniformity is traceable, to be interpreted as the result of intensified freedom of movement between the urban centres. The ancient highway that leaves Cyrene southwestward for Zavia Beida (Balagrae) is quarried in the rock and

---

[178] *Ibid.*, p. xlvi.
[179] *DAI* I Cir., ii, p. 20.
[180] But see n. 166.
[181] Thuc. VII, 50, 2.
[182] Herod. IV, 171.
[183] *BMC*, p. xlv.
[184] Periplous (Müller), 108 fin.

lined on both sides by rockcut tombs of the 5th and 4th centuries.

In the year 401 we hear of civil war at Cyrene.[185] One Ariston seized power, slew fifty aristocrats, and drove out the rest. They found refuge at Euesperitae, which still maintained, apparently, an aristocratic régime, and with the aid of 3,000 men of Messene recruited by Euesperitae to fight the Libyans,[186] who had heavily defeated the city, advanced upon Cyrene. After a severe but indecisive battle, the two factions arrived at a compromise and set up a joint polity. This account means that a moderate constitution existed in 401, participated in by both the aristocracy and the people. But Aristotle informs us [187] that a constitution modelled on the Athenian polity of Cleisthenes had been established, and had been the occasion of civil conflict (στάσις) in the city. The source for this, the *Politics*, was completed in 336, and it is known that the citizens of Cyrene had appealed to Plato to draw up a constitution for them; [188] Plato died in 346. The Stele of the Founders, which commemorates a decision of the Cyrenean demos to grant citizenship to resident or visiting Therans,[189] evidences a fully democratic constitution in the first half of the century. In the same period Cyrene was participating actively in the Panathenaic games, a clear sign of her democratic sympathies, the earliest of the known panathenaic amphorae found in Cyrenaica dating from the year 373.[190] Between the years 435-375 the city's coinage decreases, perhaps as a result of her internal conflicts; contemporarily Euesperitae was under attack from her Libyan neighbours; further, in 430/29 the plague spread from Greece to Libya,[191] and it is to be assumed that her cities suffered accordingly. But in the neighbourhood of 375 there is a change; the coins of Cyrene become more numerous, gold pieces appear in abundance, and the artistic level of the currency reaches its highest point.[192] It may accordingly be suggested that the Cleisthenic constitution was inaugurated at

---

[185] Diod. XIV, 34, 4.

[186] Paus. IV, 26, 2.

[187] Arist., *Pol.*, VI, 4 (1319b).

[188] Plut., *ad princ. inerudit.*, 1; Diog. Laertius, III, 2, who in *de vit. philos.* III, 6 records that Plato studied under the mathematician Theodorus of Cyrene, apparently in 396 BC (*PW*² V. 1934, sv. Theodorus (30)).

[189] *SEG* 9, 3; *RFC* 1928, pp. 222 sqq.

[190] G. von Brauschitsch, *Die Panathenäischen Preisamforen*, 1910, pp. 158 sqq.; E. Breccia, *Iscriz. Greci e Latini*, 1911, pp. xviii sqq.

[191] Thuc. II, 48.

[192] *BMC*, p. lxix.

Cyrene in the first half of the 5th century, probably between 375 and 373.[193] Such a date is at least appropriate to the commencement of the building of the Treasury of Cyrene at Delphi, set by Bousquet approximately in the year 373. (See p. 41).

Aristotle's information of the Cleisthenic character of Cyrene's democratic constitution poses the historian a number of problems: What were the conditions which produced it, and what the economic situation which it reflects? The problem is not simplified by the numerous differences between the history of Athens and the history of Cyrene. Does the introduction of a Cleisthenic democracy point to similar conditions and was the constitution really like the Athenian?

Aristotle says explicitly that the aims of both reforms were the same—to wit, the complete fusion of all elements of the population and the dissolution of long-standing societies (συνήθειαι)—meaning the cult associations with political aims. As he mentions the increase of the number of phratriai (φρατρίαι) [194] i.e. the organized groups of families of common kinship,—who together formed, at least in ancient times, the tribe (φυλή)—and says that Cleisthenes did not alter their structure in Attica,—we must suppose that in Cyrene their number was enlarged.[195] Newman [196] and Wade Gery [197] on the other hand, interpret Aristotle's statement, in the light of his information in the *Athenaion Politeia* [198]—that the increase of the tribes referred to in VI, 4 related only to Athens, and not to Cyrene. This conclusion is accepted apparently by Siebert [199] citing further in support of it the mention of a τριφύλια in the Cyrenean Cathartic Law of the late 4th century.[200] The conclusion may be unimpeachable in terms of an understanding of the texts, but seems unrealistic in terms of the situation in Cyrene

---

[193] Diodorus (X, 4, 1) relates that Clinias, a citizen of Tarentum, a Pythagorean and friend of Plato, travelled to Cyrene to aid one Pheroras, having heard that this man, also a Pythagorean, had lost his entire property "owing to a revolution in the state" (διὰ τινα πολιτικὴν περίστασιν). A terminus post quem for this event is probably the year 387, when Plato visited Sicily and formed ties with the Pythagorean group at Tarentum.

[194] *Pol.* VI, 4 (1319b).

[195] Wade Gery, *The Class. Quarterly*, 27, 1933, pp. 25-7.

[196] *The Politics of Aristotle*, 1902, III, p. 522.

[197] *Essays in Greek History*, 1958, p. 150.

[198] XXI, 6.

[199] *Metropolis und Apoikie*, 1963, p. 20.

[200] *SEG* 9, 72, line 134.

which can be assumed on the basis of the country's social and economic development.

One may wonder, indeed, how far an increase of phratriai is reconcilable with a non-increase of the tribes. Theoretically it is, but there may be other evidence in favour of the view that the number of the Cyrenean tribes actually was increased in the 4th century. Cleisthenes' Attic reform attained its aim by giving the tribes a new structure, each one deriving its composition from the inhabitants of three demes each located in a different trittys of Attica. The tribes thus ceased to have local political significance and the three old divisions of Attica with their individual political family interests lost their importance. The Cyrenean reform, on the other hand, would have been designed to adapt the constitution to the changes of population that had taken place since the inauguration of the democracy of Demonax, and these must have been considerable in view of the settlement of new elements by Arkesilaos II and IV, and the new groups of merchants and craftsmen doubtless attracted to the country by the growth of Cyrenean trade. It may moreover be supposed that Arkesilaos IV, in his desire to increase the population, had not hesitated to grant privileges and right of residence to newcomers. If so, the old tribes constituted by Demonax according to the origin of their members would no longer have corresponded to the composition of the free population.

Cleisthenes established the principle that the tribes no longer built their membership according to locality or origin.[201] On the other hand, the demes, which were the elective units, he made into organs of local administration. The Cyrenean democracy of 375 must have enlarged the citizen-body, the more so as Cyrene was a country of immigration and absorption to a greater degree than Attica. This is evidenced by the increase of the phratriai, whose function was, *inter alia* the initiation of the newborn infant, the bride and the young adolescent into the community. On the other hand we hear of no Cyrenean demes on the Athenian model, nor has any term parallel to the γενή of Samos, or the demes of Kalymna and Cos, come down to us. This might lead us to ask whether the Cyrenean tribes themselves did not become geographical and administrative units, as occurred at Mantineia and Elis,

---

[201] For a suggestion as to their composition in the time of Demonax, Jeffery, *Ha* 10, pp. 139 sqq.

with whom Cyrene had close relationships? We have no answer to this question at present.

There remains the problem, whether the three Demonactan tribes were superseded by a greater number. According to lines 15-16 of the "Stele of the Founders", Therans obtaining Cyrenean citizenship are to be registered [202] in a phyle of their own in the original Demonactan tribe of Therans and perioikoi, according to Siebert.[203] Yet Ptolemy Lagos' new Cyrenean constitution, given at the end of the 4th century,[204] established a boulé of 500, and five strategoi in addition to Ptolemy himself, implying the existence of five phylai.[205] Five strategoi are indeed independently attested in the 4th century (see n. 213). As Ptolemy's constitution restricted citizenship to owners of an annual income of 2000 drachmae, it may be assumed that the citizen-body of the Cleisthenic constitution was larger. For this reason, the word τριφύλια recorded in the Cathartic Law of much the same period [206] may be no more than a reference to an archaic building whose name reflected an ancient division long obsolete. On the other hand, the "Stele of the Founders" further records that each new citizen under the democracy was registered in a tribe, a patra (= phratria) and a hetairea (ἑταιρήα).[207] The nature of the last is unknown; such are recorded at Thera,[208] and in the Dorian cities of Crete they are identical with the phratriai,[209] but as units smaller than the phratriai they seem to be peculiar to Cyrene.[210] They originated as groups of kindred serving together in war,[211] but as Aristotle writes that the aim of the "Cleisthenic" reform was to break up the social-political clubs (συνήθειαι), the Cyrenean hetaireai must have had a different character. The Therans, it should be observed, are incorporated among nine hetaireai,—presumably each tribe had this number,—

---

[202] A. Ferrabino, *RFC*, 1928, p. 226.

[203] *Op. cit.*, p. 20.

[204] *SEG* 9, 1, paras 2, 4.

[205] *CERP*, p. 357.

[206] *DAI* II, Cir. i, p. 83 and line 132.

[207] G. Oliverio, *Documenti di Cirene antica*, 1926, pp. 224 sqq., line 16.

[208] *IG* 12, (3), 1898, 450, line 18.

[209] *PW* 9, 1913, sv. Ἑταιρία, col. 1373.

[210] This unit was also a feature of the constitution of Megalopolis (*IG* V (2), 495) founded in 368, not long after the inauguration of Cyrene's Cleisthenic régime.

[211] V. Ehrenberg, *Der Staat der Griechen*, I, 1957, p. 9. For a bibliography of the hetaireai, *Siebert, Metropolis und Apoikie*, 1963, p. 20.

which might be interpreted as favouring a division of each tribe into three parts. Theoretically, if the democratic constitution of Cyrene was really Cleisthenic, the entire city territory would have been divided into three or more districts, each furnishing a section of one phyle. It is indeed to be remarked, that geographically the Cyrenaican Jebel does fall into three parts—the coastal plain, the Lusaita, and the uppermost plateau.[212]

In the "Stele of the Founders" the general citizen assembly (ἐκκλησία) is the legislative body. Five strategoi are recorded in the same century,[213] and the ephors figure in the Ptolemaic constitution somewhat later.[214] They may be assumed to have existed earlier in view of the post's antiquity, for it existed in Thera; there are five under Ptolemy. The steles of the Demiurgi record three such magistrates, who officiated from the 5th to the 2nd century B.C. at least, but are unmentioned in the Ptolemaic law. This need not mean that they were unimportant under the Cleisthenic constitution. Quite the contrary; it suggests that these were the most important magistrates in the democratic régime; at Mantineia and Elis they headed the boulé. An important Cyrenean inscription of the 4th century,[215] defines the functions of the demiurgi in a given situation and adds that they are discharged by these magistrates in the cities (of Libya), by the hellenodikai in the Temple of Zeus Olympios (i.e. in Olympia), by the amphiktyons at Delphi, and by the hieromnamones in the Temple of Zeus Lykaios (the Lyceum of Arcadia). The functions concerned include the recording of claims arising from seizure of the property of one city by another as an act of reprisal in war time; hence it may well be that the demiurgi of Cyrene handled not only the revenue from the sacred lands but the city's financial affairs as a whole.[216]

We have no details of political events in the other cities of

---

[212] The name *hetairea* does not fit this function, but the geographical division of Cyrenaica is appropriate to such a partition; I do not refer here to the triple division into plateau, steppe and desert, since there is no evidence exactly when Greek settlement reached the edge of the desert. The suggestion concerns a division within the regions of primary settlement, and is of course tentative; there is no specific evidence.

[213] *DAI* II, Cir., ii, p. 160, no. 141.

[214] *SEG* 9, 1, para. 5; para 11, line 82.

[215] *ASAA* 39-40, p. 273, no. 103, pp. 8-12.

[216] Yet see the edict of Ptolemy X Soter II to Cyrene (*DAI* Cir. ii, no. 538), whose formula suggests that the Demiurgi were the city's leading magistrates.

Cyrenaica in this period. Euesperitae, despite its Cyrenean connections, had welcomed the aristocratic refugees in 401, and therefore
can be assumed to have had an aristocratic form of government.
An inscription of the 4th century [217] evidences that the city was
governed by ephors, a gerousia and a bolé (sic), and as the demos
is not mentioned, and the resolution is brought before the Bolé
by the first two instances, the city appears to have been under
aristocratic or oligarchic rule, although in the view of Fraser [218]
the inclusion of the Bolé points to a democracy. The régime perhaps
lay between the two extremes.

Barka, according to her coins, was still independent, and to
judge by her alliance with the Egyptian Akoris (383) [219] she was
still exercizing an independent foreign policy; between 435 and
375 Barka is the dominant member of a partnership with Cyrene,
but her coins cease in about 375, and Cyrene is the ruling partner
henceforth.

Cyrene's renewed activity on the inauguration of her democracy
in the second quarter of the 4th century is expressed in many ways,
nor does archaeology leave any doubt that the political change
liberated her creative powers. For the first time there are increasingly numerous inscriptions to demonstrate the growth of means
and the spread of literacy. The allusion to legal procedures common
to all the Libyan cities in the matter of reprisals is a symptom of
growing unity among the country's towns. Successful military
action is indicated not only by a contemporary campaign to the
Syrtic region and the erection of a treasury from the plunder [220] —
but also by the building of a similar treasury (called by the Italians
the "Strategeion") in the Sanctuary of Apollo by three strategoi
of Cyrene. This treasury is situated close to the wall supporting the
upper terrace of the Sanctuary, and contained the plunder of a
war whose aim is not stated.[221] The building's period is defined

---

[217] P. M. Fraser, *BSAA* 39, 1951, pp. 132 sqq.

[218] *Loc. cit.*, p. 137.

[219] Theoph., *Frag.* (ap. Phot., 176), 111.

[220] *SEG* 9, 77. The editors of *SEG* date this inscription in the 3rd century
B.C.; I permit myself to disagree, since the letters are characteristic of the
4th century at Cyrene, and Menesarchos, son of Theochrestos, one of the
strategoi of the inscription, had a son, Theochrestos son of Menesarchos, who
was buried near the city at the end of the century (*SEG* 9, 228). Even had he
not died relatively young, Menesarches could hardly have been at his acme
later than the middle of the 4th century.

[221] *TA* pp. 40 sqq.: *AI* III, 1930, pp. 203-4.

between the middle of the 4th century [222] and its last decades. In 373 approximately the building of the Treasury of Cyrene was begun in the Delphic sanctuary, but interrupted by the battle of Chaeroneia (338). Built of Pentelic and Parian marble, it was designed to demonstrate, in the view of its investigator, the mathematical theories of Theodorus of Cyrene and of his pupil Plato.[223]

The institution of democracy broke up the factions that divided the city, united the people and directed their attention to the capital. Stucchi thinks that the city's street-plan north of the main street joining the Acropolis with the Agora, originated with a lay-out along the original field-divisions in the middle of the 6th century B.C.[224] This view must presumablyt now supersede the conclusion of D. Buttle [225] and that of the writer,[226] based on the orientation of the Temple of Apollo (previously thought to be of Demeter) as rebuilt in the 4th century B.C. in the south-west corner of the Agora, that the present visible town plan originated in the same century. Stucchi bases his 6th-century date on the orientation of altars Eɪ and 2 and Sacellum Eɪ of Opheles, also of the first peribolos of the Temple of Apollo in the Agora, and its relation to the main street (the σκυρωτὰ ὁδός). It should nevertheless be noted that the insulae to the north of the Agora were observed by Stucchi himself [227] to resemble in measurement those of Priene (4th century B.C.) rather than those of Olynthos (5th century B.C.).

In the 4th century, at any rate, the city was greatly embellished; in the Agora, the heroon of Battus was replaced by a roofed structure,[228] and the Agora enlarged northward by heavy walls,

---

[222] One of the three commanders, Aristophanes son of Parabaitas, is recorded with Philon son of Annakeris and three other citizens—magistrates of the polis according to the constitution of Ptolemy Lagos—on CIG 4833 = SP pl. 178, no. 9. The latter belongs to the last thirty years of the 4th century, while the wall contemporary with the Strategeion was repaired not later than the end of the century. The building is therefore to be dated between 340 and 310 approximately.

[223] J. Bousquet, Le trésor de Cyrène; Fouilles de Delphes, II, Topographie et Architecture, 2v., 1952, p. 88; cf. Mnemosyne,[4] 6, 1953, pp. 242-243.

[224] Stucchi, Cirene, p. 41

[225] In Cyrenaican Expedn. of the Univ. of Manchester, 1952, 1956, p. 37.

[226] Expressed in the first (Hebrew) version of the present work, p. 36.

[227] Op. cit., p. 41.

[228] Stucchi, ibid., pp. 54-5; L'agora di Cirene, 1965, pp. 139 sqq.

its northern portico being replaced twice in rapid succession.[229] In the Sanctuary of Apollo, after an earthquake had caused the collapse of the cliff overlooking the area from the south in the middle of the century, the Temple of Apollo was rebuilt and enlarged. The archaic shrine was enclosed by a new wall and encompassed by an outer crepis and peristasis of great Doric columns. The altar of Apollo was encrusted with Parian marble donated by Philon son of Annakeris, whose father had redeemed the philosopher Plato from slavery in 383.[230] In the course of the second half of the century the upper terrace of the Sanctuary was laid out, while its low dividing wall (δρύφακτος), and probably at the same time the retaining wall of the lower terrace, were constructed.[231] The theatre in the west of the sanctuary was built in approximately the same period, to judge by the reuse within the structure of triglyphs from the archaic temple;[232] it may have superseded an older structure of timber.[233] The beautiful marble door of the Temple of Apollo in the Agora is stylistically dated to the same century. Furthermore, the seated figure of Zeus Lykaeos which appears on the city's coins at the end of the century [234] is perhaps to be interpreted that the Temple of Zeus on the eastern hill now received a similar image, since the head of an acrolithic statue of this type found in the temple was thought by its discoverers to be a smaller second-century copy of an original wrought by a sculptor of the school of Pheidias.[235] The building activity described, indeed finds additional expression in the increasing abundance of Cyrene's gold coins, to which allusion has already been made, and in their outstanding beauty and variety. The appearance of the names of moneyers [236] on coinage from the beginning of the century, and of masons' marks on the masonry of the dryphaktos of the upper sanctuary terrace, are signs of a technical and professional development characteristic of a commercial democracy.

Moneyers' names are known earlier on the coins of Barka, and

---

[229] *Cirene*, pp. 62 sqq.; *L'agora*, pp. 129-137.

[230] *TA* p. 69; *AI* I, 1927, p. 150.

[231] *TA* p. 64.

[232] *TA* p. 47.

[233] G. Anti, *Edifici treatrali arcaici*, 1947, p. 122 sqq.

[234] *BMC*, pp. lxxx, ccxxxix; pl. xiii, 13.

[235] E. Parabeni, *Catalogo delle Sculture di Cirene*, 1959, no. 182, Tav. 104-5; *AI* I, pp. 3 sqq.; *Dedalo* 7, Oct., 1926, pp. 273 sqq.

[236] The evidence is against their being the names of the city-magistrates; see *BMC*, p. ccxxxi.

the appearance of the name Allat(eir) between 435-322 [237] may be interpreted to mean that noble families were taking their share in the work of minting. Cyrene's influence on the Libyans of her neighbourhood finds expression in the imitations of Cyrenean staters found in Egypt.[238]

We have noted the finds of Panathenaic prize amphorae in Cyrenaica, which evidence the city's rapprochement with Athens in her democratic period. Ferrabino interpreted the granting of citizen-rights to Theran residents [239] as a first step on the part of Cyrene towards a political rapprochement with Athens' renewed maritime league, of which Thera was a member.[240] The League was reestablished in 376, shortly before the year we have thought marked the establishment of Cyrene's "Cleisthenic" democracy. Whether or not Ferrabino was right, the kindred feeling with Athens found material expression later under the rule of Ophellas, when 10,000 Athenians who had been deprived of their citizenship migrated to Cyrene.

A difficult problem is posed by the alleged war between Cyrene and Carthage. Until the Italian excavations carried out at Cyrene between 1924 and 1931, authority for this was to be found only in the works of Sallust,[241] Valerius Maximus,[242] and Pomponius Mela,[243] and as all these sources mention the event only in connection with the mythical story of the Philaenan brothers,[244] and there is no parallel Greek source, Robinson and others have rejected its authenticity. Nor does the seabattle said by Servius [245] to have been fought between Barka and Carthage find confirmation in other sources. The possibility of such a collision is nevertheless entirely reasonable on general grounds, granted the assumption that Cyrene was interested in the desert trade-routes which debouch upon the Syrtic Gulf, where the emporia appear to have lain under Punic control from the end of the 6th century. It is necessary therefore to investigate whether the desert routes played any part in Cyrenean commerce in this period.

---

[237] *BMC* p. clxxxi.
[238] *BMC*, p. lxxix.
[239] A Ferrabino, *RFC*, 1928, pp. 250 sqq.
[240] His view is doubted by A. J. Graham (*JHS* 80, 1960, p. 100).
[241] *Jug.*, 79.
[242] Val. Maximus, V, 6, 4.
[243] I, 38.
[244] Mela, *l.c.*
[245] ad *Aen.*, IV, 42.

The ancient evidence for Carthage's trade through the ports of the Syrtis is very vague.[246] The harbours themselves are not mentioned prior to Polybius, who writes of them in connection with the treaty signed between Rome and Carthage in 509 B.C. Apart from the trade in gems,[247] there is no allusion to products of Central Africa being brought through the Syrtic ports between Herodotus' time and the 2nd century B.C., and Pseudo-Scylax' report in the 4th century of the export of ivory, skins and gold from the Atlantic coast, hints only by its silence that the ports of the Syrtis may then have been entirely under Carthaginian control.[248] The whole assumption of the existence of a commerce between the north African coast and the centre of the continent, indeed, is based on the reference to emporia, on the supposition that the caravan routes have not altered in the course of time, on references to various wares from Central Africa used chiefly by the Romans, and on medieval analogies.[249] There is, indeed, no doubt that elephants from inland were exported by Lepcis Magna.[250] Yet Heywood writes: [251] "No ancient source states that there was such a trade". Nor does the outlook of recent geographers incline to assume links between Cyrene, the desert routes and Central Africa in ancient times. Cary, for example, [252] affirms that "Cyrenaica in ancient times was never the terminal region of a caravan route"; Goodchild, citing his opinion,[253] adds,[254] that the road from Aujila to Ajedabia and Bengazi could not have been as important to trade as was that traversing Fezzan to Tripoli. They are followed by Burney and Hey,[255] also by Jones and Little; [256] Burney and Hey state that there is no sign of an ancient north-south route coming from the Jebel into the Desert, and remark that the existing road from Aujila through Kufra and Tibesti was opened up only at the beginning of the 19th century.

---

[246] For historical sources, see C. Perroud, *De Syrticis Emporiis*, 1881.
[247] Theoph., *Frag.*, II, 3, who refers to the precious stones imported from Carthage.
[248] Perroud, *op. cit.*, p. 96.
[249] *RC*, para. 84, pp. 378 sqq.
[250] Aurigemma, *AI* 7, 1940, pp. 67 sqq.; J. Desanges, *Latomus*, 23, 1964, p. 713.
[251] T. Frank, *ESAR*, IV, 1938, p. 62.
[252] *The Geographical Background of Greek and Roman History*, 1949, p. 218.
[253] *GJ* 118, 1952, p. 151.
[254] *Ibid.*, n. 3.
[255] *Prehistory and Pleistocene Geology in Cyrenaican Libya*, 1955, pp. 7-8.
[256] *JRS* 61, 1971, p. 64.

So much for the arguments against Cyrenean connections with the desert routes, or at least against direct links. It may however be argued that Cyrene aspired to communication not through Aujila and Fezzan, but through the Oasis of Ammon, Fezzan and the Gulf of Syrtis; the historical and numismatic evidence, indeed, points in that direction. In the Fourth Pythiad of Pindar echoes are heard of an interest of the Cyrenean monarchy in the Syrtic region, and under Arkesilaos IV ties were formed between Cyrene and the Oasis of Ammon. Herodotus [257] knew of Ammon salt; he had heard the story of the journey of some Nasamonean Libyans into Central Africa, from Cyreneans who had visited the Oasis.[258] Rhys Carpenter [259] has shown that this journey was carried out along the desert route linking Thebes, Ḥargiyeh, Siwa (Ammon), Aujila and Fezzan, whence it turned south across the mountains of Tibesti to the region of Bodele north-east of Lake Chad. This route, he observed, is a very ancient road for the transport of salt. Herodotus also knew something of the settlements of the Libyan coast as far as the Isle of Jerba near the Syrtis, but his knowledge of the shoreline west of there was vague in the extreme.[260] This would seem to mean that the Carthaginians held the Syrtic harbours at the time, and that they were closed to Greek trade. In 503 the former expelled the Spartan expedition that had seized the Cynips region on the same coast in an attempt to settle there.[261] The situation, at any rate, is such as to explain Cyrene's interest in the Oasis of Ammon, since it stood on the route linking Egypt with the land of the Garamantes (Fezzan) and with Central Africa, and its use would have avoided the Syrtic route by going further south.

Whatever the case, gold coins appear in Cyrene in the middle of the 5th century, and in the first half of the 4th their distribution area widens.[262] In this period the city coinage bears figures of the palm tree, the prancing horse, and the horse's head, which appear

---

[257] IV, 182.

[258] II, 32.

[259] Rhys Carpenter, *AJA* 60, 1956, p. 231.

[260] Carpenter, *ibid.*

[261] Herod. V, 42.

[262] The appearance of gold coins in the Cyrenean economy cannot be explained by Persian gold delivered for political motives, since the latter came in the form of ready-minted coin. An Egyptian source evokes the question, why did it begin to arrive only in the 5th century, when Cyrene had maintained close contacts with Egypt since the 6th?

to reflect Carthaginian influence; from 375 approximately Carthaginian bronze coins are circulating in Cyrenaica, frequently restruck
by Euesperitae.[263] It is therefore difficult not to see in these phenomena an expression of commercial contacts with the Syrtic region
which lies between Cyrene and Carthage.[264] In 435, as related,
Barka and Cyrene formed an alliance, and between 413 and 401
Euesperitae was heavily engaged with the Libyan tribes, and her
enemies may be assumed to have been the inhabitants south of the
city in the direction of the Syrtic Gulf.[265] In 375 Barka's importance
declines, while Carthaginian coins begin to circulate in the area,
and Pseudo-Scylax, writing in the middle of the century, already
knew the name of Arae Philaenorum.[266] It was related that the
hostile sides (Greeks and Carthaginians) decided that the frontier
between them should be set at the point where their emissaries
should meet on a given day, each coming from his own city; but
those who had gone farthest from their homes should be put to
death. The brothers Philaeni who had left Carthage went farthest,
and were accordingly buried alive at the meeting-point, known
henceforth as Arae Philaenorum. The story bears the stamp of
legend, perhaps originating from the placename, but this does not
prove that the legend did not preserve the memory of a real war.[267]
Such a conflict would explain the sea fight between Barka and
Carthage, and also the influence of Syracuse discernible on coins of
Cyrene, Barka, and Euesperitae at the end of the 5th and the beginning of the 4th century, since between 383-378 war was being waged
between Dionysius of Syracuse and Carthage, and a rapprochement between Syracuse and Barka would have been natural. It
may be, therefore, that about 375 Barka suffered a grave defeat
from Carthage—her coin distribution now reveals a decline—the

---

[263] *BMC* p. xcvi.

[264] A find shedding light on trade between the Syrtic shore and the Sahara
are the obsidian blades found in a mausoleum near Germa (Fezzan) by the
Italian expedition of 1933. Obsidian is to be obtained from Pantalleria,
Lipari and Santorin (Thera). See R. E. M. Wheeler, *Rome Beyond the
Imperial Frontier*, 1955, p. 127.

[265] Goodchild (*GJ* 118, 1953, p. 148, cf. *Antiq.* 25, 1951, pp. 141-4), observed
that the concentration of fortified farms south of Bengazi and around
Ajedabia made it clear that the main danger came from that direction.
Although he was referring to the Roman period, it may be assumed that the
situation was much the same in the 5th century B.C.

[266] *Perip.*, 109.

[267] G. Meltzer, *Geschichte der Karthager*, 1879, I, p. 188; S. Gsell, *Hist.
ancienne de l'Afrique du Nord*, I, 1920, p. 451.

frontier between Cyrene and the Punic Syrtic cities being therefore fixed to the advantage of the latter. If so, evidently the peace agreement brought about an opening of the frontier to the merchants of the Syrtic towns.

The fact of continued hostilities between Cyrene and Carthage finds confirmation in two Cyrenean inscriptions. The first,[268] which belongs to the middle of the 4th century, was found in a treasury in the west part of the Sanctuary of Apollo, and records victories over the Nasamones and the Macae, both tribes of the Syrtic region. The other,[269] deriving from the Temple of Zeus, and of 4th-century date, is a list of soldiers and appears to mention a battle in a place called Isa on the Syrtic coast west of the Altars of the Philaeni.[270] These victories, gained far from home, are hardly credible before Cyrene's recovery in the years preceding 375, nor could such successes do other than arouse the hostility of Carthage, for both the above tribes lived in the vicinity of the emporia.[271] Cyrene is unlikely to have been without allies in such a campaign; the contacts between Syracuse, Cyrene and Barka have been noted. Syracuse was on a hostile footing with Carthage both at the beginning of the 4th century (398-2, 383-78, 368), and in the second half of the same century (339). Before 368 Cyrene was not in a position to be a partner in such a war, but the Punic War of Timoleon in 339 was an appropriate opportunity, since Syracuse had then restored her democratic régime and the influence of her coinage is again noticeable upon the currency of Euesperitae.[272] One conclusion, at least, may be drawn from the fact of this conflict; it needed the active participation of the Cyrenean cities, meaning their effectual political unification at the time and a relative stabilization of their internal régimes. Further, the war required Greek control of the Libyan tribes in their vicinity, or at least some form of accord with them.

In the last years before the entry of Cyrene into the Empire of

---

[268] *SEG* 9, 77. Cf. here pp. 40-1.

[269] *AI* III, pp. 182-31; *SEG* 9, 49.

[270] ΑΠΙΣΕΙ. Tod proposed to emend ἐπὶ πᾶσᾳ μάχῃ (*AJA* 42, 1938, p. 231, fig. 5), but the error implied seems to me to be too glaring.

[271] These two tribes fought for Carthage at Zama in the year 202 B.C.

[272] East of Euesperitae a tombstone has been found decorated with a painted relief, whose subject expresses, in Ghislanzoni's view (*DAI* I, Cir., ii, pp. 99 sqq.), patriotism for the region, a situation of warfare, and a connection with the Syrtis. I believe the stone to date from the second half of the 4th century B.C.

Alexander of Macedon, power in the state passed, it would seem, into the hands of an oligarchy. Most scholars today date the city constitution drawn up by Ptolemy Lagos, ruler of Egypt, in the last three decades of the 4th century. This constitution is engraved on a stele recovered from the Sanctuary of Apollo (see below p. 50),[273] and refers to the electorate then superseded, which numbered only a thousand.[274] It is to the introduction of this oligarchy that Aristotle apparently is referring when he writes [275] that the nobles (οἱ γνώριμοι) attacked the extreme Cleisthenic democracy in his time. This must have occurred before 336, when Aristotle completed his *Politics*. As in 339 Cyrene was, we think, allied with democratic Syracuse, the counterrevolution may have come about between the years 339 and 336, and have arisen from circumstances connected with the war against Carthage. Alexander reached Paraetonium (Gasr Madjad) the gates of Libya, in 331, on his way to the Oasis of Ammon, and a Cyrenean embassy came to welcome the conqueror.[276] In Alexander's own words,[277] Cyrene passed peacefully under his rule, one Apollonius being appointed governor.[278]

On the King's death (in 323) civil wars broke out in both Cyrene and Barka,[279] apparently the continuation of the same class-struggles which had brought about the fall of the democratic régime. The aristocratic refugees summoned an ex-officer of Alexander, Thimbron, from Crete to aid them; he came to Cyrenaica with a force of mercenaries. The conflict was prolonged with various vicissitudes, and finally the Cyreneans were forced to summon the Libyan tribes and even the Carthaginians to their aid; during the siege of Cyrene by Thimbron, moreover, the democrats drove out or butchered their aristocrats, whose faction appealed to Ptolemy Lagos, Alexander's successor in Egypt. Ptolemy despatched to Cyrene his commander Ophellas, thereupon the Cyreneans made common cause with Thimbron against Ophellas, but were defeated by him, Thimbron being captured and put to death. Victory secured, Ptolemy arrived in Cyrene to consolidate

---

[273] *SEG* 9, 1.
[274] *Ibid.*, para. 6, 1, 37.
[275] *Polit.* VI, 4 (1319b).
[276] Diod. XVII, 49, 2.
[277] Arrian, VII, 9, 6.
[278] Curtius, IV, 8, 21.
[279] Diod., XVIII, 19-20; Arrian ap. Phot., 92 (Roos, I, 16-17).

his rule throughout the territory.[280] It is more than likely that his active intervention was hastened on the one hand by the attack of the Cyrenean demos on its nobility, an attack which had revealed their determination to carry the social revolution to its final conclusion, and on the other by the alliance which the demos had formed with Carthage.

Ptolemy garrisoned Cyrene,[281] but behaved, it would seem, with moderation towards the defeated inhabitants. But the city did not yield its liberty easily. In 313, when Ptolemy was engaged with Antigonus, it rose and besieged Ophellas and his force in the Acropolis. Ptolemy, returning, sent an expedition under Agis to put down the rising.[282] Even now he did not behave with great rigour, but disarming the Cyreneans, sent the leading rebels to Alexandria. Simultaneously the city's coins begin to be replaced by issues bearing the inscription Κυραναων Πτολεμαιω, reflecting, apparently, some sort of settlement between Ptolemy and the Cyrenean polis.[283] But before many months had passed, Ophellas, left by Ptolemy as governor, seized power and declared himself king.[284] Several scholars attribute to his reign (321-309) the coins inscribed Κυραναων δαμω,[285] on the assumption that Ophellas was supported by the broader strata of the Cyrenean demos. He responded, however, to the invitation of Agathocles tyrant of Syracuse to join him in his war against Carthage, and mobilized a large number of Cyreneans as well as 10,000 Athenian volunteers lately deprived of their native citizenship, who had reached Cyrene eager for new lands. With 10,000 troops and an equal number of external elements accompanied by their women and children, Ophellas set out westward, performing in several months, under intense difficulties, the march along the Syrtic shore to Africa. His force reached Agathocles in a state of exhaustion after losing many of its members, so that it was not difficult for Agathocles to

---

[280] Diod. XVII, 108, 8; XVIII, 19, 20-21; Arr. ap. Phot., 9, 2 (Roos I, 19); Strabo XVII, 3 (826); Justin, XIII, 6; Oros. III, 23. Scholars believe that a Cyrenean inscription (DAI II, Cir., i, no. 59; SEG 9, 76) belongs to this war; it commemorates the dedication of a tithe of enemy ships captured off Cheronnesos in the east of the country, and near Euesperitae.

[281] Diod., XVIII, 21, 9.

[282] Diod., XIX, 79.

[283] A different opinion is expressed by Svoronos, Περιγραφὴ τῶν νομισμά-των τῶν Πτολεμαίων, 1907, I, p. 66.

[284] Plut., Demet., 14; Justin XXII, 7.

[285] BMC, pp. lxxxvi-lxxxvii.

4

put Ophellas to death and to merge the remnant of his force in his
own army.[286] After which events, Ptolemy was able to reassert
his control over Cyrene through the medium of his natural son
Magas.[287]

It was in the initial period of Ptolemaic rule that was drawn
up the famous Cyrenean constitution most of whose clauses have
been found inscribed on the stele to which allusion has already
been made. The constitution has produced a very wide literature,
nor have scholars reached a final decision on its date. But the
opinion of the majority is that the inscription belongs to the rule of
Ptolemy Lagos and not to the 3rd century, as some scholars
originally thought.[288] Opinions still differ, however, on the exact
time of the drafting, and whether this took place in 322,[289] 313 [290],
or 308.[291] Bengtson [292] has indeed remarked that there are few
prospects of an authoritative decision.

The new régime described in Ptolemy's constitution is timocratic i.e. the possession of citizen-rights is conditioned by the
enjoyment of a minimal yearly income of 20 Alexandrian minae
(2,000 drachmae). In harmony with these restrictions the law sets
up a body (πολίτευμα) of 10,000 citizens (in place of the restricted
body of a thousand which preceded it), within which framework
operate moderately democratic arrangements, albeit Ptolemy takes
care to retain certain powers for himself. Citizenship is open to
adults of thirty years and over. The consultative bodies are two;
the upper is the Gerousia, with a hundred and one members, to be
elected by the entire electorate for life, although the first members
are appointed by Ptolemy personally. The Council (βουλή), on the
other hand, has 500 members elected by lot, half its members
retiring annually or every second year. The number of its membership points to a division of the citizen-body into five or ten tribes
(φυλαί). Capital cases are to be tried before the Gerousia and the

---

[286] Cf. V. Ehrenberg, *RFC*[2] 16, 1939, pp. 144 sqq.; Oros. IV, 6; Diod., XX,
40-41.

[287] The date is unclear: according to Pausanias (I, 6, 8) in 301. Jones
(*CERP*, p. 358) thought that Ptolemy returned in 308, but that in 301,
following a fresh rising, he was forced to reconquer the country.

[288] Oliverio, Beloch, De Sanctis, Luzzatto.

[289] Reinach, Cary, Jones, Bengtson.

[290] Heuss, Taeger, Ehrenberg.

[291] Heichelheim.

[292] H. Bengtson, *Die Strategie in der hellenistischen Zeit*, III, 1952, p. 159,
n. 1.

Boule, whether sitting as a common court or each sitting separately; appeals are heard by a court of 1,500, elected from the entire citizen-body by lot; those condemned to death may appeal to Ptolemy during the first three years after the drafting of the constitution. The High Priest of Apollo heads the list of the city's government, but the senior magistrates are the strategoi, that is, the five elected by the citizens, and Ptolemy himself. In case of war, the people decides whether or not new strategoi are to be elected, and it is clear from this clause [293] that the city retains the right to wage war both within the frontiers of the country and beyond them.[294] The law further sets up five nomophylakes (νομο-φύλακες) [295] to serve chiefly as recorders of the laws; five ephors,[296] and five nomothetai (νομοθέται) who would have drafted the laws of the constitution.

If we ignore Ptolemy's authority, the internal procedures of the above constitution are not undemocratic. But its degree of liberalism should not be exaggerated, since the annual income that is a condition of citizenship is far from low. In Athens at the end of the 5th century B.C. many workers and craftsmen supported themselves on an annual income of 180 drachmas,[297] and if prices rose in Greece in the 4th century, the same rise had not affected Cyrene,[298] hence 2,000 dr. is a fairly high income, certainly not enjoyed by the common people, craftsmen and small peasants, and restricted, we must suppose, to the well-to-do. The law's attitude, indeed, does not particularly favour the wage-earner or the manual worker; [299] one of its clauses deprives physicians, teachers, heralds, instructors in archery, riding and the use of weapons, of the right to be elected to magistracies, and another,[300] much mutilated, reproduces a list of categories whose participation in government is restricted or

---

[293] *SEG* 9, 1, para. 4, 29-30.

[294] Bengtson, *op. cit.*, p. 160.

[295] See here, below, pp. 187 sqq.

[296] On their duties, Cary, *JHS* 1928, p. 232.

[297] Tod has calculated (*CAH* V, 1953, p. 22) that 120 drachmae were sufficient to support a bachelor. The daily wage of a building worker at the end of the 5th century in Athens was one drachma (*IG²* I, 373-4—*ibid.* pp. 24-5).

[298] This is clear from a comparison of the prices recorded by the Demiurgi Steles and those known in Greece and the islands in the same period; see *DAI* I, Cir. ii, 1933, Oliverio, I conti dei Demiurgi—*SEG* 9, 11-44; *ASAA* 39-40, 1963, p. 280, no. 104; and see here Chap. III.

[299] *SEG* 9, 1, para. 7.

[300] *SEG* 9, 1, para. 8.

prohibited; they include the manual labourer, the owner of a potter's kiln, the vendor of wine, the porter (or trader?—the word is φορτήγος) and anyone joining Ptolemy's new colonies (ἢ ἄλλοτε οἰκίας τὰς Πτολεμαϊκὰς ἐσέλθηι. But see p. 133).

The law generally reflects a situation of distress resulting from the struggle that had preceded its enactment. The new colony in the region of Thinis (Θῖνις) mentioned in the inscription,[301] shows that in this period the citizens of Cyrene had found need to seek lands at a distance, and the participation of Libyan tribes in the struggle against Thimbron may have encouraged unrest which had arisen amongst them due to the expansion of Greek settlement. The constitution, at any rate, elicits a desire to conciliate the Libyan population by granting citizen-rights to the sons of mixed marriages endowed with the necessary income, and a desire on the part of the Ptolemies to pose as Libyan sovereigns.[302]

2. PTOLEMAIC RULE

With the final consolidation of Ptolemaic control, Cyrene's real independence came to an end, despite a maintenance of the external forms, and despite the city's attempts to throw off royal control as late as the time of Ptolemy III and Ptolemy Euergetes II. The new régime was crystallized, as we have seen, in favour of the upper income groups. The Ptolemaic constitution bears traces of a situation of disorder and impoverishment,[303] of indebtedness, of the abandonment and destruction of estates,[304] of the flight and restoration of exiles. Some of the citizens are experiencing difficulties in obtaining the minimal capital required to maintain their civic rights.[305] Ptolemy's garrison is stationed in the city,[306] and the

---

[301] *SEG* 9, 1, 4.

[302] I refer to the close resemblance of the head of the goddess Libya on coins to that of the Ptolemaic queen; compare the well-known head of Berenice II, with a Libyan coiffure, from Alexandria (*Breccia, Alexandrea ad Aegyptum*, 1914, p. 197, fig. 168)—though it has recently been claimed that the coiffure is a recent addition—and further the allusions of the poet Callimachus to the Libyan wives of the Theran settlers (*Apoll.*, 87).

[303] Para 1, 9-10.

[304] *Ibid.*, Para. 11. This paragraph, much of which has been defaced, deals apparently with the assessment and restoration of lost property after political disorders. Cf. 11, 6, which refers to burnt fields.

[305] Para. 1, 9-10.

[306] Para. 11, 72-3.

danger exists of reprisals against returned political exiles.[307] The demagogic adventure of Ophellas suggests the need of diverting the resentment of the masses by an impressive project of expansion westward, while the participation of a number of Athenian emigrés in the expedition and the readiness of as many as 10,000 inhabitants of Cyrene and elsewhere to join it, indicate their depressed economic situation at the time.

The extensive emigration proceeding from Cyrenaica at the beginning of the hellenistic epoch,[308] also indicates that there were impoverished elements among the Cyrenean population from whom the emigration proceeded. Most of the Cyreneans recorded in Egypt in this period are humble people of few means—simple soldiers, owning small kleroi,[309] who had left no property in their mother-country. Their organized community (πολίτευμα) in Egypt was less esteemed from several points of view, than the other foreign communities, and most of its members were cleruch and ἐκ τῆς ἐπιγονῆς, i.e. of the second generation of military settlers. But there was also a small group of officers and government officials of Cyrenean birth.[310] The Cyreneans were, after the Macedonians, the largest contemporary group of Greek immigrants into Egypt, and certainly the largest community derived from one state. This was doubtless largely caused by Cyrene's geographical proximity to Egypt, but it should not be disassociated from the condition of Cyrene herself. Alexander's conquests had opened new sources of livelihood, new posts, occupations and fields of investment to the impoverished Greek populations, thus furnishing a temporary alleviation of their distress. This applied equally to the Greeks of Cyrenaica.

In 308 or 301 Magas, the natural son of Ptolemy the First, seized control of Cyrene,[311] In a year that appears to have fallen between 278 and 274, when his stepbrother Ptolemy II Philadelphus succeeded to the Egyptian throne, Magas seceded from his father's kingdom and became an independent monarch. Apparently out of fear of Arsinoe, Ptolemy II's queen, he signed a treaty with An-

---

[307] Para. 6, 39-41.

[308] F. Heichelheim, *ABP*, Klio Beih. 18, 5, 1925, pp. 43-6.

[309] Heichelheim, *op. cit.*, pp. 45 sqq.

[310] *Ibid.*, p. 45.

[311] Paus. I, 7; Athen., XII, 74; Justin XXVI, 3. For a detailed discussion of the date, *PW* 17, 1928, col. 293 sqq. (Geyer), sv. Magas; cf. Chamoux, *Rev. hist.*, 216, 1956, p. 21.

tiochus I of Syria and married his daughter Apamé. A little later he quitted Cyrene to fight a war against Ptolemy,[312] having strengthened the walls and acropolis of the city,[313] but was forced to return by the outbreak of a Libyan rising in his rear.[314] Not long afterwards, having become reconciled to Philadelphus, Magas betrothed his daughter Berenice to Philadelphus' son, the future Ptolemy III Euergetes.[315] Magas ruled for the rest of his reign without wars,[316] dying somewhere about 250.[317] His widow, being of the Seleucid dynasty, put aside Berenice's betrothal with Ptolemy III, and brought to Cyrene Demetrius "the Fair",[318] son of Demetrius Poliorketes, to marry her. Demetrius, however, was killed by Berenice herself;[319] she was thus able to realize her marriage to Ptolemy III, and to bring about the reunion of the kingdoms of Egypt and Cyrene (circa 246). In the Adulis inscription Libya appears among the countries subject to Ptolemy Euergetes.[320] Cyrenaica remained united with Egypt until 163/2 B.C.

Although Magas does not seem to have struck coins in his own name, but always in that of Ptolemy I or of Berenice I,[321] there is no doubt that in Cyrene itself he bore the title of king, and this is evidenced by two inscriptions, one from Cyrene[322] and one from her port of Apollonia;[323] he is also called "king" in the treaty which he signed with the Oreioi ("Ὄρειοι) of Crete.[324] His fame and power as ruler are testified to by the inscription of the Indian King Asoka, which mentions his name together with those of other hellenistic kings of his time (251 or 248).[325]

With the establishment of Ptolemaic rule Cyrenaica made her real entry into the Hellenistic world, which had been subject to

---

[312] Paus. I, 7.
[313] Polyaenus, II, 28.
[314] Paus., *loc. cit.*
[315] Justin, XXVI, 3.
[316] Agatharchides ap. Athen., XII, 74.
[317] *Ibid.*
[318] Plut., *Demetrius*, 53, 4; *Prolog. Trogi*, 26; Justin, XXVI, 31 (252); Paus. I, 7.
[319] Catul., *de coma Beren.* (Carm. LXVI), 25-8; Justin, *loc. cit.*
[320] *OGIS* 54, 6-7.
[321] *BMC*, p. clii.
[322] *SEG* 9, 112.
[323] F. Chamoux, *BCH* 82, 1958, pp. 571 sqq.
[324] M. Guarducci, *Inscriptiones Creticae*, XVII, 1935, (1), 6.
[325] Hultsch, *Corpus Inscr. Indicarum*, I, 1925, p. 25; Gercke, *RM* 42, 1887, p. 266; R. Thapar, *Asoka and the Decline of the Mauryas*[3], 1963, p. 41.

such decisive political and economic changes since the conquests of Alexander. Various factors prevented the Ptolemies from behaving towards Cyrene as they had behaved towards Egypt. Cyrene was the home of a preponderantly Greek population; the natives were divided between complete assimilants to Greek culture, and half-nomadic cultivators living at a primitive standard. Here the conquerors did not face an ancient alien culture both deep-rooted and religious in its manifestations: there was no wealthy and powerful clergy consolidated by generations, which required both appeasement and supervision. Towards the Greek cities, potential sources for the building of a civil service, a more moderate and cautious approach nevertheless was required on the part of the royal government; the sturdy democratic spirit of their broad masses obliged a special attitude, and sometimes also suppression. In consequence Ptolemaic rule in Cyrene did not on the one hand involve racial antagonism between rulers and ruled as in Egypt, nor was there need to engage systematically in the hellenization of the subject population. On the other hand from the beginning the Greek character of the country restricted the building of a consistently étatistic régime like that of Ptolemaic Egypt, nor did there exist in Cyrene that dependence on the control of Nile irrigation which had formed the basis of centralized government in Egypt for thousands of years.

Accordingly it is highly improbable that Ptolemy I saw the Cyrenaic region as "spear-won earth" (δορόκτητος χώρα), or that broad tracts fell into his hands as his personal possession immediately, for the concept of royal land no longer existed in the country. Ptolemy had gained control of Cyrene initially by a compromise and by making regulations such as could ensure his power, and it may be surmised that he reached similar accommodations with the other towns of the territory, respecting their internal autonomy. The political character of the country was such, that the series of revolts that preceded the final consolidation of Ptolemaic power there would not fundamentally have modified the necessity of such arrangements. Yet the hand of the rulers was perceptible in the economic sphere: between 308 and 304 the Cyrenean coinage undergoes modification, and silver, previously rare, becomes abundant.[326] The city's coins persist in all three metals between

---

[326] Naville, *Les monnaies d'or*, pp. 66 sq.; cf. Chamoux, *loc. cit.* (n. 34), pp. 29 sqq.

304 and 290, under Magas' rule, while the royal issues figure side
by side with them in gold and bronze. But towards 290 approximately Cyrene's gold issues disappear, and her bronze coins follow
in 277.[327] As to the internal institutions of city-government, if
they are preserved, Ptolemy's strategos is resident in the city,[328]
doubtless subsequently replaced by Magas himself, and under
Ptolemy III and his successors, by the king's deputy. At the end of
the 2nd century B.C., under Euergetes II or Ptolemy X Soter,
an inscription evidences that royal orders concerning Cyrene's
affairs were transmitted simultaneously both to the city authorities
and to the royal officials appointed over the towns (οἱ ἐπὶ τῶν
πόλεων τεταγμένοι).[329] The courtesies were observed but the king's
word was final.

The degree of internal liberty of the cities no doubt depended
on the nature of the ruler. It may be observed that the constitution
of Ptolemy Lagos, although directed only to Cyrene, nevertheless
includes an instruction that affects the other cities of the country,
to wit, the clause relating to the granting of citizenship to men of
various origins who had settled in new settlements of the countryside.[330] In this connection must be considered the problem of the
invitation of the philosophers Ecdelus and Demophanes, who were
summoned from their city of Mantineia, apparently between the
years 250 and 220,[331] in order to reform the constitution of Cyrene.
The character of their measures is unknown, nor are the circumstances of the invitation recorded. We only know that the reformers
were devoted to Greek liberty. It is possible that a connection should
be seen between their reforms and the Cyrenean coins of Magas
inscribed with the word κοινόν (federation),[332] but many scholars
have rejected the connection.[333] It has also been conjectured, on
the evidence of the letters Δημ—inscribed on some contemporary
issues, that the settlement was arrived at under the patronage of
Demetrius the Fair when he was Berenice's husband, but as no

[327] J. Machu, RM 205, 1951, p. 47.
[328] Perhaps the commander of the garrison, as Bengtson suggests in Die
Strategie, p. 162.
[329] DAI II, Cir. ii, pp. 259 sqq. = SEG 9, 5, line 70; cf. Bengtson, ibid.,
p. 164.
[330] SEG 9, 1, 3-4.
[331] Plut., Philopoem., I, 3; Polyb., X, 22, 3.
[332] BMC, pp. cli; cxxxiv-cxxxvii.
[333] The idea is supported eg. by Robinson (ibid.) and Jones (CERP,
p. 359); it is opposed by Machu (loc. cit., p. 50).

detailed information of the episode has been preserved, no decision can be made, nor can we know how to interpret the reform or the Koinon. As to the relationships between the Ptolemies and the cities of Cyrene, although the legend κοινόν overstruck on Magas' coinage seems to hint at some revolutionary event, even had the cities risen against his successors, expelled them [334] and formed a league among themselves,—no record of the episode has survived in contemporary history.

The question whether the Ptolemies appointed a permanent deputy over the entire country has not been sufficiently clarified. We hear only of one governor (Ptolemy Sympetesis) under Euergetes II, who also acted as viceroy during his visit to Rome.[335] The case of Philo son of Castor, commander of the king's body-guard and strategos under Ptolemy V,[336] is less certain, and Bengtson regards him as the governor solely of the Libyan regions, but not of the country as a whole.

There is no doubt that an administrative distinction, if not a complete separation, was made between the settled country districts and the Libyan tribal areas.[337] Ptolemy Euergetes II in his testament distinguishes between the cities and the remainder of the country; [338] this distinction satisfactorily explains the duties of Philammon the Libyarch "over the places about Cyrene" at the end of the 3rd century B.C.[339]. These tribal areas were, it seems, under the surveillance of an appropriate commissioner, and as time went on came to be regarded juridically as χώρα βασιλική, i.e. royal domain.

Despite Ophellas' failure and the demagogic motive of his expedition, Cyrene's interest in the Syrtic region, more especially under Ptolemaic rule, was serious. If some settlement had been found acceptable both to Cyrene and to Carthage in the 4th century, in the the 3rd the frontier stood 280 kilometres further west of the Altars of the Philaeni, in the vicinity of Euphrantas Pyrgos (Εὐφράντας πύργος),[340] today Gasr Zaphran in Tripolitania. It is

---

[334] The opinion of Droysden, Reinach, Tarn and Oliverio.

[335] Polyb. XXXI, 18, 6; Bengtson, *Die Strateg.*, p. 164.

[336] Bengtson, *op. cit.*, p. 158; *SEG* 9, 55.

[337] Bengtson, *op. cit.*, pp. 153-4.

[338] *DAI* I, Cir, i, p. 42, line 20 (*SEG* 9, 7).

[339] Polyb. XV, 25, 12: Λιβυάρχης τῶν κατὰ Κυρήνην τόπων; Bengtson, *op. cit.*, p. 157.

[340] Strabo XVII, 3 (836): "It was the frontier of Cyrene in the time of Ptolemy Lagos."

unknown when this Cyrenean advance took place, but it may be noted that there are traces of Jewish settlement of the 3rd century B.C. on the coast of the Syrtic Gulf,[341] and this may be a remnant of the temporary advance of the Ptolemies, whose dynasty is credited with the first settlement of Jews in Libya. Whatever the case, Ptolemaic coins are common about Carthage from this time on,[342] and the Punic capital began to strike coins on the Greek model when the Ptolemies passed from the Attic to the Phoenician standard, in order to assist their trade with both Phoenicia and Carthage. Testimony to such contacts is provided by finds of hellenistic pottery at Lepcis,[343] and Cyrenean coins bearing the palm tree are again common among Ptolemaic currency at this time.[344] These data therefore permit us to assume that even if the Ptolemaic advance westward was made in the course of a war, the collision ended with an agreement beneficial to both sides, and apparently with the withdrawal of the Ptolemies to their former frontier.[345]

The trade with the Syrtis and Egypt will help to explain the systematic development of the Cyrenean ports by the Ptolemies: Magas strikes coins bearing the representation of a trireme,[346] the seahorse [347] and the trident.[348] He may well have developed Apollonia, where a mint began to operate in the 3rd century; [349] the harbour was already well protected (πανόρμος), according to Pseudo-Scylax,[350] by the middle of the 4th century, but the city-walls are now known to belong to its last years,[351] and may have been the

---

[341] See pp. 130-1.

[342] Eg. S. P. Noe, *Bibliography of Greek Coin Hoards* [2], 1937, p. 296, no. 1129; p. 298, no. 1136.

[343] I owe this information to Professor P. Romanelli. A Greek inscription set up by Cyreneans at Marsa Delah east of Sabrata (J. B. Reynolds, J. B. Ward-Perkins, *Inscriptions of Roman Tripoli*, 1952, no. 848), belongs, apparently, to the 1st century B.C.

[344] *BMC*, p. cxxxii.

[345] The economic value of the Syrtis was no doubt enhanced by its deposits of sulphur (G. Narducci, *SCC*, p. 92)—which was prized in ancient times particularly as a fertilizer of vineyards—cf. Rostovtzeff, *SEHHW*, p. 396.

[346] *BMC*, pl. xxx, 7.

[347] *Ibid.*, pl. xxx, 8, 9.

[348] *BMC.*, pl. xxix, 12.

[349] *BMC*, p. cc.

[350] *Perip.*, 108; *JRS* 61, 1971, p. 74.

[351] *Archaeology*, 19, 1966, pp. 56-7; 1967, pp. 219-220; *AJA* 70, 1966, pp. 259-263; 71, 1967, pp. 141-147; Goodchild, *Kyrene u. Apoll.*, p. 191; Lauer, *Rev. arch.*, 1963, pp. 129 sqq.

work of Magas. The splendid tower-flanked west gate with its distinctive inner vantage-court would suit an early hellenistic date.[352] To the south-east of the enceinte, north of the present east-west main road, building remains containing 4th century and hellenistic sherds were disclosed during World War II and recorded by the writer in 1944, suggesting that the town had extended outside the hellenistic walls in that period. In the first part of the 3rd century Apollonia was separated from Cyrene and promoted to the status of an independent city, in the opinion of several scholars,[353] who base their view on the fact that the city's name does not belong to the same class as the names Ptolemais, Berenice, etc., which are associated, it is said, with the work of Ptolemy III; it would therefore be more ancient. Jones attributed the conversion of the harbour to a city to the reforms of Ecdalus and Demophanes, but his conjecture seems to be without the support of evidence, since the name Apollonia does not appear before the 1st century B.C.,[354] whereas the city of Berenice existed on its new site at least by the middle of the 3rd.

The east gate of Ptolemais belongs typologically to the earlier hellenistic age, but the city was evidently refortified under Euergetes II, for the west gate was built in 158 B.C.[355] Ptolemais became a large city, even if one excludes from its area its southernmost quarter on the mountain escarpment, which remained uninhabited although within the wall, and contained only the Akropolis.[356] The city's area approximates to that of Cyrene, and its hippodamian plan probably belongs to this period; it existed at least from the 2nd century B.C. One gets the impression that Ptolemais was designed to be the country's effective new capital, and even to rival Alexandria. Its source of agricultural supply was the Plain of Barka to the south, but the city itself was separated from the Plain by a mountainous range running parallel with the shore and commanded no more than a narrow coastal tract. Hence the in-

---

[352] Similar plans are to be seen at Megalopolis (*DS*, sv., Porta, IV, fig. 5671), Mantinea (*ib*. fig. 5672), Sidé (*Jb DAI*, 71, 1956, p. 678, Abb. 22, 27) and Perge, Pamphylia (*CAA*, 102-3, Abb. 53).

[353] Eg. Jones, *CERP*, p. 359.

[354] Strabo, XVII, 837. Chamoux, *Rev. hist.*, 216, p. 24, notes that the city's name is absent from the Delphic theoric list of the 2nd century B.C., whereas that of Cyrene appears.

[355] *DAI* I, Cir. i, p. 69, nos. 4, 5.

[356] An analogy from this point of view is the northern area of Priene, rebuilt in the middle of the 4th century B.C.

habitants must have engaged primarily in trade and crafts; Ptolemais' buildings were rich and important. Here too, Ptolemy III
opened a mint.[357]

Magas' great interest in the control of the sea arose no doubt
from his predicament as seceder from Egypt. It was also necessary
in order to protect Cyrenean commerce against piracy, a grave
factor in this period. Crete was a special centre of piratical activity,
and lay across Cyrene's approaches to the Aegean. Hence the treaty
signed by Magas with the Oreioi of Crete [358] in the second half of
his reign would have been one of his efforts to restrain piracy, at a
time when peace prevailed between himself and Ptolemy Philadelphus. This period further corresponded with that of Philadelphus'
Island League (270-250), with which he was able to control the Aegean and to check piratical raids.

Euesperitae also was an object of the dynasty's development
activity, but here the operation was more radical: the entire city,
which was situated among the lagoons along the northern shore,
was moved westward to the edge of the present harbour,[359] and its
name changed to Berenice, in honour of Magas' mother or of his
daughter, wife of Ptolemy III Euergetes. The pottery evidence
suggests this may have taken place as early as the end of the third
quarter of the 4th century, when pottery on the old site appears to
end,[360] but Vickers believed that the analysis of coin finds there
points to a transfer as late as the middle of the following century.[361]
The name of the old site represented by the initial "E", still appears
on coins at the beginning of the 3rd century,[362] while an inscription
from Alexandria belonging to the first half of the same century,
bears the text Ξενάρατος Χαρμαντίου Βερνικεὺς ἀφ' Ἑσπερίδων; [363]
hence the transfer may well have begun somewhat before Ptolemy
III's reign.[364]

Ptolemaic influence is less evident, for the time being, at Teucheira. Its name was, indeed, changed to Arsinoe, but this new title is

---

[357] *BMC*, p. clix.
[358] Guarducci, *Inscri. Cret.* XVII, 1, no. 6.
[359] This was indicated by air-photographs (Goodchild, *Antiq.*, 26, 1952,
p. 210) and also by archaeological trial-trenches. (*Ibid.*).
[360] Goodchild, *loc. cit.*
[561] *Libia Antica*, 2, 1965, pp. 91-100.
[362] *BMC*, pl. xxxviii, 20-21.
[363] E. Breccia, *Iscrizione greche e latini*, 1911, no. 284.
[364] *Antiq., loc. cit.*

not mentioned in sources before the 1st century B.C.[365] There is nevertheless hellenistic masonry in certain sectors of the city wall, and rich epigraphical material evidences the settlement of new settlers (probably katoikoi) in the city in the hellenistic period.

Changes in Cyrenaican land-tenure in this period will be discussed in greater detail elsewhere (Chap. III). Here three phenomena may be briefly noted, namely: firstly, the steady expansion of the crown domains; secondly, the colonization of extraneous elements (military settlers and the like) on the soil, on the initiative of the Ptolemaic sovereigns; thirdly, the extension of the sovereign's decisive influence over the Cyrenean temple estates and their revenues.

It is further possible in some measure to trace the evolution of the status of the native Libyans in this epoch. Under Ptolemy Lagos Libyan women were marrying Cyreneans of the well-to-do class,[366] and the allusions of the poet Callimachus to Libyan women, as well as the Libyan affectations of the royal house, have been referred to. But the active part of the Libyans in the Thimbronic war on the democratic side and their rising against Magas show that not all the Libyans were reconciled with the new rulers. They also participated in the Cyrenean revolt against Euergetes II,[367] and as late as the 1st century B.C. retained much of their independence, as is proved by the aid extended by their king Anabus to Arataphila, widow of the High Priest of Cyrene, during civil strife[368]. Yet in the same century the peasants (οἱ γεωργοί) of Cyrene belonged to the three groups of the state's non-citizens,[369] and there is little doubt that these were chiefly Libyans. We have no information concerning the process whereby this change of status took place; we do however know that in 218 B.C. Philopator, mobilizing for the Syrian war, included 3000 Libyans in the infantry commanded by Ammonius of Barka, and several thousand Libyan cavalry.[370] In 162 the Libyans are fighting on the Cyrenean side[371] in their revolt against Euergetes II, and it may be relevant to recall that the battle of Raphia (217) was the departure point

---

[365] Strabo, XVII, 3, 20, (836).
[366] *SEG* 1, 1, para. 1.
[367] Polyb. XXXI, 18, 9.
[368] Plut., *de virt. mul.*, (Arat.)
[369] Strabo ap. Jos., *Ant.* 14, 2, 7, 115.
[370] Polyb. V, 65.
[371] Polyb. XXXI, 18, 9.

among the Egyptian native soldiery, who had played a decisive part in the action, for a ferment which reached the stage of rebellion and led to various concessions in their favour on the part of the Ptolemies, the most important being the admission of the natives to the ranks of the cleruchs. This movement may well have influenced the Libyan natives, nor is it without significance that the Libyan rising against Euergetes II in 162 was led by an Egyptian, Ptolemy Sympetesis.[372] The rise of a progressive Libyan kingdom to their west, under the leadership of the capable Massinissa, in the first half of the 2nd century,[373] might also have exercized a strong influence on the Libyans of Cyrenaica and helped to intensify the ferment. At the end of the reign of Euergetes II, who died in 116, or in the early days of his successor, Ptolemy IX Soter II, a Cyrenean inscription [374] reveals a situation of agrarian disturbance in the country, which we shall endeavour to explain when we come to investigate the Cyrenean economy (See Ch. III).

In 163/2 B.C. Ptolemy Euergetes II (also known as Neoteros or Physcon) quarrelled with his brother Philometor over the throne of Egypt, and the Roman Senate,[375] called to arbitrate, adjudged to him the kingdom of Cyrene. He thereupon went to war with his brother for the possession of Cyprus, and the hostilities furnished the Cyreneans with an opportunity for revolt, which seems, however, to have ended in a compromise between themselves and the king.[376] Losing his campaign in Cyprus, Euergetes conceded the island in return for the control of certain unidentified towns, for a yearly supply of grain from Egypt, and for the hand of Philometor's daughter (159).[377] In 155, however, the King was the object of an attempted assassination, and interpreting the act as directed against both his life and his kingdom—determined to bequeath his realm to Rome in the event of his dying without heirs. The stele on which this testament was inscribed, and which was set up

---

[372] Polyb. XXXI, 18, 7.

[373] Strabo XVII, 3, 15 (833).

[374] SEG 9, 5; DAI II Cir. ii, pp. 259 sq., no. 538.

[375] Polyb. XXXI, 10; Liv. Epit. XLVI; Prolog. Trogini ad 34.

[376] Polyaenus VIII, 72; Polyb. XXXI, 26 (18). The course of events is unclear, and the conjecture that they ended with a compromise between the king and the Cyreneans arises from the fact that despite the latter's energetic resistance Euergetes was able to renew his campaign in Cyprus soon afterwards.

[377] Liv., Epit., XLVII; Polyb. XXXIX, 7 (XL, 12); Diod., frag. XXXI.

at Cyrene, has been found and still exists.[378] On the death of
Philometor in 146/5, however, Euergetes returned to rule the
reunited kingdom of Egypt and Cyrene,[379] and on his own decease
in 116 bequeathed Cyrene to his illegitimate son, Ptolemy Apion.[380]
Under Euergetes II Cyrene had entered finally into the Roman
sphere of influence, from which she never re-emerged. In his readiness to bequeath his kingdom to Rome, indeed, Euergetes was
merely acknowledging the true situation, for he had acquired his
power entirely with the assistance of the Roman Senate.

3. ROMAN RULE

We have no details of the reign of Ptolemy Apion, but he evidently followed in his father's footsteps, for on his death in 96 B.C. his
kingdom passed, by the terms of his testament, to the Roman
people.[381] The Senate resolved to restore to the cities of Cyrene
their liberty,[382] and took over only the personal property of Apion,
including his lands, which now became *ager publicus populi Romani*.[383] The remainder of the country returned to the political
position that it had enjoyed before Ptolemaic rule, in that it was
again divided between the independent cities and their territories,
five in number, Cyrene, Ptolemais, Euesperitae, Teucheira and
Apollonia;[384] it may be supposed that Ptolemais had by now
effectively assumed the place of Barka. In relation to Rome, these
cities now held the status of *civitates foederatae*.[385]

The end of monarchic rule was quickly followed by political
disturbances; somewhere between 91 and 82 B.C.[386] power was
seized at Cyrene by one Nicocrates, who had slain the High Priest
of Apollo, Melanippus, and usurped his function.[387] The position,

---

[378] *SEG* 9, 7; *DAI* I, Cir. i, pp. 11 sqq.

[379] Jos., *C. Ap.*, II, 5; Justin XXXVIII, 8.

[380] Justin, XXXIX, 5; App., *Bell. Mithr.*, 121 (600).

[381] Liv., *Epit.*, LXXXI; Tac. *Ann.*, XIV, 18; App. *Bell. Mithr.*, 121 (600);
B. Civ., I, 111; Jul. Obseq., *de prodigiis*, 49; Eutrop., VI, 11; *RC*, para. 68,
pp. 300 sqq. for differences on the exact date of his death.

[382] Liv., *Epit.*, LXX.

[383] Tac., *Ann.*, XIV, 18, 2; App. *B. Mithr.*, 121; *B. Civ.*, I, 111.

[384] Cf. P. Romanelli, *CR*, pp. 35, 43.

[385] Thus also Jones in *Anatolian Studies presented to W. H. Buckler*, 1939,
pp. 111-112. Cf. J. Colin, *Les villes libres de l'orient gréco-romain, et l'envoi au
supplice par acclamations populaires* (Collection Latomus, 82), 1965, p. 77.

[386] S. I. Oost, *Cl. Phil.*, 58, 1965, p. 15: Cyrene 96-74 BC.

[387] Plut., *De virtut. mul.*, XIX (Arat.), 255; Polyaen. VIII, 38.

however, was reversed by Melanippus' widow, Arataphila, who set
up a régime supported by the aristocrats with the aid of the Libyan
king Anabus. These events are chronologically parallel with a
prolonged war in the Egyptian Thebais, where the natives had
arisen against the Ptolemaic régime; Rostovtzeff [388] defined this
war as a rebellion of the lower orders against the government, in
which nationalism and religious fanaticism were mingled; we
shall attempt to ascertain the roots of the Cyrenean movement
below (Ch. III). At Cyrene the seizure of the High Priesthood by
Nicocrates is vital for an assessment of the situation in so far as it
shows the importance of the post after the end of Ptolemaic rule.
This is confirmed some decades later by the leading part played by
Pausanias, High Priest of Apollo, in the Marmaritan War waged
approximately between 20-2 B.C. [389] It is stated that Arataphila
was supported by the aristocracy,[390] hence her régime represented
chiefly the wealthy landowners allied with the Libyans; Cyrene
appears to have crystallized after Apion's death as a state ruled by
this group and led by the eponymous High Priest of Apollo; such a
development is also suggested by the apparent cessation of the
Demiurgi steles after the 2nd century B.C. and by the prominence
of the undemocratic post of Nomophylax in the 1st century B.C.[391]
Strabo describes the juridical structure of the city's population in
the same epoch,[392] and his account points to a complete separation
between the citizens and the peasantry, a situation that perhaps
reflects Arataphila's new order. When Lucullus procured a settlement of Cyrenean affairs about this time, indeed, it is hard to
suppose that he restored the democracy.

The precise significance of his reform is difficult to evaluate
because we do not know if his visit preceded or followed the episode
of Nicocrates and Arataphila. Lucullus' citation from Plato, who,
after alluding to Cyrene's previous flourishing state, had added
that no one was easier to govern than he who had been brought
low by fortune, indicates that the city had been in a bad way, and

---

[388] *SEHHW*, pp. 876-7.

[389] *SEG* 9, 63; *DAI* II Cir., i, no. 67.

[390] *De virt. mul.*, XXV: ἦν δὲ θυγάτηρ ... γνωρίμων ἀνδρῶν ... ἠξιοῦν
δὲ τὴν 'Αρατάφιλαν συνάρχειν καὶ συνδιοικεῖν τοῖς ἀρίστοις ἀνδράσι τὴν πολιτείαν.

[391] On the nomophylakes *RL* VI, 1, pp. 414 sqq; *PP* 97, 1964, pp. 291-303;
see also Pugliesi-Cartarelli, *QAL* 4, 1961, p. 16; no. 2.

[392] Strabo ap. Jos., *Ant.* 14, 2, 7, 115.

was therefore ready to consent to unpalatable measures;[393] but it can hardly be supposed that these were fundamentally to the detriment of an aristocratic régime, since Rome's permanent policy was to intervene in favour of such régimes. Generally, it looks as though Lucullus' visit took place after Arataphila's restoration of aristocratic government rather than before it.

Fifty years later (between 31 and 13 B.C.) it is true, M. Agrippa, minister of Augustus, addressed the city as "the people, the archons and the council of Cyrene",[394] which would mean, theoretically, that a more democratic form of rule had meantime been reintroduced—yet this need be no more than a conventional diplomatic formula.[395]

In 88/6 B.C., when Lucullus reached Cyrene to mobilize ships,[396] he also found need, according to Strabo as cited by Josephus,[397] to put down a Jewish disturbance (στάσις). The reasons for this disturbance will be discussed elsewhere (see Ch. V), for this is the first appearance of the Jews in the country's history as an independent political factor, and in the second half of the century (31-13 B.C.) they were again at odds with the city over their right to transmit the half-sheqel to the Temple of Jerusalem.[398]

The political disturbances and conflicts in Cyrene, however, do not seem to have ceased with Lucullus' visit, and in 74 B.C. the Roman Senate saw need to intervene directly, assigning the task to a magistrate with the junior rank of quaestor.[399] If this was a decision to annex the country as a province, it may have been influenced by the pressure of a group of Roman citizens, including publicani, possessed of economic and financial interests, already settled in the country, and whose existence is evidenced by an inscription of 67 B.C. dedicated to Cornelius Lentulus Marcellinus,[400] Pompey's legate. Mentioned also in another source,[401] they had perhaps arrived earlier to take over the exploitation of the agri publici. Oost, on the other hand sees the Senate's shortage of

---

[393] Plut., Luc., 2.
[394] Ant. 16, 6, 169.
[395] Yet see CIG 5186 from Ptolemais—δῆμος Πτολεμαίεων.
[396] Plut. Luc., 2.
[397] Ant. 14, 7, 114.
[398] Ant., 16, 6, 169.
[399] Reynolds, JRS 52, 1962, pp. 97 sqq.; PW 7, 1900, col. 1390, no. 231.
[400] Reynolds, loc. cit., p. 98, no. 4.
[401] Plin., HN, 19, 3 (15).

money as the main inducement for the annexation, and Badian finds no evidence of publicani before 67,[402] when Crete was added to the Roman dominions; by 63 Cyrene was certainly a province, and the administration of the island was merged with that of Cyrenaica.[403]

Several scholars [404] have assumed, that on the establishment of the province Cyrene lost her freedom. This however is doubtful, since the city's officers and troops took part in the war against the Marmaritae at the end of the century under the leadership of their High Priest,[405] hence Cyrene may have retained her position as a free ally. Nevertheless, several inscriptions, particularly one group belonging to the year 67 B.C.,[406] indicate the continuation of an unstable internal situation. That year Pompey's legate Lentulus Marcellinus arrived in the country during his commander's great drive against the eastern Mediterranean pirates. The law which had given Pompey command of the campaign (the *Lex Gabinia de piratis*) had granted to him and his lieutenants control over a zone of 400 stades (80 kilometres) inland from all the coasts concerned, and Marcellinus apparently found it necessary to use this authority in Cyrenaica. According to the above inscriptions, a group of Roman citizens expressed its thanks to Cornelius Marcellinus for suppressing pirates,[407] and the legate settled on land near Ptolemais a mixed body of settlers, including some Cyreneans, but also people from Cilicia and Illyria; [408] this is likely enough to have been the settlement of a group of captured pirates on the model of similar colonization work carried out by Pompey in Asia, Greece and Italy.[409] Marcellinus further arbitrated in a dispute between Apollonia and Cyrene,[410] and collected contributions

---

[402] Oost, *Cl. Phil.* 58, 1965, p. 19; Badian, *JRS* 55, 1965, pp. 119 sqq.

[403] See generally *CAH* 11, 1956, pp. 659 sq.; *CR* p. 50; Cyrene is mentioned as united with Crete for the first time by Cicero, *Pro Plancio*, 63, cf. 85; for the numismatic evidence, *BMC*, pp. ccvii sq.

[404] Eg. Jones, *Anat. Stud. pres. Buckler*, p. 111.

[405] *SEG* 9, 631; *OGIS* II, 767.

[406] Reynolds, *loc. cit.*, pp. 97 sqq.

[407] *Ibid.*, p. 98, no. 4.

[408] *Ibid.*, pp. 99-100, no. 7.

[409] Strabo VIII, 7, 5 (388); XIV, 3, 3 (665); Plut., *Pomp.*, 28, 3-4; App. *B. Mithr.*, XIV, 96; Serv. ad Virg., *Georg.*, IV, 127. The inscription indicates that the people concerned were settled on plots of state land divided by *limitatio* (centuriation), and abandoned by their previous occupants.

[410] Reynolds, *loc. cit.*, p. 99, no. 6; *AI* II, pp. 112, 142-3.

towards some project of watersupply or irrigation.[411] All this suggests that the country's government had been so enfeebled that Marcellinus had been forced to intervene in its internal affairs to the point of suppressing banditry; the Cyreneans at any rate felt bound to honour him with the title of "saviour" (σωτήρ),[412] an appellation hitherto reserved by them for the Ptolemies and in a later period for Hadrian and Antoninus Pius.

This period seems, nevertheless, to have been one of prosperity for Ptolemais. The remains of the "palace", a wealthy residence excavated in the centre of the city (il Palazzo dei Colonne) [413], if they belong initially to this period, reveal wealth and good taste influenced both by the eastern and western Mediterranean. The Roman governor Crassus (23-19 B.C.) opened a mint in Ptolemais,[414] which already exceeded Cyrene in importance, and hardly fell behind the more ancient city in its *objets d'art*; its system of water supply was more up to date, its dwellings were larger and more magnificent. Ptolemais also boasted an academy and several gymnasia. Its commercial and economic contacts are evidenced by finds of Italian Arretine red glaze pottery, and of abundant Gallic terra sigillata. Stlaccius, whose name appears in the city's neighbourhood,[415] perhaps belonged to the Puteolan family of that name, freed slaves engaged in the eastern trade; two brothers of this name are mentioned contemporaneously in the edicts which Augustus directed to Cyrene.[416] West of the city of Ptolemais, a majestic mausoleum was built in the second half of the 1st century B.C., and later passed, on epigraphical evidence, into the hands of the Stlaccii themselves.[417] The palace of columns possessed roomy cellars, and attached shops on the north and east. In the 1st century B.C. and A.D. there were changes and improvements in the building. Although an analysis of the personal Latin names recorded at Teucheira, Ptolemais and Cyrene in the early imperial period is not yet available, the impression is that the province absorbed a considerable group of Italian immigrants after the death of Apion and in the reign of Augustus.

---

[411] Reynolds, *loc. cit.*, p. 99, no. 5.

[412] *SEG* 9, 56.

[413] G. Pesce, '*Il Palazzo delle Colonne' a Tolemaide di Cirenaica*, 1950, pp. 92 sqq.

[414] *BMC*, pp. ccvi, ccxxii.

[415] *CIG* III, 5216.

[416] *SEG* 9, 8, para. 2, 42-3; Anderson, *JRS* 17, 1927, p. 39.

[417] *DAI* II, Cir. ii, p. 482.

Nor was building activity lacking at Cyrene in the 1st century
B.C. A stele dating before the middle of the century carries a long
list of contributors and the sums contributed presumably for the
erection of a large public building in which it was set up at the
east end of the present village of Shahat, where the west and east
hills of the ancient city meet. Several sums recorded amount to a
thousand drachmas, at least two to two-thousand drachmas, and
one to three thousand. The wealth of some citizens is further
demonstrated by the inscriptions of Claudia Venusta, who erected
no less than four temples, to Athena, Persephone, Dionysus and
Demeter respectively, at her own expense.[418]

The civil war between Julius Caesar and Pompey did not pass
Cyrene by. Pompey held the province, but after the battle of
Pharsalia (48 B.C.) the city refused to receive his lieutenant
Labienus,[419] and was subsequently captured by Cato. From Berenice
Cato set out on his famous march along the Syrtic shore.[420] It has
been shown by numismatic study that the port of Cyrene served as
a Roman naval base from Pompey's time and throughout the civil
wars.[421] In 43 Cassius held the country,[422] but Antony gave it to
the children of Cleopatra.[423] It passed officially under the administration of the Senate in 27 B.C.[424]

As Roman authority was still largely restricted, it would seem,
to the city territories, the Libyan tribes had begun, probably as
early as 96 B.C., to spread northward; the hand of Rome under the
Republic and during the Civil Wars that preceded its fall had been
unable to check them. But in the year 20 B.C. Cornelius Balbus
mounted a campaign from Africa against the Garamantes who
occupied Fezzan south of the Syrtis,[425] and perhaps simultaneously
Sulpicius Quirinius opened a wide attack on the Marmaritae (or
Marmaridae [426]) to east of the Cyrenes; [427] the war, in which Cyrene

[418] SEG 9, 163; SGDI 4848; CIG 5139; SEG 9, 164.
[419] Lucan, Phars. IX, 297-8; Cf. Plut., Cato, 56.
[420] Strabo XVII, 3, 20 (836); Lucan, Phars. IX, 524.
[421] Alföldi ap. Mélanges d'archéologie, d'épigraphie et d'histoire offerts à
J. Carcopino, 1966, pp. 25 sqq.
[422] App., B. Civ., III, 8.
[423] Cf. Monum. Ancyr., V, 31-2; Plut. Ant., 54.
[424] Dio, LIII, 12, 4 (27 B.C.): "Crete with that part of Libya around Cyrene."
[425] Plin., HN, V, 5, 36.
[426] Florus, II, 71; CAH XI, 1936, pp. 667-668.
[427] Strabo XVII, 3, 23 (838); Plin. HN, V, 5, 33; Ps.-Scylax, 108.

took an active part, apparently reached a pause in 2 B.C.,[428] but Desanges [429] believes that the murder of L. Cornelius Lentulus, possibly proconsul of Africa at this time, by the Nasamones, should be linked with the campaign conducted by Cossus Cornelius Lentulus, who contemporarily pacified the Gaetuli of the Syrtic coast. If this is right, then Gsell's theory that the Syrtic coast was in 25 B.C. temporarily reattached for purposes of the campaign to Cyrene (a position reflected in Agrippa's survey of the Empire, according to which Cyrenaica extended to the Isle of Jerba) [430] must be abandoned, and the war would have taken place towards 2 B.C., after the survey had been completed. In A.D. 14, at all events, Lepcis Magna was again under control of the African province.[431] To 1 B.C., and to Cyrenaica, in the view of Desanges, belongs a passage of Dio [432] recording the repulse of an enemy advancing from Egypt—presumably Libyans—by a praetorian commander despatched by L. Domitius Ahenobarbus.

Valuable light on the state of the province under Augustus is thrown by that ruler's edicts, found inscribed on slabs in the Agora of the city, and promulgated in the years 7-4 B.C.[433] The Emperor's rescripts concern three principal subjects, namely, the province's judicial system, the taxability of citizens, and the recovery of money extracted contrary to law by the governing instances. Subsequent to the inauguration of direct Roman rule, service on the juries in the country had become concentrated in the hands of a small group of Roman citizens, and at the time when the edict was promulgated there were among them only 215 enjoying incomes of 2,500 denarii or more, the minimal sum qualifying for the judicial function. This group had abused its authority by

---

[428] *SEG* 9, 63, the inscription of Lucius Orbius, testifying to the rôle of the High Priest Pausanias in the campaign. See *CR*, p. 77 for the possibility that Quirinius' campaign was conducted in the year 6 B.C.

[429] *Hommages à Marcel Renard*, II (Coll. Latomus), 1969, pp. 197-213.

[430] Plin., *HN* V, 4, 28; 5, 38; A. Riese, *Geog. minores*, 13, 19.

[431] S. Gsell, *Hist. Afr. Nord*, VIII, p. 165, n. 1.

[432] Dio LV, 10a, 1; Desanges, *Hommages . . . Renard* (n. 429), 204.

[433] *SEG* 9, 8, where the relevant literature down to 1944 will be found. The principal discussions are: G. Oliverio, *NAMC* IV, 1927, pp. 13 sqq; Arangio-Ruiz, *RFC* 56, 1928, pp. 321 sqq.; J. G. Anderson, *JRS* 17, 1927, pp. 33 sqq.; J. Stroux, L. Wenger, *Abh. Bayr. Ak.* 34, 1928, *Die August-Inschrift auf den Marktplatz von Kyrene*; F. de Visscher, *Les édits d'Auguste découvertes à Cyrène*, 1940. See now also Oliver, *Hesperia*, 29, 1960, pp. 324 sqq.; cf. *AE* 1961, p. 176; *Bull. Épig.* 1961, p. 262, no. 841; K. M. T. Atkinson, in *Ancient Society and Institutions: Studies presented to Victor Ehrenberg*, 1966, p. 24.

condemning innocent Cyreneans to death, and to remedy this state
of affairs, Augustus ordered the governor to appoint an equal
number of Roman and Cyrenean judges to hear capital charges,
fixing the minimal census qualifying for service at 7,500 denarii.
He further permitted Greek defendants to decide if they desired
a court composed solely of Roman judges, or a court composed
of Greeks and Romans on a parity basis. He further prohibited the
bringing of murder-charges against Greeks by Romans, except
when the plaintiff was a Greek with Roman citizenship.

In cases between the Greeks themselves, with the exception of
those involving capital charges, Greek judges were to be nominated,
but not from among the fellow-citizens of the offendant or of the
plaintiff. Capital charges were to be heard before the governor or
before a court nominated by him.

The second edict (the third clause of the inscription, but the
second theme among those detailed above) obliged citizens of
Cyrene who had obtained Roman citizenship to fulfil their obliga-
tions in respect of the expenses of special duties laid upon them by
the city (liturgies, *munera*) in its interest, unless they had been
explicitly exempted on receipt of citizenship. The third edict
concerned the important subject of *de pecuniis repetundis* that is,
the claims of provincials for the recovery of money levied from them
contrary to law by the Roman administrators. In his rescript on
this question, Augustus cites the senatorial decree of the same
year (4 B.C.), designed to facilitate citizens to secure an investigation of their claims. Previously they had been compelled to spend
prolonged periods at Rome before obtaining redress; now the
senatorial decree enabled the claimant to nominate a legal representative (*patronus*) to present his case to the Senate, and a
regulation provided for the appointment within a defined period
of a tribunal of Senators to assess the claim.

The edicts of Augustus have for many years constituted a
central object of interest among historians of the legal and administrative history of the imperial provinces, nor is it our object to
enter into the various problems involved. Analysts of the document
have emphasized Augustus' rôle in provincial reform, and his
personal intervention in the affairs of a province which was theoretically subject to senatorial supervision; they have seen herein
an expression of the overriding authority (*imperium maius*) of
the Princeps. No small importance attaches to the document, in so

far as from it we learn for the first time of a senatorial decree intended to facilitate claims made *de repetundis*.

Roman care for the public good in these years was not confined to the judicial and financial spheres. Progress in the economic field is also discernible in the country's life. Improvements in the water-supply are to be seen at Cyrene and Ptolemais,[434] and a fragmentary inscription from Apollonia may refer to the erection of an aqueduct.[435] The magnificent Caesareum of Cyrene, in origin a hellenistic structure, was modified in the reigns of Augustus and Tiberius,[436] when it appears to have been re-adapted and dedicated to Julius Caesar.[437] An Aqua Augusta was repaired in Tiberius' reign.[438] In the early days of the Principate the north portico of the Agora was rededicated to Zeus Soter, Rome and Augustus,[439] and a late hellenistic ornamental well-house in the north-west corner of the Agora transformed into a sanctuary of the Divine Augustus, identified with Apollo.[440] The east front of the Acropolis was refortified by a wall of fine drafted masonry.[441] The large walled enclosure on the south-eastern angle of the city walls, which contained a number of circular cisterns, does not seem, according to the style of its construction, to be later than the first half of the first century of the current era.[442]

The Augustan edicts provide evidence that some Cyrenean citizens received Roman citizenship from Julius Caesar and Augustus.[443] A larger number subsequently obtained *civitas* from Claudius or Nero, and confirmation of Tiberius' favour is perhaps to be seen in the placing of his statue in the so-called "Strategeion" in the Sanctuary by Sufenas Proculus.[444] In Tiberius' reign, it

---

[434] Ptolemais, *DAI* II, Cir. 11, no. 508, recording the repair of *valvae* and *hydrogogiae* in the early Roman period. The city had a complete system of earthenware pipes supplying water to its houses. The great cisterns under the Agora seem to have been built in the hellenistic period, but the vaulting was renewed under Roman rule (G. Caputo, *L'Illustrazione Italiana*, Jan. 5th, 1936).

[435] *CIL* III, 12.

[436] *PBSR* 26, 1958, pp. 160-1.

[437] Stucchi, *Cirene*, pp. 96 sqq.; Goodchild, *Kyrene u. Apollonia*, p. 71.

[438] *AA* 1938, p. 730.

[439] *SEG* 9, 127.

[440] Stucchi, *Cirene*, pp. 65 sqq.

[441] *DAI* I, Cir. ii, no. 49.

[442] *JRS* 49, 1959, pp. 98-9; cf. *QAL* 4, 1961, p. 86.

[443] *SEG* 9, 8, para. 3.

[444] *AI* III, pp. 198-201. Reynolds (*JRS* 49, 1959, p. 97) ascribes the grant

should be noted, the city's coinage experienced a brief rehabilitation, before it was replaced completely by Roman issues.[445] In 8
B.C. the well-to-do Jewish community of Berenice repaired and
readorned its amphitheatre, designed to house its periodical
gatherings.[446]

Little is known of the Cyrenean countryside in the first days
of Roman rule. A bath-installation at Messa west of Cyrene belongs
to this period, and the regular distribution of farmsteads east of
the same area suggests that the lands here were contemporarily
divided into fairly large farm-units. The inhabitants of the village
of al-Gubba, east of Cyrene, found some reason to express their
loyalty to the Emperor Claudius in an inscription set up in a public
place.[447] A Roman military highway linked Cyrene with Phykus,
the ancient harbour northwest of the city (today Ras al-Ḥammam),
and can be plainly seen in air-photographs. Pliny the Elder wrote
of the measuring of the distance from Phykus to Cape Criumetopon
in Crete in the time of M. Vipsanius Agrippa,[448] and this operation
may have had as its object the establishment of a mail-packet
service between the two parts of the province. If so, the aforesaid
highway was probably an Augustan work; several of Cyrenaica's
important roads, however, were paved or repaired, according to
their milestones, by Claudius, among them being the routes from
Cyrene to Apollonia and from Balagrae to Cyrene.[449]

The estates of Cyrene's temples continued to exist and flourish,
in the Roman period, on epigraphical evidence, since the revenues
of Apollo (πρόσοδοι) are referred to under Augustus,[450] Nero,[451]
Trajan,[452] and Hadrian,[453] also between the years 161-180.[454]
The management of these domains was in all probability under the
influence of the Roman government, for under Augustus (before
20 B.C.) the proconsul G. Lucanius Proculus made a dedication to

---

of *civitas* to Claudius. The identity of the emperor portrayed by the statue in
the Strategeion has recently been questioned.

[445] On the grant of *civitas* to inhabitants of Cyrene, see Reynolds, *loc. cit.*
[446] *CIG* III, 5362.
[447] *SB* no. 5904.
[448] *HN* IV, 5, 10.
[449] *PBSA* 18, 1959, pp. 83-91.
[450] *SEG* 9, 4.
[451] *SEG* 9, 75.
[452] *SEG* 9, 101.
[453] *SEG* 9, 171.
[454] *SEG* 9, 174-5.

Caesar with money given to him by the priests of Apollo.[455] The future emperor Vespasian, when serving as quaestor of Cyrene,[456] also discharged the priesthood of that deity,[457] and the same post was held in 111 by a relative of Antonius Flamma, who had governed the province till the year 69.[458] The latter, indeed, was sued by the Cyreneans for corruption and brutality, and punished by exile.[459] This incident was by no means isolated, for the governors Caesius Cordus [460] and Pedius Blaesus [461] were called to account in a similar fashion for their misdeeds in Cyrene. The successful prosecution of these Cyrenean governors for robbery and fraud by the inhabitants they had governed, shows that Augustus' machinery for the protection of the property of the subject was needed, and was not completely ineffective. Such action on the part of the people of Cyrene also permits the conjecture that they possessed a *concilium* or *conventus provinciae* participated in by the provincial notables; a similar institution existed in Crete,[462] and such assemblies in some measure secured representation of the provincials and protected their interests; the existence of such at Cyrene is the more likely in view of the title of "High Priest" (ἀρχιερεύς),[463] borne by the priest of Apollo at Cyrene and applied elsewhere to the priest of the imperial cult which formed the raison d'être for these provincial conventions.

---

[455] *SEG* 9, 96.

[456] Suet. *Vesp.*, 2.

[457] *CIG* III, 5154 c.

[458] Reynolds, *JRS* 49, 1959, pp. 96 sqq.; *SP*, p. 115, no. 24.

[459] Tac., *Hist.*, IV, 45.

[460] Tac., *Ann*, III, 70.

[461] *Ibid*. XIV, 18.

[462] E. de Ruggiero, *Dizionario epig.*, II², 1910, p. 1435, sv. Cyrenae; cf. Tac., *Ann.*, XV, 20.

[463] *DAI* Cir., ii, 271 (Augustan); *SEG* 9, 184, 6-8 (Flavian).

CHAPTER THREE

THE ECONOMY AND AGRICULTURE
OF ANCIENT CYRENE

I. PHYSIOGRAPHY

Cyrenaica resembles most of the countries of the Mediterranean littoral in its division into a limestone belt and a tertiary plateau which intervenes between the mountains and the maritime plain.* But it differs from other mediterranean lands in that the red soils produced by the Miocene limestone, are to be found solely on the coastal terraces to north of the mountain plateau, or in depressions scattered along the plateau itself, while the alluvial valleys formed by the seaward runoff are very restricted in extent. On the southern plateau-slope the limestone is replaced by white-soil steppe, which finally fades into the Saharah. The red soils created by the insoluble limestone residues are in Cyrenaica not so leached by the rains as to lose their alkaline content, hence they are the most fertile soils of the region; they are also situated in areas where the rainfall is sufficient for cultivation, that is, north of the plateau and on it, at the most suitable altitudes for corn-growing, i.e. at 300-750 m above sea level. The red soils of the Jebel and its northern terraces have indeed been described as containing all the elements required for agriculture, possessing as they do a high percentage of phosphoric pentoxide.[1] On the other hand the qualities of these soils are offset by their restricted area and by the limited water supply at their disposal.

The country's precipitation, concentrated between the months of October and May, varies in quantity from 10 to 1000 mm. according to locality, the highest rainfall being in the vicinity of Cyrene, a fact justifying the Libyan observation concerning that district (as reported by Herodotus) that "here the sky leaks" (ὁ οὐρανὸς τέτραται).[2] But average rainfall varies greatly from year to

---

* For this chapter, end-maps 1-4 should be consulted.

[1] J. W. Gregory, *Jewish Territorial Organization, Report on Jewish Settlement in Cyrenaica*, 1909, p. 7.

[2] Herod. IV, 158, 3. Theophrastus, after describing the increase of trees and the growth of their bark as a result of heavier rainfall, "as in Cyrene",

year, and a drought is expected every fourth year. The seasonal incidence, nevertheless, is of maximum utility to the cultivator, since it comes at a time when cool weather restricts evaporation. On the other hand the country suffers from a rainless summer of five months; and unlike several Mediterranean lands, the permeable miocene rocks of Cyrenaica do not overlie impermeable strata over which quantities of subterranean water can accumulate to break out as springs from the escarpments, or to be tapped by means of artesian wells. This function is discharged by marl strata of limited extent distributed over the plateau in comparatively few localities, such as Cyrene, al-Gubba and Messa, and the plains of Barka and Silene (al-Abbiar). The winter concentration of rainfall enables the accumulation to runoff in cisterns or by means of dams, but its quantity is not such as to make possible the irrigation of wide areas. According to one estimate made in recent years.[3] the entire spring-water of the Plateau is sufficient to irrigate no more than 4,000 hectares fully or 10,000 has. partially.

The cultivable areas themselves are also restricted in area. The Italian colonists in 1932 claimed that there were in Cyrenaica over 150,000 has. of cultivable land, and another 100,000 has. fit for "less intensive exploitation and pasture".[4] In 1931 the Italian colonizing institutions had acquired 120,150 has., of which 82,225 has. had been confiscated from Sanussi "zaviet" (lodges). The same year, the soil of the latter amounted to 200,000 has., much of

---

writes: (HP III, 1, 6): 'Thus woodland grew where there had been none before: and it is said that the silphium also, previously non-existent, appeared for the same reason'. This observation, cited from a Cyrenean tradition, is connected with the tradition that the silphium originated in the country seven years before the city was founded by the Greeks (Theophrastus, HP VI, 3, 3). Theophrastus seems to have based his observations on a personal visit to Cyrene, according to the convincing arguments of W. Capelle (RM² 97, 1954, pp. 169 sqq.). Theophrastus' evidence concerning the silphium suggests the possibility that the Greek settlement took place during a time of climatic change in the direction of increased precipitation. Cf. Herodotus' report (IV, 150) that the Theran emigration was preceded by seven years' drought in the island—a southward shift of the winter rain-bearing winds is a possible explanation. A climatic change in the direction of greater rainfall and lower temperatures in the 8th-7th centuries B.C. in areas as far apart as America, the eastern Mediterranean, Europe and India, now seems certain in the light of palaeobotanical and archaeological evidence summarized by W. Wendland and R. A. Bryson, Quaternary Research, 4, 1974, pp. 9-24: Dating climatic episodes of the Holocene.

[3] The International Bank of Reconstruction and Development, The Economic Development of Libya, 1960, p. 111.

[4] BMA 11, p. 8, n. 4.

it the best land in the country.[5] According to these figures it can be calculated that there are in Cyrenaica not less than 220,000 has. of cultivable land (cf. here, p. 128). Newer estimates do not differ appreciably; a report of 1960 estimated the cultivable area at 200,000 has., and the area of pasture at 5 million has.[6] Another expert [7] put the area of Cyrenaica fit for permanent agriculture at 145,000 has., the tracts suitable for seasonal shifting agriculture at 500,000 has., and the area of pasture at 37 million has. It should not be forgotten, however, that the areas of fertile soil in Cyrenaica have decreased to a certain extent since ancient times due to soil erosion. Some experts have found no evidence of this phenomenon,[8] but anyone who travels in the territory can prove to himself that this phenomenon has in fact diminished soil-areas, as for example between Teucheira and Bengazi or in the Safsaf district. In the neighbourhood of Teucheira ancient farmsteads remain in places where the soil has been eroded to bedrock. The Roman bridge east of Ptolemais is twice as long as the present width of the gorge, as the stream bed has moved westward and stratified erosion silt can be seen exposed against the eastern arch of the bridge. East of Ras-al-Hillal the entrance to an ancient tomb-chamber cut in the rocky flank of the gorge, has been blocked by the erosion soil which fills the wadi. The process of erosion had apparently begun by the 4th century A.D., since Synesius [9] writes from Phykus (Ras-al-Ḥammam) that residence there was dangerous due to the stagnant water and its noisome vapours, a phenomenon attributable to the formation of swamps near the coast due to the blocking of the watercourses by erosion soil swept down from the Plateau.[10] The reality of the erosion factor in the past was confirmed by an agricultural survey of Libya made in 1960.[11]

---

[5] *Op. cit.*, p. 6, n. 1.

[6] Int. Bank. Rec. and Dev., *Ec. Dev. Lib.*, 1960, p. 109.

[7] W. B. Fisher, *GJ* 119, 1953, p. 189.

[8] B. A. Keen, Middle East Supply Centre: *The Agricultural Development of the Middle East*, 1946, p. 11.

[9] *Epp.*, 114.

[10] In *Pap. Vaticanus* 11 (Norsa and Vitelli), a survey of landed property in eastern Cyrenaica, carried out under the Severan dynasty, fields whose soil has been swept away (ἐξεσυρμένη) by runoff are recorded in two localities (VIII, 2214; VII, 4718).

[11] *Ec. Dev. Lib.*, pp. 127-8; cf. Vita-Finzi, Wilmott, Clarke, *Field Studies in Libya*, 1960, pp. 46 sqq. for alluvial erosion in the Wadi Lebda (Tripolitania) after the Byzantine period.

The destruction of the forests must also be numbered among the factors that have diminished fertile soils, and an example is the Teucheira region, today surrounded by a barren rocky terrain, yet wooded as late as the 14th century.[12] Gregory indeed stated [13] that the diminution of wooded areas in Cyrenaica was apt to decrease the volume of existent springs. Although there is no decisive published evidence for a change in the country's climate since ancient times,[14] the greater extent of wooded land in the Greek and Roman periods no doubt aided the more effective concentration and use of precipitation.

The restriction and decay of the country's woodlands occurred inevitably with the growth of population, since the woods are concentrated in the limited region in which rain suffices for permanent settlement, that is, on the Plateau. Today remains of real woodlands survive north of Lamluda and Safsaf, south of Messa, in the vicinity of Wadi al-Kuf, Slonta, Mameli and Barka, and south of Teucheira on the north edge of the al-Abbiar district. Pliny [15] stated that Cyrenaica was rich in trees for a distance of 15,000 paces from the coast. Both he and Theophrastus [16] speak of the thuon tree (θύον), whose wood was esteemed for furniture-making, and was exported in the Roman period.[17] Theophrastus writes of the country's cypress trees.[18] The Cyrenean Cathartic Law of Apollo, which reaches us in a 4th-century version, contains a clause (no. 2) permitting the felling of the trees of the sacred groves by license of the temple authorities.[19] Remains of ancient olive groves survive on the plateau, and very numerous are the ancient olive-presses which point to the presence of olive-plantations over considerable areas in Greek and Roman times.[20] Today the dew precipitation of the Plateau is sufficient to support summer pasturage, composed mainly of bushes and maquis for cattle and goats.

---

[12] Edrisi, trans. R. Dozy, M. J. de Goeje, *Description de l'Afrique et de l'Espagne*, 1866, p. 162.

[13] *Op. cit.*, (n. 1), 19.

[14] Bonacelli, *AC* 16, 1922, pp. 386 sqq.; E. C. Semple, *The Geography of the Mediterranean Region*, 1932, pp. 99 sqq.

[15] *HN* V, 5 (33).

[16] Plin., *HN* XIII, 16; Theoph., *HP* V, 3.

[17] Athen., V, 38 (205); Paus. VIII, 17, 2; Strabo, IV, 6, 2 (202); Plin., *HN.*, XIII, 30 (100).

[18] *HP* IV, 3, 1, 17; cf. n. 2.

[19] *SEG* 9, 72; *DAI* II, Cir. ii, no. 57.

[20] The ancient oil-presses are especially numerous to east of Cyrene, and a remarkable concentration exists at Lamluda.

Cyrenaica's decisive characteristic is, as stated, the division of its non-desertic area into two zones, differing from one another in climate and soil: the plateau, whose characteristic features are red soil, woodland, springs and sufficient winter rainfall; and the steppe where white soils prevail, wells replace springs, low scrub replaces woodland, and herbage is confined to winter owing to the decrease of precipitation southward. These contrasts constitute the difference between permanent tillage and nomadism based on the rearing of pastoral sheep and camels. Today the camels and sheep predominate on the steppe, while cattle and goats rule the plateau. The camel does not have to go north in the summer as his need of water is restricted, and in any case camels were not present in Cyrenaica before the late 2nd century A.D.[21] Sheep, by contrast, need to drink in April and May and must migrate northward, as the southern wells dry up at the end of the rainy months. On the other hand the flocks go south with the opening of the rainy season (December), when the steppe is once again covered with grass. The tribes which have ascended the plateau in the summer, plough and sow the southern plateau in October and November, the coastal region a little later, and the Plateau itself in December. The harvest begins on the Barka Plan and in the southern plateau in April; on the Plateau from May to August; accordingly the tribes return from the south in the spring in order to harvest their grain. In accordance with the climatic conditions of the Plateau the population there is permanently settled, moving only such distances as are necessary to find fresh pasture for their cattle and goats, which are their chief livestock. In this region land is held in individual possession, whereas on the steppe, only the wells are regarded as private property. Hence a rhythmic seasonal transhumance characterizes the life of the country, necessitated by its climatic requirements (water supply, pasture, sowing), and this transhumance takes the form of the movement of nomads from the steppe to the plateau and back. Such a process can proceed without friction between the southern nomads and the permanent settlers of the plateau, just so long as the latter are not densely settled and vacant areas remain amongst them to furnish annual summer grazing and corn-land for the southerners. But if the plateau population grows and begins to expand southward and itself

---

[21] See n. 24.

becomes interested in the winter grazing of the steppe, friction and even conflict will develop between the inhabitants of the two areas.

It would therefore be logical to suppose that this annual trans-humance, which was till recently a regular phenomenon in Cyrenaica, also existed among the Libyans in the Greek and Roman period. Both Egyptian and classical sources testify that they included a nomadic and a settled element living side by side, and that the Libyans also practised agriculture. The sources show that they possessed horses, cattle, asses, goats and sheep,[22] while Herodotus and Strabo call them "nomads" (νομάδες),[23] Annual migrations are mentioned in connection with the Nasamones, the Macae, and the Garamantes, and a permanent condition of nomadism among the population of the interior was observed and recorded by Roman writers. The steppe land flockowners of Cyrene faced, then as now, the necessity of a seasonal migration to the plateau in order to water their stock.[24]

2. THE AREAS OF SETTLEMENT

The areas of primary settlement and the order of the colonization of the various parts of Cyrenaica can be determined with some certainty by an examination of the country's climate and physiography. The first settlement area of the men of Thera, according to Herodotus' narrative, stands out prominently on Professor Pantanelli's map,[25] which divides the territory according to regions distinguished respectively by springs, by wells, and by storage cisterns. Prominent is the Martuba region, which includes the shoreline from Ras al-Tin to Bomba, as a well-defined isolated district of wells and cisterns at the east end of the Plateau, and is probably identical with the region of Aziris,[26] the settlement area of the Theran pioneers after they had crossed to the mainland.[27] This bloc is separated from the area of springs to westward by a broad belt containing only cisterns, but no wells or springs.

---

[22] The ancient sources on the livestock of the Libyans are collected by O. Bates, *The Eastern Libyans*, 1914, pp. 91-100.

[23] Strabo, XVII, 3 (837): εἰσὶ δὲ νόμαδες; Herod. IV, 199; Diod. III, 49, 2.

[24] The camel appears in Libya only in the hellenistic period—see M. Schnebel, *Die Landwirtschaft im hellenistischen Ägypten*, 1925, pp. 332-4.

[25] *RIC*, 1940.

[26] Herod. IV, 157.

[27] Goodchild, *GJ* 118, 1952, p. 149.

The location of the areas of springs, wells and cisterns, explains better than any other factor the distribution of ancient settlement in Cyrenaica.[28] This distribution is determined by the interaction of rainfall and the geological structure. The area of high precipitation in Cyrene and its vicinity itself stands out as the region of primary settlement after the transitional period of experiment and exploration. In this region, owing to the restriction of springs to localities in which the geological strata constitute water tables suitable for the accumulation of subsoil water, the more habitable areas constitute well-defined blocs, the largest of which is bounded on the north by the coast between Derna and Apollonia, and by the second escarpment from Cyrene westward to 'Ein Targuna; from here its southern limit passes north of Slonta to al-Fayyidieh and then returns eastward to the coast along Wadi Derna. This bloc contains the ancient settlements of Cyrene, Messa, Zawia Beida, Safsaf, Labrakh, Tert, Lamluda, al-Gubba, 'Ein Mara, Negharnes, and many more. There are in addition other smaller settlement-blocs centered on springs at al-Jarib, Tecnis (separated from the former by the broken waterless area containing Wadi al-Kuf) and Barka, although in the Barka Plain water is available chiefly from wells.

The region of wells is defined by the Barka Plain, and by the coastal belt at the foot of the el-Aḥmar mountain between Ptolemais and Bengazi. This belt continues southward as the coast region from Bengazi to Rejima and Ghemines, narrowing towards Ajedabia. Isolated areas of wells also exist in the Plain of Silene (al-Abbiar) and the blocs centering on Tecnis, Mirwah, Jaulan and al-Mekhili—all, except the last, on the southern slopes of the Plateau on the line where the red soils meet the white. Al-Mekhili is a sort of 'island' in the steppe. These areas, in which wells are normal and springs rare, were among the regions of secondary settlement, and in all probability their first colonization was restricted to trading stations (e.g. Ptolemais), although points with plentiful wells adapted to oasis-cultivation were early occupied; such are found in the coastal sector between Teucheira and Bengazi, and at Bengazi itself, in whose vicinity is the River Lethe.

---

[28] A Fantoli, *RIC*, Oct. 1933, pp. 780 sqq.; F. Mühlhofer, *Spelealogica Cirenaica*, 1928; *EI* 10, 1931, sv. Cirenaica, pp. 417 sq.; E. Pantanelli, *RIC*, 1940; F. Franchi, *La Cirenaica dal punto di vista zooeconomico e zootechnico*.

But a third important factor influenced the choice of settlement, namely, the distribution of the red-soil areas, whose chemical qualities and resistivity to drought make them especially suitable for the growing of cereals. The southern limit of these areas coincides approximately with the line dividing the area of 150 mm. rainfall to the north, and the area with a lower precipitation in the south, i.e. with the southern fringes of the Plateau. This line commences at the coast between Ghemines and Bengazi, takes in the plain of al-Abbiar on the south, and passing south of al-Gerdes, Mirwah and Jaulan, reaches the eastern shore of Cyrenaica in the neighbourhood of Bomba. The red soil must by its nature coincide in area with the extent of the karst areas of the Plateau, although they are not continuous within it. The most concentrated and extensive areas are situated on the Lusaita north of Cyrene, east of the city; in the quadrilateral of Safsaf—al-Gubba—'Ein Mara—al-Fayyidiyeh; in the area west of Derna, and on the plains of Barka and al-Abbiar. The initial points of settlement were the regions in which high rainfall, springs and red soil were combined, and only in the second phase were settlers attracted to the red-soil areas of Barka and al-Abbiar, despite their comparative lack of plentiful springs, and the quality of those soils induced the settlers to depend solely on wells in order to exploit their agricultural potentialities.

Rockcut cisterns are not restricted to any one area of the country. As a secondary source of water they are to be found even in the plentifully watered plateau areas, and in the regions of Martuba, the Barka Plain, and the coastal plain between Teucheira, Bengazi, Ghemines and Ajedabia, where they supplemented the wells as sources of supply. In areas without wells or springs they are the only source, provided the nature of the soil permits them to be dug and the rainfall suffices to fill them. Areas like these are to be found in the mountainous region between the Barka Plain and al-Jarib, and in the coastal plain between Teucheira, Ptolemais and al-Haniyah. The widest region deriving its water solely from cisterns is the southern slope of the Jebel al-Ahdar, south of the line al-Rejima, al-Abbiar, Gerdes, Mirwah, Jaulan and Derna. Its southern limit, leaving the Syrtic shore north of Ghemines, passes eastward to the region of a-Sirwal and al-Mekhili, swings northward towards Jaulan and returns through al-Hawat to reach the coast near Wadi Temimi. It should be noted that this zone coincides approximately with the area of rainfall whose yearly average is 150-200 mm.; its northern limit coinciding with the ancient route, the Tarik al-'Aziza, is also the final limit of Greek and Roman settlement, since the plateau ends and the steppe commences along this line. Some military stations, however, existed beyond it—such were al-Mesus and Saunu.[29] The southern area of cisterns itself, apparently held no more than poor Libyan settlements.

The settlement-zones deriving their water entirely from the storage of runoff or rain-water, doubtless served in the third phase of colonization, after the primary and secondary areas had been taken and settled to maximum density, but the digging of cisterns continued well into the Roman period. The areas of primary settlement deriving their water-supply from springs continued to absorb settlers in the 7th and 6th centuries B.C., and as early as the middle of the 6th, with the foundation of Barka, began the colonization of the more fertile areas supplied by wells; Euesperitae existed in the first quarter of the century. In discussing the character of the country's ancient agriculture we may regard it as reasonable to suppose that overcrowding and a shortage of vacant land was being felt on the plateau in the 4th century B.C., when the attempt had already begun to settle the arid areas in exclusive dependence on the storage of runoff. We shall indeed find evidence in the course of discussion that the temple estates of Cyrene extended over the southern slope of the Jebel in the hellenistic period.

3. GREEK AGRICULTURE IN CYRENAICA

The pioneers of Thera and the other Grecian settlers reached Libya equipped with a good knowledge of agriculture,[30] but some time certainly passed before they achieved the full development and exploitation of the country's natural resources, and it may be assumed that in the first phase they imitated the agriculture of the Libyans. Italian experts have remarked [31] that the natural course

---

[29] Coster ap. Coleman-Norton (ed.), *Studies in Roman Economic and Social History in Honour of Allen Chester Johnson*, 1951, pp. 3 sqq.; 8, n. 3. Pentanelli (*op. cit.*, p. 12) believed that the fringe of the southern belt was a fortified frontier in the Roman period, but archaeological reconnaissance conducted subsequently has not confirmed his conjecture.

[30] Thera, for instance, already possessed a reputation for its wine.—Glotz, *Ancient Greece at Work*, 1926, p. 25.

[31] G. Piani, *La Valorizazzione dei Colonie*, 1933, pp. 173-4.

of agricultural development in Cyrenaica is from livestock breeding through the cultivation of cereals to the growing of fruit and other specialized crops.

Cyrene achieved renown in the ancient world for her fertility. We find among the epithets applied to her the expressions "fruit-bearing" (καρπόφορος); [32] "not without her share of all fruitful plants" (οὐ παγκάρπων φυτῶν νήποινος); [33] "deep-soiled" (βαθύ-γειος), [34] and "bearer of fair fruits" (καλλίκαρπος). [35] Herodotus writes of the district round Cyrene [36] that "it has abundant fruits", and Strabo speaks of it as a fertile area; [37] both he and Pliny state that its climate favours agriculture. [38] But there is no doubt that Cyrene's principal reputation was initially derived from her live-stock,—her flocks, cattle and horses. Thus her name was associated with the terms "flock-feeding" (μηλοτρόφος), [39] and "of many sheep" (πολύμηλος). [40] Arrian speaks of her abundance of sheep and cattle. [41] Her cattle are mentioned by Herodotus [42] and Hermippus, [43] and Cyrene is variously described as "mother of horses", "owner of fair horses" (κάλλιππος, εὔιππος), [44] "horse-pursuing" (διώξιππος), [45] "best of horserearers" (ἀρίστη ἱπποτρόφος), [46] "mother of renowned steeds" (clarorum mater equorum), [47] and "mistress of horse-pasture" (ἱππόβατος). [48] Horse-breeding in the Plain of Barka is explicitly referred to by Arrian, [49] and the poetry of Pindar in the 5th century celebrates in lyric language the victories of Cyrene in the races held at Olympia, Corinth, and Delphi. The city's pastures are also praised: she is "mistress of broad meadows"

---

[32] Pind., IV Pyth., 6 (10).
[33] Pind., IX Pyth., 58 (101).
[34] Callim., Apoll., 65.
[35] Strabo, XVII, 3, 21, (837).
[36] III, 50, 1.
[37] Loc. cit.
[38] Plin., HN XVIII, 21; Strabo, II, 5, 33, (131); XVI, 3, 21 (837).
[39] Herod. IV, 155.
[40] Hom., Od., IV, 85-9; cf. Pind., IX Pyth., 6.
[41] Arrian, Ind., 43, 13.
[42] Herod. IV, 186.
[43] Ap. Athen. I, 49, 10.
[44] Strabo XVII, 3, 21 (837); Pind. IV Pyth. 2.
[45] Pind., IX Pyth., 4.
[46] Strabo XVII, 3, 21 (837).
[47] Priscian, Perieg., 197.
[48] Oppian, Cyneg., II, 253.
[49] Arrian, Ind., 43, 13.

(εὐρυλείμμων).[50] With one exception indeed, these expressions do
not precede the 5th century B.C., but it may be assumed that the
livestock branch was already well-developed when the people of
Thera arrived in Cyrene, for the Libyan tribes owned numerous
cattle and goats in the 12th century B.C. during their wars with
Egypt,[51] and also possessed horses.[52] Homer already speaks of
"Libya of the numerous flocks",[53] whence it may be supposed
that the rearing of sheep, cattle and horses was important in the
Cyrenean economy from the first. When Barka was founded in the
middle of the 6th century the figure of a bull appeared on her coins,
and the kylix of Arkesilaos II is evidence of the royal trade in
wool. Although we hear nothing of horserearing before Pindar,
Herodotus tells us that the Cyreneans learned the use of the
quadriga from the Libyan Asbystae,[54] showing that the branch was
then an ancient one.[55] The monopoly of the silphium trade was
associated with Battus I,[56] and the plant is represented on the
city's first coins in the 6th century.[57] The silphium plant grew,
according to Herodotus [58] and Theophrastus,[59] throughout Libya,
but more especially in the west in the vicinity of Berenice and the
Syrtic Gulf,[60] and it is clear that it belonged essentially to Libyan
life, for Theophrastus informs us [61] that only the Libyans knew
how to treat it. Hence Jones was probably right in his belief [62]
that this produce was paid by the Libyans to the Battiads as
tribute. It is known that the silphium had to be protected from the
flocks which coveted the plant,[63] and a synthesis of the details
makes it clear that the growing of silphium and the rearing of
sheep were carried on in large measure on the fringes of the plateau
among the native tribes living about the Greek settlements, so that
their direct association with these branches, and the feudal pa-

---

[50] Pind., IX Pyth., 55 (95).
[51] Bates, op. cit.. p. 95.
[52] Ibid., p. 96.
[53] Od., IV, 85-9.
[54] Herod. IV, 170.
[55] Bates, op. cit., p. 146.
[56] Schol. Aristoph., Plut., 925 and other sources.
[57] BMC, p. xxx. The nature of the plant, see Chap. II, n. 59.
[58] IV, 169.
[59] HP VI, 3, 3.
[60] Theoph., HP VI 3, 3.
[61] HP IX, 1, 7.
[62] CERP, p. 356.
[63] Plin., HN XIX, 15 (43).

triarchal relationship apt to develop between the Libyans and the royal house in these circumstances, induce the supposition that the areas concerned became in course of time the property of the dynasty.

Arable farming, on the other hand, began to develop as an export-branch, it would seem, in a later period. Pindar in the 5th century knew Cyrene as "grain-bearing" (πυροφόρος),[64] and Herodotus reports that the soil of Euesperitae produced a hundred-fold.[65] Under Darius (521-485 B.C.) the country together with Egypt and Libya paid the Persian king a tribute of 120,000 artabae of wheat,[66] although Cyrene's share in this payment cannot be determined. Only in the 4th century do we encounter the testimony of Theophrastus that Cyrenean wheat was being sent to Athens.[67] At the end of that century a well-known inscription reveals that Cyrenaica was growing wheat on a considerable scale, sufficient to supply a number of Greek cities and islands in a time of shortage. This event will be discussed below (see p. 97). Theophrastus reproduces technical details on the development of Libyan wheat, which was a quick grower, needed a "strong" soil and possessed a stout stalk.[68] Pliny states of this wheat that it needed no cultivation during the growing period.[69]

We know little of the plantation economy of Cyrene. Vineyard products appear first in the Demiurgi stele of the 5th century, together with olives and figs.[70] Pseudo-Scylax (mid-4th century [71]) and Diodorus (3rd century) [72] record the country's vineyards, but apparently their produce was not of the best; Marmarica at any rate, gained a reputation for inferior wine; over forty vineyards or groups of vines are nevertheless recorded in the Martuba district at the end of the 2nd century A.D.[73] In the first century B.C. Strabo wrote that wine was being smuggled into the country from

---

[64] Pind., IV *Isthm.*, (3), 54.
[65] IV, 198, 3.
[66] Herod., III, 91, 3.
[67] Theoph., *HP*, VIII, 4.
[68] Theoph., *HP* VIII, 4, 3; *CP* III, 21, 2.
[69] Plin., *HN* XVIII, 21 (186).
[70] *DAI* I, Cir., ii, nos. 10-14.
[71] Ps.-Scylax, 108, 109,—cf. the name Ampelos; Schol. Aristoph. *Plut.* 925; Steph. Byz., 75 etc.
[72] III, 50, 1.
[73] Strabo XVII, 14 (799). Over forty vineyards of groups of vines: *N.V.*

the region of Carthage.[74] Theophrastus, Scylax and Diodorus speak of the olives of Cyrene, and the large number of presses scattered over the plateau, especially on the eastern Jebel, witness that oil-production flourished at least in the Roman and Byzantine periods. In the 1st century B.C. Barkaios son of Theochrestos bequeathed to the gymnasium of Cyrene an olive grove and its oil produce.[75] The numerous cisterns in the enclosure on the south-east edge of the city, it has been suggested, were for the storage of olive oil; were this correct, they would testify to the scale of production at the beginning of the Roman period, but the theory is disputable. Cyrenaica was also well-known for its growing of vegetables, table-herbs and perfume-plants, and some of these will be noted in the course of the discussion on Cyrenean agriculture.

Herodotus' remark on the reforms of Demonax, to the effect that "(Demonax) made over to the people all remaining affairs previously the kings', excepting their private domains and priestly functions",[76] suggests that in the 6th century the royal estates had become very extensive, and it may be supposed that the nobility also possessed estates of some size. The "large private tower"[77] of Aglomachos, where the enemies of Arkesilaos III found refuge, was doubtless a fortified farmhouse and the centre of a large agricultural estate on the far fringes of the territory. The establishment of the mixed settlement of Barka by Arkesilaos's brothers in cooperation with the Libyans, and the renowned horse-rearing of that town, point to the close connection between the live-stock branch and the Cyrenean nobility, paralleled in several other Greek states.[78] It may be assumed that in Cyrene too the aristocratic estates took the form of large units engaging in the rearing of horses, cattle and sheep and exploiting the labour of the natives in semi-feudal conditions. On the other hand both Battus II and Arkesilaos III brought new settlers to Libya under the

---

[74] Strabo XVII, 20 (836).
[75] SEG 9, 4, 43-6.
[76] Herod. IV, 161, 3.
[77] Herod. IV, 164, 2.
[78] P. Guirard, La propriété foncière en Grèce, 1893, pp. 111 sqq.; J. Hase-broek, Griechische Wirtschaft u. Gesellschaftsgeschichte bis zur Perserzeit, 1931, pp. 217 sqq.; cf. Hom. Il. II, 106, 705; IX, 154, and many other allusions, especially Arist. Pol., 1289b that horse-rearing states are most suitable for oligarchies, as Chalcis, Eretria, and Magnesia on the Maeander.

slogan of "new land-allotments" (ἀναδασμὸς γῆς), hence Cyrene also possessed a class of smallholding peasants, in part descended from the first settlers and in part colonists of the 6th century. This class subsequently included mercenaries settled in the Euesperitan region by Arkesilaos IV in the 5th century. As already suggested, the introduction of coinage in the 6th century may at first have impoverished the smallholder, and it is probable that we should see in contemporary royal policy the aim of intensifying agriculture by breaking up the aristocratic estates and settling smallholders on them, while the Delphic denunciation of Arkesilaos III may have been directed against royal centralization of authority and the development of economic étatism. The last Battiads seem to have devoted themselves to increasing the population of small-holders and also to extending the royal branches of silphium pro-duction and stock-farming.

4. CYRENEAN AGRICULTURE IN THE FOURTH CENTURY: THE DEMIURGI STELES

The known Demiurgi steles begin in the middle of the 5th century B.C. The two examples that survive from that time are unfortunately much mutilated, any record of the crops grown contemporarily being lost. But to judge by the uniformity of the records during the 4th century, it may be permissible to assume that they included similar items in the preceding century. The official character of these documents is made clear from the for-mulation and order of the opening lines: after the appeal to the gods (Θεοί, Θεός, Θεὸς Τύχα), comes a record of the year under the name of the eponymous priest of Apollo. Then the Demiurgi, the three officials responsible for the matters concerned, are named, and finally appears a list of agricultural produce and the price of each product with the total income of the year, followed by the items of expenditure from the recorded revenue and the balance in hand. It is therefore clear that we are dealing with an estate or estates administered by the Demiurgi for the polis of Cyrene. The produce of these lands was sold, all or in part, and the proceeds were devoted to the requirements of the cults. The place where most of these steles were found shows that the administrative office of the Demiurgi was in the Agora, perhaps in the Temple of Apollo (previously thought to have been the Temple of Demeter) or near it, although the fund supported several other cults, among them those of Artemis and Athene.[79]

It is not difficult to discover the source of the lands concerned. The king was the high priest of Apollo and also disposed of royal domains (τεμένεα). On the deposition of the Battiad dynasty these lands doubtless passed to the city and to the management of the priests of Apollo who took the place of the kings, or of other magistrates of the polis. As we have seen, the relations of the Battiads with the Libyans and the confiscation of the property of their numerous enemies had led to the growth of their estates. It is clear from the Cathartic Laws of Apollo, which reach us in a fourth-century copy, that the god's domains also included sacred groves, from which timber was cut and sold for secular purposes.[80] The temple property is likely enough to have grown still larger as a result of bequests on the part of worshippers such as Barkaios son of Theochrestos, who bequeathed an olive plantation to the revenues of Apollo, Artemis, Hermes and Heracles in the first century B.C.[81] The name of one temple estate has come down to us, in the Ἀρτά-μιτος Κώμη recorded by Ptolemy [82] in the western or southern Jebel in the middle of the 2nd century of the current era. The expression "from the revenues of Apollo" (ἐκ τῶν τοῦ Ἀπολλώνος προσόδων) appears in the middle of the 4th century B.C. in the Stele of the Founders,[83] and part of these revenues was doubtless derived from the sacred lands. In the same period the administrators included accountants (ἐπιστάντες ἐπὶ τὸς ἀπολόγος),[84] and in the same instance the revenues bear the expenses involved in the setting up of the "Stele of the Founders". The officials receiving salaries from the fund in the 4th century included the ἐπίσκοποι [85] who, according to an analogy from Rhodes [86] were in charge of funds and sacred fields;[87] both the ἐπιστάντες and the ἐπίσκοποι may be regarded as working under the supervision of the Demiurgi.

It may reasonably be supposed then, that the produce recorded

---

[79] *DAI* I, Cir., ii, no. 12, 12.
[80] *SEG* 9, 72, para. 2.
[81] *SEG* 9, 4; *DAI* II, Cir. ii, no. 547, paras. 2, 3.
[82] IV, 4, 7.
[83] *SEG* 9, 3. 22.
[84] *Ibid.*, line 22.
[85] *DAI* II, Cir. i, no. 12, 17.
[86] *SIG* 619, 43; n. 6.
[87] *DAI* I, Cir. ii, p. 36.

in the inscriptions is that of the temple lands, its prices being
fixed by the Demiurgi. An analogy may be found in the law of
Samos [88] which lays down that "they (the officials concerned)
will sell the wheat levied as a tax of twenty percent. from the Anaoi,
valuing it at five drachmas and two obols, not less than was previously fixed by the people." The government of Cyrene spends the
proceeds of these sales on the celebration of given civic festivals
and on sacrifices. The steles, however, do not inform us what
percentage of the produce was levied or sold, hence the size of the
estate or estates whence it came cannot be determined with any
confidence. The total annual income from the produce in a normal
year was 30,000 drachmas,[89] and while certainty is impossible, it is
not improbable that the revenue was derived from no more than a
percentage of the total produce, for most Greek temples leased
their land to tenants by contract for a fixed percentage of the
crops.[90] Unfortunately, our knowledge of rents in ancient Greece
is scanty. The 20 percent. corn tax as levied by the Samos temples
has been mentioned. Eleusis took 8 percent. tax on annual produce;[91]
the estate of Phainippos yielded an interest of 9.5 percent. per
year; [92] Delos imposed a ten percent. tax on wheat crops in the
2nd century B.C.; [93] in Elis rents of 10 percent. were paid; [94]
at Heracleia—of 8 percent.[95] Michell [96] thinks that rents of 8-10
percent. were usual in Greece in the 4th century. But it should not

---

[88] *SIG* 976, 23.

[89] Stele no. 10 (*DAI* I, Cir. ii): 37, 293 drachmas; no. 11 : 30, 237 dr.; no.
12 : 30, 875; no. 13 : 38,052 dr.; no. 14 : 33,647. The estate of Phainippos, in
Attica, brought in an annual income of 31,700 dr. in the late 4th century BC,
according to Demosthenes (*Phaen.*, 1040, 1045). Its area was some 390
hectares, including 86 hectares of arable and 10 hectares of vineyards. The
remainder was covered by woodland or scrub. But the prices brought in by
crops in Attica differed greatly at that time from those in Cyrene (they were
normally six times those of Libya), nor do we know the distribution and
proportions of the crops grown on the Cyrenean temple estate. On Phainippos' estate, see A. Jardé, *Les céréales dans l'antiquité grecque*, 1925,
pp. 48 sqq.; 157 sqq.

[90] J. Kent, *Hesperia*, 17, 1948, pp. 243 sqq.; Ziebart, *Hermes* 61, 1926, pp.
87 sqq.; Durrbach, *REG* 32, 1919, pp. 167 sqq.; *IG*[1] II, 2492 sq.

[91] Plut., *Vit.*, X; *Orat.* 849d; Jardé, *op. cit.*, p. 92, n. 2; 116, n. 2; cf. *id.*,
op. cit., p. 155, n. 1.

[92] Jardé, *op. cit.*, p. 162.

[93] *SEHHW*, p. 235.

[94] Jardé, *op. cit.*, p. 151 n.

[95] *Ibid.*

[96] *The Economics of Ancient Greece*, 1940, pp. 44-5.

be forgotten that the farms of Apollo at Delos, for example, were leased by auction, hence the rents varied according to circumstances.[97]

Let us now endeavour to analyse the type of cultivation reflected in the Demiurgi steles in the 4th century B.C. The crops recorded are: barley, wheat, legumes (ὄσπρια), cummin, hay (sown and natural), grapes (table and wine), figs, raisins, olives and olive oil. Barley today is sown in Cyrenaica on areas far exceeding those sown to wheat, and the country is generally regarded as more suitable to the former than to the latter.[98] The yield of barley in present-day Greece is approximately double that of wheat, and the same applies to Crete. Of the ten demes recorded in the well-known Eleusinian inscription of 329/8 B.C.[99] only three devote less than sixty percent. of their areas to barley-growing, and thirteen sow barley on over seventy percent. of them. The percentage of land down to wheat may have been larger in Cyrene, to judge by the "Cereal Stele" of the years 330-325 B.C., which will be discussed below. Generally barley brought lower prices (1-2 drachmas, in the 4th century)[100] than wheat (2-3 drachmas). The Italian experts were agreed that wheat predominates on the Plateau, while barley does better on its southern slopes and in the wadis bordering on the steppe.[101] This view concurs with the ancient sources. Strabo[102] states that the silphium region, despite its dry and sandy nature, was suitable to the growing of grains adapted to resisting dry conditions; he also writes[103] that ὄρυζα was grown in the central grain-zone owing to its dryness. As ὄρυζα means rice, this word is obviously the result of a corruption of the text, and

---

[97] J. Kent, The Temple Estates of Delos, *Hesperia* 17, 1948, pp. 243 sqq. The actual sums paid in rent by individual farms are not recorded; we know only the total annual rents of five farm-units over six years of the 4th and 3rd centuries B.C.

[98] *BMA* 7, p. 10.

[99] *IG* II², 834b. This inscription records the amounts of tithe (ἀπαρχή) sent to Demeter the same year from the lands of Attica.

[100] *DAI* I, Cir. ii, nos. 10, 11, 12, 14, 21, 24.

[101] N. Scaetta, *Nozioni della Agricoltura Libica*, 1924, p. 38; A. Maugini, *Le Colonie Italiane, Flora ed Economia Agraria degli Indigeni*, 1934, p. 89.

[102] XVII, 3, 23 (838): 'The country nurtures trees for a hundred stades; for a distance of another hundred stades there is (soil) which is suitable only as arable and grows rice (ὄρυζα—certainly to be emended ὄλυρα = emmer-wheat) owing to its dryness. Beyond these zones (the soil produces) silphium.'

[103] *Ibid.*

should be amended as Bonacelli has suggested,[104] to ὄλυρα, meaning emmer (*Triticum dicoccum*). According to Piani,[105] barley was grown in larger quantities than wheat in Cyrenaica, as it ripens more quickly and needs less rain. Bonacelli, indeed,[106] shows that the drought resistance and early ripening of barley in February and at the beginning of March, are better adapted to the hard conditions of the critical growing season in Cyrenaica.

In 1934/5 the Italian farms had 13,173 hectares under wheat, and 2,574 hectares under barley. The same year the Arabs had sown 7,809 to wheat, and 58,496 hectares to barley.[107] It is therefore clear that wheat was sown chiefly on the plateau and in the Barka Plain, where the Italian colonies were concentrated, while the natives remained preponderantly growers of barley. On the other hand in 1939 Cyrenaica grew more wheat than barley, the general yield being 234,915 quintals of wheat and 170,946 quintals of barley,[108] that is, 293,643 and 284,910 kilograms respectively. This change arose doubtless from an increase in wheat production in the expanding Italian settlement area, and it is probable that the barley-yield tends to increase in dry seasons, which are to be expected every fourth year. Piani indeed notes [109] that the unstable character of the rainfall even on the Jebel makes difficult the maintenance of fixed rotations and requires the reduction of arable areas in certain years. Accordingly it is impossible to form an estimate of the relationship between barley and wheat; nevertheless a summarization of the phenomena enables us to state, that if the two crops might be nearly equal in good years—although the balance tends permanently in favour of barley—the sowing of barley exceeds that of wheat in drought years, while barley and emmer were probably the chief grains of the small peasant interested in subsistence rather than export, as well as the peculiar crops of the Libyan, and more especially of the nomad.

The general lines of the Cyrenean farm of the 4th century B.C. may be reconstructed on the basis of the crops recorded on the contemporary steles, and on the authority of our general knowledge of the Greek agriculture of the time. Of the crops recorded and

[104] Bonacelli, *REC*, 1931, p. 228.
[105] *La Valorizazzione dei Col. Ital.*, 1933, p. 176.
[106] *REC* 1931, p. 225.
[107] L. V. Bertarelli, *Guida d'Italia, Libia*, 1937, p. 125.
[108] *SCC*, p. 148.
[109] *Valorizazzione*, pp. 176 sqq.

listed above, the grains were mainly winter crops, the normal
practice being to alternate the sowing of grain with fallow in
successive years.[110] In the Mediterranean region as a whole and in
middle eastern lands in particular, where summer rain is rare or
entirely absent, extensive irrigation not feasible and modern
rotations and manuring not practised, it is essential to fallow the
land in winter in order to conserve moisture for summer growth;
soil which has borne a winter crop must therefore remain unsown
during the following summer. Summer-grains, indeed, were not
frequent among the Greeks except in one or two areas. They were
rare even among the Romans, being limited to regions of especially
fertile soil or to areas of permanent summer rainfall. In these conditions, the only solution was to divide the arable equally between
crop and fallow. The sown half received wheat and barley in one
season, this being clear not only from the Demiurgi steles, but also
from the 4th-century Sunium inscription in Attica, which says: [111]
"(the lessee must sow) half with wheat and barley, and the fallow
half with legumes (ὄσπριοις); the rest of the (fallow) land he shall not
sow". The same arrangement appears in a lease from Dyaleis,[112]
which divides the plot into corn (σῖτος) and legumes (ὄσπρια).
A similar plan is probable in Ptolemaic Egypt, where a clause in
a contract dictates [113] that "after the appointed time I shall hand
over the plot leased, half under wheat, a quarter under various
seeds, and the remaining quarter under fodder for cattle." [114]
Here the fodder (χόρτος) is sown on the winter fallow; the ὄσπρια
occupying the second half of the fallow, included such crops as
beans, peas, lentils, clover, lucerne and vetch, and served as fodder,
or, after ploughing in, as green manure.

The advantage of the long summer-season, when no grains were
sown, lay in the leisure it afforded to the Greek farmer to plough
his fallow, to work it deep, and to tend his vines and fruit-trees
which ripened only at the end of the summer. Pliny, as we have
seen, remarked that corn in Libya required none of the hoeing or

---

[110] Xen., *Oec.* XVI, 12, 14; Theoph. *CP* III, 20, 1-2.

[111] *IG* II², 2493-339/8 BC.

[112] *IG* II², 1241, 21-4.

[113] *Pap. Hamb.* Inv. 319; Schnebel, *Landwirtschaft*, pp. 112, 223.

[114] *Ibid.* καὶ μετὰ τὸν χρόνον μεταδώσω τὸν κλῆρον τὸ μὲν ἥμισυ πυρῷ καὶ
ἄλλο τέταρτον ἀπὸ σπορᾶς γένων, τὸ δὲ λοιπὸν τέταρτον ἀπὸ χόρτου βρώματος
βοῶν.

weeding normally needed in the growing season in other countries,[115] and this saved labour and cheapened the produce. On the other hand a serious loss was involved in the necessary fallowing of half the arable which remained unsown throughout the summer, and obviously the farmer sought summer crops which could be sown on or next to the areas from which the winter grains had been harvested. Theophrastus draws up a list of such crops: [116] summer wheat ripening in three months, and a variety of late-sown barley which matured after earlier varieties; also lentils, pulse, peas, vetch, chickpeas (*Lathyrus sativus*), beans, millet and lupin. We know too little to say how far the Cyrenean farmer of the 4th century grew summer-crops without irrigation. We read of two summer crops in ancient Cyrenaica, to wit, cummin [117] and saffron. Cummin was sown in the same season as pulse [118] and appears to have been a commercial plant used, like silphium, as a source of condiments and drugs. Apicius writes of Libyan cummin in his cookery book,[119] hence it was exported. Saffron figures among Cyrenean products in the 4th century, and in Ptolemaic Egypt was sown as a summer crop on unirrigated land; [120] it may accordingly be listed among the summer plants of the Cyrenean farmer. As to the ὄσπρια of the Demiurgi steles, this class seems to have connoted both winter vegetables and summer legumes, the latter being required as green fodder after the corn had been cut.[121] The growing of summer legumes is not impracticable on the Plateau, which enjoys a high dew precipitation in the hot season, explicitly referred to by Theophrastus, who says: [122] "In Egypt, Babylonia and Bactria, where the country enjoys little rain, the dew nourishes everything; this it does also about Cyrene and Euesperitae." Real "dry farming" is possible only on the highest part of the Plateau,[123] in the region which receives over 400 mm. of precipitation annually, but here summer-sown pulse, lentils and chickpeas do well,[124] thanks to

---

[115] Plin., *HN* XVIII, 21 (186).

[116] *HP* VIII, 4.

[117] *DAI* II, Cir. ii, nos. 10, 12.

[118] Theoph., *HP* VIII, 6, 1.

[119] III, 105. It should however be remarked that his work is late and not dated with certainty.

[120] M. Schnebel, *Landwirtschaft hell. Äg.*, p. 202.

[121] Cf. Xen., *Oecon.*, XVII, 10.

[122] *HP* VIII, 6, 6.

[123] *RIC*, p. 85.

[124] Piani, *Valorizazzione*, p. 176.

the water-retentive qualities of the red soil in the dry season.[125]
The area of summer legumes, therefore, is limited to the red soils
that extend between the line Tocra-al-Abbiar on the west and
al-Gubba on the east; their northern limit is the escarpment of the
middle terrace (the Lusaita), and their southern limit the line from
Gerdes/Marawa to Slonta. But to succeed after a grain crop on
the Plateau, legumes would have to be swift-growing late varieties,
as the Plateau cereals were usually cut in August. It is more probable, then, that they were sown on the fallow, and this has been
the actual practice down to the present in Cyprus,[126] as part of a
cropping plan which has altered little since antiquity. Due to the
lateness of the plateau harvest, the sowing of summer grains is
improbable, nor does sowing succeed in Cyrenaica after the December rains, which are essential to the ripening of the crop.[127] On the
other hand corn is cut in the southern Jebel and in the Barka
Plain as early as April, hence it is possible to envisage the utilization
of the very long summer for a second sowing. But it is improbable
that the moisture in Cyrenaica was adequate for sowing such
crops except in an unusually rainy season. Exceptional was ὄρυζα =
ὄλυρα emmer, which grew in the country's central region in dry
conditions. If a three-field division was practised in ancient times
on the plateau, it probably involved the growing of early barley,
since this crop ripened sooner than wheat and required less moisture,[128] and could be followed by another crop.

The decisive characteristic in the division of the country's
arable tracts into three climatic zones (the Jebel, the southern
Jebel and the maritime plain including the Barka Plain), in each
of which the harvest took place at a different time, enabled the
farmer to prolong his growing season during most months of the
year, if he owned land in all three zones. This fundamental fact
made Cyrene an exporter of corn so long as grain-growing was in
the hands of the big landowner. The peculiar character of the
country's climate was grasped by Herodotus, although he exaggerated the length of the harvest-season,[129] which lasts not eight
but five months. It need not be doubted that there were then

---

[125] Mühlhofer, *Speleal. Cir.*, pp. 24-5.
[126] Keen, *Agric. Devel.*, pp. 13-14.
[127] Piani, *op. cit.*, p. 174.
[128] Bonacelli, *REC*, 1931, p. 225.
[129] IV, 199.

proprietors owning land in all three regions of the country. In the 4th century A.D. Synesius' family held tracts near the coast (at Phykus) and also in the extreme south; [130] the name of the settlement of 'Αρίμμαντος Κώμη south-east of Cyrene,[131] can hardly be unconnected with the aristocratic family which appears in the poems of Callimachus [132] and also in inscriptions at Cyrene in the 4th and 1st centuries B.C.[133]

Access to the south slope of the Plateau was important to the farmer in search of winter grazing for his sheep, but when spring came the steppe dried up and the flock had to return north. This need both created and solved a problem; on the one hand, summer pasture had to be found in the north, where arable was restricted and valuable; on the other hand the seasonal transhumance made an important contribution to the fertility of the fields. In many areas of the Mediterranean lands summer pasture is confined to the hills, and the arable being restricted to the plain, does not benefit from the organic manure, a deficiency which caused a decline of agricultural production in the Mediterranean area in ancient times,[134] since in winter, when the livestock descended to the valleys, the fields had been sown and the grazing so restricted. The winter maintenance of cattle was further hampered in ancient times by ignorance of rootcrops, which restricted the quantity of manure accumulating in the byres and sheep pens. In Cyrenaica, the situation was different, since the livestock came north to the Plateau after the grain had been harvested on the Barka Plain, on the southern Plateau and in its northern district. On the central Plateau grain was harvested between May and August and thus additional tracts were freed for grazing. Thus the livestock could invade the stubble at the end of cutting, also benefiting from the rough grazing about the arable. In such conditions it is unlikely that the Cyrenean farmer sowed his arable to summer grains, for half the area was needed for grazing. Sown hay was doubtless limited to the winter (since he seldom possessed sources for irrigation); what was left of it was needed for the livestock during the summer months, and new-mown hay had to be

---

[130] *Epp.* 114, 148.
[131] Ptol. IV, 4, 7.
[132] *Epig.* 13. Cf. also Φίλωνος κώμη—Ptol. IV, 4, 6.
[133] *SEG* IX, 1, 77; *TA* p. 102; *SH* VII, 1961, pp. 36-37.
[134] C. E. Stevens, *Cambridge Economic History I*, 1942, pp. 91-2; C. Parain, *ibid.*, p. 127.

got in from the field before August, when grass seeds in Libya.

It was this important difference between Cyrene and the other regions of Greece, namely, the manuring of the summer fallow by the seasonal migration of livestock—as determined by the physiography of the country (the identity of arable lands with a plateau which is also the region of high rainfall), that determined the relatively high grain yields of Cyrene. Here the arable enjoyed a greater quantity of organic manure, and larger flocks and herds could be maintained throughout the year.

But this coordination of branches had its own dangers. Its success depended on a balance between stock and arable, and on the maintenance of security in the southern steppe, the grazing ground of the Libyan nomad tribes. An overdevelopment of herds and flocks on the one hand, or of arable and fodder crops on the other, was apt to lead to a sharp conflict between the pastoralist and the plateau farmer in the summer months, and this conflict might continue in the winter when the settled farmer wished to send his flock southward. This situation would become acuter in years of drought or low rainfall, when the nomads tend to concentrate in the neighbourhood of the springs and to sow wider areas.[135] The decline of security in the southern region would have made difficult the seasonal transhumance of flocks and thus have caused a fall in arable yields and the degeneration of the livestock. The loss of the early grains of the south would also have compelled the inhabitants of the plateau to resort to summer sowings of corn (especially if he was under pressure of taxation). To do this he faced the alternative of enlarging his plot in an already overcrowded area, or of adopting a three-course rotation not usually favoured by the climate, which meant the fragmentation and overworking of his plot.[136]

On the evidence discussed, then, the cropping plan of the Cyre-

---

[135] Maugini, *Le Colonie Italiane*, p. 87.

[136] The closest parallel to the normal form of agriculture prevalent in ancient Cyrene, survives on the unmodernized farms of Cyprus (Keen, *Agric. Development*, pp. 13, 14). These are worked on a two-field system ; the more fertile tracts are sown to wheat, the less fertile to barley.Two thirds of the unsown are left fallow, and the rest is devoted to summer vetches. The soil gets its manure from the grazing of the livestock on the stubbles and the fallow. Summer legumes, vegetables etc. are grown by irrigation from runoff or from the watertable. In Cyprus the shortage of summer pasture still causes a constant struggle between the shepherd and the settled farmer.

nean farmer in the 4th century B.C. may be represented in approximately in the following table:

PLATEAU			COAST			S. PLATEAU		
December			*November*			*October-December*		
Vegetables or Legumes ploughed in	Hay	Wheat Barley	Hay	Vegetables Legumes ploughed in	Wheat	Vegetables Legumes	Hay	Wheat Barley Emmer
May-August			*May-June*			*April*		
3 ploughings Part Legumes?	Legumes Cummin Saffron	Sheep	3 ploughings part Legumes?	Legumes ploughed in Cummin Saffron	Sheep	3 ploughings? part Legumes	Legumes ploughed in Cummin Saffron	Sheep
December			*November*			*October-November*		
Wheat Barley	Hay	Vegetables Legumes ploughed in	Wheat	Hay	Vegetables Legumes ploughed in	Wheat Barley Emmer	Hay	Vegetables Beans
May-August			*May-June*			*April*		
Legumes Cummin etc.			Legumes Vegetables	Sheep	3 ploughings	Legumes Vegetables	Sheep	3 ploughings

5. THE CEREAL STELE

Not a few problems concerning the agrarian and agricultural state of Cyrene in the last decades of the 4th century B.C. are raised by the contents of the well-known Cyrenean inscription which records the despatch of 805,000 medimini [137] of grain (σῖτος) to a number of Greek cities and islands, and a few other towns, in the reign of Alexander the Great.[138] The recipient communities were apparently Macedonian allies, which had been hit by a scarcity of grain artificially created by the Egyptian monopoly. The inscription has been dated between 330 and 328 by Oliverio,[139]

[137] The Attic medimnus was the equivalent of 51.84 litres.
[138] *SEG* 9, 2; DAI II, Cir. i, pp. 31 sqq., n. 58.
[139] *Loc. cit.*, p. 86.

between 330 and 325 by Ferri,[140] and between 331 and 328 by
Zebelev.[141] For the purposes of the present discussion the exact
date and political background are not so important, but three
questions require an answer and these are: What was the unit of
volume used in the inscription? What does σῖτος mean in relation
to the consignment? and over how many years did the consignments extend?

Oliverio [142] assumes that the Attic medimnus is the unit of
measurement used in the cereal inscription; de Sanctis [143] thought
that the Aeginetan medimnus, the equivalent of 1.5 Attic medimni,
was meant. But if we consider the wheat prices of the Demiurgi
steles, we shall see at once that Oliverio was right, since Cyrenean
grain was sold in the 4th century at prices below those of mainland Greece,[144] and if we assume the Aeginetan medimnus, Cyrenean
prices fall by an additional third. On this point, Heichelheim [145]
concurs with Oliverio.

Wilamowitz-Moellendorf interprets σῖτος as wheat.[146]   The free
inhabitants of Athens, which received not less than 10,000 medimni
of the total consignments, habitually ate wheat, as did most of the
Greek cities with the exception of Sparta,[147] which was not among
the recipients. Barley in the 4th century had become the food of
slaves and animals, except in times of extreme scarcity.[148] It is
probable, therefore, that most of the consignments were wheat,
though certainty is impossible.

As regards the time occupied by the consignments, it is clear that
the items on the list have been recorded not in chronological order,
but in the order of the amounts sent, beginning with the largest. It
is further evident that each city did not receive more than two
consignments; Chios received four, but each was sent to a different
settlement of the island. Segré [149] remarked that there is no need to

---

[140] *Ha* III (Ital.), 1929, p. 396..
[141] S. Zebelev, *Contes rendues de l'Acad. des Sciences URSS*, 1929, pp. 97
sqq. which has not been available to me.
[142] *Loc. cit,*
[143] *RFC* 83, 1935, pp. 124-5.
[144] Eg. the price of wheat at Cyrene: 1 dr. 4/5; in Greece: 3-9 dr.;
Cyrene, barley, 1-2 dr.; Greece, 2-5 dr.
[145] *PW* Supp. 6, 1935, col. 890, sv. Sitos, Tafel.
[146] *Cirene*, p. 23.
[147] Jardé, *op. cit.*, pp. 123-4.
[148] *Ibid.*, p. 124.
[149] *Il Mondo Classico*, 4, p. 401.

assume that all were sent simultaneously, as the list seems to be a summing up at the end of the undertaking.[150] He considered that they had been despatched throughout the period of scarcity (331-325). Yet if we suppose that the price was normal (and nothing to the contrary is mentioned), and that the consignments were spread over five years—why should the trouble have been taken to commemorate them? The argument that the exports were a special concession, as Greek cities normally prohibited the export of corn,[151] does not apply here, since such prohibitions did not hold good in states producing grain in large quantities, Cyrene being one of them. The stele then had no point unless it commemorated a special effort, that is, a maximum consignment in the shortest possible time during a period of special stress. Here therefore we must agree with Oliverio [152] and Zebelev [153] when they date the consignments between the years 331 and 328, and it is even more probable, since no city received grain more than twice, that the whole project occupied two years. If this conclusion is correct, the total export in one of the two years concerned could not have been less than 402,000 medimni, or 221,420,41 hectolitres on Oliverio's calculation.

Can the area of cultivation necessary to produce this quantity be estimated? Any calculation must be rendered more doubtful by the possibility that part of the consignments came from stocks stored from the previous year. But in order to arrive at some notion of the area concerned we have no alternative but to assume as a hypothesis that all the grain came from one year's harvest. The possibility of despatch from the granaries is at any rate less probable in the second year. Jardé [154] estimated the maximum yield in ancient Greece at 16.80 hectolitres per hectare, on a basis of a yield of seven to one. The Cyrenean yield was certainly higher—the Arabs estimate their yield in the plain of Bengazi as 35:1, that in the wadis of the southern plateau at 50/60:1; in Marmarica, at 8:1.[155] The yields would not have seemed to have changed much in Marmarica from ancient times; the Vatican Payrus of the late 2nd century A.D. cites for Marmarica barley yields of 7-12 to 1 and

[150] *Ibid.*
[151] Francotte, *Mélanges du droit publique grecque*, 1910, p. 293.
[152] *Loc. cit.*, p. 86.
[153] *Loc. cit.*
[154] *Op. cit.*, p. 59.
[155] Information from the late Professor Sir E. Evans-Pritchard.

wheat yields of 4.5-10 to 1.[156] Barley yields of 30 hectolitres the
hectare and 180:1 have been cited from the wadis south of Bengazi.[157] Bertarelli [158] ascribes yields of 30/40 to 1 to some years,
although the average, he admits, is 5/7. Scaetta [159] has estimated
Arab crops on the plateau between 12.5 and 25 hectolitres the
hectare, at 25/40 to 1. The Italian farms, however, seem to have
obtained less impressive crops, their averages being 10 hectolitres
the hectare.[160] There is no doubt that yields vary greatly from
year to year with the variations of the annual rainfall, but taking
into account the Greek average of Jardé, Cyrene's ancient reputation for plentiful crops, and Scaetta's figures for wheat on the Jebel,
it may be permissible to put the ancient yield at 20 hl. the hectare
in a good year. On this assumption, and adding the fallow area,
we may evaluate the area reflected by the consignments of 331-328
at 21,124 hectares. The Cyreneans, however, would not have
exported their total year's crop, as they needed to keep enough for
their own consumption and for seed in the coming autumn. If so,
we are faced with the task of estimating the size of the population
of 4th-century Cyrene.

This is rendered easier by one factor at least; the stele says
explicitly: "To which (cities) the city gave wheat", meaning, that
we have to consider only Cyrene and her territory, excluding the
other cities of the Pentapolis. It is said that 7,000 Cyreneans fell
at the battle of Leukon in the middle of the 6th century.[161] The
city recruited 10,000 foot, 600 horse and 100 chariots for Ophellas; [162] 8,000 infantry and 500 horse against Euergetes II.[163] These
figures point to a citizen population of not less than 50,000 souls.
The citizens with the franchise in the city at the end of the 4th
century B.C. (not long after the grain consignments under discussion) numbered, as we have seen, 10,000, at a time when the city
was apparently approaching its peak population; but this body
was limited to men of a minimal annual income of 20 minae. As

---

[156] Johnson ap. Frank, *ESAR* II, 1936, Egypt, p. 59.
[157] Cf. Herod. IV, 198, 3; Maugini, *Flora ed Economia*, p. 99.
[158] *Guida*, p. 120.
[159] *Nozioni*, p. 38.
[160] *Agricoltura Coloniale*, Nov. 1939, p. 636; *Annuario Generale della Libia*, 1938, p. 218.
[161] Herod., IV, 160, 3.
[162] Diod., XX, 41.
[163] Polyb., XXXI, 18.

already noted, workmen were supporting themselves in fourth-century Athens on 180 drachmas a year, and even if this income was inadequate in the face of steadily rising prices,[164] prices in Cyrene had not then risen considerably and were generally lower than those of mainland Greece. If then we estimate the electorate of 10,000 as representing 30,000 souls (a very modest estimate), we can hardly add fewer than three times that number to account for free Greeks with incomes lower than the minimum census, metics, slaves and Libyans.[165] And in this connection it were well to recall that when Antipater in 312 restricted citizen-rights in Athens to 9,000 inhabitants, 12,000 Athenians remained without them.[166] There was also a considerable number of Greeks permanently resident at Cyrene who were not born in the city: [167] these constituted, according to Strabo,[168] a well-defined community in the 1st century B.C. The proportion of metics at Athens in the 4th century has been estimated at 30-40 percent. of the Athenians; [169] this percentage is doubtless too high for Cyrene, and 25 percent. might be a more realistic guess. The number of slaves can hardly be estimated at less than one for each of the 10,000 with incomes of 20 minae per annum or more; this is obviously too low a figure. The number of Libyans, by contrast, is much harder to evaluate, since there were among them many nomads and most of the natives would have lived dispersed over the city territory, the boundaries of which cannot be determined with confidence. But evidence will presently appear suggesting that the Cyrenian territory embraced not less than 80 percent. of the country in the hellenistic period, excluding chiefly the coastal areas of Ptolemais, Teucheira and Berenice. Accordingly the Libyan population associated with Cyrene may be seen as identical with the Jebel al-Aḥdar, which today contains the tribes of al-Dorsa, al-Braasah, al-Hassa, the Ailat Fayyid, and al-Abiad, numbering 77,250 souls in 1923.[170]

---

[164] *WGA*, p. 319.

[165] Most of the poorer citizens may be identified with the Cyreneans who followed Ophellas in his African adventure.

[166] *GS* I, 189; Diod. XVIII, 18; Plut. *Phoc.*, 28, 14; 9,000 possessed an income of 2000 dr. or above; 12,000 an average of 200-240 dr.

[167] See above, p. 35.

[168] Ap. Jos., *Ant.*, XIV, 7, 2 (115).

[169] V. Ehrenberg, *Der Griechische und der Hellenistische Staat* (Gercke u. Norden. *Einleitung*, III, 3) 1932, p. 13.

[170] Da Agostino ap. *EI*, 10, p. 421, sv. Cirenaica.

Gregory estimated the Libyan population at 50,000.[171] Hence we shall not be exaggerating if we number the Libyans of the territory of classical Cyrene in the neighbourhood of the same figure (50,000). We therefore arrive at the following cautious and hypothetical result:

Citizens and their families (under the democracy)	60,000
Metics (25 percent.)	15,000
Slaves	10,000
Libyans	50,000
Total	135,000

It is a reasonable assumption that the slaves and Libyans ate barley-bread, just as do the Arabs of Cyrenaica today, hence we must subtract their number from the number of wheat-consumers. If we suppose that the needs of adult males were 7.5 medimni of wheat per head per year, of women (one third), 4.5 medimni per head, of children (one third) 3.5 medimni per head,[172] then 413,437 medimni of wheat were needed annually for the population of Cyrene. Sufficient seed was further required for sowing 405,000 + 413,437 = 818,437 medimni. If the average yield is estimated at 20:1, there was need to grow an additional 40,402 medimni for seed. Thus the hypothetical yearly production totals some 858,839 medimni, or approximately 429,419 hl. With the addition of an equal area of fallow, then, we attain, on a yield of 20 hectolitres per hectare, an arable area of 42,942 hectares. But on the assumption that this area was devoted entirely to wheat, we must add an area for barley and its associated fallow. As the ratio of barley to wheat was apt to be 1:1 in good years, with a steady tendency for barley to preponderate, both on the analogy of modern Greece and in the light of presentday conditions in Cyrenaica, and because the years 331-328 were good years—we may conclude that the arable area totalled not less than 85,570 hectares.

If the quantity of barley needed to feed 60,000 Libyans and slaves is regarded as 5 hectolitres per head annually (according to Jardé's consumption-figure),[173] and add the seed for the following year, it would have been necessary to produce 315,000 hectolitres, for which 31,500 hectares were needed including fallow, and if the

---

[171] *Jew. Terr. Org. Rpt.*, p. 11.
[172] Jardé, *Céréales*, pp. 134-5.
[173] *Op. cit.*, p. 135.

country's livestock is regarded as not less than it was under Turkish rule,[174] an additional 55,200 hectares (including fallow) had to be cultivated in order to produce its fodder, which amounted to 552,028 hectolitres. Accordingly the total area of arable, including fallow, extended over not less than 129,642 hectares.

What was the ratio of this area to the total cultivated land of the country at that time? At the beginning of the 4th century B.C. 85-90 percent. of Athenian citizens, whose composition was decidedly biased in the direction of trade and the crafts, still possessed plots of land.[175] In contemporary Cyrene, although the commercial element was not lacking, the proportion of landowners was hardly inferior to that of the same group among the citizens of Athens. The Italian colonial institutions allotted an area of 31 hectares of arable per settler, containing 6 hectares of irrigated land, or 30-70 hectares of unirrigated land,[176] but it should not be forgotten that these farms were worked by modern methods. If 8,500 (85 percent.) of Cyreneans with civic rights under the Ptolemaic constitution, held plots of only 30 hectares,[177] (a purely mathematical average), the total area owned would have amounted to 255,000 hectares. We have seen that the area fit for permanent cultivation in Cyrenaica amounted to 150,000-200,000 hectares; [178] Fisher's estimate (1953) gives some 145,000 hectares for permanent cultivation and 500,000 hectares for shifting agriculture. But not all the cultivable lands of the country were available to the founder city: Barka, Berenice and Teucheira also needed soil to feed them.[179] We have no evidence at present of the agricultural areas

---

[174] Evans Pritchard, *BMA* 7, p. 12, according to the figures of Ahlmann, *op. cit.*

[175] *WGA*, p. 388; when the Athenian statesman Phormisios proposed at the end of the 4th BC to abolish the citizen rights of all Athenians not owing landed property, it was found that this step would affect 5,000 adult male citizens only, in a population of some 35,000-50,000 citizens.

[176] Keen, *op. cit.*, p. 32.

[177] This area would have been sufficient to furnish the necessary income in normal years; half of it would have brought in, on a yield of 20 hl. the hectare 600 medimni, to be sold at Cyrene at that time at 3 dr. the medimnus, or 1440 dr. after the deduction of a tenth for seed and food, and a tenth for rent. Even after additional deductions for overheads, the income could be supplemented from the vineyards and the plantations.

[178] See above, pp. 75-2.

[179] It may be supposed that the other four cities of the country possessed not less than 100,000-150,000 inhabitants in this period. Beloch estimated the total ancient population at 240,000-300,000 (*Die Bevölkerung der griechisch*

of those cities, but there may be indirect evidence for the proportion
of land held by Cyrene in the country in the 3rd century B.C.
Segré [180] observed that of the 101 names of Cyrenean immigrants
to Egypt in that century, recorded by Heichelheim,[181] 90 percent.
came from the city of Cyrene, the remainder being from Apollonia,
Barka, and Berenice. Moreover, 16 of the 17 names of people from
Cyrenaica whose period is unknown, were from Cyrene, and from
a total of 133 Greeks of Cyrenaica recorded in the hellenistic,
119 were from the founder city. This evidence caused Segré to
conclude, that the territory of Cyrene in the 3rd century stretched
from Katabathma (Sollum) to Thinis (Θῖνις), the settlement to
which Cyrenean citizens had been sent as colonists not long, it
would seem, before the drafting of the Ptolemaic constitution,
which mentions the place specifically.[182] Clearly the settlement
was outside the recognized city-territory at the time of the founding
of the new colony, but its whereabouts is unknown.[183] On the other
hand the Ptolemaic constitution fixes the frontiers beyond which
the sons of Cyrenean fathers and Libyan mothers could not obtain
citizenship, at Katabathma and Automalax (perhaps bu-Shifah
near al-Ajela).[184] According to this Cyrene would have controlled
the greater part of the country from east to west. There is no doubt
that her territory reached Ras al-Tin on the east in the 4th century.[185] De Sanctis however interpreted the frontiers as stated in
the constitution as evidence for the existence of a city league
(κοινόν) in Cyrenaica, but there is still no evidence for such in the

---

-römischen Welt, 1886, p. 259), and perhaps more in the Ptolemaic period.
In 1923 the population of Cyrenaica numbered 185,000 (da Agostini), in
1944, 200,000. Gregory (Jew. Terr. Org. Rpt., p. 8) believed that the country
was capable of supporting 240,000 souls with modern methods of water-
conservation, whereas Mühlhofer (Spel. Cir., p. 19) estimated its absorptive
capacity at 350,000 on the basis of the ancient cisterns.

[180] BIDR 1928, pp. 15 sqq.

[181] F. Heichelheim, ABP, p. 43.

[182] SEG 9, 1, 4.

[183] Segré thought (ibid.) that Θῖνις was identical with the Ἡρακλέους
Θῖνοι of Ptolemy (IV, 4, 5-6), which appear to have been situated in the
mountainous region south of Bengazi. This identification, however, is far
from certain; it should be emphasized that θῖνοι means "coastal sand-banks",
so that the name may be connected with the shores of the Syrtis and with
new colonization in the direction of that gulf following the war with Carthage
in the second half of the 4th century.

[184] SEG 9, 1, para. 1, 3.

[185] Ps. Scylax, 108. (Χερρονῆσσοι).

period concerned. More convincing is Jones' suggestion [186] that these limits were fixed to prevent Egyptians and Carthaginians obtaining Cyrenean citizenship. In either case, the evidence of names in the 3rd century must be interpreted to mean that Cyrenean territory was the largest of the city-territories of the country, and amounted to 80-90 percent. of its total area. If so:

Total cultivable area (permanent cultivation)	200,000 has
80 percent. of the above	160,000
Minimal cultivated area of Cyrene 335-31	129,642
Minimal cultivated area of 85 percent.	
of citizens of Cyrene	285,000
(according to the Ptolemaic constitution)	

These figures present us with several interesting conclusions, but before discussing them we should observe that these are extremely cautious. The above estimate of the population of Cyrene, if it is erroneous, errs on the side of an underestimate. A population of 30,000 free citizens implies many more than 60,000 souls, while 10,000 slaves is palpably far below the mark. If it was larger, the problem of a land shortage which emerges prominently from these figures, becomes even more acute. In any case the same problem is reflected by the predicament of the ten-thousand citizens of the Ptolemaic constitution—and the number is well-established.

In order to assess the rightness or wrongness of the argument, let us review several other possibilities:

1) that the citizen-body of ten thousand included not only the inhabitants of Cyrene, but also all those of all five cities who possessed the required income;

2) that the estimate of the percentage of the 10,000 citizens owning land (85 percent.) is exaggerated, and that a smaller percentage must be assumed;

3) that we have underestimated the fertility of the country's soils, and should put their yields at a higher rate;

4) that the lands suitable for permanent cultivation extended over a wider area than that estimated by the Italians and by the authors of surveys carried out since the Second World War;

5) that a land-shortage prevailed among the citizens and other inhabitants of Cyrene in the second half of the 4th century B.C.,

---

[186] *CERP* p. 485, n. 9.

due to population growth and perhaps to the concentration of considerable tracts in the hands of a restricted group of proprietors;

6) that the consignments of grain, under Alexander continued for a period longer than two years;

7) that part of the consignments of the Cereal Stele were derived from previous years' crops stored in the granaries.

As to the first possibility, it finds no basis in the Ptolemaic constitution. The only clause which might suggest a city federation is that defining the area outside which the sons of mixed marriages might not obtain citizenship, but this cannot substantiate the existence of a federal organization, for the detailed arrangements of the constitution contain no regulation to ensure representation of the other cities of the country; there is here no trace of a κοινόν, and examination of the legal form of the Greek city federations of the period shows that their existence was based, not on the supremacy of one city but on equality of rights and on common institutions.[187]

The second possibility breaks down on the face of evidence furnished by the Ptolemaic constitution itself, which expresses a pronounced prejudice against craftsmen and merchants; its outlook is conservative in the spirit of Aristotle and his school, and obliges us to conclude that the ownership of land was the chief basis for guaranteeing the franchise in the régime of the ten thousand.[188] Even if this principle was not completely applied, the reality discernible in the spirit of this constitution obliges the assumption that the percentage of landed proprietors in the ten thousand was a high one.[189] Nevertheless, there is no absolute certainty that the

---

[187] Tarn, Griffiths, *Hellenistic Civilization* [3], 1959, pp. 68 sqq.; *PW* 7, 1931, col. 1102 sqq. sv. Συμμαχία.

[188] *SEG* 9, 1, paras. 7, 8; cf. Xen., *Oecon.*, IV, 2; 'and in certain cities, especially those deemed successful in war, no citizen is permitted to practise a handicraft'.

[189] Cf. again Xen., *Oecon.* IV, 4 (which comes immediately after the sentence disqualifying craftsmen for political rights): 'Among the most respectable and necessary (livelihoods) are considered to be agriculture and the art of war, and both should be attended to with all energy.' These words are put into the mouth of the King of Persia, but in the following chapters Socrates endeavours to prove that they are justified. Cf. also Arist. *Pol.*, 1260a, 1278a, 1319a for the disqualifying of craftsmen and people earning their living by manual work. The main opposition was to craftsmen and labourers (cf. *SEG* 9, 1, para. 8), and perhaps affected traders—cf. *SEG loc. cit.*: "Whoever sells wine. . . or becomes a merchant (φορτηγός). Φορτηγός indeed can here also be interpreted as "porter" instead of "merchant". Aristotle

percentage of landowners was not declining among the citizens of Cyrene, and we shall presently notice signs that this was the case.

The third possibility, that we have underestimated the grain yields of ancient times, is also unlikely. If the Italian farms could not raise their output beyond 10 hectolitres per hectare before the British occupation, we certainly cannot put the ancient Greek yields at more than 20 hectolitres in good years. This estimate can only be reduced if we enlarge the agricultural areas at the disposal of the Greek population, meaning that possibly the ancient areas of permanent cultivation have not been estimated at their true extent (Possibility 4). But we have seen that even the highest estimate, that of the Italians in 1931, amounted to no more than 220,000 has., and the survey of 1953, which assumed cultivable areas at 645,000 has., stated that 145,000 has. were fit for permanent tillage and the remainder only for shifting cultivation. The modern estimates could be enlarged by taking into account tracts today eroded of their soil-cover, but their area may well be offset by the wider previous area of woodlands which have been destroyed by indiscriminate felling and by the depredations of the goat. The seventh possibility, that part of the consignments of the Cereal Stele was derived from the crops of previous years, is the least disputable, and, indeed, highly probable. Yet it can only serve to reduce the 21,000 has. estimated to be additional to the minimum required to feed the existing Cyrenean population. It can do nothing to reduce the minimum cultivated area needed by some 85 percent. of the enfranchised 10,000 of the Ptolemaic constitution (225,000 has.).

This being the case, if we believe in the existence of, say, 8,500 landowners within the Cyrenean régime of the ten thousand, we shall be obliged to conclude that a considerable percentage of Cyrenean citizens were forced to be content with restricted plots (perhaps also divided and scattered), and with farms on inferior soil on the southern, eastern and western fringes of the Plateau. The conclusion also presents itself, that the Greek settlement area had reached its maximum expansion in this period, at the expense of the Libyan natives. In the course of this study we shall see that the Demiurgi Steles provide actual evidence of this possibility.

elicits suspicion of those engaging in maritime commerce (*Pol.* 1327a), admitting reluctantly their necessity and the benefits derived from them by the state.

This situation does not, however, contradict the fifth possibility, that there was a dearth of land and that a considerable part
of the Greek population of Cyrene could not find an independent
livelihood. There are in fact some indications that such a situation
existed at the end of the 4th century B.C. and at the beginning of
the Ptolemaic period; the readiness of a large number of Cyreneans
to follow Ophellas in search of new lands in Africa; the new settlement of Cyrenean citizens (who possessed incomes of 20 minae or
more!) outside the city territories at Thinis; the growing emigration
from Cyrene to Egypt in the 3rd century— and the possible mention
of Cyreneans joining Ptolemy's colonies, if this reference did really
appear in the Ptolemaic constitution of Cyrene.[190] If there was
insufficient land for elements among the possessors of 20 minae or
more, the situation among the remaining disenfranchised inhabitants of Cyrene is likely to have been even worse in this respect.
If this was the case, the sixth possibility, that the grain consignments lasted more than two years, might lower the extent of the
cultivated area reflected, but would not alter the minimal area
required for the population of Cyrene.

Another important factor may provide the key to an understanding of the situation, namely, the considerable difference
between the prices of grain at Cyrene and its prices in the rest of
the contemporary Greek world. A medimnus of wheat at Cyrene
in the later 4th century cost 1, 4/5-2,2/5 drachmas, and a medimnus
of barley 1-1,2/5 drachmas; in mainland Greece the price of wheat
was 3-5 drachmas the medimnus, that of barley 1.5-2.5 drachmas.[191]
This difference would have induced the Cyrenean farmer to export
his grain, especially his wheat, overseas. The well-to-do proprietor
would have sought to expand his property in order to enlarge his
profit in the export trade, and the owner of a small farm would
have seen in the increased price obtainable for his grain abroad
the only way to make ends meet. But the instability of the Cyrenean
climate would have been apt to ruin the small man in a year of
drought, if he had invested all his efforts in sowing wheat at the
expense of other crops, and he possessed no reserve to support
himself in a difficult year. In such a year he would have fallen into
debt, and would have been forced to restrict his fallow so that his
over-exploited land would in the end have passed to the wealthy

---

[190] *SEG* 9, 1, para. 8, 4: .. ἢ ἄλλοτε οἰκίας τὰς [Πτ]ολεμαικὰς ἐσέλ-θηι . . .
[191] *DAI* I, Cir., ii, p. 63.

estate-owner. The situation of the farmer who owned land in each of the three climatic zones of the country would have been easier, for the distribution of his land over these three regions could maintain production and export for four or five months of the year, from April to August.[192] If therefore we take into account the country's physiography and natural conditions against the economic background of the time, we shall see that they were favourable to the owner of large estates, and were such as to bring about a concentration of lands in the hands of the wealthy, and the transformation of many of the small peasants into debtors and landless proletarians.

The timocratic régime of Cyrene in the time of Ptolemy Lagos reflects the city's situation after the destructive war against Thimbron and the uprisings and class conflicts that took place on the appearance of the first hellenistic rulers. These struggles must have led to a fall in the population and to the ravaging of the country and in fact we may perceive in the land-shortage and pushing out of the smallholding peasant by the big proprietor, the social background of the oligarchic reaction which took place at Cyrene in the second half of the 4th century, and of the revolutionary storms which swept the state after the death of Alexander the Great.

6. CYRENEAN AGRICULTURE IN THE HELLENISTIC PERIOD

The view has been put forward that the Ptolemies did not at first treat the land of Cyrenaica as "spear-won land", and it is doubtful if broad acres of βασιλικὴ γῆ were immediately gathered

---

[192] Cf. p. 95, above, on Synesius' estates at Phycus, near the coast, and in the south of the Plateau (*Epp.* 114, 148). Here may be mentioned "Arimmas' Village" ("Αριμμαντος κώμη—Ptol. IV, 4, 7) somewhere in the south of the country. The name Arimmas first appears among the city magistrates recorded in the constitution of Ptolemy Lagos (*SEG* 9, 1, para. 11, 77) at the end of the 4th century B.C.; it recurs in the 3rd century in the verse of Callimachus (*Epig.* 13) as the name of a Cyrenean nobleman, and appears in the 1st century B.C. on an inscription in the Temple of Apollo in the city (*TA* p. 102). The name occurs at least 14 times among the sepulchral and other inscriptions of Teucheira in the 1st centuries BC and AD, chiefly among elements that had reached the town in the Ptolemaic period. It is possible that they had taken the name of one of the Ptolemies' trusted aides who had carried out the settlement at Teucheira. (See *SH* 7, 1961, pp. 36-7). We may therefore see Arimmas as one of Cyrene's notables, loyal to the Ptolemaic dynasty, who had obtained influence under Ptolemy Lagos, also as a proprietor of estates which included areas, and a village-centre named after him, in the south of the Jebel.

into their hands in their earlier period. Although an agrarian problem of hardship and land shortage is reflected in the events of the latter forty years of the 4th century, these events also took toll of the Cyrenean population, and echoes are heard in the Ptolemaic constitution of estates abandoned or burnt,[193] while the settlement of Ptolemaic mercenaries on the land is mentioned.[194]

We further perhaps read (although the text is doubtful) of the withholding of the franchise from Cyrenean citizens who join Ptolemy's colonies [195] ([αἱ] οἰκίαι Πτολεμαϊκαί). New settlement schemes initiated by the sovereigns existed in all the Ptolemaic dominions, part of the land being allotted to serving soldiers or veterans (κληροῦχοι, κάτοικοι).[196] Most of the information on such settlement schemes in the Ptolemaic empire, indeed, begins in the time of Ptolemy II Philadelphus and his successors,[197] but such projects would have been needed in Cyrenaica to repopulate deserted tracts and to strengthen Ptolemy's control of the territory, a function also fulfilled there, on Josephus' evidence, by Jewish settlers.[198] The areas made available to these new elements, by political confiscation or the death of their owners, would have constituted the first nuclei of the royal lands (βασιλικὴ γῆ) which were to assume wide dimensions in the course of time.

Available material is not such as to enable us to date certain important changes in the tenurial situation whose influence is discernible in Cyrenaica at the end of the hellenistic period. In the year 155, Euergetes II regarded the entire country as legally his own, as we have seen, and by the end of Ptolemaic rule the royal domains had become very extensive, for they were converted by the Romans to *ager publicus populi Romani* on the death of his son Apion in 96 B.C. Part of these tracts can be identified from literary sources, by archaeological observation, or by means of Roman boundary-stones such as have been found at various points near Cyrene,[199] at 'Ein Targuna,[200] and at Marazig: [201] an area north-

---

[193] SEG 9, 1, para. 11, 1. 66.
[194] Ibid. line 63: μισθοφόροι τῶμ Πτολεμαίωι.
[195] See p. 108.
[196] SEHHW pp. 149 sqq.
[197] J. Lesquier, *Institutions militaires des Lagides*, 1911, pp. 162 sqq.
[198] C. Ap., II, 4 (44).
[199] Cf. Tac. Ann. XIV, 18.
[200] SEG 9, 352.
[201] Goodchild, *Tab. Imp. Rom., Cyren.*, p. 16. A third boundary stone with a similar inscription is at Cyrene; its place of origin is unknown to me.

west of Safsaf, divided by a centurial grid, corresponds to the
description of Hyginus,[202] which reports the division of Apion's
estates (agri Apionis) by this method. Not far to the east of this
area occurs the name Ḥirbet Maga,[203] which supports the evidence
for the existence of royal property in that district. Another such
tract is indicated, apparently near al-Gubba- where air photographs
reveal fields divided by the chessboard method of centuriation.[204]
Other tracts of state land, probably to be located near Ptolemais,[205]
were divided up by Roman surveying methods; Kraeling interpreted a boundary-stone west of the city in the same way.[206]
More complicated is the question, whether the boundary-stones
found near the walls of Cyrene also relate to Ptolemaic royal
lands.[207] The payment of silphium as tribute to Rome [208] after the
"liberation" of the country's cities in 96 B.C., before the country
became a Roman province (74 B.C.), has been taken to show that
the silphium areas of southern Cyrenaica also became ager publicus,
and had therefore been crown land before that, whence it is to be
deduced that the plant had passed into the hands of the Ptolemies
as a royal monopoly, its areas being regarded juridically as βασιλικὴ γῆ. Badian [209] does not think the silphium sent to Rome was
tribute, but a normal purchase, yet does seem to admit that the
silphium fields were state land in 73.[210] It would be entirely reasonable to expect that the first Ptolemies should appropriate this lucra-
tive area for their revenue. Hyginus writes that Apion's domains
were divided by the Roman surveyors into units called plinthides,
each of 6,000 foot-side and an area of 1,250 iugera.[211] These units
are six times as large as those usual in measured tracts of the
Roman Empire, hence it may be supposed that the dimensions of
the agri Apionis were very large indeed, occupying no inconsiderable

---

[202] De cond. agror., Lachmann, 122.

[203] Cyrenaica 1:100,000, Part 2, 5048.

[204] I have been unable to locate the precise position of these remains.

[205] Reynolds, JRS 52, 1962, pp. 100-101. Jones (CERP, p. 362) held,
perhaps on less reliable evidence, that royal land existed also between
Teucheira and Euesperitae. My own conclusion, that part of the community
of the former town consisted of katoikoi, might confirm his belief.

[206] SEG 9, 350.

[207] See p. 212.

[208] Plin. HN, XIX, 3 (15).

[209] JRS 55, 1965, pp. 119 sqq.; cf. Oost, Cl. Phil., 58, 1965, pp. 12, 13.

[210] Ibid., p. 120.

[211] One iugerum is the approximate equivalent of 2.5 dunams (0.25 hectare).

part of the entire country.[212] A second-century B.C. inscription from Cyrene, recording an edict of Ptolemy Neoteros Euergetes II or Ptolemy X Soter II,[213] mentions ownerless lands escheated to the government (ἀδέσποτα), so providing one instance of how the landed property of the monarchs expanded during the period. Another fragmentary inscription, published by Fraser,[214] refers to farmlands allotted to cover the expenses of the royal cult at Cyrene. A further interesting phenomenon is the location of a bloc of royal land near Safsaf, in an area which had been part of the territory of Cyrene in the 4th century according to Pseudo-Scylax.[215] This infringement of the city's boundaries meant the restriction or division of Cyrene's immense city land, and perhaps we should connect this with the establishment of Apollonia as an independent city. The objective necessity of such a reform will easily be understood in view of the disproportion between the territory of Cyrene (as revealed in papyrological statistics) and the territories of the remaining cities of Cyrenaica. If Heichelheim's conclusion was correct these changes were carried out before the middle of the 3rd century B.C.

The Jewish inscription from Berenice,[216] recording the despatch of Sextus Tittius to the country "on public affairs" (ἐπὶ δημοσίων πραγμάτων), has been interpreted to indicate the proximity of public land to the city (see below, p. 170).

The existence of royal land in the form of plots leased for rent (γῆ ἐν ἀφέσει) is shown by the settlement of cleruchs. We shall see later that Ngharnes, east of Cyrene, was settled by such, and Rostovtzeff [217] held that the royal edict of the 2nd century B.C. found at Cyrene (above), related to landholders of this category. The inscriptions of Teucheira, most of which belong to the 1st century B.C., contain much evidence for the immigration of new settlers to the country, among those who record their origin being settlers from Didyma, Thrace, Egypt, Judaea, Demetrias (Thessaly?), Aksine (Sicily), Nysa and Bithynia. To the same period of

---

[212] Cf. Jones, *CERP*, p. 362.
[213] *SEG* 9, 5; *DAI* II, Cir., ii, no. 538.
[214] *Berytus*, 1958, 12, p. 101, no. 1.
[215] 108.
[216] *CIG* 5361 = *REG* 62, 1949, pp. 283 sqq., line 11.
[217] *SEHHW*, p. 916.

immigration belongs the establishment of the Jewish community shown by the Teucheira epitaphs (see Ch. IV). Reasons will later be seen for thinking that this community began as a group of military settlers colonized by the government, and the places of origin of part of the non-Jewish settlers (Thrace, Thessaly, Bithynia) favour the supposition, since they were among the undeveloped countries from which mercenaries were frequently recruited in this period.

We have evidence, albeit indirect, for the relations of the Ptolemies with the temple estates of Cyrene. The Demiurgi steles testify to the existence of these estates in the period concerned, and Apollo's revenues (οἱ τοῦ Ἀπολλῶνος πρόσοδοι) are known in the Roman period, hence it is certain that they remained a unit in the Ptolemaic period as well. Their perpetuation is further indicated by the settlement of Ἀρτάμιτις κώμη recorded in the 2nd century A.D.,[218] but it is an important fact that both Magas and Euergetes II officiated as priests of Apollo,[219] and the desire to control the temple estates and revenues, or at least to introduce reforms in their administration, accords excellently with the wide organizational activities of Magas and with the aggressive and covetous character of Euergetes II. The political importance of the priesthood of Apollo has already been noted.[220] The steles of the Demiurgi, who were in charge of the revenues, at least part of which came from the estates in question, cease in the 2nd century B.C., while the absence of any later records and the silence of the Roman period on the subject, suggest that an important change had taken place in their administration. An examination of the steles which belong to the hellenistic period also reveals various hints of technical changes, probably introduced under royal supervision; these will be discussed below. Actual royal control of the temple property is disclosed in the edict of the 2nd century B.C.[221] in which the king orders the priests to draw from the temple revenues (πρόσοδοι) for the expenses of the royal cult; the creation of the cult of Arsinoe II in Egypt enabled the later Ptolemies to draw considerable sums

---

[218] Ptol. IV, 4, 7. On internal evidence Ptolemy's information on Cyrene derives from a time near to the conclusion of his work, i.e. c. AD. 150.

[219] SEG 9, 112; Euergetes, Comment., viii, ap. Athen., XII, 73.

[220] See above, p. 64.

[221] SEG 9, 5, 26.

from the temple revenues and to use the balance left over as they saw fit [222] after the holding of the cult ceremonies.

There is no reason to believe, however, that private estates ceased to exist in the country under Ptolemaic rule; on general considerations the Ptolemies inclined to make grants of large areas (δωρεαί) to individuals, in order to encourage agricultural experimentation and improvement such as small owners could not afford to carry out.[223] The name of Arimmas has already been cited as evidence for the estates of a prominent Cyrenean family between the 4th and 1st centuries B.C. The citizen body established by Ptolemy was apparently based for the most part on the large and medium landowners, and in 16 B.C. Barkaios son of Theochrestos left lands to Apollo and other deities.[224] The fine funerary monuments of Messa and a-Zawani point to the existence of well-to-do landowners in the hellenistic period, and the cleruchs who set up similar monuments near their village at Ngharnes can have differed little from them.

In Chapter II we have traced the fortunes of the native Libyans, and concluded that a strict administrative and legal barrier grew up between them and the citizens living in the cities and their territories. The Libyans, indeed, were ruled by a distinct governor, and according to Strabo in the 1st century B.C. were classed among the inhabitants of Cyrene not possessed of citizen rights. The conclusion appears justified that those not resident on the Greek lands as tenants and labourers were mainly concentrated in the southern region, and it is to be supposed that they engaged in shifting and seasonal agriculture on lands regarded juridically as state land, i.e. βασιλικὴ γῆ. It is nevertheless hard to believe that these wandering elements, who moved northward in summer and southward in winter, performed the functions of "royal peasants" (βασιλικοὶ γεωργοί) on the contemporary Egyptian model, yet there is no doubt (to judge by Strabo) that they included permanent agricultural workers near the territorial boundaries of Cyrene and the other cities, and these doubtless belonged to the class of "royal cultivators" and worked under the conditions characteristic of their class.

---

[222] *SEHHE*, p. 283.
[223] *SEHHW*, p. 289.
[224] *SEG* 9, 4.

The representation of a plough appears on two coin types of Cyrene in the Ptolemaic period, the first [225] of the years 322-308 (Ptolemy Lagos), and the second in the reign of Magas.[226] The identification on the first is not completely certain, but no doubt attaches to that of the second. It is not beyond possibility that this is more than an arbitrary adjunct, and rather reflects Magas' drive to revive and improve the agriculture of his kingdom. The actual type of plough represented is interesting; it possesses a stout horizontal share beam, into whose upper face the stilt and plough-beam are inserted as two distinct parts. The stilt is almost vertical, and a horizontal grip projects from its rear side near the head. The plough-beam rises obliquely from the share-beam and turns parallel to it through a rightangle. The position of the horizontal share-beam shows that this is not an implement for deep ploughing, nor can it be determined if the share was of iron, but the plough today used by the Beduin in the Tripolitanian steppe [227] resembles it in every detail: it has the same horizontal share-beam, the same vertical stilt with horizontal grip; its share is made of iron. It is therefore evident that the coins represent a steppe-plough, and it would seem likely that the figure reflects an interest in the cultivation of the southern fringes of the plateau. This interpretation may well find confirmation in the appearance of a corn-ear as an adjunct on contemporary coins bearing the form of the silphium plant.[228]

The Demiurgi steles of this period reveal interesting innovations from which relevant information can be derived.[229] The first striking change is, that the prices of agricultural produce are now fixed twice yearly instead of once, this being clearly proved by the division of the face of each stele into two parallel columns, headed respectively by the words πράτη ἐξαμήνις and δευτέρα ἐξαμήνις viz. the first and second half of the year, each half repeating exactly (in so far as restoration is possible) the items of the other. It would be possible to suppose that this change was required by the more extreme fluctuations in prices which became frequent in the 3rd century B.C. The great influence of these fluctuations

---

[225] *BMC*, no. 208, p. 47.
[226] *BMC*, no. 223, p. 49.
[227] Maugini, *Flora ed. econ.*, p. 43.
[228] *BMC*, p. lxvi.
[229] *DAI* I, Cir. ii, nos. 30-43.

in Cyrene is made clear by the steles themselves, and Cyrenaica was affected by the same general rise in prices which prevailed over the rest of the Greek world. Cyrene, which till then had generally enjoyed relative economic stability and prices lower than those of mainland Greece, now became part of the wider Greek economy whose unity had been promoted and in a measure achieved by Alexander's empire. Cyrene's prices now begin to fluctuate, and do not differ in some cases from other prices in the eastern Mediterranean. Nevertheless, owing to the mutilated state of the steles, we know only two instances (cummin, no. 40; legumes no. 41) of price-changes—in these cases rises—from one price-fixing to the next. Was there therefore some other reason for a second fixing of prices in the latter half of the year?

The first solution that suggests itself is that an annual two-crop course had been adopted. This innovation would explain why wheat, barley, fruit and legumes are recorded on both halves of the steles. But the appearance of legumes and vegetables ready for sale at the end of summer could also be the result of an increase in irrigated areas. Before we accept this solution, it would be well to enquire, when the Cyrenean year began, and when it ended.

It would be natural to assume that the calendar accepted at Cyrene would be the Dorian, as at Sparta, Elis, Argos, Delphi and in other Dorian states.[230] Loios (Λῶιος). the tenth month of the Dorian year, is in fact mentioned in the testament of Euergetes II,[231] but other hellenistic documents at Cyrene use the Egyptian calendar (e.g. the Ptolemaic constitution and numerous epitaphs). The royal edicts in the middle of the 2nd century cite both the Dorian (Γορπαῖος) and the Egyptian month (§ ii, lines 27-28), while § ii, 1.13 dates by the month of Theudaisios (Θευδαισιός). This month derives from a calendar known also at Lato in Crete, at Cos, Mitylene and Rhodes; its year began in September. The Ptolemaic year likewise began in the autumn, in 300 B.C. in November, in 200 B.C. in October.[232] The Dorian year too opened at the autumn equinox.[233]

---

[230] *PW* XX, 1919, col. 1578, sv. Kalendar.
[231] *SEG* 9, 7; *DAI* I, Cir. i, p. 11.
[232] W. Kubitscheck, *Grundriss der Antiken Zeitrechnungen*, 1928, pp. 222-3.
[233] *PW*, *loc. cit.*. 1578 sq.

A first fixing of prices in October and a second in April would indeed have been appropriate to the agricultural reality of the country. In October all the plateau crops had been harvested, the latest being gathered in August and September. But the harvest in the southern plateau began in April, on the plateau itself in May. Thus the April price-fixing marked the first month of harvest in the plain and the southern plateau; the October price-fixing relates to the crops got in between May and October, mainly on the plateau. The April price-fixing corresponds, in short, to the beginning of the harvest season, and the September fixing to its end. The introduction of a fixing of prices twice a year does not itself prove the introduction of summer-cropping in the hellenistic period, or a use of the three-course system associated with it; but it does tell us that the temple estates which form the subject of the Demiurgi steles had now been extended to the southern fringes of the Jebel.

The steles of this period further contain another innovation which is bound up with the same question, namely, the more detailed listing of the legumes. Down to the 3rd century B.C. only ὄσπρια are mentioned. From the beginning of that century, pulse, beans, lentils and other legumes (ἄλλα ὄσπρια) appear.[234] It would seem that the legumes had become more numerous and of greater variety. This phenomenon is susceptible to two interpretations: it indicates either an extension of cultivated areas, or a restriction of "dead" fallow. There is no support for the assumption that the cultivated areas were capable of continuous expansion. The two 2nd-century steles which we possess show a steep decline in yearly income,[235] although this may have been the result of temporary climatic, social or economic causes. It is more probable on general grounds, and in the light of the contemporary evidence in Egypt and Greece, that the greater detail in which legumes are listed points to closer attention to rotations and that half the arable, instead of being divided into "dead" and "green" fallow, was now wholly devoted to green crops.[236] According to the lease-contracts of Sunium and Dyaleis in the 4th century B.C., not more than half the plot was sown to grain, but in Egyptian farms at the end

---

[234] *DAI* I, Cir. ii, no. 40.

[235] *Ibid.*, nos. 38, 40.

[236] This division is termed by Schnebel (*Landwirtschaft in hellenistischen Ägypten*, p. 218), "the improved two-field system".

of the 2nd century B.C., we find that half the plot is fallowed
every third year, and a third in the intervening years.[237] However,
the three-course system does not necessarily mean that summer-
sown crops were grown. A possible interpretation is that a third
of the arable received grain in the autumns of two successive years,
a mere summer fallow intervening between the two crops, since
summer sowings did not do well over most of Cyrenaica. Such
were possible, as we have seen, on the Plateau, although there the
harvest was as late as August, hence summer sowing was not
essential unless additional ground was available. It should nevertheless be recalled that the earlier Ptolemies conducted experiments in quickly ripening summer crops of wheat,[238] and the
sowing of such seems to have spread at the end of the 2nd century
B.C.[239] The said evidence relates to Egypt, where grain growing
was assisted by Nile-irrigation, but the wheat referred to came
from Syria.[240]

Several other indications are to be found of the desire of the
Ptolemies to improve the agriculture of the Cyrenean temple
estates. One is the appearance of garlic among the plants recorded
on the steles of the hellenistic period.[241] Attempts to improve this
plant were made in the Fayyum in the 3rd century B.C., by
introducing external varieties from the south and from Greece,[242]
and garlic from Tlos was then being sown in Fayyum on stony
ground.[243] This information suggests that the introduction of this
crop on Cyrenean temple lands was the result of governmental
initiative and designed to enable the exploitation of hitherto
uncultivated tracts, in conformity with the desire to expand
cultivated areas.[244]

---

[237] *Pap. Tebt.* 115, for example—116-113 B.C.

[238] Schnebel, *op. cit.*, pp. 145-7; P. Zeno (C. C. Edgar, *Catalogue générale
des antiquités égyptiennes du Musée du Caïre: Zenon Papyri*), 59155; *AP* 9,
1928-30, pp. 207 sqq.

[239] Schnebel, *op. cit.*, pp. 230-1.

[240] See the works referred to above.

[241] *DAI* I, Cir. ii, no. 40.

[242] Schnebel, *op. cit.*, p. 207; M. Rostovtzeff, *A Large Estate in Egypt in the
Third Century BC*, 1922, p. 85 and refs.

[243] *SEHHW* p. 357.

[244] In the stele *SEG* 9, 35 (*DAI* I, Cir. ii, no. 34), Oliverio read πισσά to
mean pitch, and this reading would have added interesting evidence for the
fostering of conifers by the Ptolemies, perhaps for purposes of shipbuilding.
But a new stele published by Fraser (*Berytus*, 12, 1958, p. 104, no. 2), and
dating to the period 290-280 approximately, makes it clear that πισσά is

The following data may now be assembled:

1) The agriculture reflected in the Demiurgi steles shows the extension of cultivation to the southern Jebel, an intensification of the growing of legumes, and experimentation with the utilization of uncultivated tracts.

2) In the 3rd century B.C. a change takes place from annual to semi-annual price-fixing. It is further known that King Magas held the post of high priest to Apollo.

3) An alteration of the system of numerals used on the Demiurgi steles took place at the end of the 3rd century.[245]

4) Euergetes II (161-116 B.C.) officiated as high priest of Apollo.

5) In 155 Euergetes included as a clause in his agreement with his brother Philometor, the obtaining of a yearly consignment of grain from Egypt: [246]

6) The edict of Euergetes II or Ptolemy X Soter II [247] evidences royal control of the revenues of Apollo at Cyrene.

It may be concluded from these data: a) that an intensification of the economy was being promoted by royal initiative; b) that there was increasing royal control over the temple-estates; c) that the kings took over their administration in the 2nd century; d) that the country's agriculture reveals symptoms of decline, despite the above intensification, on the evidence of Clause 5, which informs us of the agreement to furnish Egyptian grain to Cyrene. How is the conjunction of these four items to be explained?

The evidence for the improvements made in Cyrenean agriculture, as a result of royal interference, fits well with our suggested interpretation of the plough figured on the coins of Magas, and perhaps on those of Ptolemy I. It may also be remarked that all these phenomena find analogies in contemporary Egypt, where the intensification and improvement of agricultural exploitation was carried out by the Ptolemies by étatistic methods. But this state policy was increasingly infringed and weakened as time went

---

to be translated as "peas". One plant, though unmentioned in the steles, was probably promoted by the Ptolemies in Cyrene, namely, the lentisk. This tree was introduced by them into Egypt (*SEHHW*, p. 1165), and is to-day very common in the rocky areas of the Jebel. In 1934 it covered some 200,000 hectares (Narducci, *La colonizzazione della Cirenaica nell' Antichità e nel Presente*, 1934, p. 87).

[245] *DAI* I, Cir. ii, p. 52, nos. 35-42.
[246] Diod. XXXI, 33 and see here p. 62.
[247] *SEG* 9, 5.

on by concessions to private enterprise (the temples; land-grants to individuals; private ownership; hereditary cleruchic tenure; emphyteutic leases), and by the growing opposition of the masses, resulting in the abandonment of lands and economic decline. There is little doubt that the general factors which caused difficulties in the Egyptian economy from the end of the 3rd century onward, also affected Cyrenaica. The general contraction of the mainland Greek markets between 200-150 B.C.,[218] loss of the Syrian caravan-route after the conquest of Palestine by Antiochus III (c. 200 B.C.), the interruption to the Sudanese trade route caused by disorders in Upper Egypt (206-185 B.C.), the rise of Rhodes as a dominating commercial power in the Aegean, the loss of the Ptolemaic colonies in the same area (246/5 B.C.), and the interruptions to the western Mediterranean markets caused by the Second Punic War (218-201 B.C.)—not to mention the impairment of security in the Aegean by the spread of piracy [249]—would have affected Cyrenaica as much as they affected Egypt, both directly and by diminishing the revenues of the Ptolemies and so increasing the weight of internal taxation. On the other hand the price records that have reached us do not confirm the view that the 2nd-century inflation of the Ptolemaic currency affected Cyrenaica, although our evidence on the question is inadequate. As to the grain-trade, African wheat appeared on the market after the Second Punic War and began to compete in the eastern Mediterranean zone.[250] In the 2nd century, Pergamum, Bithynia and Pontus also developed as grain-growers.[251] All these factors combined to add to the pressure of taxation in Egypt and to intensify the struggle between bureaucracy and subject. The antinomy between étatism and the private economy grew sharper, clashes grew more frequent between the Greek rulers and the Egyptian peasantry, and as a result came the abandonment of lands, the impoverishment of the population, a decline of production and further economic disintegration.

A temporary turn for the better occurred in the economy of the Aegean area after 170 B.C., while between 155 and 145 Cyrenaica was separated from Egypt, remaining under Euergetes II, and this may have saved the country from the full burden of impositions

---

[248] *SEHHW*, pp. 205 sq.; 615 sq.
[249] *SEHHW*, pp. 195 sq.
[250] *SEHHW*, p. 619.
[251] *SEHHW*, pp. 917-8.

to which it had been formerly, and was to be subsequently, subject. Yet precisely in 162 Cyrene is found in a state of revolt, and Euergetes' arrangement to obtain consignments of wheat from Egypt was made in the year 155.

Do these factors find expression in the prices of the Demiurgi steles, and if they do, in what form? The recorded prices reveal several fluctuations during the 3rd and 2nd centuries B.C.: wheat varies between 8; 5; 2. 2/6 and 3. 1/6 dr.; barley between 16; 2; 2.4/6 and 1.4/6 dr.; pulse between 12; 5; 5 7.2/6 and 3 dr. The prices on nos. 31 and 34 (3rd century) and on 35 (end of the 3rd century?) are all unusually high (wheat—8 dr.; hay 40 dr.; cummin and raisins, 20 dr.). The prices tend to fall after 170 B.C., to judge from nos. 38 and 42, in harmony with the general improvement in the contemporary Greek world. It may be that Euergetes II, who was both unscrupulous and able, took steps to amend the economic situation by taking over the management of the temple estates. In the 3rd century, at all events, Cyrenean wheat was being sold at prices like those current in mainland Greece. Between 270 and 170 wheat prices were at first lower than those of Greece (no. 40), then fell considerably (no. 31—2.2 dr.), approximating to those in Egypt (1-2 dr. the artaba = 1.1/4-2 1/2 dr. the medimmus). This phenomenon reflects the general decline of grain prices which took place after 270 B.C.; [252] Cyrenean prices seem to have been depressed by the steady rise of Egyptian production and by the competition of other countries overseas. Barley prices fluctuate less throughout the period and approximate closely to those of Greece, indicating that they were less prone to be influenced by temporary market conditions, meteorological variations, and the fluctuations of the international market. Notwithstanding, the price soars to 16 dr. at the end of the 3rd century or at the beginning of the 2nd (no. 35) in an exceptional year. As to olive oil, although our evidence is limited, it should be noted (nos. 38, 40), that the oil marketed stood at the same nominal price as in the 4th century B.C., implying that its real price had fallen by fifty percent. The Ptolemies had developed oil production in Egypt as a state monopoly by every means in their power, and imposed an excise of 50 percent. on the imported product, even when brought from

---

[252] *SEHHW*, p. 235.

their own overseas dominions: [253] the reason for the fall of the price of Cyrenean olive oil is therefore clear.[254]

As has been observed, Cyrenean wheat production seems to have been adversely affected by external competition in the 3rd and at the beginning of the 2nd century, and in 155 B.C. Euergetes was forced to demand wheat from Egypt. Cyrenean wheat rose in price after 170, yet the stability of the prices of barley and oil throughout the period shows that the position of Cyrenean agriculture had not been seriously impaired before the beginning of the 2nd century; it was apparently the wheat export that was the chief sufferer. Why then did Euergetes need wheat from abroad?

It has already been suggested that the upsetting of the balance between the livestock branch and arable farming in the Plateau and steppe areas was apt to bring about social conflict, insecurity, and a decline in the fertility of both branches. It may be accepted that the silphium-growing areas passed into the hands of the Ptolemies as royal property, a view that finds support from the information [255] that the product was being smuggled out of the country by the inhabitants of Charax (Χάραξ) on the shore of the Syrtic Gulf, which suggests a strict state supervision of its export. The silphium areas had shrunk as time went on, probably due to the expansion and intensification of agriculture in the territory. This restriction is deducible from the ancient sources, for while Herodotus [256] knew its area was identical with the greater part of the country, and Theophrastus reports that it flourished in the greater part of Libya,[257]—Strabo [258] places its region as a distance of 200 stades (25 miles) from the sea, Pliny,[259] south of the cultivated zone, Arrian [260] and Ptolemy,[261] on the fringes of the desert. Most interesting is the difference between the indications of Theophrastus

---

[253] *SEHHW*, p. 305.

[254] Rostovtzeff explained the low prices of oil and wine in Greece in the 2nd century B.C. by the existence of an adverse balance of imports and exports. (*SEHHW*, p. 628).

[255] Strabo XVII, 3, 20 (836).

[256] IV, 169.

[257] VI, 3, 3: "It occupies a large area of Libya—it is said more than 4,000 stadia. It grows in great abundance around the Syrtis from Euesperitae onward."

[258] XVII, 3 (838 fin.).

[259] *HN*, V, 5 (34).

[260] *Anab*. III, 28.

[261] IV, 4, 6.

and Strabo. The retreat of the plant to the edges of the desert, then, took place mainly between the late 4th and the 1st centuries B.C., i.e. in the period when Cyrenean agriculture was being intensified and the cultivated areas extended over the Plateau and southward. Bonacelli [262] noted that Theophrastus [263] described a plant (ἀβρότονον) which was fed on by the flocks in the silphium area; this he identified as Artemisia herba alba (wormwood). This plant's northern limit of growth is the meeting point of the terra rossa with the reddish yellow soils of the southern plateau slopes, but this does not necessarily contradict Theophrastus' statement [264] that silphium grew on the greater part of the country, since he writes in the same place that silphium "is absent from the mountain in spring and winter." The silphium, in point of fact, flowered in winter,[265] when the flocks were grazing the steppe, and Arrian tells us that it needed fencing to protect it from the sheep; [266] moreover Theophrastus himself evidences that the sheep grazed the silphium zone in that season.[267] Accordingly we are forced to conclude from Theophrastus, that the plant flourished chiefly in the south of Cyrenaica in his day. Its limitation to the south and the expansion of the royal lands in this direction were found to restrict the winter pasture of the Libyan tribes, especially when the plant's areas diminished and needed stricter protection. Capelle, following other scholars,[268] has indeed pointed out that the report of Strabo and Solinus [269] that the Berber nomads uprooted the plant out of hostility and owing to oppressive taxation, is not later than c. 200 B.C., being derived from Eratosthenes.

Other factors may have contributed to the contraction of pasture areas. It is reasonable to think that the Ptolemies conducted the horserearing branch as a royal monopoly. Real evidence for this conjecture with regard to Cyrenaica is not abundant: Rostovtzeff, who voices it three times,[270] finally confesses that "We may think that they (sc. the Ptolemies) had large horse-studs in Cyrenaica.

---

[262] *AC* 1922, p. 257.
[263] *HP* VI, 3, 6.
[264] *HP* VI, 3, 4.
[265] Plin., *HN* XIX, 3 (15).
[266] *Anab.* III, 28, 7.
[267] *HP* VI, 3, 1.
[268] *RM²* 97, 1964, pp. 185 sqq.
[269] Solinus 27; Strabo XVII, 3, 22 (837) and see here n. p. 16.
[270] *SEHHW*, pp. 293, 333, 385.

But this is no more than a guess". Yet one document is such as to strengthen the belief, namely, a dedication by Stolos son of Theon to Ptolemy Soter II at Cyrene in the year 115 B.C.[271] Stolos, an associate of the sovereign and one of his "first friends" (τῶν πρώτων φίλων), is here termed "in charge of the horses" (ἐπὶ τῶν ἡνιῶν), and this office is probably no mere title. Fraser[272] remarked that it is recorded only in the present case, and was bestowed on its bearer in Cyrenaica itself. The horse-breeding branch would have required the supervision of the appropriate grazing areas, chiefly in the Plain of Barka, and also the levying of contributions from the growers of sown fodder grass, especially if the branch was intensified and improved by the Lagids in the manner characteristically theirs. As the natural conditions for the large-scale breeding of horses within the Ptolemaic Empire were to be found preponderantly in Cyrenaica, the probability of such having been carried on there under the later Ptolemies, especially after the loss of Southern Syria in 200 B.C., is very great. The pasture-areas as a whole may also have constituted an object of taxation in this period; indirect evidence is to be found for this in Solinus' information[273] that the Libyans destroyed the silphium owing to over-taxation, and the tax involved in these areas could only have been the hellenistic ἐννομίον.[274]

The representation of the plough that appears on the coins of Magas points also to the intensified and extended exploitation of the of the southern plateau for corn-growing in this epoch, and this evidence fits the reports of Solinus and Strabo concerning the Libyans' destruction of the silphium. We have already seen that

---

[271] *DAI* I, Cir., i, p. 71, no. 9; *SEG* 9, 62.

[272] *Berytus*, 12, 1958, p. 113, no. 7. Cf. F. Durrbach, *Choix d'inscriptions de Délos*, 1921-2, p. 207: "les titulaires étaient préposés aux écuries royales." In the 4th century A.D., Cyrene was still exporting horses, mules and asses (Synes., *Ep.* 109). The donkeys of Libya are also mentioned in Jewish literature (M. *Kilaim*, VIII, 4; *Shab.* V, 1).

[273] 27.

[274] C. Préaux, *L'économie des Lagides*, 1939, p. 225; *SEHHW*, p. 295, for this tax. See below for other taxes in Cyrene, evidently of the Ptolemies, as evidenced by the Negharnes inscription. The latter testifies to a cult of Dionysus in that village; this cult was organized in Egypt by Ptolemy IV at the end of the 3rd century as a means of binding the peasantry to the monarchy, and Negharnes may have derived its internal organization from that time. The compulsory participation in the fight against locusts in Cyrene, described by Pliny (*HN* XI, 49 (105)), may have been an extension of the liturgies referred to in the Negharnes document.

the temple estates of Cyrene extended to the same region under the Ptolemies. The sowing of garlic also indicates the extension of cultivation to stonier terrains, and the enlargement of the areas devoted to legumes and green fodders in the arable regions of the Plateau would have restricted still further the grazing available to cattle and sheep in the summer season, when the livestock concentrated on that area.[275] The growing of saffron, known to us as a summer crop in Cyrene and as a royal monopoly in Egypt,[276] would also have been an object of intensification under Ptolemaic rule.

The factors thus described, taken together, may well explain the Libyan ferment in the reign of Euergetes II and the general social unrest—presumably partly agrarian—expressed in the royal edict of that sovereign or of Soter II already referred to. The restriction of the pasture areas of the Libyan nomads was apt to cause collisions and to hinder the winter movement of the flocks from the plateau southward, also leading to a general fall in cereal yields by depriving the fields of their manure and so impairing the condition of the livestock. This situation had evidently begun even before 200, when the Libyans tore up the silphium, and might explain the rise of wheat-prices and wheat-shortages after 170. A consequence could have been the extension of wheat-growing areas on the Plateau, and the sowing of early barley to replace the southern crops; such action, however, would have restricted the pasture areas still more; the alternative was the overworking and exhaustion of the soil.

If we consider the above agrarian situation in the light of the general difficulties with which Egypt was struggling in the same period, or if we recall the influence of Massinissa's kingdom on the west, as well as the revival of Egyptian nationalism on the east—we shall be approaching a comprehensive explanation of the decline of Cyrenaica at the end of the hellenistic age. In brief, the Ptolemaic policy of agricultural intensification had contradicted itself: it had exceeded the capacity of the country as defined by its peculiar conditions, and had generated a reaction. This reaction arose from overpopulation, and probably from a decline of fertility due to the upsetting of the balance between the livestock branch and arable farming. Cyrenean emigration to Egypt had indeed fallen off in

---

[275] Cf. *IG* XIV, 645, which prohibits grazing on fallow sown to green fodder.

[276] *SEHHW*, p. 302.

the 2nd century,[277] but this is to be explained, not by an improved situation in Cyrenaica itself, but by the situation in Egypt, which had now ceased to absorb newcomers.

7. TRADE AND HANDICRAFTS

The Cyrenean economy was based, like all the economies of the ancient world, primarily on agriculture. But how did the population supply its non-agricultural needs, composed chiefly of metal products, pottery and the like? To what extent were they furnished by imports, and how far could Cyrene produce them at home?

From the beginning of the colonization imported pottery evidences trade connections with Rhodes, the Cyclades, Ionian Greece, Crete, Chios and Attica, while stray finds suggest contacts with areas as far afield as Syria, Palestine and even Babylonia. Generally throughout the late 7th and 6th centuries the imports from the Cyclades and Rhodes pre-dominate, but Attic blackware becomes common from about 550, and blackware bowls are numerous during the 5th and 4th centuries. Attic fishplates appear between 320 and 290. During this period local, somewhat coarser wares prevail, but imports continue; "Megarian" and hellenistic Pergamene come in after the 4th century. As connections with the western Mediterranean become closer in the course of the last three centuries before the common era, Arretine, South Gaulish terra sigillata, and Roman (but also Asiatic), Pergamene are found, and in the 2nd century, Trajanic and Hadrianic terra sigillata from Greece, Italy and Alexandria enters the Cyrenean market.[278] Marble from Thasos arrived at Cyrene as early as in the 7th century.[279] The city's first silver coinage (c. 560 B.C.) imitates the Athenian, and by adopting the monetary standard of Solon Cyrene was able to strengthen her commercial ties whith the Greek centres of the west and the Corinthian market. Her attachment to the eastern Aegean nevertheless persists, and its influence is again perceptible in the city coinage in about 525.[280] Oliverio [281] considered that Cyrene's system of weights and measures, as reflected in the Demiurgi steles, was introduced in the 6th century, during

---

[277] Heichelheim, *ABP*, p. 46.
[278] Stucchi, *Cirene*, pp. 150-162, esp. 161.
[279] Wilamowitz-Moellendorf, *Cirene*, 1930, p. 18, n. 9.
[280] *BMC* pp. xxx, xxxi.
[281] *DAI* I, Cir., ii, p. 69.

the second wave of immigration initiated by Battus II: he based this conclusion on the similarity of the Cyrenean system to the systems of the Peloponnese, more especially to those of Argolis and Arcadia. But Oliverio also weighed the possibility that the Cyrenean system was introduced under Battus III, as part of the constitutional and economic reforms of Demonax of Mantineia,[282] which aimed at adapting to a new commercial rôle a state hitherto based on a predominantly agricultural economy. It should however be observed that the decimal system associated with the steles of the Demiurgi is not reflected in the city's coinage before about 430.[283]

At the end of the 5th century the finds in the Temple of Artemis evidence increased imports from Egypt,[284] and Cyrenean coins are numerous in that country.[285] Their distribution is also considerable in other lands, more particularly in Crete, during the 5th century. The abundance of Cyrene's coins and of other metal finds poses the problem, what was the source of the country's metals?

Cyrenaica's only mineral is salt, produced chiefly along her north-western shore in the salt-lagoons near Bengazi; in the south of the country rock salt exists [286] and salammoniac is found in the Oasis of Ammon, whence it was traded into Egypt [287] and perhaps to Cyrene. Despite the absence of other minerals in his kingdom, Arkesilaos III could send Cambyses 500 minae of silver,[288] and Cyrene could import marble and various other products. Iron was present in Crete and the Peloponnese, nor are Cyrene's trade relations with those lands in doubt; the commonness of her coins in Crete may be explicable by the purchase of iron. The nearest source of copper was Cyprus, contacts with which may be indicated by the flight of Pheretime to the island. Cyrene's close contacts with Lycia, as reflected by Lycian coinage in the years 450-430,[289] are likely to have been based on the import of her silver into Libya. Egypt doubtless was the primary source of Cyrene's gold; the problem of whether the city got gold directly from central Africa

[282] *Ibid.*, p. 71.
[283] B. V. Head, *Historia Nummorum*, 1910, 868.
[284] See p. 17.
[285] Cf. *BMC*, p. lxxix.
[286] Herod. IV, 181, 2; Synes. *Ep.* 148.
[287] Arrian, *Anab.*, III, 4, 3.
[288] Herod. III, 13.
[289] *BMC* p. xliii.

has been examined, and relates to the same period, since her gold currency does not begin before the 5th century.

It is not easy to find an answer to the question, how Cyrene paid for her imports and what she produced at home. There has been little study of the local finds of coins derived from other Greek centres, hence we cannot utilize them to assess the scale of the country's exports to them.

At the end of the 7th century nevertheless, Cyrenean potters were copying proto-Corinthian wares and also Attic blackware.[290] By the 5th century she was using her own pottery which was somewhat coarser than the imported wares. On the other hand the famous kylix of Arkesilaos II, manifesting a close acquaintance with Cyrene, was made in Laconia.[291] Finds of amber in the archaic Temple of Apollo hint at trade-contacts with Northern Europe and of exports in that direction; Cyrene sent grain to Illyria in the reign of Alexander the Great,[292] and Flavius Josephus saw a Cyrenean ship in the Adriatic in the 1st century A.D.[293] Numerous 4th-century Carthaginian coins found in Cyrene point to trade in the Syrtic region. The quantity of local coinage struck from imported metals proves that the country's exports were considerable, and it may be noted that Cyrene enjoyed an advantage over Attica and many other Greek mainland cities, in that she needed no corn from overseas, and disposed of sufficient timber.[294] For this reason, she could devote her exports to paying for Greek goods such as metals and other craft-products. If this was the case, a certain slowness in the development of her own local industries would be probable, and might explain why no Cyrenean school of exportable painted pottery or other craft product is known. Much glazed table-pottery reached the country both from the eastern and the western Mediterranean in the hellenistic and Roman periods; the imported terra sigillata found in the "Palace of Columns" at Ptolemais lasts to the end of the 2nd century at least.[295] On the other hand owners of pottery kilns are mentioned in the

---

[290] *AI* IV, p. 190.

[291] See pp. 19 sqq.

[292] *SEG* 9, 2, 54; *DAI* II, Cir. i, pp. 31 sq. no. 58, para. 54.

[293] Jos. *Vita*, I, 3 (15).

[294] On the roofing of houses in Cyrene with the timbers of the *thuon*, see Theoph. *HP* V, 3, 7.

[295] *NAMC* I, pp. 85, 95; cf. Rostovtzeff, *SEHHW*, pl. xli, 2.

Ptolemaic constitution,[296] and Vatican Papyrus no. 11, of the late 2nd century A.D., informs us of brick kilns in two localities of the Martuba district in the east of the country.[297] At least one type of lamp manufactured locally is known.[298] and its probable centre of manufacture was found by Wright at Teucheira.[299]

In view of all this, it would appear that most of Cyrene's exports consisted of agricultural produce: wheat, silphium, wool, hides,[300] perfumes,[301] the wood of the thuon,[302] olives, dates, honey, vegetables,[303] horses, donkeys and mules. How far these were supplemented by luxury goods arriving from Central Africa along the Saharah caravan routes, depends on a solution of the general problem which these routes present. Yet in the absence of information concerning the export of craft products (excepting, probably, sealstones),[304] we are bound to ask whether Cyrene could have attained the level of wealth attributed to her by Plato and others,[305] unless she had possessed a share of the export trade in such goods from Central Africa.

---

[296] *SEG* 9, 1, para. 8, 48.

[297] *NV*, V, 22/30 V, 31/33.

[298] B. Walters, *Catalogue of Greek and Roman Lamps in the British Museum*, 1914, nos. 851, 1059, 1125; O. Bronneer, *Corinth*, Type XXV; cf. *IEJ* 7, 1957, pp. 154 sqq.

[299] G. R. H. Wright, *PEJ* 1963, pp. 27 and 29; fig. 2.

[300] Hermippus ap. Athen., I, 49.

[301] Plin. *HN*, XXI, 6 (saffron); Theoph. *HP*, IV, 3, 1 (saffron); Athen. XV, 29, 38; 689a (roses). An inscription at Cyrene of the 4th century AD refers to the perfume dealers' quarter of the city (ἀγρὸς Μυροπωλάς)—*ASAA*, I, 1914, p. 164.

[302] Theoph. *HP* IV, 3, 1.

[303] Cucumbers—Plin. *HN*, XX, 1 (3); truffles—Athen. I, 62; beans—Jer. *Kilaim*, VIII, 1, 31b.

[304] Plut. *Luc.*, 2; cf. Aelian, *Varia histor.*, XII, 30, 4.

[305] Plut., *ad princip. inerud.*, XII, 89.

CHAPTER FOUR

THE JEWS OF ANCIENT CYRENAICA

1. The Circumstances of Settlement

The earliest known find of Jewish significance in Cyrenaica is the seal bearing the archaic Hebrew inscription:

לעבדיו
בן ישב

(of ʿAvadyu son of Yashav)

It was found, apparently, at Cyrene itself.[1] As Diringer could not date the seal more closely, it can only be placed within the broad period to which seals of this type belong, namely, between the 10th and 4th centuries B.C.

Isolated Jews may have found their way to Cyrene before the hellenistic period. One apparently Semitic name, at any rate, is known to us from a Cyrenean inscription of the end of the 4th century; this is a list of soldiers, set up in the Temple of Zeus,[2] among its names being Baraibis son of Moiristheneus (Βάραιβις Μαρισθενεύς). Baraibis seems to be a transliteration of Bar-Ḥibbas.[3] Furthermore, it will be noted (p. 131) that the Jewish population of the Syrtic region was very ancient, and it is hard to know whether it reached the Gulf from Africa or from Cyrene. An archaic Hebrew inscription has been found at Zliten,[4] also a seal with the name of the owner, Elyashiv.[5] A number of 3rd-century B.C. amphorae discovered at Busetta bore inscriptions, one of which was in Hebrew.[6] As previously stated, the Cyrenean frontier reached Purgos Euphrantas (Gasr Zifrin), under Ptolemy Lagos, and only

---

[1] M. A. Levy, *Siegel und Gemmen*, 1869, no. 19; D. Diringer, *Le iscrizione antico-ebraiche Palestinesi*, 1934, p. 193, no. 34.

[2] *SP* pl. 79, no. 7.

[3] Cf. Εἴβας, an Aramaic name (Arabic—Ḥibbeh)—Preisigke *NMA*, p. 518; Maspéro, *Papirus grecs d'époque Byzantine*, III, 67.328, 3. (6th century), also *SEG* 15, 851; *Berytus*, 11, 1954-5, p. 53, n. 691: Εἰαειβᾶς, from Dura-Europos.

[4] *Memoires de l'Académie d'Inscriptions*, 12, 1913, pp. 513-4, pl. i, 1.

[5] N. Slouchz, *My Travels in Libya*, II, 1943, p. 239, n. 1.

[6] Levi della Vida, *AI* I, pp. 224-5.

subsequently resumed its former position further eastward, hence it is possible that Jewish settlement on the Gulf began in the same period, since the arrival of Jews in Cyrenaica itself is connected by Josephus with the first Ptolemy. The question, however, must remain without a definite answer for the time being, as the seal from Zliten may well indicate an earlier arrival. In this connection may be mentioned the Jewish settlement at Boreion (Bu-Grada) [7] on the south-western Cyrenaican coast, i.e. on the east shore of the Syrtic Gulf. In the Byzantine period the Jews of this place claimed that their ancestors had reached the place in the days of Solomon,[8] and even if the tradition is far-fetched, it is doubtless evidence that the settlement was very old. In short, the chief value of the remains of early Jewish settlement on the Gulf lies in this, that if there were Jews there as early as the 3rd century B.C., they can hardly have been absent from Cyrenaica in the same century.

Flavius Josephus attributes Jewish settlement in Cyrene to the time of Ptolemy Lagos, and in the light of historical reality we must connect the establishment of a Jewish population in the country with the growth of the hellenistic Jewish community of Egypt. Josephus writes that Ptolemy entrusted fortresses to Jews in Egypt, and desiring to strengthen his hold over Cyrene and the other cities of Libya, sent part (μέρος) of the Jews to inhabit them.[9] Elsewhere [10] he says that since Cyrene and Egypt had been placed under united rule, Cyrene had supported numerous organized groups (συντάγματα) of Jews, which flourished and continued to practise their Jewish laws. This information follows immediately after Josephus' reference to a Jewish political disturbance (στάσις) at Cyrene in the time of Sulla, hence it is to be assumed that it relates to the period after the unification of Cyrene and Egypt under the rule of Euergetes II, in 145 B.C. Josephus further relates that Ptolemy Lagos settled Jewish prisoners from Judaea in Egypt and distributed them among his garrisons, while other Jews emigrated

---

[7] Goodchild, *GJ* 118, 1952, p. 147.

[8] Procopius, *de Aedif.*, VI, 2, 21-3.

[9] *C. Ap.* II, 4 (44): "Ptolemy son of Lagos and Alexander entertained the same opinion concerning those (Jews) who settled in Alexandria; Ptolemy entrusted to them fortresses throughout Egypt, assuming that they would guard them loyally and well, and as he desired to strengthen his hold on Cyrene and the other cities of Libya, he sent part of the Jews to inhabit them."

[10] *Ant.* XIV, 7, 2 (116).

to the country voluntarily.[11] In the same book he writes that
Ptolemy II freed 120,000 Jewish prisoners in Egypt.[12] This report,
and that on the formation of Jewich garrisons, are repeated shortly
afterwards in the same work.[13] The liberation of Jewish prisoners is
confirmed by the *Aristeas Letter*,[14] which says that Ptolemy brought
a number of Jews from Syria, some of them prisoners of war, to
settle in Egypt, placing 30,000 of them in his fortresses.

Three salient facts can be distinguished among these quotations:
1) that the Jewish colonization in Libya was connected in Josephus'
view with their settlement in Egypt, and took place in similar
conditions; 2) that with regard to Cyrene, Josephus speaks of two
periods or stages of Jewish immigration, namely of the first settlement and subsequently of the situation created by the union of
Egypt and Cyrenaica in the second half of the 2nd century B.C.;
3) Josephus' writings produce the clear impression that the first
Jewish settlement in Egypt and Libya was of a decidedly military
character. His account of the despatch of Jews to Cyrene and the
country's other cities, does not indeed state explicitly that they
were sent as garrisons or to discharge military duties. Only the
fact that his report comes immediately after the description of
the Jewish settlement in garrisons (φρούρια) in Egypt, leads us
to this assumption. But his words clearly mean that the Jews
were sent to be a loyal element among the population and supporters of the Ptolemaic régime. Very interesting, moreover, is the
term applied by Josephus when he reports the "organized groups",
(συντάγματα) of Libyan Jews, as the word is derived first and
foremost from the sphere of military organization.

We therefore face two questions: What was the character of this
first settlement—military, agricultural or other; and when did it
take place?

Some scholars have seen in the first clause of the Ptolemaic
constitution of Cyrene a loophole for the introduction of newcomers, including Jews, into the ranks of the citizens of Cyrene;
the reference is to the clause which permits Ptolemy to grant
Cyrenean citizenship to anyone he chooses.[15] But it is very im-

---

[11] *Op. cit.*, XII, 1 (7-8).
[12] *Op. cit.*, XII, 3 (24).
[13] *Ibid.*, XII, 5 (45).
[14] 12-14 (Thackeray).
[15] *SEG* 9, 1, para. 1, 5; K. Friedmann, *GSAI*, ns. 2, iv. 1934, pp. 324-5.

probable that Ptolemy would at this stage have intruded a non-Greek group into a citizen-body whose affairs he was endeavouring to compose by compromise, with the object of restoring stability and healing rifts after a stormy period. On the other hand the evidence from Egypt and perhaps from the Syrtis confirms that Jews were brought in at this period as a colonizing factor, hence there are two possibilities: either that Jews figured among the Ptolemaic garrisons of Cyrene and the remaining Libyan cities, or that Jews were included among the new military settlers planted by Ptolemy on the soil of the conquered country. If we could be certain that the clauses of the constitution disqualifying for citizenship those joining "Ptolemy's colonies" was rightly read by Oliverio (Fraser was unable to find the words on the inscription), this would be good proof of contemporary cleruchic settlement. Unfortunately, we cannot be sure if the proof exists. As to the first possibility, there is no evidence for Jews serving in garrisons in Cyrenaica; the information of Ptolemy's constitution is simply that his garrison was stationed at Cyrene.[16] We therefore have no alternative but to examine the question of the form and date of the first Jewish settlement by the method of analogy, that is, in the light of the contemporary situation in Egypt and elsewhere.

There were Jewish troops in Alexandria, on archaeological evidence, as early as in the 3rd century. This is shown by the tombs of al-Ibramiyeh.[17] We also know of Jewish garrisons in the Egyptian Delta, indicated by the names Castra Iudaeorum [18] and Στρατόπεδον 'Ιουδαίων (the Jewish camp); [19] a third is recorded at Pelusium.[20] Unfortunately the records belong to the 1st century B.C. or later, and we do not know when they originated. A "phyle" (φυλή) of Jewish "Macedonians" existed in Alexandria in the 1st century A.D.,[21] and it seems highly probable that Tcherikover was right in interpreting the designation "Macedonians" as a "pseudo-ethnic" indicating merely the type of unit to which they belonged,[22] "phyle" being thus, not a tribe of the polis but a military formation. The date when this body originated is equally

---

[16] *SEG* 9, 1, para. 11, 72.
[17] *BSAA* 9, 1907, pp. 35 sqq.; 25, 1930, p. 108.
[18] *Not. Dig. Or.*, (Seeck), XXVIII, 42.
[19] Jos., *BJ* I, 9, 4 (191); *Ant.* XIV, 8, 2 (133).
[20] Jos., *BJ* I, 8, 7 (175).
[21] Jos., *C. Ap.*, II, 36; *BJ* II, 18, 7 (488).
[22] *The Jews in Egypt* ², 1963, p. 43.

unknown, and it may well have been formed during the 2nd century B.C. when Jewish prestige as a military factor was high for both external and internal political reasons, and the independent Jewish katoikia of Onias was set up at Leontopolis for a body of Jewish katoikoi.[23] The Egyptian analogy, then, does not help us to answer the question, whether the Jews composed garrisons in early Ptolemaic Libya.

On the other hand the question of whether the first Cyrenean Jews were military cultivators (cleruchs, katoikoi), invites two other considerations. Firstly, the word κατοικῆσον ("in order to settle there") is used by Josephus when he reports the despatch of Jews to the cities of Cyrenaica. Possibly he was influenced to use this word by the conditions of a period later than the event he was describing, since the word κάτοικος replaced that of κληροῦχος in Egypt only in the 2nd century B.C.[24] in application to a soldier settler who received his plot in return for military service. But the term κάτοικος for such a settler appears in the 3rd century B.C. in Asia,[25] and the Jews of Hierapolis (Phrygia) not only called themselves κατοικοῦντες, a broad term without specific meaning (cf. the Latin word *consistentes*) but their communal organization was known as a κατοικία, and we have reliable testimony from Josephus that Jews were settled in the cities and countryside of Phrygia in organized military colonies under Antiochus III in the years 223-197 B.C. [26] Accordingly it is possible that Josephus himself, at least, believed that the Jews of Cyrene had been sent from Egypt as an organized body of military settlers.

Antiochus III's settlement of Jews in Asia may indeed assist our study, since its circumstances were decidedly parallel to those in which the Cyrenean Jews were originally settled, to judge by Josephus' account. Two thousand Jewish families were then sent from Babylonia to Phrygia and Lydia to prop Seleucid rule after serious risings had occurred in those countries. In Antiochus' instructions to his governor Zeuxis, preserved in Josephus' text, the King directs his deputy to settle the immigrants in "garrisons (or fortresses) and at the most vital points (εἰς τὰ φρούρια καὶ τοὺς

---

[23] Tcherikover, Fuks, *CPJ* I, 1957, 3, 17, 44-6; Tcherikover, *HCJ*, pp. 275 sqq.

[24] *CPJ* I, 1957, 13.

[25] *OGIS* 229, 72 (Magnesia).

[26] Jos., *Ant* XII, 3, 4 (147) sqq.

ἀναγκαιοτάτους τόπους), the orders being explicit to allot them plots of land and plantations.[27] Recently Sardis has yielded epigraphical confirmation of the background of the colonization, in the form of a fragmentary inscription discovered in the city's synagogue, and containing parts of the orders of Antiochus to Zeuxis, the destruction of the city in the course of disorders being referred to, and instructions issued to repair the damage.[28] If analogy is here permissible, we shall understand the Jewish colonization in Cyrenaica described by Josephus as the settlement of these newcomers in organized bodies, some in the town and some outside it, but all with plots of land assigned from tracts in royal possession. Here again, Asia Minor offers us an instructive analogy. Sources consistently refer to the Jews of Cyrenaica as "the Jews about Cyrene" (see further p. 196) e.g. οἱ κατὰ Κυρήνην Ἰουδαῖοι. A not dissimilar phrase was used in 281 B.C. to designate the Macedonian military katoikoi settled round Thyateira (Phrygia) in the hellenistic period.[29] This being the case, there can be little doubt that the Jewish settlers of the period did not obtain citizenship in the cities concerned, and it may be stated that as noncitizens did not normally enjoy the right to acquire landed property (γῆς ἔγκτησις) within the territory of a Greek city,[30] the new immigrants of the period must have been mostly absorbed, in so far as they took up agriculture, by royal lands. This inference is important, and apt to influence our estimate of events in a subsequent period.

We have little information on the behaviour of the Ptolemies towards the landed property of the older free Greek states which they controlled, but an instance from Thera, Cyrene's own mother-city, throws some light on what may have occurred in Cyrene. Thera became a Ptolemaic naval base between 296 and 146 B.C., and in 164-160 B.C. Ptolemy III is known to have awarded the income of four local farms, which had been confiscated for reasons unknown, to support the gymnasium used by his garrison there.[31] These troops, it is true, were not cleruchs, but the action shows

---

[27] *Ibid.*, para. 151, and cf. Schalit, *JQR* 50, 1960, pp. 289 sqq.

[28] *Illustrated London News*, Mar. 21, 1964, no. 6503, p. 432.

[29] *OGI* I, 211; cf. Strabo, XIII, 4, 4, 625. Cf. also *OGI* 290 (Acrasos, Asia)—which Robert, *REA* 1934, p. 523, restored οἱ περὶ Ἄ]κρασον Μακεδό-νες, and Jones, *CERP*, p. 44, and n. 26 generally.

[30] P. Guiraud, *Histoire de la propriété foncière en Grèce*, 1893, pp. 153 sqq.

[31] *IG* XII, 3, no. 327; *Klio*, 17, 1920, p. 94, n. 1.

that the Ptolemaic kings regarded it as within their power to exploit the land of a free Greek city in the interests of their own military forces. Another instance may be cited. Some hellenistic king whose name has not come down to us appropriated the lands ot the Temple of Zeus at Aezani (Phrygia) for distribution among cleruchs, as is proved by an inscription.[32] Here, however, part of the rent paid by the military settlers was returned to the city concerned.

Evidence of cleruchic settlement is absent in Egypt until 275 B.C.[33] although it is generally thought to have begun earlier.[34] From 259 B.C. we hear of Jews settled on the land, always as individuals among non-Jews, among them cleruchs, men of the epigoné, and simple peasants (λαοί) [35]. We further learn of "prisoners from Asia" settled on the soil in 224,[36] partly on crown land, but it is not clear if they included Jews. On the other hand we know from Hecataeus of a group of Jews who came from Judaea to settle in Egypt at this time, and appear to have obtained a distinct charter from Ptolemy Lagos; [37] the conclusion is therefore natural that this was organized colonization in defined conditions. Egyptian epigraphy and papyrology show the existence of Jewish villages as early as the 3rd century B.C.; such were Athribis,[38] Psenyris,[39] Schedia,[40] Alexandrounesos,[41] and an unidentified place in Lower Egypt.[42] All these had synagogues, hence probably also organized corporations with their own internal regulations (πολιτεύματα).

An analysis of the status of all these Jewish settlers during the 3rd century and later shows, that whether or not they included prisoners settled as λαοί, or leasing land from cleruchs, others were simple peasants on crown land (βασιλικοὶ λαοί), cleruchs, or their second generation (τῆς ἐπιγονῆς). In sum, the evidence in Egypt for

---

[32] CIL III, 355.
[33] J. Lesquier, Inst. Mil. Lag., pp. 162 sqq.
[34] Op. cit., p. 164; F. Uebel. Die Kleruchen Ägyptens unter den ersten sechs Ptolemäer, 1968, p. 3.
[35] For a list, Tcherikover, op. cit., (n. 22), pp. 35-43; CPJ I, Sect. iii, pp. 147 sqq.
[36] Pap. Petrie, xxix.
[37] Jos. C. Ap., I, 186-9; compare especially Tcherikover, HCJ, p. 300.
[38] OGIS 96.
[39] L. Mitteis, U. W. Wilcken, Grundzüge u. Chrestomathie der Papyruskunde, 1911, p. 55; CPJ I, no. 33.
[40] OGIS 726.
[41] Pap. Lille, II, 235.
[42] CIL III, Supp. (i-ii), 6583.

the period under discussion shows plainly that the Jews settled as peasants, or cleruchs, and that by the middle of the 3rd century were already living in concentrated villages or were organized in village communities. But none of this material confirms the literary testimony concerning Jewish garrisons in the same early period. Yet the Egyptian evidence, if it does not strengthen the literary evidence concerning Cyrene, does not contradict it. And it is proper to note an important difference between the position in Egypt and that in Cyrenaica in this period. No rebellions broke out in Egypt against the Ptolemies in the 4th and 3rd centuries, whereas in Cyrenaica the Lagid conquest was marked by civil war at home and resistance to the conqueror from without for a period of twenty years. It is with this difference in mind that we must gauge the degree of truth in Josephus' report on the character of the first Jewish colonization in the Libyan cities.

Can the date of the Jewish settlement in Cyrene by Ptolemy Lagos be dated more closely? Ptolemy captured Cyrene in 322; in 313 a rebellion of the city was suppressed, but this was carried out by his general Agis, and Ptolemy himself did not visit the country. In 308 he reestablished his control of the city after the death of Ophellas and seems to have been there personally. If there was a fourth reconquest in 301, this was led by Magas, his son. An appreciable Jewish settlement is unlikely to have taken place before a considerable number of Jews had reached Egypt, and this could only have been the result of a campaign of conquest in Judaea itself, which had led to the transfer of numerous inhabitants as prisoners or refugees. Ptolemy invaded Judaea in the years 320, 312, 302 and 301. In one of these campaigns, according to Agathar-chides,[43] he captured Jerusalem, and Appian [44] also mentions this event, adding that Ptolemy then took many prisoners to Egypt and sold them into slavery. Hecataeus relates that after much fighting in 312, Ptolemy was accompanied back to Egypt by many of the inhabitants, including the high priest Hezeqiah and his followers.[45] As Tcherikover has shown,[46] there is no evidence that Ptolemy took Jerusalem in 320 or 312, but the conditions for the taking of the city by storm and the transporting of prisoners-of-war to Egypt

---

[43] Ap. Jos., *Ant.* XII, 1, 5 (1).
[44] *Syr.*, 50 (viii).
[45] Ap. Jos., *C. Ap.* I, 186 sq.
[46] *HCJ*, pp. 55-8.

existed in 302.[47] It is however evident that Ptolemy would hardly
have settled a hostile group just uprooted from its own homeland
for sedition, in a country that had recently risen against him, with
the object of using them to strengthen his domination. The year
302, then, is unlikely to have been the year of the Cyrenaican
colonization; and a better choice would be 312,[48] when Hezeqiah
and his people went down to Egypt voluntarily out of friendship
for Ptolemy and perhaps because they were hostile to Antigonus.
In that year, indeed, according to Diodorus [49] Ptolemy settled
8000 prisoners of war in Egypt. We possess moreover, as stated,
evidence that Hezeqiah's group were settled by a written agreement,
and this could have been part of a general movement which enabled
the settlement of a larger Jewish group as far afield as Cyrenaica.

The Ptolemaic colonization of Jews in Cyrene may therefore be
regarded as finding confirmation in contemporary circumstances,
and Josephus' account of it may be accepted in a broad sense.
We may further believe that the newcomers were settled chiefly as
cleruchs, i.e. as soldiers and cultivators who received their plots in
return for their readiness to serve when required. It may on the
whole be assumed, that the Jewish population of Cyrene at this
period did not differ in its composition from that of contemporary
Egypt, i.e. that it included cultivators, soldiers, military settlers,
craftsmen and, in course of time, traders and perhaps even government officials.[50]

2. THE SECOND JEWISH IMMIGRATION

Besides the literary evidence just discussed, we have at present
no reliable archaeological evidence for the existence in Cyrene of a
Jewish population in the time of the first Ptolemies. Slouschz saw
the name "Adam" inscribed in Hebrew near the city of Cyrene [51]
It may reflect the initial period of settlement when the newcomers
still spoke their own language. On the other hand the Greek name
"Adamas" appears in Egypt in company with two Cyreneans in a
3rd-century B.C. inscription at Hiera Sykaminos (Maharaka). [52]

---

[47] Ib., p. 55.
[48] As V. Ehrenberg, Hermes 65, 1930, pp. 332 sqq.; also Heuss and Taeger.
[49] Diod. XIX, 85, 4.
[50] See p. 175.
[51] Inscribed on a tomb near a spring called Gigi, according to Slouschz
(Travels, II, p. 227). I have not succeeded in identifying this spot.
[52] SB, 302: Πασιμένης Κυρηναῖος β' Ἰάσων Κυρηναῖος α' Ἀδάμας.

A more reliable testimony of early Jewish settlement in the territory is the Hebrew village name Kappharodos ("New village")
recorded by Synesius (see p. 197); such a name could only have
originated with Jewish immigrants who had come directly from an
unhellenized Judaea.

Our information on the Jews of the country begins to assume a
more substantial character in the 2nd century B.C. when Jewish
immigration to Cyrenaica appears to have increased, according to
the report of Strabo, (as reproduced by Josephus) [53] which we have
quoted above (p. 132), and is to be related to a time shortly after
145 B.C.; by 140/39 B.C. the Jewish community of the country was
important enough to earn a mention in the Roman Senate's circular letter to various states and cities containing Jewish populations.[54] The new migration would seem to have inaugurated the
golden age of Cyrenaican Jewry. In the same decade the first
Hasmoneans broke through to the coast of Judaea by capturing
Jaffa (142 B.C.) and other maritime cities, and the reputation of
the Jews as a fighting nation was established. The national war, as
well as the accompanying social and political struggle between
hellenists and nationalists among the Jews of Judaea itself, caused
the departure from the country of not a few Jews who settled in
Egypt and in other neighbouring lands. Hence the general situation
led to an increase of Jewish traders, slaves, soldiers and colonists
throughout the eastern Mediterranean area, and Cyrene was
doubtless one of the beneficiaries of this outflow.

The influence of the Maccabees and of the Jewish national
movement in Judaea on the Jews of Cyrenaica is known to us only
from one source, namely, from the composition of the *Second Book
of the Maccabees*, the original version of which was written by
Jason of Cyrene. Had we possessed the full original version, we
might perhaps have been able to gather from it further information
on Cyrenean Jewry, but fate has decreed otherwise.[55] The book,
at any rate, reveals the links of that Jewish community with its
homeland and also the contemporary level of Greek culture among
Libyan Jews of the period. The contents of the existing epitome
proves, in the view of some scholars, that the author had been

---

[53] *Ant.* XIV, 7, 2 (116).
[54] I *Macc.* 16, 15-23.
[55] The sacrifices for the dead alluded to in II *Macc.* 12:39 and quite alien
to the Judaism of Judaea, may be a trace of Libyan Jewish influence.

an eyewitness of the events he described,[56] and if this is correct, it shows that individual volunteers or groups reached Judaea from Libya to take part in the Jewish war against the Seleucids.

There may be indirect evidence for such participation. In the 1st century A.D. we know the name of a Jew who discharged a prominent function in the life of the city of Cyrene, serving in the important post of nomophylax in the civic authority,—Eleazar son of Jason (see below, pp. 186sq.). The *Second Book of Maccabees* [57] relates that Judah the Maccabee sent to Rome a diplomatic mission consisting of Eupolemos son of Johanan and Jason son of Eleazar. Tcherikover has noted that the author of *II Maccabees*, Jason of Cyrene, mentions Eupolemos in a way that shows him to have been his contemporary and personal acquaintance. Jason son of Eleazar may therefore also have been a Cyrenean and an ancestor of Eleazar son of Jason, nomophylax of the city under Nero.[58]

Epigraphy may have given us yet another echo of the events of the Maccabean wars against the Seleucids and the Jewish hellenizers.

In 1960 the writer republished four inscriptions inscribed on the north wall of the town of Teucheira, the names in which suggested that they were of Jews who had migrated to Cyrene from Judaea as a result of the Maccabean struggle against the Seleucids.[59] He there voiced the opinion that they may have become military settlers, but it subsequently became clear that the inscriptions are those of ephebes, or pupils of the city's gymnasium who appear in couples,

---

[56] Schürer believed (*GJV* III⁴, 1909, pp. 482 sqq.) that the author used eyewitnesses who were contemporaries of the Maccabees, but some years after the events described; Willrich regarded the book as unreliable. Others (Büchler, Laqueur, Wellhausen) thought the book contained authentic information mingled with fable. Torrey ((*The Aocryphal Literature*, 1946, pp. 76 sqq.) stated that the work contained vivid touches which point to the evidence of eye-witnesses. Pfeiffer (*Hist. N.T. Times*, p. 516) expresses the view that the book used written sources rather than eyewitness accounts. For a new summing up of the problems involved, and a conclusion in favour of the work as a source contemporary with the events described, Tcherikover, *HCJ*, pp. 381-90.

[57] II *Macc.* 4, 11; cf. I, 8, 17.

[58] *HCJ*, pp. 384-5: several scholars have suggested that Jason son of Elea'zar, Judah the Maccabee's contemporary, was the same as Jason author of II *Maccabees*; thus Keil, *Comm. über die Bücher der Makk.*, 1875, p. 275.

[59] *BIES* 22, 1958, pp. 74 sqq.; *SH* 7, 1961, p. 40. The present treatment supersedes the above interpretations.

evidently as lovers.[60] The fourth inscription undoubtedly includes Jewish names,

Τελ[χι]ναῖος Δα[- - Δο]σίθεο[ς] / [61] Αἰνέας Θεοξῆ / νω

The three other inscriptions in their revised form, are:

1) Ἴσχος ὁ Αιδυ<μ>αῖ<ος> Ἀρχίβιος Χυλδαῖος Τιμοκράτη(ς) [62]
2) Μένι[ο]ς- - ν Ἀριβαῖ[ος] (ἔτους) ι Φιλ - - (ἔτους) ιδ᾽ Ἀριστέας [63]
3) Ἀλέξων ψυχὴ Ἀδδι(δ)α <ῖος> [64]

My first conjecture was that the names Huldaios, Aribaios and Addidaios were the places of origin of the men concerned, referring to the three ancient Judaean villages of Ḥuldah, Ḥadid [65] (the Arabic Ḥaditah) and Ḥarib (the Arabic Kefar Ḥarrubbah),[66] all of which are situated in the same region of south Judaea, in the vicinity of Lydda. Two of these, Ḥarib and Ḥadid, were preponderantly Jewish in the Second Temple period and subsequently,[67] while Ḥuldah has yielded remains of a Jewish building, probably for ritual immersion, containing mosaic floors adorned with Jewish symbols and Greek inscriptions of Jewish content.[68] The names at

---

[60] SEG 9, 440.

[61] See Tcherikover, *Jews of Egypt*, p. 290, on the Jewish associations of the name Dositheos.

[62] SEG 9, 424.

[63] SEG 9, 439.

[64] SEG 9, 441.

[65] *Ant.* XIII, 6, 5 (203). In several places the name is spelt with one *delta* only.

[66] Jer. *Ta'an.*, IV 69a; *Mid. Lam. R.*, II, 2; *Sepher Ha-Yishuv*, 1939, I, p. 92.

[67] There are clear proofs that Haddid was a Jewish settlement at least down to the period of the Mishnah. It had been walled, according to tradition, since the days of Joshua (*M.'Arakh.* IX, 6), was resettled by Babylonian exiles, (*Ezra*, 2:33; Neh. 7:37), and was fortified by Simon the Hasmonean. (I *Macc.* 12:35). It was Simon's base against Tryphon, was captured by Vespasian in the Great Rebellion (*BJ*, IV, 9, 1-486), and was subsequently a residence of mishnaic scholars. Its population would therefore appear to have been overwhelmingly Jewish for a prolonged period. Our information on Kephar Ḥarrubah is sparser; it was improbably the village of that name associated with the outbreak of the revolt of Ben Kosba, but rather the place known east of Lydda.

[68] *Bull. of the Louis Rabbinowitz Fund for the Exploration of Ancient Synagogues*, III, 1960, pp. 57 sqq.; *Studi Biblici Franciscani*, 4, 1953-4, p. 228 ad voc.; *IEJ* 3, 1953, p. 133. The name of the village is otherwise mentioned first in Byzantine sources; see E. H. Palmer, *The Desert of the Exodus*, II, 1871, Appendix D, p. 552, containing the episcopal list of the year 534.

Teucheira, however, must now be regarded as personal, and the names Archibios and Huldaios seem to have been written by two different people. Yet even if this be accepted, we are bound to ask, how can we explain the proximity of two Jewish names (Dositheos, Theoxenos), to those of three other people, the name of each of whom takes the form of that of an ancient village in Judaea, each situated in the same region of that country? Even the assumption that the Libyan language contained Semitic elements (the place name Ḥarrubbah occurs in Cyrenaica; it simply means a "carob tree") is hardly a convincing explanation in the present circumstances, and the question must be left unanswered, but it does furnish evidence that among the pupils of the gymnasium in the hellenistic period were several young Jews, among them perhaps sons of émigrés from Judaea, and if these were émigrés, it is difficult not to connect their presence with the events of the Hasmonean revolt. It should nevertheless be noted that the name Ḥaled today occurs three kilometres east of Teucheira, that of Ḥarrubbah 28 kilometres east of the town. Further, Addida could conceivably represent the Aramaic form of Kephar Ḥaddash (cf. above, p. 139).

The national struggle in Judaea not only resulted in the dispersal of refugees and émigrés over the neighbouring countries, but also strengthened the position of the Jewish community outside Judaea for a certain period. In Egypt a conjunction of political circumstances at home and abroad in the second half of the 2nd century B.C. led to a growth in the military importance of the Jewish community and to the establishment of several defined districts in which Jewish troops were concentrated as settlers, perhaps also to the stationing of a Jewish unit at Alexandria as part of the garrison. In the same period several Jews gained prominence as commanders in the Ptolemaic forces.[69] We do not know how these developments influenced the standing of the Jews of Cyrenaica; at this time the leaders of Egyptian Jewry supported Ptolemy VI Philometor and Cleopatra in their struggle against Euergetes II, then ruling Cyrene, and in 145 the latter invaded Egypt to win power.[70] His attack ended in a compromise with Cleopatra, but archaeological evidence suggests that the forti-

---

[69] For these developments, Tcherikover, Fuks, *CPJ* I, pp. 23-4; Tcherikover, *The Jews in Egypt*, pp. 39, 46: *HCJ*, p. 334.

[70] Justin VIII, 2; Polyb. XXXIV, 6 (1314); cf. Oliverio, *DAI* I, Cir. i, pp. 16 sqq.

fications of the Jewish temple at Leontopolis, in the military district of Onias, were then taken by storm;[71] hence, in all probability, the story of Euergetes' persecution of Egyptian Jewry.[72] This ended not (as Josephus relates) with a divine miracle or thanks to the prayers of Irene, mistress of the king, but owing to his reconciliation with Cleopatra, whom he duly wedded.[73] Nor do we know whether Euergetes' wrath against the Jews of Egypt, due to their stand in the conflict, was extended to the Jews of Cyrene after the union of Egypt and Cyrene under his rule; it may however be noted, that previously in 162, Euergetes had been faced with a revolt of the Cyrenean Greeks and of the Libyans, nor was the territory without social ferment in the later years of his reign.[74] Euergetes may therefore have taken care not to attack the Jewish element in Cyrenaica; in Egypt he is known to have come to terms with the Jewish community after the crisis and behaved to them favourably: this at least, is what the inscriptions would imply.[75]

In Euergetes' later years, indeed, the Jewish community of Cyrene grew stronger, and probably when Judaea gained access to the sea an influential commercial element began to develop amongst its members. This is perhaps reflected in the coins of Cyrene between the years 140-96 B.C., since Robinson noted[76] that in that period mutual influence between the Cyrenean coins and those of Judaea is discernible, which affects particularly the coins of the later Hasmonaeans and Herod.[77] This influence is chiefly detectable in technical characteristics,—roughness of execution and the clipping of the edges; on the other hand the only figured type common to both countries is that of the double

---

[71] But I have been unable to find in the relevant excavation report any authority that the attack, which is shown to have taken place by the presence of the ballista-balls fired by the attackers, was not mounted by the forces of Vespasian in A.D. 73 (*BJ* VIII, 8, 10, 3-483) rather than by those of Euergetes II. Cf. *Tarbiz*, 25, 1959, p. 422, n. 10.

[72] Jos., *C. Ap.* II, 53-5. Cf. III *Macc.* II, 25 sq., which, presumably in error, attributes the event to the reign of Ptolemy IV Philopator; see Tcherikover, *Zion.* 10, 1935, pp. 1 sqq.; also in *The Jews in the Greek and Roman World*, 1961, pp. 339 sqq. (Heb.); *CPJ* I, pp. 21-3.

[73] Tcherikover, *Zion*, 10, 1945, pp. 1 sqq. (Heb.); *SH* 7, 1961, pp. 1 sqq.

[74] *SEG* 9, 5.

[75] Tcherikover, *HCJ*, p. 282; *SB* 5862, 7454.

[76] *BMC* p. clxi.

[77] *BMC* pl. xxxii, pp. 8-17; G. F. Hill, *Brit. Mus. Cat. Greek Coins, Palestine*, 1914, pl. xxii-xxiv.

cornucopia struck on contemporary Cyrenean coins [78] and also on Hasmonaean issues from John Hyrcanus to Matthias Antigonus, then on those of Herod.[79] However, the double cornucopia is also to be seen on coins of Ptolemy III at Cyrene.

The drawing closer of ties between Cyrenean Jewry and Judaea is nevertheless not in doubt, particularly in the first century B.C. The "Tyrians of Akko", alone among the Levantine coastal towns, had received a consignment of grain from Cyrene, during the dearth of Alexander's time, albeit the smallest on the list (1000 medimni); [80] later, apparently in the 2nd century A.D., Cyrenean Jews and even Libyan proselytes were resident at Jaffa.[81]

3. THE JEWS OF TEUCHEIRA

The increased immigration of the 2nd and especially of the 1st century B.C., is shown most strikingly by the cemetery of Teucheira to which allusion has already been made. Of some 440 tomb inscriptions published in learned periodicals,[82] and located in the quarries to east and west of the city, 109 can be identified as Jewish by reason of the Jewish, Aramaic or theophoric names among them, but there are some 144 identifiable as Jewish because of their location in tombs in which other identifiable Jews were buried. With two exceptions, all these are in the eastern cemetery, since only a few of those to west of the town have been read or published.[83] The proportion of Jewish names is roughly 30 percent. of the total known, but other Jews are certainly unidentifiable because of their Greek or Latin names, since such are known in tombs in which undoubted Jews were interred. If therefore we

---

[78] *BMC* p. 87, Gp. viii, 83.

[79] Israel Numismatic Society Publications: A. Kindler, apud *The Dating and Meaning of the Ancient Jewish Coins and Symbols* (Pubns. Numis. Soc. Studies, II), 1958, p. 11; A. Reifenberg, *Ancient Jewish Coins*, 1940, pl. iii, 33a.

[80] *SEG* 9, 2, 57; *DAI* II, Cir. i, p. 31, no. 58.

[81] *Sepher ha-Yishuv*, I, pp. 79 sqq., and see here pp. 306-7.

[82] *SEG* 9, 1938, 559-567, 569, 572-724; *SEG* 16, 1959, 876-930; 20, 1964, 769-771; *DAI* II, Cir. ii, 1936, pp. 198 sqq.; Rowe et al, *MUC* 1952, ch. vii, pp. 43 sqq.; S. Applebaum, *SH* 7, 1961, pp. 27 sqq.: The Jewish Community of Hellenistic and Roman Teucheira in Cyrenaica; G. R. R. Wright, *PEQ* 1963, pp. 22 sqq.: Excavations at Tocra.

[83] For these, Wright, *ibid.* (n. 1), pp. 27, 36 sq. The discussion on date concerns all the known burial courts (*latomie*) near the town, whether gentile or Jewish. The Jewish burials will be discussed separately.

cannot know the percentage of Jews in the total population, and not all the known burials have been published, there is nevertheless proof that the Jews composed a considerable section of it. As stated, most of the recorded epitaphs are in the quarries to the east of the city, those inscriptions published to the west of it being graffiti cut on the stones of the city-wall or the wall of the gymnasium.[84]

The period of the interments is not easy to determine. Some tombs are of the 1st century A.D., but the regnal and other dates figuring in the associated epitaphs make it more likely that they began twenty to thirty years earlier. (See below). Most of the epitaphs to east of the town open with a record of the year, but it is not always clear which era is used. In some cases it is difficult to decide if the figures indicate the era of Actium, the era of the province or the regnal years of a ruler. Some with high figures may be assumed to reckon by the era of Actium and their figures generally coincide with the regnal years of Augustus.[85] One inscription demonstrates explicitly the use of the regnal year, as it mentions Domitian.[86] The use of the era of Actium is proven for certain inscriptions in Cyrene, eg. SEG IX, 128,[87] while the use of the era of the province has not been proved with certainty, to the best of my knowledge, though it may be conjectured in one or two cases.[88]

In the discussion of this problem, it were well to utilize the archaeological evidence of the finds made in excavations carried

---

[84] In his previous study of the Teucheira Jewish epitaphs, the writer was under the impression that part of the inscriptions published by Oliverio in *DAI* and by *SEG* were from tombs to the west of the town. This impression was based on the assumption that Oliverio had followed Halbherr (to whose plan the writer had access) in the numbering of the tomb-courts. In effect the western inscriptions are cut in the city-wall and in the wall of the adjacent gymnasium. The present study, therefore, is a revision of the author's previous publication.

[85] Eg. *SEG* 9, 612: Λη λ' = the thirty-eighth year of Augustus or of the era of Actium, ie. A.D. 7.

[86] *SEG* 9, 498: Αὐτοκράτορος Δομιτιανοῦ Καίσαρος. The attempt of J. Gray (*MUC* 1952, pp. 54-55) to prove the use of the era of Actium, is not convincing. See *SH* 7, p. 31.

[87] Lονδ' τοῦ καὶ γ' αὐτοκρατόρος Μ Αὐρηλίου Σεβήρου 'Αλεξάνδρου ... Cf. *CIG* III, 2, 5145b; *SEG* 9, 184.

[88] It should be remarked that there is no certainty if the year of the constitution of the province was regarded as 74 or as 67 B.C. when Cyrene was administratively merged with Crete. See Appian, *Bell. Civ.*, I, 111; *RC* para. 73.

out by Webster in the east cemetery.[89] The following epitaphs associated with the group of tombs dug by him and published by Gray and Wright,[90] may be noted:

SEG XVI	No. (Gray)	Year in Inscription	Date acc. to Provincial Era (74 B.C.)	Date acc. to Era of Actium (31 B.C.)
880	5	105	A.D. 31	A.D. 73
887	8	2		
901	18	13		
905	21	11		
908	24	8		
921	33	95	A.D. 21	A.D. 64

According to the finds made in the tombs, these burials were all of the same period, and their pottery was thought to date them approximately to A.D. 100. It therefore becomes clear that two eras were used side by side, nor is there any relationship between the high and the low figures. The higher represent a "political" era (of a city or régime), and the lower, the regnal years of a ruler or rulers. Accordingly the figures of the Era of Actium are more appropriate to the archaeological finds. As regards the regnal dates, these probably belong to Flavian emperors, in which case the third (13 years) can only be that of Domitian (A.D. 81-96). Thus Wright's dating of the pottery was correct, but only for the latest deposited in the tomb. We must therefore assume the Era of Actium in regard to a number of tombs at Teucheira, but it is hard to know whether some of the low figures do not indicate regnal years of the Ptolemaic dynasty. However, if we assume the Era of Actium for the high figures, then the tombs so dated extend from 5 B.C. to A.D. 94.[91]

---

[89] *PEQ* 1963, pp. 37 sqq., tombs A-E.

[90] *Ibid.* = J. Gray, ap. *MUC*, 1952, Chap, vii, pp. 43 et sqq.

[91] This after much rereading and revision of inscriptions by Miss Joyce Reynolds. Known dates of Teucheira epitaphs, according to the era of Actium. All reference numbers are those of *SEG* with the exception of that marked W4, which was recorded by Webster.

895	20 BC	882	AD 18
885	19	877	27
904	19	561	60
905	19	921	64
913	16	884	68
704	11	W4	70
650	10	880	73

There may be one burial under Commodus, to judge by the name of the dead man recorded in the epitaph.[92] A number of epitaphs are dated in the Roman period by their names.[93] In four of these only the *nomen* and *praenomen* occur, and are therefore evidently to be dated down to or in the reign of Tiberius. One family among the bearers of the *tria nomina* received citizenship under Claudius or Nero.

The problem of date must also be considered from the point of view of the letter-style of the inscriptions. This did not alter much in the period when the tombs were used, and in contrast to the position at Cyrene, the forms C and W are common at Teucheira (as in the other coastal towns and in Egypt) before the 2nd and 3rd centuries A.D., apparently owing to the influence of Egypt, where these forms appear in half-cursive inscriptions as early as the 3rd century B.C.,[94] also on painted steles[95] and on Jewish tomb-monuments at El-Ibramiyeh.[96] On the other hand the open sigma (Σ) is completely absent at Teucheira, likewise the irregularly sized letters characteristic of the 3rd century BC in hellenistic inscriptions; this would suggest that the epitaphs begin later. Nor are there parallels to the inscriptions dated to the 2nd century B.C. at Cyrene, with letters of irregular height, adorned with cerifs. In addition, the shape of the frames enclosing the epitaphs must be considered. Many of them resemble those of the epitaphs of Tel el-Yehudiyeh (Leontopolis—The land of Honio or Onias)[97]

670	10 BC	889	AD 73
681	10	880	74
917	9	639	76
705	8	640	76
612	7	641	76
888	6	593	78
923	5	594	78
653	4	600	77
		883	79
		894	79
		909	80
		498	87
		901	94

[92] *SEG* 9, 591—Λ Αἰλίω; 522—Μ Αὐρ[ήλ]ιος Νιγ [ρῖνο]ς.

[93] 522, 582, 583, 585, 591, 615, 712, 602, 620, 623, 624, 644, 668, 674, 676, 724; Gray nos. 1, 8, 9, 12, 25, 41.

[94] Breccia, *Iscriz. gr. e lat.*, nos. 27, 28.

[95] Eg. *ibid.*, nos. 238, 242, 246.

[96] *Ibid.*, nos. 251, 253.

[97] *Annales du service des antiquités d'Égypte*, 19, 1920, p. 216; 22, 1923, pp. 7-16; *ZNTW*, 22, 1923, pp. 280 sqq.

and of other Egyptian sites. The resemblance is particularly close to the stones at Tel el-Yehudiyeh, with their apicidal gable tops; these begin in the 2nd century B.C. On the other hand there is a striking absence at Teucheira of such formulae as "Farewell, no one is immortal", or "I am not and I don't care", so common on Egyptian epitaphs. Egyptian influence at Teucheira will be discussed presently.

Discussion of the distribution of the tombs requires caution, since, as stated, Jews may be concealed among apparently gentile epitaphs. Nevertheless, several features can be indicated. Obvious Jewish names are absent in Courts I, II-VII, X, XIII, XVI and XX. II has only one identifiable Jewish name, although it contains a symbol interpretable as a sort of *menorah*, with three instead of seven branches. There are Roman citizens in V, VI, VII, VIII, XI, XIII, XV and XVIII. Of these, V, VII and XIII contain no identifiable Jewish names, XI only three, although other names here are suspect. But the large number of Jewish names in XV and perhaps XVIII, justifies the view that there were Jews among the Roman citizens whose names are incised there. The overwhelming majority of the tombs at present known to be of Jews are situated to east of the town, yet only one other was here adorned with a true *menorah*-symbol; it was found by Wright.[98]

Larger or smaller groups of Jewish graves can be identified in VIII, XI, XII, XIV, XV and XVIII. The largest is in XV, where no fewer than fifty names appear in *Supplementum Epigraphicum Graecum*. Webster, Gray and Reynolds add 26 more. It is therefore evident that one court was overwhelmingly Jewish, but smaller concentrations are found in other courts, and in a number there are no identifiable Jewish graves, or only a few. On the assumption that not all the burials to the east of the town are Jewish—which is hard to prove or disprove—the situation corresponds to that prevailing in the hellenistic and early Roman periods between Jews and Greeks in Alexandria:[99] there two quarters were inhabited preponderantly, if not entirely, by Jews, but Jews lived dispersed also throughout the other quarters.[100]

---

[98] Wright, *PEQ* (n. 1), pp. 54-5 (Tomb A).

[99] Jos. *C. Ap.*, II, 4 (33-6); cf. *Ant.* XIV, 7, 2 (117); I, Bell, *Juden und Griechen in römischen Alexandrien*, 1926, p. 19.

[100] This statement is correct, of course, only if the writer's view is justified that not all the Teucheira quarry-tombs were Jewish. If on the other hand the opinion of some scholars is accepted, that they were all Jewish, then it

The Jewish epitaphs of Teucheira can only be distinguished by the character of the names or because they are found in tombs together with obvious Jewish names. Even the few Hebrew words to be seen, for example, at the end of Jewish epitaphs in Rome, do not appear here, and the same applies to religious symbols (the menorah, etrog, lulav, shophar, etc.) with two exceptions. As stated, one such, a menorah, was rediscovered by Wright to west of the town.[101] The language of the known epitaphs is Greek, with one doubtful exception, Hebrew letters being perhaps incised over an inscription dated in A.D. 69.[102] The fewness of symbols, the apparent dispersal of burials among the Greeks, and the almost complete dominance of the Greek language at Teucheira, show a good deal of assimilation on the part of its Jews; the composition and character of their names point in the same direction.

Of the 144 names under discussion, only 39 are Hebrew. These are Sarah (2); David (Dados) (1); Simon (4); Musaeos (2); Jesus (3); Judas (6); Judais (2); Judion (1); Sepphoris (Tzipporah) (1); Sabbatis (1); Josippos (2); Isuphon (= Josipon) (1); Joses (1); Josecos (Isaac?) (1); Maria (2); Mara (1); Joannos or Joannes (5); Tubias (2); and apparently Simux (Heb. *tzimuq*—raisin).[103] Some of the names are probably Greek translations of Hebrew names; such are Irene (? Shulamit) and Pothetos (Shaul?). The Hebrew names constitute 31 percent. of the total known Jewish names at Teucheira; in Egypt they were about 25 percent.[104] There are also some Aramaic names, and it cannot be determined with certainty if they belong to Jews, although circumstances

may in any case be assumed that a large cemetery of this sort is fair testimony to an organized Jewish community.

[101] Above, n. 98.

[102] This inscription was published in *SEG* 16 (894) with the note: *infra titulum Hebraicum expressum*. I have examined the photograph of this inscription, sent to me by the kindness of Miss J. Reynolds, but it is so faint as to be indecipherable, and its Hebrew character cannot be regarded as certain.

[103] *JJS* 13, 1962, p. 34; *SEG* 9, 596. Gray thought to see in "Hermon" a transliteration of Hiram, and in Herennos a form of Aaron, but I am not convinced. One of his suggestions, however, that Arimmas is Ahiram, or Jehoram, requires additional comment, which will be found below.

[104] *CPJ* I, p. 28; *SEG* 9, 446. Θαννύρας (cf. Heb. *tanur* = oven) is also found as a Semitic name (cf. H. Wuthnow, *Die semitische Menschennamen in griechischen Inschriften und Papyri des Vorderen Orients*, 1930, ad voc.). It appears in the area to the west of the town of Teucheira, but cf. *SEG* 9, 135, 348; Herod. III, 15 (Θαννύρας), where it is Libyan.

favour this. They are Abbias, Martha, Marin and Marinicos; Marin
and Marinicos have perhaps been influenced by a similar Libyan
name.[105] Beischa (Βεῖσχα)[106] and Nonna [107] are found on Jewish
tombs elsewhere, and are paralleled on one epitaph at Jaffa; the
second is common both in masculine and feminine forms. Nonos
or Nonnas are found in various instances in Jewish or Semitic
contexts.[108] Beischa is a Libyan name, to be compared with the
district of Bassachis (Βασσαχέως Παρατόμη) in Marmarica, recorded
in Papyrus Vatican 11,[109] also with the Bessachitae, a Libyan tribe
mentioned in the same area by Ptolemy.[110]

Theophoric names are common, and most of them must be
regarded as Jewish in this context. To this class belong Theodoria,
Theodotos, Dositheos (9 cases), Dosithea, Theogiton, Theocles,
Theoxenos, Theodorus, Theodora and Theologos. Didosas (Διδώσας)
although not strictly theophoric, must be seen specifically as
Jewish, a sort of pseudo-theophoric, or a translation of Nathan.
Gray also noted that the name Ptolemy, found in three instances
among the Jewish names, is probably an indication of the presence
of the descendants of Jews who had come as military settlers.

A few words must be devoted to the name Arimmas (Ἄριμμας).
This name is found at Teucheira in four cases among Jews and not
less than ten times in non-Jewish inscriptions. We have already
seen that it was associated with a wealthy and influential Cyrenean
family, which can be traced from the 4th down to the 1st century
B.C. (see p. 95, nn. 132, 133). We have already suggested that the
name's frequency among the settlers of Teucheira is to be explained
by the possibility that a member of this family in the Ptolemaic
period discharged the function of assigning land near Teucheira
to katoikoi on behalf of the king, since cases are known in Egypt
under Euergetes II, in which cleruchs took the name of the official
in charge of the allotment.[111] The period of these parallels is ap-

---

[105] Cf. *SB* 6651 (Tel el-Yehudieh); Philo, *In Flaccum*, VI, 39.
[106] *SEG* 9, 703.
[107] *SEG* 9, 642.
[108] C. Clermont-Ganneau, *Archaeological Researches in Palestine*, 1899, II,
p. 145, no. 7; Diehl, *CICV*, II, 1924,—Tituli Judaici, 4895a, 4858a, 4858;
L. Jalabert, R. Mouterde, *Inscr. grecques et latines de la Syrie*, (1929-),
459b, 487, 625.
[109] *NV* VI, 28/30; cf. V, 24: Βασσαχέως; VI, 42/3, ἐν τῷ Βασσάχι.
[110] Ptol. IV, 5, 21.
[111] P. Tebt. 64 (e) iii; 72, 322 etc.; *ib.*, 61 (a) 19 etc.; Lesquier, *Inst. mil.*

propriate to the present case, and it therefore becomes possible
that the evidence at Teucheira indicates that katoikoi or cleruchs
formed the first nucleus of the settlers whose tombs survive near
the town. Chronological considerations have shown that these do
not precede the 2nd century B.C. Nevertheless the fact that only
four of the 14 cases of the name Arimmas occur east of the town,
among the known Jewish concentration, should mean that the
colony of katoikoi was not limited to Jews.[112]

Besides the general hellenization manifested by the high proportion of Greek names among the Jews of Teucheira, certain names
are such as to throw light on their outlook. Euterpe, daughter of
Theodotos,[113] is called after one of the Muses, and no name can
point more clearly to pretensions to hellenic culture. Yet we have
a parallel at Beth She'arim in Israel, in the 3rd or 4th century
A.D., where a Jewess of Byblos, called after Calliope, the chief
Muse, is buried.[114] Schwabe wrote of this name: "I have not found
a Jewess with a name like this anywhere else, in Eretz Yisrael or
outside it . . . but it is known that the Jews of Phoenicia were some
of the most hellenized." It may be noted that Calliope is called
"matrona" in her epitaph, and was therefore a woman of rank, yet
nevertheless was brought to be buried in Eretz Yisrael near the
resting place of Rabbi Judah the Prince. Thus such names do not
so much indicate complete assimilation as a synthesis between
Greek culture and Judaism. It has already been suggested, indeed,
that some young Jews were being educated in the gymnasium of
Teucheira. But generally it must be admitted that the Jews here
do not exhibit signs of a high level of hellenic culture. There is
here no known example of a metrical epitaph of the sort so common
among the Greeks of Cyrene and Ptolemais, and the like of which
can be found among hellenized Jews at Leontopolis and even at
Beth She'arim in Eretz Yisrael. Two such [115] occur among the
non-Jewish tombs of Teucheira. Nor do we find here the brief,
almost cynical farewells so characteristic of Greeks and sometimes

---

Lagides, pp. 193-5. In P. Tebt. I, 32, we read of the establishment of cle-
ruchies by a high-ranking personage holding the rank of "first friend".

[112] The name Arimmas is also found in a list of settlers settled near
Ptolemais in the time of Pompey (circa 67 BC)—Reynolds, *JRS* 52, 1962,
p. 100, no. 5.

[113] *CIG.* 5265.

[114] *BIES* 18, 1954, pp. 32-3, nos. 202-3.

[115] *SEG* 9, 557, 558.

adopted by Jews. Such expressions are generally absent in the Teucheira cemetery. One inscription found by Wright [116] to west of the town, however, greets the deceased, the young "Adonis Hyacinthus", who died at the age of seventeen, with the word "Be of stout heart (εὐψύχι) Hyacinthus, child." Most of the line before the word εὐψύχι is uninterpretable. It is true that this tomb, although inscribed with the menorah symbol, is of pronounced hellenizing complexion, on the evidence of the names and the formula; but the greeting εὐψύχι is also common at Beth She'arim, where it has been interpreted by scholars to relate to the future resurrection of the dead.[117]

Very instructive on the outlook of some of the Jews of Teucheira is the name Timocrates son of Theodotus.[118] Timocrates was born in A.D. 75, five years after the destruction of the Second Temple and two years after the disastrous rising of part of the Jewish population of Cyrene led by Jonathan the Weaver, yet Timocrates was given a pronouncedly non-Jewish name. There is no doubt as to his Jewish identity, for he was buried in the same tomb as four other people possessed of theophoric names, one Dositheos, another his son or daughter. We may further note three names of Jewish context,[119] all derived from the name of the god Apollo-Apollonius, Apollonidas and Apollodorus. This phenomenon is not restricted to Teucheira in the Jewish world of the period, and points to a measure of external assimilation.[120]

Although the evidence of names does not solve the problem of the geographical derivation of the Teucheira Jewish community, it does throw light on the question, and some conclusions may be drawn from it.

A comparison of 144 names with a list of Jewish names occurring in Egyptian papyri of the hellenistic and Roman periods,[121]

---

[116] *PEJ* 1963, p. 55. For an amplified reading, which unfortunately adds nothing comprehensible, *SEG* 16, 771.

[117] One may recall in this connection the supposed belief of Jason of Cyrene, author of the original book of which II *Macc.* is an epitome, in the resurrection of the dead (II *Macc.* 12:39-45). Cf. Lévi, RE 29, 1894, pp. 43 sqq.; *REJ* 41, 1900, pp. 161 sqq.

[118] *SEG* 9, 641.

[119] 683, 709, 722.

[120] On names of this category borne by Jews, see Tcherikover, *Jews in Egypt*, p. 192.

[121] The comparison was made with the aid of the card-catalogue of the late Professor Tcherikover, and I would like to record his generous assistance in this matter.

gives the following picture: 31 names at Teucheira find parallels
among Jewish names recorded in papyri, but 23 of them are so
common among Jews of the period as a whole that the parallels
permit no deductions. But eight names of Teucheiran Jews paralleled in the papyri are not very common, hence it is probably that
part of the town's Jewish community came from Egypt, and that
it continued to maintain contacts with that country. A similarity
between the tomb-tablets at Leontopolis and those at Teucheira
has already been noted, and important from this point of view is
the inscribed stele found by Webster in one of the tombs he investigated.[122] The inscription was not completely legible and in
itself does not prove the Jewish character of the tomb, but steles of
this type were found in the Jewish tombs of Tel el-Yehudiyeh.[123]

One detail may be important for an understanding of the character of the graves to east of the town. This is, that the Egyptian
calendar is the accepted calendar of the eastern cemetery, and the
recording of the ages of the deceased is the rule. Both features
make the impression of belonging to a common tradition, and
whatever the reason, this loyalty to the Egyptian calendar suggests either an Egyptian origin or a strong attachment to a political
régime centered there, i.e. to the Ptolemaic dynasty. It would not be
wise to decide on this evidence whether the majority, and not
merely some of the burials to the east of Teucheira were Jewish.
But it may be suggested with a greater degree of probability that
this cemetery was that of people descended from katoikoi and soldiers settled in the town by the Ptolemies.

On the other hand it is an interesting fact that the place of
origin of the deceased is inscribed in the eastern cemetery in one
case only (661).[124] By contrast, people from Didyma, Thrace,
Demetrias (Thessaly or Damascus), Aksine (Sicily?), Bithynia
and Nysa (the town of Asia Minor, or perhaps Beth Shean) are
recorded on graffiti on the city-wall or associated buildings in the
west of the city.

As stated, two cases only are known in which menorah symbols
are incised by the graves. Unfortunately we do not know what was

---

[122] Wright, *PEJ*, 1963, p. 40, (Tomb C), does not publish the text of the
inscription, nor is the stele mentioned by Gray, but the late M. N. Tod had
a copy of the epitaph and I have seen the stele in Tocra Museum.

[123] E. Naville, *The Mound of the Jew and the City of Onias*, Egyptian
Exploration Fund, 1888-9, pp. 13 sqq.

[124] The case, indeed, is doubtful; see below.

the inscription associated with one of them and the inscription associated with that in the western cemetery included no date. But the accepted view is that the menorah symbol was not cut on funerary monuments prior to the destruction of the Second Temple.[125] Two such symbols do indeed appear in the Alfasi Street tomb in Jerusalem, not used after the reign of Tiberius,[126] and show that it could appear earlier, but there is little doubt that its wide popularity as a funerary and decorative figure began only after 70. We shall see later that there is reason to believe that its first centre of diffusion was Cyrenaica itself; the Teucheira evidence supports the view that its main diffusion took place after the Destruction, for the presence of no more than two examples is appropriate to a cemetery where the Jewish burials are not later than A.D. 115 and the datable majority are before 94/5.

Another symptom of a Jewish religious consciousness at Teucheira is indicated by the Hebrew and theophoric names of the members of the community.

A third symptom is the presence among them of proselytes. Libyan letters appear in some of the epitaphs, and, as we have seen, the name Beischa daughter of Theogeiton is Libyan; her father's name, moreover, is perhaps to be translated as "proselyte".[127] The name Sarah, which occurs twice, denotes proselytes or their daughters, and may do so here, as both the women so called had fathers with Greek names; a Cyrenean inscription, indeed, mentions "Sarah, a proselyte" (Σάρρα προσήλυτος) explicitly.[128] Libyan customs may also have influenced the Jews of Teucheira, for in one tomb Webster found a skull reposing in an amphora, one of several containing skeletons, and this form of burial is an ancient local form, while Nicolaus of Damascus knew of the Libyan custom of decapitating the dead.[129]

---

[125] Cf. *IEJ* 7, 1957, pp. 155 sqq.

[126] *IEJ* 6, 1956, pp. 127-8.

[127] But the name occurs among gentiles, eg. in Attica (*SEG* 15, 111; 23, 86, line 284).

[128] *SB* 1742. For Sarah as a name taken by proselytes, Baron, *SRHJ* I, 1935, p. 142. Cf. the Jew with a Libyan name ("Αλζαν Συμώνος) found in the Jaffa cemetery—*Sepher Ha-Yishuv.* I, p. 85, no. 41.

[129] Müller, *FHG*, frag. 141 = Jacoby, *FGH*, II, frag. 123. This practice was common among many primitive peoples, eg. among certain strata of the British population in the Roman period; cf. *Proceedings of the Dorset Natural History and Archaeological Society*, 69, pp. 33 sqq.; but the case at Teucheira might also be interpreted as the result of the custom of *liquṭ ha-'atzamot* (M. *Mo'ed Qatan*, I, 5).

The lack of evidence for Greek culture among the Jews of Teu-cheira has been remarked upon, but evidence of this sort is scarce throughout the cemetery. It is not easy to decide how far the inscriptions reflect literacy in the community, but evidence exists that Jewish stonecutters worked in Cyrenaica,[130] and usually an illiterate stonecutter reveals illiteracy on the part of his employers. Thus, Δωσίθεος (637) appears side by side with Δοσίθεος, the name Εἰρήνα (680) together with Ἰρήνα (622). The forms Theukles and Theudoros, instead of Theokles and Theodoros, reflect Libyan influence, which regularly converted the omicron to an upsilon.[131] In some epitaphs barbarous letters appear which are undoubtedly Libyan. This should mean that we have here inscriptions cut by Libyan craftsmen, or that their employers were used to the Libyan alphabet, as these signs are not used, except in one or two instances, in their Libyan value.[132]

Several interesting sociological facts can be derived from the Teucheira inscriptions on the life of the town as a whole and on the Jewish community in particular. Firstly, the size of Jewish families. Their reconstruction, of course, involves some risk, as there is no certainty that all the epitaphs are known, and given families may have buried some of their children elsewhere. The reconstruction of fourteen Jewish families is based on the assumption that children with the same patronymic and interred in the same tomb or in adjacent tombs, belong to the same family. On this method, seven families have two children, five have three, one has four, and one five. These results, although limited, do not differ greatly from Tcherikover's finding [133] concerning the Jewish community of

---

[130] *CIG* III, 5167 = *SB* 5886- AD 88-9 (Cyrene).

[131] *NAMC* 2, pp. 173, 177 n.

[132] The letters concerned correspond to the first, third and twenty-fifth letters as listed by Halévi-Tourneau (O. Bates, *The Eastern Libyans*, 1914, p. 86). A fourth perhaps corresponds to their twenty-first. The presence of these letters was first noted by the writer in *Zion*, 19, pp. 46-7. Gray has no hint of them, but there is no reason to cast doubt on the reliability of the readings of Col. Thackrah made available to the writer, and they also appear on the sketches made by Halbherr, which I have been able to examine.

[133] *HCJ*, p. 293; n. 87, p. 505. The evidence was assembled by Manteufel, *Tell Edfu*, 1937, p. 147. Cf. Tarn, Griffiths, *HC*³, 1952, pp. 100-102, who wrote concerning the family situation in the Hellenistic period: "The general conclusion from c. 230 onwards seems certain: the one-child family was commonest, but there was a certain desire for two sons (to allow for a death in war); families of four or five were very rare; more than one daughter was very seldom reared; and infanticide on a considerable scale, particularly of girls, is not in doubt."

Edfu (Apollonipolis) in Egypt, in the Roman period: "There is no trace of families burdened by numerous children, and in so far as the matter can be examined, there is no family the number of whose children exceeds three."

To this information on the size of Jewish families can be added impressive evidence on the mortality of Jews and gentiles in ancient Teucheira. It is clear that caution must be exercized in regard to a statistical analysis, since the number of people—163—whose ages are preserved, is not large. One phenomenon nevertheless stands out; of 101 males and 63 females whose age of death is recorded, 44.5 percent. of the males and 34.9 percent. of the females died up to or at the age of twenty. As a number of children probably died immediately after birth and were not recorded at all, the real mortality must actually have been higher. The figures are:

Jews

0-20 years		Total recorded	Percentage
Males	28	60	46.6
Females	17	44	38.6

Not proven to be Jews

0-20 years		Total recorded	Percentage
Males	21	41	51.2
Females	5	19	26.3

B. E. Richardson, who analysed the average longevity of Greeks on epigraphical evidence,[134] reached similar conclusions to the above; she also found 42.3 percent. cases of death up and at the age of 20, the highest mortality being between 16 and 20. These findings are apt to alter on the one hand on account of the numerous old people whose ages were unknown at the time of death, and on the other due to the death of unrecorded infants; yet at Teucheira 13 deaths are recorded of people of 70 and over. Nor is it credible that any unknown figures would greatly alter the impression of the high death-rate up to age of 20.

It may be asked how the community perpetuated itself, with so high a mortality which included the ages of adolescence and marriage. There is indeed evidence for marriage at an early age among the Jews of Teucheira. According to no. 622, Mousaios son of Euphrosynos died in Year 1 at the age of 30, and his son Simon died in

---

[134] *Old Age among the Greeks*, 1933, pp. 231 sqq.

year 6, at the age of 20. Simon was therefore fourteen when his father died, and was born when his father was 16. Hence the latter's marriage took place at latest at the age of fifteen, and it may be accepted that marriage at this age was a regular practice if the community was to overcome so high a mortality in its younger age-groups. Frey also found cases of marriage at the ages of 15-16 [135] among the Jews of Rome. This high death rate among the Teucheira young also reflects the economic condition of the community, for there was certainly some connection between longevity and conditions of life. It is a logical conclusion that the high mortality among their younger generation was caused not only by the absence of medical aid, but also by a low standard of living and by gruelling physical labour which affected more especially the men.

Although the information is slight and the evidence incomplete, the epitaphs can tell us something of the social position and economic function of part of the Jews of Teucheira. We have seen that some of the deceased were Roman citizens, and the existence of names demonstrating this in two courts where there were numerous Jewish names suggests that there were Jews among them. The name T. Flavius in epitaph no. 615 invites the interpretation that there were here freed slaves of the Flavian Caesars,[136] and manumission was doubtless one of the ways in which some Jews had obtained Roman citizenship. The evidence for slaves in the Jewish community of Teucheira is fairly clear, for no. 619 commemmorates Maker son of Irene (Μάχερ Ἰρήνας), and the recording of his parentage by his mother instead of his father points, in my opinion, to birth outside wedlock. The case is paralleled by no. 658, not certainly Jewish, but it is in Court XV, where most of the burials are those of Jews. Frey indeed explained the recording of some of the deceased by their mothers' names in the Roman catacombs as evidence that their parents were divorced;[137] it is difficult to refute him, but a third inscription from Teucheira,[138] recording Epikles (born) to the slave-woman Antylla (Ἐπίχλ[η]ς ἐκ δούλης Ἀντύλλας) shows that the first explanation has something to go on,

---

[135] *CIJ* I, p. cxvi. Cf. at Teucheira *SEG* 9, 713: "Secunda daughter of Fabius and wife of Aristos; deceased at the age of twelve."

[136] Cf. the tombstone of Bassara, imperial slave-woman, at Ptolemais (Βάσσαρας Καίσαρο[ς] δούλης)—Pacho, *Relation d'un voyage dans la Marmarique*, 1827-9, pl. lxxv.

[137] *CIJ* I, p. cxv.

[138] Robinson, *AJA*² 17, 1913, p. 191, n. 108.

i.e. that this form alludes to a servile origin. There is no evidence whether these slaves were Jews or gentiles. Jewish slavery had virtually disappeared in Judaea at this time,[139] but not necessarily in the Diaspora. In Cyrenaica these may have been Jews redeemed by their brethren, but it is more probable that they were non-Jews who had been circumcised by their Jewish owners.

Various indications have already been noted suggesting that not a few of the Teucheira community were descended from military settlers settled by the Ptolemies. This and the cultural tradition of the eastern cemetery mean that the community included katoikoi or cleruchs holding crown land in the vicinity of the town. The evidence derivable from the name Arimmas points to the formation of the colony in the 2nd century B.C., probably under Euergetes II (163-116 B.C.),[140] and we may note the title "Macedonian" attached to an anonymous epitaph in the eastern cemetery; it is likely that the term is not ethnic but relates to membership of a military unit trained and armed in the Macedonian manner, like the Jewish "phyle" in the garrison of Alexandria. (p. 133).[141]

Both the character and topographical position of the town of Teucheira are such as to confirm that the Jews there worked in agriculture. The city appears to have possessed no harbour; there are traces of a fishing-quay or sea wall. The immediate vicinity was wooded in ancient times, and the remains of small ancient farmhouses can be seen on the coastal plain to south, east and west of Teucheira,[142] which, like most Greek towns, subsisted mainly on agriculture and to a lesser extent on crafts, eked out with fishing

---

[139] Cf. B. *Gittin*, 65a; '*Arachin*, 25a.

[140] Wright, summing up previous excavations, finds that all the tombs in the quarries to east of the town are Roman, but discovers earlier elements among those to west of it. His finding is appropriate to our own conclusion. It should be stressed that we see the epitaphs of the eastern sector as representing the generation of Teucheira Jews of the Roman period, but not the first generation of their community, which belonged to the hellenistic period.

[141] On the term "Macedonian" in Ptolemaic Egypt, see Tcherikover, *Jews in Egypt*, pp. 42 sqq.; *CPJ* I, p. 14; M. Launey, *Recherches sur les armées hellénistiques*, 1949-50, I, pp. 308 sqq.

[142] Cf. Wright on Teucheira (*PEQ* 1963, p. 23): "The terrain is characterized by rocky outcrops, the steeply-dipping strata of which are visible on the surface. The soil, however, is good, and numerous wells once supplied fresh water, so that the city must have been something of an agricultural centre. It was this and not its position on the coast *per se* which must have prompted settlement for. . . facilities for harbourage are completely lacking."

and perhaps a little coastwise trade. The town's area seems to have altered little from the 4th century B.C. to the Byzantine epoch, and even larger cities contained a majority of cultivators who worked the land about them; Teucheira hardly differed in this respect. Most of those interred were probably humble tenants on royal estates or labourers on the city-land, a status appropriate to their low standard of living, revealed by their high mortality before the age of 20. After the rebellion of 115-117 the town of Hadrianopolis was founded in the coastal plain to west of Teucheira. This means that much of the area remained vacant for settlement, a fact which points to a large Jewish population in the same region before the rising.

We may now sum up the information on the Jews of Teucheira that has been derived from their tombs.

The Jews constituted a considerable part of the city's inhabitants. One section of them evidently reached the town from Egypt, but possibly a group came as emigrants from Judaea in the 2nd century B.C., and appear to have become assimilated to Greek society. The community included Roman citizens and freed slaves, also military settlers or their descendants, and it may be deduced that a number were engaged in cultivation near the city. They possessed particular links, political and social, with the Ptolemaic régime. Their standard of living, at least in the 1st century A.D., was low, and their deathrate up to the age of 20 shocking, although in this respect their lot was probably no different from that of the gentiles. The sizes of their families did not exceed those usual in the times. A high percentage of the Jews possessed hellenized names, so that they are not recognizable as Jews by their names alone. A small group seems to have received a gymnasium education. On the other hand there is no evidence of a high level of Greek culture among most of them, and the suspicion of illiteracy attaches to some of them. Yet the names of one or two indicate an aspiration to hellenism on the part of their parents. The Jews of Teucheira probably had an organization, although their religious consciousness is hardly revealed before the destruction of the Temple, except by the Hebrew and theophoric names of some of them. They nevertheless included proselytes won over to Judaism by individual influence or by ownership of slaves. These included Libyans, and there was reciprocal influence, linguistic and perhaps not only linguistic, between them and the Jewish community.

Teucheira therefore furnishes the picture of a community which was certainly not wealthy, and was, in part, poor; which lived a life of hard manual labour as soldiers and cultivators, was influenced not a little both by its Greek environment and by its contact with the Libyan population, yet still preserved its adherence to Judaism.

4. BERENICE

The discoveries at the city of Berenice, today Bengazi in the west of Cyrenaica, reveal a different picture. This city, one of the five towns of the Pentapolis,[143] formerly Euesperitae, was transferred, as we have stated, to the vicinity of the present port at the latest by the middle of the 3rd century B.C. It is to be assumed that from that time, if not earlier, a Jewish community existed in the city. It probably contained many poor members and people of humble means, but the three Jewish inscriptions found at Bengazi inform us of a comfortable and even wealthy stratum which constituted the leadership of the community.

The first inscription was found two centuries ago, but was not read rightly, being the most fragmentary and mutilated of the three documents. It has been restudied in recent years,[144] when its Jewish character was established, and its contents throw light on a number of points in the second inscription. It belongs to the years 8-6 B.C., being a resolution of the Jewish archontes (ἄρχοντες) and the politeuma (πολίτευμα) of the city—meaning, of the wardens of the organized community, and of the community itself—to express their thanks and esteem to one Decmus Valerius Dionysius for his services to the community, in so far as he had plastered and adorned the amphitheatre. The community resolves to set up a stele in the amphitheatre in his honour, to free him from liturgies and to crown him publicly at every monthly gathering.[145] The archons, to the

---

[143] The name "Pentapolis" does not appear before the 1st century BC, when Pliny (HN V, 5 (31)) enumerates as the five cities of Libya, Berenice, Arsinoe (Teucheira), Ptolemais, Apollonia and Cyrene. According to his evidence, the group of cities associated with this name did not precede the conversion of Apollonia to an independent city, an event not anterior to the 2nd century B.C. See p. 59, n. 354.

[144] CIG III, 5362 and the reexamination of G. and J. Roux, REG 62, 1949, pp. 290 sqq.

[145] An honorary inscription closely akin to the present tablet in language and circumstances is OGI 737, of the 2nd century B.C., from Memphis. The politeuma of the Idumaeans here thanks a high official for painting and

extent that their names can be read, number seven, and it should be noted that the community imposed liturgies on its members (it may be assumed, on the richer families among them), i.e., the execution of projects on behalf of the community involving monetary expenditure.

The amphitheatre is mentioned also in the second inscription, which dates 30 years after the first, and in some measure clarifies the building's character and identity. It shows that the building did not belong to the gentile city, but was a specifically Jewish structure, apparently designed for the community's gatherings. This is made clear by the word used to describe the reconditioning of the edifice in the first inscription, viz. "a contribution to the politeuma" (ἐπίδομα τῶι πολιτεύματι).

The word ζωγράφειν used in the first inscription if of special interest, as it means "to paint", more especially animal figures and even human beings; hence the building may have been adorned with wall-paintings and pictures like those to be seen at a later period in the synagogue of Dura-Europos. But the very existence of such a structure as an assembly hall of the Jewish community in a gentile city of the period is unique. We shall see presently, that there are two other contemporary Jewish buildings which perhaps belong to the same tradition.

The second Berenice inscription,[146] which is also the best-known, as it is complete, appears to have been incised in A.D. 24/25. It commemorates a resolution of the archons and politeuma of the Jews of Berenice, taken at the Festival of Tabernacles (Sukkot) the same year. The archontes now number nine, and the resolution honours the Roman official M. Tittius, who had been sent to Cyrene to look after "public affairs" (ἐπὶ τῶν δημοσίων πραγμάτων), for his courteous attitude both to the Greek citizens of the city and to the members of Jewish community. It is therefore resolved to set up a stele of white Parian marble in the amphitheatre in his honour, also to crown it and to praise the Roman publicly in the assemblies held on the sabbaths and at New Year.

The third inscription was executed in A.D. 56 under the Emperor Nero. It was discovered in the city in 1938 and subsequently lost,

---

plastering (τὴν τε καταλιφὴν καὶ κονίασιν) the Temple of Apollo which belonged to the politeuma.

[146] *REG* 62, 1949, pp. 284 sqq.; *CIG* III, 5361.

but its photograph has been preserved.[147] The slab was broken, and its lower part was missing, but what remained of its upper part was sufficient to show the contents and purpose of the text and to prove that the missing portion was not large. This too is a resolution of the community commemorating monetary donations made by its wardens and members for the repair of the synagogue. The photograph of the inscription, taken when it was *in situ*, shows stretches of wall each side of it, leaving no doubt that it was found in its original position within the synagogue building to which it refers. Thus the discovery gives us the site of the synagogue, which stood facing the sea, like the synagogues in several other Greek cities such as Miletus, Ephesus, and Caesarea Palaestinae. The slab differs in several features from the two former inscriptions, whose styles were similar, their language precise and their lettering elegant; the letters of the third inscription are less refined, and several errors are discernible in its drafting and grammar.[148]

The most important difference between this inscription and the earlier ones concerns the body adopting the resolution. While the two earlier resolutions were taken by the archons and the politeuma, the deciding body in this inscription is the synagogue (συναγωγή), here denoting the community, and subsequently the building. Secondly, the list of contributors, eighteen in number, begins with the archons, of whom there are now ten; they are not, as formerly, named before the community as a whole. The reason for the change in the name of the deciding body may have been that the archons were themselves among the contributors and could not therefore propose a vote of thanks to themselves; hence the thanks are expressed by the entire synagogue. But this explanation does not account for the absence of any reference to the politeuma. Whether this change implies a change in the constitution of the community between the years A.D. 25 and 56, must remain undecided.[149]

---

[147] *BIES* 25, 1961, pp. 167 sqq.; *PP* 12, 1957, pp. 132 sqq.; *REG* 72, 1959, pp. 275-6; *SEG* 17, 823.

[148] Eg. line 3 τῆ(ι)συναγωγῆ(ι); line 4, ἐπιδόντας has been corrected to ἐπιδόντες, when it ought to be ἐπιδόντος; in line 12 Ἡρακλείδης and Ἡρακλαίδου appear in propinquity; in line 16 Ἀντίγον(ο)ς is read.

[149] It can be argued that the reference is to one synagogue among several contemporarily existent in the city, and that the archontes belonged to it. But this suggestion seems to be disproved by the inscription's expression "resolved by the synagogue of the Jews of Berenice and its vicinity" (ἐφάνη τῆ(ι) συναγωγῆ(ι) τῶν ἐν Βερνεικίδι Ἰουδαίων).

The increase of the number of archons from seven in the year 8/6 B.C. to ten under Nero, is also of interest. It is difficult to believe that this increase was without significance; probably it arose from the growth of the community. Naturally this fact itself is no proof of the election of the community wardens by democratic methods, but there does appear to have been a certain coordination between the size of the community and the number of its wardens, and therefore we should not be too positive concerning the non-democratic structure of the Jewish communities of the hellenistic and Roman world.[150]

The third inscription records thirty-five names in all (13 men and three women). Most of the names of these members of the community and their fathers are Greek; only two (Jonathas, Marion) are Hebrew. In the first inscription only one is Hebrew (Iosippos); in the second, in so far as the names of the archontes can be read, no Hebrew name is to be found except Simon, which is both a Hebrew and a Greek name. On the other hand the third inscription lists several Greek names which were particularly common among Jews in the hellenistic and Roman periods, such as Dositheos (twice), Jason, Isidorus (cf. Isidora in the same inscription, line 8), Alexandros and Theophilos. The name Zosimeter (Ζωσιμήτηρ), which occurs on this stele, must be a translation of "mother of all life", in other words, Eve.[151] By contrast, no fewer than twelve names among those on the third inscription recur at Cyrene as those of non-Jews: in other words, these are normal and characteristic Cyrenean names.[152] Thus the composition of these names at Berenice reflects assimilation to the Cyrenean environment and to the peculiar onomasticon of Cyrenean personal names. It may also be remarked that four of the names on the third inscription recur on Jewish epitaphs at Apollonia and Teucheira.[153] Straton and Euphranor further appear in the second Berenice

---

[150] Cf. *CPJ* I, 9-10, n. 25; *HCJ* p. 303.

[151] *Gen.* 3:20. It was my late wife who drew my attention to the meaning of the Greek name.

[152] Names especially characteristic of Cyrene are Euphranor, Pratomedes and Carnedas, while Ammonios and Serapion are common in Egypt. The following names, present in the third inscription from Berenice, all recur together among hundreds of names on a stele at Cyrene (unpublished) which lists gentile contributors of the 1st century B.C.: Carnedas, Euphranor, Lysanias, Jason, Pratis, Pratomedes, Straton, Cartisthenes, Thaliarchos, Zoilos.

[153] Alexandros, Euphranor, Lysanias, Marion.

inscription. An innovation in the third document is the listing of women together with the men. This phenomenon is not without parallel in the Jewish world, and in the later Roman imperial period, at least, we encounter the names of Jewish women taking part in the paving of synagogue floors,[154] or honoured with the title of "mothers of the synagogue". It is worthy of note that at the head of the list of donors and at the end of the list of archons, appears the name of a priest, Cartisthenes son of Archias, who occupies, it would seem, the first place of honour in the lists of simple congregants.

It is not evident whether the synagogue of Berenice was destroyed or damaged by enemies, or whether the inscription commemorates a repair of the building after damage by nature or the passing of time. However, the recorded contributions, which are not large, suggest simple repairs rather than reconstruction. The symbol ∠ which appears before every sum stands for "drachmai",[155] and the contributions, in so far as they are preserved, add up to 283 drachmas. This is a considerable sum, but not sufficient to erect a complete new structure.

What kind of building was the amphitheatre in which the Jewish community of Berenice assembled on the first day of the month, on festivals, and on sabbaths?

Scholars disagree whether it was Jewish, or a building of the Greek city, in which the Jews had received permission to set up their commemorative and honorary steles.[156] J. and G. Roux [157] reached no conclusion on this question; L. Robert expressed the view that the building was Jewish.[158] The writer's opinion is that already expressed, to wit, that the words describing the work of Decmus Valerius Dionysius at the end of the first inscription, that he had plastered the floor (?) and the amphitheatre, and also adorned it with figure-paintings at his own expense, as a gift to the community (Τὸ ἔ[δ]αφος ἐκονίασεν καὶ τὸ ἀμφιθέατρον καὶ ἐζωγράφη-σεν τοῖς ἰδίοις δαπανήμασιν, ἐπίδομα τῶι πολιτεύματι), prove that it

---

[154] At Ḥamat Gader and Apamea, for instance.

[155] G. Foucart, *RA²*, 1864, p. 465; S. Reinach, *Traité d'épig. grecque*, 1885, p. 549; C. Kraeling, *Gerasa*, 1938, no. 365 = *SEG* 7, 894: and cf. Galen, Περὶ μέτρων καὶ σταθμῶν, ii.

[156] P. Wesseling, *Diatribe de Judaeorum Archontibus*, 1738; for the second view; also G. Caputo, *Anthemon*, (Scritti di arch. e di antichità in onore de C. Anti), 1955, pp. 281-291.

[157] *REG* 62, pp. 290-1.

[158] *Ibid.*

was Jewish property. Had the building belonged to the city rather than the Jews, the word "polis" would have taken the place of "politeuma", and it is hardly to be imagined that the community (however assimilated to Greek habits) would have met to pray in a building contaminated by gentile idolatry.

The word "amphitheatre" was comparatively new when the said inscription was set up: such buildings begin to be built at Rome, still of timber, only in the time of Julius Caesar. The oldest known stonebuilt amphitheatre is that at Pompeii, erected in 70 approximately: [159] it was called "spectacula".[160] The Greek term "amphitheatre" is first found in the writings of Strabo,[161] (64/3 B.C.-A.D. 21) and Flavius Josephus mentioned it in connexion with Herod's building-activity about 25 B.C.[162] We learn from the inscriptions honoring Valerius Dionysius that the building at Berenice was already standing in 8/6 B.C., and its language means that the repairs were on a considerable scale, hence the amphitheatre had then existed some decades, and was probably built at approximately the same time as Herod's amphitheatres at Jerusalem and Caesarea, not long after the first experiments at Rome. The Berenice inscription, to the best of my knowledge, is the first known that mentions an amphitheatre in Greek (the Latin word appears later, in Pliny). It must therefore be stressed that the word's meaning was then elastic and fluid, nor was the building's form necessarily like that of the crystallized amphitheatres known in Italy or the East. But the name obliges one of two assumptions: either that it was circular or elliptical, or that the seats of the audience were ranged on two sides opposite to one another (ἄμφω means "on both sides"). It is nevertheless difficult to suppose that the Jews derived the idea from a structure designed only for wild-beast hunts and gladiatorial contests, much less in Greek Berenice, the heads of whose community were deeply imbued with hellenistic culture.

The Greek world had known for centuries assembly halls in which the seats were ranged around three or four sides of the buildings, beginning with the third telesterion (τελεστήριον) built at Eleusis by Pisistratos. The Greeks also knew a circular assembly

---

[159] M. Bieber, *History of the Greek and Roman Theater*², 1961, p. 170.
[160] *CIL* X, 852.
[161] Strabo XIV, 143 (649)—Mesogis near Nysa.
[162] Jos, *Ant.*, XV, 8, 1 (268); cf. A. Smith, *Jerusalem*, 1908, pp. 493-4.

hall in at least one city, the Tholos (θόλος) in the Athenian Agora, where the prytaneis met.[163] This however was designed for only fifty people, whereas Berenice must have possessed some hundreds, if not thousands, of Jews. From the fact that Dionysius plastered the floor—if the restoration ἔ[δ]αφος is correct—scholars have deduced that the hall was roofed,[164] This is is not inevitable, as is demonstrated by the plaster floors found in the theatres of Caesarea and Lepcis Magna, yet it is altogether probable that the Berenice building was covered, since the Jews met in it throughout the year. There are two possibilities: either it was of limited area, as the roof was supported internally by columns or piers, or the building was open to the sky. The first possibility is unlikely, for though the Roman world possessed small roofed theatres, called odeia, which were used as council-houses in various cities (one at Ptolemais of Cyrenaica),[165] no instance of a circular roofed amphitheatre is known. We are therefore bound to conclude that the Jewish amphitheatre of Berenice was square or rectangular in plan, like the archaic bouleuterion at Athens (6th century B.C.), or various later assembly halls at Megalopolis, Priene and elsewhere.

New excavations have disclosed two buildings in Eretz Yisrael which are undoubtedly Jewish, and constitute a chronological link with the Greek assembly-halls and the Jewish amphitheatre of Berenice. These are the halls of assembly and prayer found in the excavations at Masada (1964) and Herodeion (1962-3). At the time of its occupation by the Zealots the Masada hall took the form of a chamber surrounded by seats ranged along the interior walls, the ceiling being supported by internal columns.[166] But when Masada was fortified by Herod in 37-31 B.C.,[167] the prayer hall then had the form of a basilica; only during the Sicarian occupation did it become a hypostyle hall with seats around the walls, and it may be supposed that this plan was more appropriate to the democratic notions of the insurgents. The same initial plan and a similar replanning by the Sicarii were revealed by the excavations of the Herodian stronghold of Herodeion.[168] The plan of the two halls

---

[163] I. T. Hill, *The Ancient City of Athens*, 1953, pp. 55 sqq.

[164] *REG loc. cit.*, p. 291.

[165] C. Kraeling, *Ptolemais, City of the Libyan Pentapolis*, 1961, pp. 89 sqq.

[166] *IEJ* 15, 1965, pp. 76 sqq.

[167] M. Avi-Yonah, et al., *Masada, Survey and Excavations*, 1957, pp. 4-5; Jos., *BJ*, VII, 8, 4 (300).

[168] *Arch. News of the Dept. of Antiquities of Israel*, 30, 1969, p. 28 (Heb.).

thus shows that this system of constructing an assembly hall was known to the Jews in the same period and was copied from the Greek and hellenistic hypostyle halls, such as those built at Delos and Notion (Asia Minor) in the 3rd and 2nd centuries before the common era.[169]

If the assembly hall of the Berenice Jews was a square or oblong structure, with a roof supported by internal columns, and the seats ranged along the walls, why was it called an amphitheatre? This will be understood if we imagine the building's plan as similar to that of the Ekklesterion (ἐκκληστήριον) of Priene (Asia Minor), built about 200 B.C.[170] to hold some 700 people. The seats are ranged to a depth of nine rows on the east and west, and of fifteen on the north, being absent only on the south. If we assume that at Berenice there were also a few rows on the fourth side a plan is obtained to which the term "amphitheatre" may fitly be applied.

5. PTOLEMAIS

Although Ptolemais was larger and more important than Eues-peritae-Berenice, its prosperity belonged only to the hellenistic and the early Roman periods. Ancient Jewish remains in and round the city are not numerous; most of them are tomb-inscriptions, among which four are known to be Jewish and one is doubtfully so,[171] We also know of one Jewess born at Ptolemais, who was buried in the Valley of Qidron near Jerusalem in the 1st century B.C.[172] Two other inscriptions are important for determining the status of Cyrenean Jews vis-à-vis the Greek cities: the first is a stele of the ephebes, or senior pupils of the gymnasium, found at Ptolemais, and recording a list of pupils,[173] which includes the name Itthalammon son of Apellas ('Ιτθάλαμμον τοῦ 'Απέλλα). The same man's name is also recorded on another dedication at

---

[169] For a survey of various examples of the hypostyle hall, see C. Anti, *Teatri greci arcaici*, 1947, ch. vi, pp. 153 sqq.

[170] D. S. Robertson, *A Handbook of Greek and Roman Architecture*[2], 1943, pp. 176 sq.; T. Wiegand, H. Schrader, *Priene*, 1904, pp. 176 sqq.

[171] *SB* 5918; *NAMC* I, 1915, p. 152; fig. 42; *CIG* III, 5328; Kraeling, *Ptolemais*, pp. 111 sq.; p. 215, nos. 48-51.

[172] N. Avigad, *IEJ* 12, 1962, pp. 1 sqq., no. 7 (a).

[173] Unpublished. It were well to remark that the list contains six theophoric names, hence it is possible that there were other Jews in the list who cannot be identified; cf. especially Timostheus son of Onasion; the latter name appears also on the second inscription of the Berenice politeuma, *CIG* III, 5361.

Lanuvium in Italy;[174] this is a bilingual inscription in honour of Aulus Terentius Varro Murena, their patron, by Itthalammon son of Apellas and Simon son of Simon on behalf of the Ptolemaei Cyrenens(es). The letter-style indicates that the inscription is not a "local product", but was cut by a Cyrenean mason, while the presence of the name Itthalammon among the ephebes of Ptolemais shows that the deputation had come to Terentius from a Cyrenean city. The stele of the ephebes, of whom Itthalammon was one, opens with the date Lχη', and its style belongs to the first century B.C. According to the Era of Actium, this would be 3/2 B.C., and as Itthalammon was a pupil of eighteen in that year, the Lanuvium dedication must have been set up several decades later, when he had attained an age at which he could participate in the public affairs of his city.

Who were these two emissaries who went to Italy to represent the affairs of their city to a Roman patron and were successful in their mission? Itthalammon looks at first sight like a Libyan name:[175] it appears also at Cyrene, in one case in an ephebe list which includes some Jewish names,[176] and the name of the father of Itthalammon of Ptolemais,—Apellas,—like that of his colleague, Simon son of Simon, arouses suspicion of a Jewish derivation; moreover a small plaque found at Naples bore the name "Yitshalom" in Hebrew.[177] The name of Itthalammon's father, indeed, was regarded by the poet Horace as sufficiently characteristic of Jews to be a synonym for any Jew.[178]

The question therefore arises, why did the Greek city of Ptolemais send two Jews to represent its interests to people of influence in Rome in one of the years of the first half-century of the common era?

The Lanuvium inscription does not refer to the city of Ptolemais specifically, either in Latin or in Greek. It refers neither to the polis nor to the *civitas Ptolemensium*; all that appears is *Ptolemaei Cyrenens(es)*. Now the form of the first of these two words is unusual as the title of the citizens of Ptolemais; it actually means

---

[174] *ILS* 897; *CIL* XIV, 2109. The slab is now in the Capitoline Museum at Rome, where I have been able to examine it.

[175] Cf. *NV* IV, 12: 'Ιθαννύρον; VII, 6: 'Ι θάλατος.

[176] *QAL* 4, 1961, p. 20, no. 7, (c) 3.

[177] *CIJ* I, 555.

[178] Hor., *Sat.*, I, v, 100; Credat Iudaeus Apella.

"the people of Ptolemy".[179] Frank,[180] indeed, accepts this interpretation, and understands the term as referring to the settlers of
the past lands of the Ptolemaic kings, the Roman *agri publici*,
the οὐσιάι or βασιλικὴ γῆ of the former hellenistic rulers. Several
features support this assumption. Firstly the letter-style of the
inscription honoring Terentius is characteristic of the rural inscriptions of Cyrenaica; secondly, Itthalammon's name, which
reflects assimilation to a Libyan environment. There can of course
be no doubt that Itthalammon was a citizen of Ptolemais, for which
reason he was selected as a representative of the public, whether
this was the urban public or the rural tenants of the state domain.

There are difficulties as to the identity of Terentius. Two scholars [181] have thought him to be the consul of 23 B.C., put to death
the same year by Augustus on a charge of conspiring against his
life.[182] This identification is possible only if we agree to date the
year of the ephebe list in which Itthalammon figures, according to
the era of the establishment of the province of Cyrene (alleged to
have begun in 74 B.C.), in which case Itthalammon would then
have been eighteen in 46 B.C. and have travelled to Italy well
before Terentius' death in 23 B.C. There is, indeed, no information
of a later Terentius Varro who lived in the first half of the 1st
century A.D., hence no final decision is possible on the problem
of his identity. All that we can say is, that no use of the provincial
era on Cyrenean inscriptions has been proved. It is moreover
difficult to see the two emissaries, Simon son of Simon and Itthalammon son of Apellas, as emissaries of the city of Ptolemais,
and as no simple decision is possible on this question either, we
are obliged to reexamine the connection of the Jews of Cyrenaica

---

[179] The inhabitants of the city are called in a Cyrenean inscription of the
time of Domitian (A.D. 88—*CR* p. 102, n. 3) Ptolemaenses. The form
Πτυλιμαϊκή appears on a Jewish ossuary of the 1st century AD in Jerusalem
(see p. 216, n.), the substitution of 'o' for 'υ' here showing that the inscription is that of a Jewess of Cyrene. The citizens of Egyptian and Phoenician
Ptolemais are called by the *Digesta* (50, 15, 1) and the *Vulgata* (I *Mach.* xii,
48; II *Mach.* xiii, 25) Ptolemenses, whereas the adjective Ptolemaieus (Cic.,
de fin., 5, 1, 1) means "that which belongs to Ptolemy". The citizens of
Cyrenean Ptolemais and Ptolemais of Egypt are also Πτολεμαιεῖς (*CIG*
5186; *OGIS* 49; 50).
[180] *JRS* 17, 1927, p. 150, n. 2.
[181] Dessau, *ILS* ad 897; B. Borghesi, *Oeuvres complètes*, 1862-97, VII. p.
488.
[182] *PW* IX, 1934, sv. Terentius (92), col. 708.

with the *agri Apionis*, the Ptolemaic royal lands of the hellenistic period.

In 25 B.C. the Jews of Berenice expressed their gratitude to M. Tittius for his assistance; this official had been sent to deal with "public affairs" (ἐπὶ δημοσίων πραγμάτων) in Cyrenaica. We may state at once that he was not the governor of the province, who was of praetorian rank and this would have been mentioned on the complementary inscription had it been directed to him. The document's language, which states that M. Tittius had "arrived" (παραγενηθείς) in the country on public affairs, precludes the rank of governor. He had come to the province on some special administrative duty, probably involving finance, hence Paribeni was perhaps right in tentatively connecting his business with the property of the Roman state, i.e. the *agri publici*.[183] But the expression δημόσια πράγματα can be more broadly interpreted, to mean simply "on affairs of government administration". Only if we are prepared to assume the existence of a strong Egyptian influence on Cyrenean administrative terminology, are we bound to accept Paribeni's interpretation.[184] The discussion that follows may help us to a solution of the problem.

6. 'EIN TARGHUNA

On the Cyrenean plateau, 27 kilometres west of the city of Cyrene and six kilometres west of the ancient village of Messa, is to be found a Graeco-Roman site called 'Ein or Gasr Targhuna or Targhuniyeh.[185] The site is also known to the local Libyan inhabitants as Ḥirbet al-Yahud. The representation of a menorah, cut deeply in the ancient rockcut road a short distance south of the site, is proof that the name reflects historical reality,[186] and ancient

---

[183] Ap. de Ruggiero, *Dizz. Epig.*, II, 1910, 1436.

[184] In the 2nd century B.C. the words δημόσια πράγματα meant "public affairs" (*SIG³* 674, 72) or "the public interest" (*ib.* 646, 35); in the 1st century B.C. we find the expression used to translate the word *respublica* (*SB* 4224, 2). In Roman Egypt δημόσια generally was used to denote state property and especially imposts levied by the state, also state domain. (F. Preisgke, *Wörterbuch der griechischen Papyruskunde*, 1925, p. 337; cf. *Suidas* (Adler), II, p. 47, no. 461: Δημοσίων πραγμάτων διοικέτης, οἷον φροντιστὴς χορηγίας. . .

[185] Cyrenaica map 1:100,000, Section 2, (1942), 5036, where it appears as 'Ein Targhuna. *EI* X, 1931, p. 428, has Taurguni; the local pronunciation is "Targuna" or "Tarkhuna". See here end-map 5.

[186] *DAI* II, Cir. i, 1933, fig. 106; *CR* fig. 32.

rockcut tombs here have been described as Jewish.[187] The character of the settlement can be demonstrated by the discovery near the menorah of a Roman boundary-stone (*cippus*),[188] recording the restoration of public land (*ager publicus*) to the Roman state by the legate Acilius Strabo, who was active in the years A.D. 55-56 under the Emperor Nero. It cannot be determined if the settlement originally stood within the limits of the *ager publicus* or near them, but a consideration of its position may give reason to favour the belief that the former was the case.

The geographical situation of 'Ein Targhuna is instructive from every point of view. It lies on the line of the main Roman road linking Cyrene with Ptolemais,[189] and at the western end of a natural pass through the wooded area west of Cyrene. It also occupies the extreme western point of a spur of the Jebel which looks out over the middle terrace (the Lusaita) to the sea on the 500 metre contour above sea-level. 'Ein Targhuna, moreover, is situated a short distance north-east of the entrance to Wadi al-Kuf, a wild and rocky region traversed by a narrow gorge which constituted a grave danger because it served as a concealed approach through which the desert tribes could penetrate to the heart of the plateau from the south-west. The area as a whole was nevertheless a natural barrier between the eastern and western parts of the Jebel. The security problem in the region is graphically emphasized by the presence of Gasr ibn Igdem, six kilometres south-west of 'Ein Targhuna, one of the largest hellenistic forts in the country; [190] its task was to watch the pass, the many caves in which could furnish ready shelter to robbers and outlaws.

The topographical position of 'Ein Targhuna stands out even more clearly when defined in relation to the areas of settlement, as determined by the distribution of springs and wells. The site lies in the extreme north-west angle of the area of springs, defined by the lines Targhuna-Cyrene-Apollonia-Derna-al-Fayyidieh-Slonta.[191] To west, there are no wells or springs till al-Gharib is reached, but

---

[187] *DAI* II, Cir. i, p. 128, figs. 104-5; *AA* 1926, col. 450.

[188] *SEG* 9, 352 = *DAI* II, Cir. i, p. 129, no. 137; *Tab. Imp. Rom.* HI 34, Cyrene, pref. pp. 16-17.

[189] The place where the stone was found is called Gasr Nuara by Goodchild, *ibid.*, opposite p. 16.

[190] *Bull. Amer. Inst. Arch.*, 2, 1910-1911, p. 136, pl. xxxviii; *CR* p. 201; fig. 19.

[191] See p. 80 and fig. 5.

to east the land is fertile. This is in brief, first and foremost a
frontier position placed on a salient,—an ideal point for a unit of
military settlers.

As to the name 'Ein Targhuna, ancient Greek rural placenames
have survived here and there on the Cyrenean Plateau down to the
present day.[192] The name Targhuna recalls the Aramaic form of the
Greek name (Τράχων) applied to the el-Lejja region of Hauran; [193]
the *Targum Jonathan* has the form Targuna (טַרְגּוּנָא). That this was
not merely a corruption of the text, is to be seen from Greek-
Hebrew parallels in which the *patah* and *resh* change places.[195]
Later Arabic parallels also occur of the addition of the suffix iyeh
to names previously without it.[196] The meaning of the name Targhuniyeh is therefore likely to be "the people of Targhuna", and it is
probable that the name Targhuna originated from the Greek
τράχων, "the rocky place", from which the Greek name for al-
Lejja was derived—Trachonitis.[197] Near this latter area Herod
settled a unit of Jewish mounted archers probably in 7-6 B.C.,
under the command of one Zamaris,[198] who had come to Syria
from Babylonia in 10 B.C.[199] The aim of this settlement in so
difficult an area was, of course, to hold in check its cave-dwellers,
who were plundering the neighbouring villages.[200] The area had
been first annexed by M. Terentius Varro, governor of Syria, in
the year 23 B.C. He was a brother of Aulus Terentius Varro and a
relative of the Terentius Varro whose name appears on the Lanuvium inscription discussed above. It may be added that at the
end of the 4th century A.D., according to Synesius,[201] a unit of

---

[192] Examples are Gasr Belgara (1:100,000 (2), 4947) near Zavia Beda,
the ancient Βαλάκραι (Paus. II, 26); Siret Maga, apparently derived from
the name of the Cyrenean king Magas, east of Cyrene (1:100,000 (2), 5048);
Meneqret, the name of a Greek rockcut tomb south of Barce, derivable
from the Greek name Menecrates (W. Papé, G. Benseler, *WGE*, 1911, II,
p. 897, ad voc.); Negharnes, the Graeco-Roman village east of Cyrene,
evidently to be identified with Ptolemy's Ἀρχίλη, (IV, 4, 6)—1:100,000 (2),
5874.

[193] Y. Press, *Encyc. of Eretz Yisrael*, 1948, II, p. 381, ad voc. (Heb.).

[194] *Targ. Jonathan.* (Argov), Deut. 3; 4, *Yalqut Shim'oni*, Deut. 'Eqev,
תתע"ד.

[195] Eg. Heb. פַּרְצוּף (Greek πρόσωπον); Heb. פְּלָתֵר (Greek πρατήρ).

[196] Eg. Adamah—Ademiyeh; Gilgal—Jaljulieh; Parod—Faradiyeh.

[197] Jos., *Ant.* XVI, 9, 3 (292); Strabo XVI, 2, 16 (755); 2, 20 (756).

[198] Jos., *Ant.* XVII, 2, 1 (24-5).

[199] *Ibid.* XVIII, 2, 1 (24).

[200] *Ibid.* XV, 10, 1 (346).

[201] *Epp.* 132.

mounted archers (ἱπποτόξοται) recruited or stationed at Balagrae (Zawia Beida), 13 kilometres east of Targhuna, was stationed in the Jebel. Although they were called Balagritae, their permanent station is unknown, but their existence teaches that there was a tradition of mounted archery in the district, and it would seem that the Roman command of the 4th century, wishing to beat the Libyan tribes with their own tactics, raised a unit of mounted archers among the local natives to protect the district.[202]

On the basis of the above evidence, the following conjunction emerges. 'Ein Targhuna was a Jewish settlement whose topographical position shows that it was settled by the government with military settlers (katoikoi or similar) to protect the area from raids conducted from the west. The place's present name is Aramaic-Greek in origin, and the same name was attached to the rocky area of the Hauranite Trachonitis near which Jewish mounted archers were settled for police purposes. The Targhuna area possessed a tradition of mounted archery like that of the Jewish Babylonian settlers, and the Roman governor who annexed Trachonitis in 23 B.C. belonged to the family of the Terentius who received a deputation of two Jews representing either Ptolemais, or the settlers of the public lands, in the early decades of the 1st century of the present era.

With these facts in mind, we may infer that the Jewish settlement of 'Ein Targhuna, in view of its clear paramilitary function, was included within the area of the Roman *ager publicus*, the previous Ptolemaic royal lands, where plots had doubtless been allotted by the government to the settlers; this inference agrees with the view already expressed, that Jews and other immigrants of the hellenistic period who entered agriculture, could only settle on the royal land, i.e. on the king's personal estates (οὐσίαι) or on crown domain (βασιλικὴ γῆ).

The precise date of the establishment of the Jewish settlement at 'Ein Targhuna cannot be determined. The menorah symbol merely furnishes an approximate *terminus post quem* for the existence of

---

[202] For mounted archers in Libya, cf. those illustrated in *AI* 4, 1931, pp. 191, 195, on a gold placque of the 5th century B.C. from the Temple of Apollo at Cyrene. Libyan archers are mentioned in inscriptions of the Pharaoh Mereneptah—J. H. Breasted, *Records of Egypt*, 1927, III, paras. 579, 609. For Libyan cavalry, Caes, *Bell. Afric.*, VII, 5. Cf. Coh. III Cyrenaica Sagittariorum, *AE* 1896, 10; Cyrenean archers in the Roman army of Cappadocia in the early 2nd century C.E.—Arrian, *Ekt. Alan.*, I, 18.

occupation after 70, but does not establish its commencement. A Jewish military colony hardly suits conditions much after the beginning of Roman rule, and is more apposite to the policy of the hellenistic monarchs. The close parallel between the conditions of the colonization of 'Ein Targhuna and those of the Babylonian-Jewish settlement in Bashan, as well as the identity of geographical names, encourages the conjecture that the 'Ein Targhuna Jews were also brought to Libya at that time, in the last decades of the 1st century B.C., and this is more probable since the form of the placename is Aramaic.[203] This date, indeed, cannot be proved, but two additional remarks can be made: a) a transfer of Roman forces from Syria to Cyrenaica is known in the period of Augustus; b) not a few instances are known in the Ptolemaic kingdom and in Roman Egypt, in which the names of foreign communities or of their former settlements, whether of soldiers or of civilians, were transferred to their new places of colonization. The stationing of Syrian units in Cyrenaica under Augustus is proved by inscriptions at Ajadabia south of Bengazi,[204] and at Zawiat-Mesus on the desert fringe in the south-west of the country.[205] These garrisons included troops from Apameia, and their presence was apparently connected with the great Roman campaign against the Garamantes, the Marmaritae and the Gaetuli between 20 and 2 B.C. approximately.[206] Examples of the transfer of the names of immigrants or of their villages are Samareia, Magdola, Chana'anain and Sandalion in Egypt, all of migrants from Syria;[207] a similar instance is to be found in eastern Cyrenaica itself, namely, Magdalis in the Martuba region,[208] and very probably the name Targhuna was likewise transferred in this way from the Trachon of Auranitis.

---

[203] The transfer of part of the Babylonian unit from Bathanea to Cyrene, if it took place, was apposite to the period; somewhere about 9 BC Herod moved Idumaeans to Bathanea; cf. Sulpicius Quirinius' expulsion of Ituraeans from their hillforts in 6 B.C. (*Eph. Ep.* IV, 537). There are several hints of Herodian contacts with Cyrene; cf. Idumaean inscriptions in the cult cave of Budrash near Cyrene—*NAMC* 3,1971, p. 99; Nicolaus of Damascus had information on Libyan burial customs—see here p. 154.

[204] *SEG* 9, 773, 775, 781.

[205] S. Ferri, *Rivista di Tripolitania* 2, 1925-6, pp. 363 sqq.; *CR*, p. 77; *JRS* 43, 1953, p. 76.

[206] See pp. 68-9 sqq.

[207] Tcherikover, *The Jews in Egypt*, p. 19.

[208] *Zion*, 19, pp. 26, 48; *NV* I/35; IV 12/15.

7. CYRENE

By surveying the remains relating to the Jews of Teucheira, Berenice, Ptolemais and 'Ein Targhuna, we have been able to arrive at a certain appreciation of the economic and social position of the Jews of Cyrenaica. The literary and epigraphical evidence suggests that no small part of the Jews of Libya were soldiers and cultivators, but there are some indications that from the 2nd century B.C. a commercial element existed amongst them. Concerning the presence of Jewish craftsmen we can only conjecture. The very restricted archaeological evidence points to stonemasons,[209] potters,[210] perhaps a painter,[211] and mint-workers,[212] weavers,[213] and sailors.[214] We also know of a Jewish slavewoman at Ptolemais,[215] and, of the female slave of publicani at Apollonia.[216] We hear of 3,000 well-to-do Jews at Cyrene in A.D. 73 (εὐπορίᾳ χρημάτων διαφέροντες),[217] and, by contrast, contemporarily, of 2,000 Jews without means (ἄποροι).[218]

Bound up with any estimate of the social and economic position of the Jewish community of the country, is the question of its citizen status. We are forced to assume that the Jewish cultivators, by reason of the circumstances of the settlement of most of them at the beginning of the hellenistic period and in the 2nd century B.C., were concentrated on the crown land and royal estates of the Ptolemies, and did not therefore qualify for citizenship in the Greek towns. The constitutions of the latter, indeed, prohibited

---

[209] The name of the mason Sidonius Selumaio engraved on a funerary monument of A.D. 88-99 (*CIG* III, 5176 = *SB* 5880); cf. *CIL* VIII, 21900; 14106; *RA* 4, p. 373.

[210] Clay lamps from Cyrene; see pp. 235 sqq.

[211] The painter of the ζωγραφήματα in the Berenice amphitheatre.

[212] The influence of Jewish coinage on that of Cyrene; see p. 143.

[213] Coster, in *Studies in Economic and Social History in honour of A. C. Johnson*, ed. Coleman Norton, 1951, p. 15, n. 68, states erroneously that Jonathan the Weaver was a Jew of Cyrene; it is however possible that the found supporters among Jewish weavers in that city.

[214] We read of a 4th-century Jewish ship sailing from Alexandria to Cyrene (Synes. *Ep.*, 4). Cf. inscriptions of Libyan Jews at Jaffa (*Sepher ha-Yishuv*, nos. 41, 54, 85), and links between Cyrene and 'Akko which hint as sea-communication between Cyrene and Judaea from very early times. There may also be evidence that the rising of 115-117 affected Jaffa (see here p. 306).

[215] Pacho, *Relation d'un voyage en Marmarique*, pl. LXXV.

[216] *REG*, 1969, p. 535, no. 618.

[217] Jos., *BJ*, VIII, 11, 2 (445).

[218] *Ibid.* 1 (438).

non-citizens from acquiring land in their territories.[219] Hence opportunities of obtaining citizenship in the Cyrenean cities would have been open only to those Jews who settled in the cities themselves and got their livelihoods in other branches, i.e. by trade and the handicrafts, but the constitution of Cyrene under Ptolemy Lagos was strongly prejudiced against those engaged in trade and the crafts (pp. 51-2), nor is there reason to think that this situation changed until the Roman period. It is clear, then, that the Jews of the Pentapolis had little prospect of penetrating the ranks of the Greek citizens, and the question whether the Cyrenaican Jews possessed civic rights in the Greek *poleis* can be answered in advance: if any did possess them, they were not numerous. But this reply is not sufficient, for there are sources that make certain statements on the question; these are both literary and epigraphical.

Flavius Josephus writes that the Jews of Cyrene enjoyed equal rights before the law (ἰσονομία) with the inhabitants of their city — and had received this privilege "from the ancient kings".[220] He further reports [221] that Augustus reconfirmed to them the privilege of ἰσοτελεία (equality in payment of taxes). Strabo [222] had stated that the Jews constituted one of the four classes into which Cyrene was divided, namely, the Cyreneans, the aliens of Greek origin (μέτοικοι), the peasants and the Jews. Josephus' statement was made in relation to events under Augustus (circa 31-13 B.C.), but he says that their status was granted to the Jews by the "ancient kings". Strabo's grouping belongs to the period of transition from Ptolemaic to Roman provincial rule, that is, between 96 and 74 B.C., and in relation to the happenings of the year 88/6 B.C., when Lucullus arrived at Cyrene. The two writers' statements appear to conflict, since Strabo's classification puts the Jews, to all appearance, outside the ranks of the citizens, and the question is whether the status of Cyrenean Jewry changed between the Ptolemaic period and the imposition of Roman rule, or whether one of the two statements is erroneous.

The very fact that the Jews belonged, according to Strabo,

---

[219] *OGIS* 760; *SIG*[3] 108 etc.; *CIG* 90, 92 etc.; P. Guiraud, *Propriété foncière*, pp. 152-7; Busolt, *GS* pp. 297, 302.

[220] *Ant.* XVI, 6, 1 (160): "The cities had dealt evilly with the Jews who dwelt in Asia and in the neighbourhood of Cyrene of Libya, to whom the former kings had granted *isonomia*.".

[221] *Ant.* XVI, 6, 1 (161).

[222] Strabo ap. Jos., *Ant.* XIV, 7, 2 (115).

neither to the metics nor to the peasants suggests that they held a special position. Rostovtzeff rightly observed [223] that Strabo's fourfold division corresponded to that of the population of hellenistic Egypt, namely, the citizens of Greek cities, Greeks who were not citizens of such, aliens organized in their own organizations (πο-λιτεύματα), and native Egyptians. The question is, of course, how far the Egyptian analogy may be applied to Cyrene. As for Josephus, scholarly criticism suspects him of inaccuracy, and sometimes of distortion of the truth, since his statements were made in the heat of controversy concerning Jewish status in the Empire as a whole and in Greek society in particular, and with an apologetic motive.

Cyrenean inscriptions, nevertheless, contain evidence, of which part has been already cited, which shows that there were Jews among the citizens of Ptolemais, such as Itthalammon son of Apellas, and very probably his fellow delegate Simon son of Simon. The ephebe stele of 3-2 B.C. records, as we may note, several other theophoric names, especially Timotheus son of Onasion, which perhaps belonged to Jews. In 1961 an ephebe stele from Cyrene was published [224] figuring several names whose Jewish identity is indisputable. They begin in the year A.D. 3-4, and among 88 names appear five obvious Jews: Bar Tubas son of Bar Tub[r]as, Bar Tubas son of Bar Tubas (a second time), Ela(s)zaros son of Elazaros, Agathocles son of Elazaros, and Julius son of Jesus. Simion (Σιμίων) son of Pothion may also be Jewish, as the second *iota* of his name must indicate a transliteration of the Hebrew letter ʿayin. The list may include other Jews whose identity is concealed from us by their purely Greek names.[225] Additional lists for the years 20, 23, 24, 27 and 28 were incised on the left and right sides of the same stele in inferior and irregular letters; the years are numbered by the era of Actium. They include the names Cheirias son of Jesus and Itthalammon son of Itthalammon. Finally the city

---

[223] Rostovtzeff, *SEHHW*, p. 333.

[224] *QAL* 4, 1961, p. 20, no. 7.

[225] Cf. for example Theochrestos son of Theochrestos, Theodotos son of Theodotos and Theodoros son of Nicanor. We also find Simon son of Orion, of ambiguous origin. It is not quite clear to me whether Professor K. M. T. Atkinson (*Ancient Society and Institutions: Studies presented to Victor Ehrenberg*, 1966, The Third Cyrene Edict of Augustus, p. 24), thinks that *all* the Jews of Cyrene possessed citizenship on the evidence here discussed; I suggest below (pp. 234-5) that only a minority obtained the privilege.

of Cyrene has yielded a list of high ranking magistrates, the nomophylakes (νομοφύλακες) for the years A.D. 60 and 61, among
them being recorded the name Elazaros son of Jason.[226] We shall
speak of this man and of the Jewish ephebes, at a later stage; in
the meantime the evidence suffices to show that some Jews had
penetrated the gymnasium of the city of Ptolemais at the end of
the 1st century B.C., and were citizens of their polis; [227] by the
beginning of the 1st century of the present era a group of young
Jews were pupils in the gymnasium of Cyrene, so that it may be
assumed that they were prospective citizens as well, as is demonstrated by the election of Elazaros son of Jason to the responsible
office of nomophylax under Nero.

But in order to clarify how large a section of the Jewish inhabitants achieved citizenship in their cities, and when this process
began, a broader discussion of the whole problem is desirable.

It may be said at once that in discussing the question of Jewish
rights in the hellenistic and Roman towns of the eastern Mediterranean, scholars have generally paid far too much attention to
the problem as reflected in Alexandria, and tended to assume that
any conclusion drawn from the material affecting the Egyptian
capital must apply also to other Greek towns. For all that, it is
necessary to begin by examining what Josephus has to say on this
and other cities, and to determine how his statements are to be
interpreted.

He refers to Jewish status in Alexandria five times. In *Antiquities* XII, 8, he says that the Jews of the capital were made
citizens with rights equal (ἰσοπολίτας) to the Macedonians by
Alexander the Great, after he had recruited them to the garrison.
This is supplemented by the information (*Against Apion*, II, 35),
that a phylé of Jewish "Macedonians" still existed in his own day.
In *Antiquities* XIV, 188 he alludes to the stele set up in the town by
Julius Caesar (he probably meant Augustus) recording Jewish
rights, which included their citizenship of the city. He repeats
this information in *Against Apion* (II, 37-8). A third passage (*Ant..*
XIX, 281 sq.) cites what has been held to be the famous letter of the
Emperor Claudius to Alexandria,[228] written in A.D. 41, to settle

---

[226] *QAL* 4, 1961, p. 16, no. 2.
[227] See *SEG* 8, 641, apparently from Ptolemais in Egypt, for the connection
between gymnasium education and the obtaining of citizen rights.
[228] P.Lon. 1912; I. Bell, *Jews and Christians in Egypt*, 1924, pp. 23 sq.;
CPJ II, no. 153.

the dispute that had led to riots between the Jews and Greeks there under his predecessor Gaius. Another view however, holds that the citation relates to an earlier rescript of the Emperor. Here he writes: "As we have long known that the Jews of Alexandria who are called Alexandrians have lived from the earliest times together with the Alexandrians and obtained equal citizen rights (ἴσης πολιτείας) from the kings, as is made clear by letters which they possess and also by orders etc." Finally Josephus writes in the *Jewish War* (II, 487) that Alexander had granted the Jews the right of residence in the city and equal status (ἰσομοιρίας) with the Greeks, including the permission to call themselves "Macedonians".

There is no point in discussing here the question of whether Jewish troops served under Alexander the Great in Egypt,[129] but the information on their membership of the garrison and their title "Macedonians" is open to more than one interpretation; Tcherikover [230] considered that it meant simply that the Jews who bore the title "Macedonians" were troops of a "pseudo-ethnic" unit trained and armed to fight after the Macedonian manner, their phylé being, not a division of the citizen body, but a military formation. Whether or not this had nothing to do with citizen rights, however, is open to argument, for one of these Jewish "Macedonians", recorded in the early Roman period, held land in the Alexandrian city-territory, and was therefore almost certainly a citizen.[231] Josephus' alleged version of Claudius' rescript, on the other hand, although based on a genuine document sent by the Emperor to Alexandria to settle several issues, including that of Jewish status, faces the fact of the discovery of another, perhaps later papyrus version of a similar letter,[232] which states in clear language that "I order the Jews not to aspire to more than they already have had till now in a city not theirs." [233] Thus, even if we argue that the papyrus document was preceded by another, that cited by Josephus, which said something different, i.e. that two distinct pronouncements by the Emperor are involved, this would not resolve the difficulties created by the differences between the

---

[229] Tcherikover, *HCJ*, p. 323; 513, n. 77.

[230] *Loc. cit.*

[231] *CPJ* II, no. 141.

[232] Tcherikover, *l.c.*

[233] *Ibid.* lines 89-95: καὶ 'Ιουδείους δὲ ἄντικρυς μηδὲν πλήωι ὧν πρότερον ἔσχον περιεργάζεσθαι . . . ἐν ἀλλοτρίᾳ πόλει.

two.[234] It is in any case difficult to trust the accuracy of Josephus' report on the Alexandrian stele which allegedly recorded Jewish rights in the city: it may, indeed, have recorded the internal rights enjoyed by the Jewish communal organization (politeuma) in the city, but these do not bear on the problem of citizen status.[235]

On the other hand, some individual Jews did hold Alexandrian citizenship. Philo Judaeus certainly possessed it (*Ant.* XVIII, 159, 259; XIX, 276; XX 100; cf. *Philo, quod omnis probus liber*, 6), as did the father of the Jewish petitioner Helenos in the early Roman period.[236] The Jewish "Macedonians" were probably citizens, and others may have obtained the status in the Ptolemaic period by medium of a gymnasium education (Cf. *CPJ*, I, p. 23, n. 58). But there is no evidence that their number was ever large.

What then are we to make of Josephus' various other seemingly unequivocal statements concerning the ἰσονομία, ἰσοτιμία and ἰσο-μοιρία, of the Jews of Alexandria, of the ἰσονομία and ἰσοτελεία of the Jews of Cyrene—or of his attribution to the Jews of the status of πολῖται and ἰσότιμοι in the cities of Asia Minor and in Antioch (*Ant.* XII, 119-121), where they enjoyed an "equal share" of the city (ἐξ ἴσου ... τῆς πόλεως μετέχειν) with the Greeks?

Before we seek a solution for this problem, we must consider the evidence of Philo Judaeus, who, as an Alexandrian and leader of the city's Jewish community, was directly concerned with Jewish status when it was under critical attack. Philo does not use the terms ἰσοπολιτεία, ἴσης μοιρᾶς or ἴσης τιμῆς with regard to Jewish status in the two works in which he deals directly with the problem, the *Legatio* and the *In Flaccum*. Only once, in *de Vita Mosis*, does he use the expression ἰσοτιμία in relation to metics aspiring to the status of ἀστοί (I, 34-6). For him πολιτεία denotes the rights enjoyed by Jews within their organized community, which he also calls a πολιτεία. These rights he terms δίκαια; in one place (*Flacc.*, 53) he calls them τὰ πολιτικὰ δίκαια. But he consistently refers to the Jews as Ἀλεξανδρεῖς, and appears to use the expression in a

---

[234] The independent identity of each document has been argued by Dr. A. Kasher in his Ph. D. dissertation "The civic status of the Jews of Egypt in the Hellenistic and Roman periods" (Tel Aviv University, 1972), chap. 9, pp. 299 sqq. See also I. D. Amusin, The Letter and Edict of Claudius Caesar, *Westnik Drevnoj Istorii*, 1949 (2), pp. 221-8, cited by Dr. Kasher, and not available to me.

[235] *HCJ* p. 325; cf. *CPJ* I, p. 56, n. 20.

[236] *BGU* IV, 1140 = *CPJ* II, no. 151.

purely general geographical sense. For him, it had no strictly juridical meaning with reference to citizen status.

Let us now revert to the terms used by Josephus. If we scrutinize them, we shall discover that only ἰσοπολιτεία and ἰσοτελεία are terms of status susceptible to precise legal definition. Ἰσοτιμία means "equality of privilege",[237] ἰσομοιρία an equal share in wealth and power;[238] ἰσονομία denoted in classical times "equality among peers"; later the ideal of a community in which the citizens had their equal share.[239] These are, then, general expressions describing not a legal status, but a situation. We are left with ἰσοτελεία and ἰσοπολιτεία. Ἰσοτελεία was the privilege sometimes bestowed by a Greek city on metics releasing them from payment of the μετοίκιον— a tax to which they were otherwise subject.[240] Ἰσοπολιτεία was the potential citizenship granted by a Greek city to citizens of another city. It was part of a reciprocal agreement called συμ-πολιτεία, whereby the citizenship granted to the partner's citizens became effective in the event of their settling in the granting city, and *vice versa*.[241] We shall presently see that ἰσοτελεία, as applied to the Jews of Cyrene, was a genuine grant which can be historically demonstrated.

As to ἰσοπολιτεία, some scholars have seen in it an indication, where the Jews of Alexandria are concerned, that they held potential citizenship in the Greek polis, and this became actual if they chose to participate in the pagan rites involved in entry into the ranks of the citizens of Alexandria.[242] But this interpretation is very doubtful, for two reasons. Firstly, all known agreements involving ἰσοπολιτεία were concluded between two Greek cities, and none is known between a Greek city and a non-Greek corporation. Secondly, it is inherently unlikely that an agreement existed between the Jewish politeuma and the Greek polis, providing that any Jew prepared to desert his faith should be admitted to Alexandrian citizenship. Whatever Josephus' term ἰσοπολιτεία meant, it was not that.

---

[237] Xenoph., *Hieron*, VIII, 10; Strabo VIII, 5, 4 (365).

[238] Ehrenberg, *The Greek State*, 1960, p. 51.

[239] Ehrenberg, *Polis and Imperium*, 1965, pp. 279 sqq.; *op. cit.* p. 285.

[240] Eg. *SEG* 3, 122; cf. A. Heuss, *Staat und Herrscher des Hellenismus*, pp. 64 sq., Klio Beih. 39, 1937.

[241] E. Szanto, *Das griechisches Bürgerrecht*, 1892, pp. 67 sqq.; Busolt, *GS*, 1920 pp. 295 sqq.

[242] F. Griffiths, Tarn, *Hellenistic Civilization*[3], 1952, p. 222.

Now an examination of the relevant documents, including both literary sources (Josephus, Philo) and Jewish inscriptions of the Roman period in various Jewish centres, shows that the term πολῖται was applied to the members of Jewish politeumata existing in gentile cities or elsewhere. We have seen that Philo called the Jewish communal organization a πολιτεία; its constitution was a πολιτεία, its laws were τὸ πολιτικὸν δίκαιον; its members πολῖται. The Jews of Sardes are termed by a Roman document (Ant., XIV, 235) οἱ Ἰουδαῖοι πολῖται ὑμέτεροι; the city of Sardes refers to them officially as οἱ κατοικοῦντες ἐν τῇ πόλει Ἰουδαῖοι πολῖται (ib., 259). The president of the Leontopolis Jewish community in Egypt, was entitled a πολιτάρχης and had held the same office in another unidentified Egyptian Jewish community (CPJ., III, no. 1530). Josephus (Ant., XII, 123-4) speaks of the communal rights of the Antioch community as τὰ δίκαια τὰ τῆς πολιτείας.

It therefore appears that nearly all Josephus' statements regarding Jewish citizen status in Alexandria and other Greek cities can be understood to refer to their status as members of their own organized communities. It is, indeed, highly improbable that many Jews in the Roman period (in relation to the hellenistic epoch we have little information on this question) were interested in obtaining citizenship in the Greek polis of Alexandria, which stood in a relation of almost continual conflict with the Jewish population. The problem may have interested a small group of Jewish hellenizers who already held that status, or were impelled to seek it to escape the situation created by Roman policy in Egypt, which chose to class the Jews with the despised native Egyptian population. The real conflict in the Egyptian capital and in other Greek cities possessing Jewish populations, however, was created by the claim of the Jewish politeumata to equal status with the Greek citizen communities, and the endeavours of the latter to liquidate the power and existence of the Jewish organizations. If then Josephus' use of the term ἰσοπολιτεία was in any sense meaningful, it meant to him the claim to equality of status between these two bodies. This indeed perhaps emerges from his use of the word in the context of the conflict between the Jews and Greeks in Caesarea Maritima in the years before the great revolt (Ant., XX, 173).[243]

---

[243] I owe this point to Dr. A. Kasher.

Bearing this solution in mind, we may now return to the situation in Cyrenaica. One important document here furnishes evidence that the Jews of a Greek city were not as a body citizens of the polis. This is the resolution of the Jewish politeuma of Berenice, in honour of M. Tittius (A.D. 24/25).[244] which reads "not only did he manifest himself as accommodating in these matters, but behaved in like manner both towards the citizens whom he encountered privately, and also (ἐτὶ δὲ καί) towards the Jews of our politeuma in matters public and private." The expression ἐτὶ δὲ καί in this text distinguishes clearly between the citizens of Berenice and the members of the Jewish community; there is no doubt that the two groups were regarded as two separate bodies.[245]

It is another question whether a Jew who obtained Greek citizenship remained a member of his politeuma. But in Egypt, at least, a native Egyptian could only be a Roman citizen if he was also a citizen of Alexandria.[246] The politeuma of Berenice certainly had some Roman citizens amongst it,[247] and we may note that Augustus' edict [248] compelled Cyreneans possessing Roman citizenship to assume or maintain their civic responsibilities in the Greek polis. It seems very likely therefore, that on the same principle Jews who held *civitas* either became citizens of the Greek city, or were obliged to continue to bear the responsibilities involved in membership of their politeuma.

As we have seen, some Jewish pupils were already training in the gymnasium of Cyrene in the reign of Augustus; this means they were being accepted as citizens, and the first known Jewish graduates recorded for the year A.D. 2/3 must have begun their education in 7-8 B.C.

The fourfold division of the Cyrenean population reported by Strabo belongs to the first half of the 1st century B.C., and shows that at that time the Jews were not, as a body, Greek citizens. This is also indicated by the reason given by the city for withholding permission from its Jews to despatch the half-shequel payment to

---

[244] *CIG* 5361, 15 sq.

[245] The same interpretation is adopted by Taubenschlag, *The Law of Greco-Roman Egypt in the Light of the Papyri, 332 BC-640 AD*, 1948, p. 19, n. 2.

[246] Plin. *Ep.* x, 6, 10; also *ib.* 7.

[247] Decmus Valerius Dionysius and M. Laelius Onasion.

[248] *SEG* 9, 8, para. III, 56-62.

the Temple of Jerusalem.[249] This was, that the Jews had defaulted
in the payment of certain taxes (τέλη).[250] which indicates that the
community paid them as a body, and not as individuals. This is
clearly not a reference to *tributa*, which were collected and for-
warded by the city: in no case outside Judaea do we hear of Jews
paying *tributa* as a separate body, but here collective responsibility
is inferred, hence city-taxes must be meant. Josephus describing
this or a similar previous incident [251] says that the impounding
of the half-sheqel was an act of "the cities", but even so, M.
Agrippa's letter cited by the historian in connection with the
affair is addressed to Cyrene in particular. According to Josephus,
the Jews complained to Agrippa that the money had been stopped
as the result of the act of informers (συκοφάνται); this may be taken
to mean that certain citizens had risen in the council or assembly of
Cyrene, and claiming that the Jews had defaulted in their tax-
payments, had proposed taking measures against them by delaying
the despatch of the Temple dues. The normal translation of the
words τέλη μὴ ὀφελόμενα is "taxes not owed" because they had
already been paid. But if the Jewish community really owed
taxes, why were informers needed to tell the city so? Informers do
not deal with complete communities, but with individuals, and it is
improbable that even an anti-Semitic polis would have stopped the
despatch of the sheqel merely on account of a few individual
defaulters. For one thing, the Jews believed in the justice of their
cause, otherwise they would not have appealed to higher authority;
for another, the city had reason to think that their charge had
substance. What then was the subject of dispute?

If the city was so certain of its case as to impose sanctions for
non-payment, the meaning of Josephus' τελὴ μὴ ὀφειλόμενα should
be, not "taxes not owed because they had already been paid",
but "taxes not owed because they were being demanded (in the
Jewish view) illegally." As this was a tax for the discharge of which
the Jews were responsible as a group, yet saw themselves as exempt
from it, there are two possible alternatives: either this was an
exceptional imposition to which the Jews had not agreed, or it was

---

[249] Jos. *Ant.*, XVI, 6, 5 (169-170).

[250] *Ibid.* For a detailed discussion of this episode, and of Jewish status
in the Greek cities of the period, see the writer, *The Jewish People in the
First Century*, ed. Safrai, Stern, 1974, I, Chap. viii, pp. 434-454.

[251] *Ant.* XVI, 6, 1 (160).

a regular tax whose payment was now refused by the community. Generally both citizens and non-citizens of Greek cities were liable to pay the same taxes, but alien residents (μέτοικοι, κάτοικοι) paid a special impost (the μετοίκιον), and this only can have been the tax concerned in the present dispute. In other words, the subject of the conflict was the status of the Jews as citizens or non-citizens. Their position, indeed, was sufficiently ambiguous to expose them to attack; as we have seen, Strabo's information tells us that they were neither citizens nor metics. This being the case, the function of the συκοφάνται was to cast doubt on the validity of their status and of their privileges. This analysis, indeed, can be confirmed by Josephus' own account, which relates that Augustus, reasserting the Jewish right to transmit the half-sheqel, granted them τὴν αὐτὴν ἰσοτελείαν (Ant. XVI, 161), indicating that he confirmed an existent status that had been challenged by the city of Cyrene. 'Ισοτελεία, as stated, was exemption of metics from the μετοίκιον. The Jews, though not citizens, were exempt from this tax; they were in fact especially privileged aliens, and the Greeks of Cyrene saw no reason why, if they annually sent large sums of money out of the state, they should enjoy such exemption, which gave them a status superior to that of the Greek metics. We do not know whether as a result of Augustus' confirmation the opportunity was also given to certain Cyrenean Jews to obtain full citizen status. But there are some hints that such was the case.

In the first half of the century, on Strabo's evidence, the Jews did not possess citizenship in Cyrene. The year when Agrippa confirmed this right to send the half-sheqel, is not known; in Juster's opinion [252] it was between 23 and 13 B.C., when Agrippa was in charge of the Near East, and issued a similar order on the half-sheqel to the city of Ephesus. He died in 13 B.C. Agrippa himself refers in his letter to a previous instruction on the matter sent by Augustus to Flavius, governor of Crete and Cyrene; [253] probably, then, his second instruction was given nearer to the year 13. At Ptolemais we find Jews as ephebes as early as 3/2 B.C., hence they had begun their education in the gymnasium in 13 B.C. approximately. In Cyrene Jews had begun to obtain the same education by 7/6 B.C.

On this evidence, Agrippa's letter was sent to the Cyrene author-

---

[252] Les Juifs dans l'Empire romaine, I, 1914, p. 150 and n. 3.
[253] Ant. XVI, 6, 5 (169).

ities not long before his death, and it would seem that in this or
another order issued in connection with the same problem Augustus
(probably with Agrippa's advice) decided that a number of Jews of
Cyrene, Ptolemais, and perhaps of the other Pentapolis towns,
could acquire Greek citizenship. Such an order would indeed
have been appropriate to Augustus' general eastern policy in those
years, for between 2 B.C. and A.D. 2 he reconfirmed by a general
declaration the internal rights of the Jewish organizations throughout the Empire.[254] Josephus reports this confirmation immediately
after mentioning for the first time the attempts of the cities of
Cyrene and Asia to prevent the transfer of the Temple dues.

Further light is thrown on the status of the Jews of Cyrene in the
1st century A.D. by an inscription of the nomophylakes of Cyrene,
published in 1961.[255] This is a dedication by the nomophylakes of
the city to some deity (the stone is broken below and its lower part
has been severely damaged). It belongs to the years 60 and 61 of
the current era, opening with a date and the names of the priest of
Apollo who is completing his term of office, and of his successor.
There follow the names of ten or eleven and perhaps additional
nomophylakes. As the inscription records these posts for two years,
and other known dedications of this class do not mention more
than nine and generally fewer persons. it may be deduced that the
names here represent two successive colleges of magistrates, each
of which functioned for a year. In this case Eleazar son of Jason,
who is listed second on the list of nomophylakes, served in the
year 60.

To the best of my knowledge this is, with one possible exception,[256]
the first Jew serving as a senior magistrate in a Greek polis who can
be identified as a Jew. It may be supposed that he had not re-
nounced his faith, since he did not follow a common fashion of
changing his name to a Greek one, as did many Cyrenean Jews—
including some active in their communities—who, as we have
seen, bore purely Greek names. It is probably right to suppose that
Eleazar belonged to the local Jewish aristocracy, and that his
ancestors had reached Cyrene in the hellenistic period.[257]

---

[254] *Ant.* XVI, 6, 2 (162).

[255] *QAL* 4, 1961, p. 16, no. 2.

[256] In Asia Minor Jews appear as city-magistrates in the 3rd century
A.D. after the Constitutio Antoniniana—cf. especially *CIJ* 788 (Corycus)
and 760 (Blaundos).

[257] The name Ele'azar (Elasaros) was common among Cyrenean Jews in

The complete dedications of the Cyrenean nomophylakes [258] known hitherto were dedicated respectively to Apollo Nomios, Homonoia and Aphrodite (two), and all belonged to the period of Augustus. Four of them were found in a hall situated to south of the Agora, separated from it by a small building through which the hall was entered. On the floor of the latter were discovered 4,000 stamped pyramidal clay seals (cretulae), of the sort made to be attached to documents and certificates.[259] This was, therefore, the city's registry, which was administered, as the inscriptions showed, by the nomophylakes. The hall communicated south-eastward with a building of no great size possessing a two-storeyed colonnade on its north front, repaired in the reign of Domitian.[260] North of it an alley-way led into the nomophylakeion by a side door, but the nomophylakeion itself was much older, and was apparently built before the hellenistic period. The interior of its hall elicited clear signs of burning, the result of a conflagration at an unknown date.[261]

The college of nomophylakes at Cyrene varied from six to nine members, and they were aided if necessary by three scribes (γραμματεῖς), whom Ghislanzoni [262] considered as belonging to the college. These magistrates are first heard of in the constitution of Ptolemy Lagos, at the end of the 4th century B.C., when their

---

the Hellenistic period. It appears four times in Egypt on inscriptions (Tcherikover, *Jews in Egypt* [2], p. 186; cf. *CPJ*, I, p. 84). It occurs twice in Cyrene (*QAL* 4, no. 7, 48). It is interesting to find that the hellenistic writer Lobon (*FHG* III, para. 209) mentions the Libyan king of Barka, Aladdeir (*CIG* 5147; Herodot. IV, 164, 4) under the form 'Ελεάζαρ, which perhaps reflects Jewish influence among the Libyans.

[258] E. Ghislanzoni, *RAL*[6] I, 1925, pp. 406 sqq.; I Νομοφύλακες di Cirene; *SEG* 9, 131-5.

[259] For examples elsewhere, *DS* II[2], 1483.

[260] *RAL*[6] I, p. 420; *AE* 1927, no. 142. The name of the proconsul Didius Gallus is incised on the architrave of the building; this man restored public land to the city of Ptolemais in A.D. 88 (cf. *CR*, p. 101). The Cyrene structure resembles the Tabularium at Rome, hence its proximity to the Nomophylakeion creates the impression that it served as a land-registry.

[261] The signs of burning on the interior of the walls pass behind the pilasters, which were inserted at a secondary stage in the building's history to support the walls. The placques recording the nomophylakes of the time of Augustus were incorporated into the pilasters. It is therefore logical to suppose that the conflagration that damaged the building occurred in the hellenistic period. This possibility is ignored by G. Madolle, Les cretales del Nomophylakion di Cirene, *ASAA*, 41-42, 1965, pp. 39 sqq.

[262] *Loc. cit.*, p. 427.

number was fixed at nine.[263] They were then appointed from the electorate of ten thousand, and signed the constitution together with the priest of Apollo, six strategoi, the five ephors and the four nomothetae; one of the last officials was also a nomophylax. This fact and the dedication to Apollo Nomios make it clear that the functions of the nomophylakes included the recording of the city's laws, and probably their drafting. Their post may indeed have been created earlier, if Pernier was right in identifying ten names incised on the lintel of the Temple of Artemis in the mid-4th century B.C., as belonging to the same magistrates.[264]

Everything then known of these magistrates was assembled in 1925 by Ghislanzoni.[265] In the classical and hellenistic periods their duties varied: in late 4th-century Athens, in the period of anti-democratic reaction, they wielded a right of vetoing the acts of the magistrates and popular assembly; at Sparta they were responsible for the state records; at Elis, where they were called "Thesmothetae", they administered to the bearers of office the oath of loyalty to the alliance with Athens; at Corcyra in the 2nd century B.C. they were in charge of sacred and public funds, as they appear to have been at Thespiae in about 200 B.C.; at Chios they assigned new citizens to their tribes and trittyes. They recorded the decisions of the government at Abdera, also appointing ambassadors and reimbursing them for their expenses. At Pergamum in the hellenistic period they supervised the magistrates and were authorized to fine them for neglect of duty or abuse of powers; they also recorded legislation. In these functions they correspond to the accounts of Xenophon [266] and Cicero,[267] who define their duties as supervision of the proper implementation of the laws. Aristotle [268] characterizes the nomophylakes as typical of oligarchies, in which they exercized a "pro-bouleutic" function, and elsewhere [269] states that they are appropriate to aristocratic régimes. The post continued to exist in the Roman period, especially in the cities of Asia Minor, where it retained a measure of importance and much the same character.[270]

---

[263] *SEG* 9, 1, 78-82.
[264] *TA*, p. 95.
[265] *Loc. cit.*, pp. 427 sqq.
[266] *Oecon.*, IX, 14.
[267] *De legibus*, III, 20, 46.
[268] *Polit.*, IV, 1298b.
[269] *Ibid.* VI, 1323a.
[270] A. H. M. Jones, *The Greek City*, 1940, p. 329.

To sum up, the duties of the nomphylakes were connected with registration and recording, with finance and with supervision over the proper administration of the laws. Their connection with the records and registration is proved at Cyrene equally by archaeological and epigraphical evidence. Accordingly a man elected to this post must be imagined to have been a capable administrator, knowledgeable in the law and of sufficient moral courage to impose observance of the law when it was abused by the magistrates. The members of this college discharged in some measure the modern tasks of town clerk and state comptroller.

We know little of the constitution of Cyrene in the Roman period; whether or not changes were introduced into the Ptolemaic constitution in the time of Demophanes and Ecdalus,[271] it may be supposed that no radical democratization took place, while after the counter-revolution of Aretaphila the régime was pronouncedly aristocratic, headed, apparently, by the High Priest of Apollo. It is difficult to imagine that Lucullus altered these fundamentals, or that the rights of the common people were enlarged with the inauguration of Roman rule; Rome generally confirmed the political *status quo*, and if she intervened in the class-struggle which raged in the Greek cities, threw her weight onto the scales on the side of the well-to-do.[272] In view of this, when Agrippa addressed his letter (according to Josephus) to "the magistrates, council and people of Cyrene" (Κυρηναίων ἄρχουσιν βουλῇ δήμῳ),[273] the greeting can be regarded as no more than a convention; more decisive is the complete silence of Cyrenean inscriptions of the imperial period as to any democratic institution in the city. Nor can the formula used in the dedication to Germanicus at Ptolemais in the year A.D. 19, δῆμος Πτολεμαιέων,[274] furnish a different conclusion. It may safely be assumed that the power in the Cyrenean cities in the 1st centuries B.C. and A.D. remained in the hands of the wealthy, even if the skeletons of the ancient institutions were preserved. It follows, that in general lines the timocratic basis of government continued to hold good, hence it is improbable that more than a

---

[271] Stucchi (*Cirene*, p. 170) publishes an inscription from the Agora (*ibid.* no. 23) which records an eponymous priest of Apollo and six ephors in the 3rd or 2nd century BC, instead of the usual five; this suggests an unusual situation which probably involved the city's constitution.

[272] Jones, *op. cit.*, pp. 120-1; Griffiths, Tarn, *HC³* pp. 123-5.

[273] Jos., *Ant.* XVI, 6, 5 (169).

[274] *CIG* 5186.

minority of well-to-do Jews was admitted to citizenship at the end of the 1st century before the common era.

Of the Jews in this period, then, we know three things; they took an active part in political life, since round about 88 B.C. they were involved in some internal conflict (στάσις), of whose nature we are ignorant; [275] about the same time they held a position intermediate between metics and citizens in the city; [276] and they were forced to defend this status in the last decades of the century.[277] At this time, when the importance of the nomophylakes had increased in the city, evidently as a result of the aristocratic trend in government and the special association of these magistrates with such régimes, as noted by Aristotle, the Jews were in conflict with the polis. But in the course of several decades the position had changed somewhat; the Greek and Jewish aristocracies had reached an accommodation, expressed in the admission to citizenship of the latter, and in the subsequent appointment of Eleazar son of Jason to a highly responsible government board, for whose work men of knowledge commanding the public confidence were required.

Josephus, in his account of the events of the year A.D. 73, states that there were then 3,000 well-to-do Jews in the city (εὔπο-ροι).[278] Even among the Cyrenean civic body, which was of considerable size as fixed by Ptolemy Lagos, and numbered 10,000 members,—but was probably smaller in the Roman period—the Jewish element may have carried considerable weight. Josephus' figures are seldom reliable, and in this case his 3,000 Jews may have included the Jewish upper class of the entire Pentapolis, yet even this supposition would do little to alter the position, for one can hardly attribute to Cyrene less than a third of Josephus' 3,000 well-to-do members. If we add the Jews of lesser status, who were certainly numerous—for they survived to create the revolt of 115—we shall begin to understand the reason for the tension prevailing at Cyrene in the 1st century A.D., which ultimately produced the great explosion under Trajan.

---

[275] Plut., *Luc.*, 2: Strabo ap. Jos., *Ant.*, XIV, 7, 2 (114); see below pp. 202-3 sqq.

[276] Ap. *Ant.*, *loc. cit.* (115).

[277] *Ant.*, XVI, 6, 5 (169-70).

[278] *BJ* VII, 11, 2 (445).

8. The Organization of the Communities

Having learned something of the civic status of the Jews of Cyrenaica, we must sketch what is known of their internal organization. The right to an internal organization which enabled the Jews to maintain their ancestral customs and commandments, was recognized throughout the diaspora of the hellenistic and Roman periods. In the Greek cities of the hellenistic monarchies the Jews received such recognition because the variegated and cosmopolitan composition of these towns influenced both their rulers and the city authorities to accept voluntary organizations of aliens, soldiers, craftsmen, followers of various cults and other types of association within their general frameworks. The Roman Empire permitted the existence of such bodies, but took care that they should not possess any political content. The Jewish bodies, indeed, went beyond the functional terms of reference of most of the other politeumata of the hellenistic monarchies and the Greek cities, since besides the functions of welfare, cult or simple social enjoyment performed by the other societies, the Jewish bodies performed two more: they administered a system of justice based on Jewish law, and exercized the right of sending the contributions of their members to the Temple of Jerusalem. These functions also involved the recognition on the part of the government of certain tacit privileges, namely, the right not to worship the deities of the city or the monarchy (or, under Rome, the Capitoline triad and the Genius of the Emperor), and the right not to appear in court on Sabbaths or festivals.[279] These privileges gave rise to broader practical corollaries beyond the religious and social spheres, such as the ineligibility of observant Jews to serve in the municipalities of their cities. The internal autonomy of the Jews of the Diaspora in the period concerned found practical expression in the erection

---

[279] Despite the statements of some scholars, I do not think that there is specific evidence that the Jews of the Roman Empire enjoyed a general exemption in military service. Such exemption was given on several occasions in Asia Minor to Jews possessing Roman citizenship, and then in the special circumstances of civil war in the late republican period. The fewness of Jews from the Roman army in the 1st and 2nd centuries AD was caused principally by political factors, and in the 3rd and 4th centuries they are found serving in the imperial forces. For some cases in the 1st and 2nd centuries, see the author, *The Katz Memorial Volume*, (*Commentationes ad Antiquitatem Classicam Pertinentes*), 1970, pp. 3 sqq.; for my general views on the question, *Roman Frontier Studies* 1967, 1971, pp. 181 sqq.; *The Jewish People in the First Century*, ed. Safrai, Stern, 1974, I, pp. 458-60.

of buildings (prayer-houses, assembly places, hostels and the like), in the maintenance of of burial places, in the exercise of internal jurisdiction, the collection of money, in welfare work, and in the maintenance of registries and the administrative machinery required by all the above functions. The evidence of such activities in Cyrenaica is not abundant, nor does it illustrate them all.

Communal Institutions. Specific evidence on the details of organization is to be found only at Berenice, where the organized body is called a πολίτευμα in the years 8 B.C.[280] and A.D. 24/5; [281] in A.D. 56, it is called συναγωγή.[282]

The interference with the despatch of the Temple moneys under Augustus is ascribed by Josephus to "the cities" of Cyrenaica.[283] This ascription suffices to indicate what could have been assumed— that organized Jewish communities existed in each of the chief cities of the country (Cyrene, Berenice, Ptolemais, Apollonia, Teucheira and perhaps Barka). This may be confirmed by the words of the same account,[284] "and if the sacred money of any of the cities has been seized" (καὶ εἰ τινῶν ἱερὰ χρήματα ἀφήρηνται τῶν πόλεων); this is clearly a corrupt text, but the Latin translation reads, instead of *civitatium, civium*, showing that the original had read πολῖτων instead of πόλεων—and, as we have seen, the members of Jewish politeumata were also known as πολῖται (see p. 182).

In Book XIV of the *Antiquities*,[285] Josephus calls the Jewish communities of Egypt and Libya συντάγματα. This is an interesting term, normally used for military formations, and certainly points to the strongly organized character of the Jewish groups in Cyrenaica.[286] The Jewish tombs of Teucheira may legitimately be understood to mean that there was an organized Jewish community in the city.

---

[280] See p. 160.
[281] *CIG* 5361.
[282] *SEG* 17, 823; *REG* 72, 1959, pp. 275-6; *PP* 12, 1957, pp. 132 sqq.; *BIES* 25, 1965, pp. 167 sqq.
[283] *Ant.* XVI, 6, 1 (160): "The cities had dealt evilly with the Jews. . ."
[284] *Ant.* XVI, 6, 5 (169).
[285] XIV, 7, 2 (116).
[286] Eg. P. Petr. III, 14, 17: ὁ δεῖνα Κυρηναῖος τῶν Ἰδαίου σύνταγμα κληροῦχος. The other meanings of the word (political constitution, social class—F. Passow, *Handwörterbuch der griechischen Sprache*, 1857, ad voc.) are not appropriate in this context.

Procopius' report [287] of a Jewish "temple" at Boreion (Βόρειον), the modern Bu-Grada on the shore of the Syrtis between Augila and Ajedabia,[288] can be interpreted to mean that corporate Jewish communities existed at other points in Cyrenaica beside the five towns. Moreover the Berenice Jewish inscription of A.D. 56 calls the congregation ἡ συναγωγὴ τῶν ἐν Βερνικίδι᾽Ιουδαίων; this form of the city's name applied not only to the city, but also to its territory (χώρα), i.e. to its rural area.[289] It may therefore be inferred that Jews who lived in the country area round the city also belonged to the latter's politeuma, and the same principle may be applied equally to the other more important settlements of the country.

Only the Berenice inscriptions furnish any information on the officers of the Jewish corporations of the country. These show that the communal leaders here were the archons, whose number grew from seven in the period of 7-8 B.C., to nine in A.D. 24/5, and to ten in A.D. 56. The names of these magistrates, who formed a board possessed of both initiative and executive powers, headed the recorded decisions taken by the general meeting of the community (the politeuma), and in A.D. 56 by the synagogue. The names of the archons head the list of contributors, followed by a priest and concluding with the names of several female congregants. The community meets on sabbaths, on the first day of each month, and on festivals. The politeuma further imposes liturgies and confers honours upon both Jewish and gentile benefactors. The second Berenice inscription and the incidents affecting the half-sheqel show, that the wardens conducted negotiations with Roman officials and sent complaints to the authorities. The politeuma seems also to have borne responsibility for the defrayment of certain taxes to the city.

Places of Prayer. The Jewish place of worship in Berenice in A.D. 56 was known as the synagogue, and this word contemporarily denoted both the community and the building. A fragment of a marble stele found at Cyrene and published in 1963 bore a Greek inscription including the two words [τ]ὴν συναγωγ[ήν]; its letter-

---

[287] *de Aedif.*, VI, 2 (B 334).

[288] R. G. Goodchild, *JRS* 41, 1951, pp. 11 sqq.; *Antiq.* 25, 1951, pp. 132, 140, 143; *GJ* 118, 1952, p. 9.

[289] Cf. the forms Thebais, Argolis and the like.

style dated it to the 1st century B.C. while the appearance of the
Roman name Dekmos shows that the inscription was incised after
the beginning of Roman rule.[290] The fragment preserved belonged
to the righthand side of the top of the stele, comprising four lines of
private names, while the fifth mentioned the synagogue. The upper
edge of the stone was rounded off by a moulding, over which were
remains of a curved plant-tendril or stalk, and a leaf; it is evident
that the head of the stele took the form of a pediment. The legible
names are Dekmos, Sosandros, Teimarchos and Leonides, and the
accusative form of the word συναγωγή implies that we have here
the commemoration of people who had aided in the repair or
building of the edifice. We cannot be completely certain that the
dedicators were Jews, but the form of the stele, which resembles
two of the Berenice resolutions, is in favour of a Jewish identity.

On the other hand P. M. Fraser has published another fragmentary inscription found at Cyrene,[291] dedicated to Ptolemy
Euergetes II and referring to the erection of an unidentified building and its συ[γκύροντα] or annexes, a word used in Egypt in this
period for the outbuildings of a Jewish prayerhouse; [292] accordingly
he proposed that the Cyrenean dedication was probably that of a
Jewish synagogue.[293] Unfortunately the places where the two
above inscriptions were found have not been recorded, and the
building south of the Wadi Belgadir, opposite the Agora, which
this writer tentatively suggested might be a synagogue,[293] has
turned out on excavation to be an early temenos devoted to Demeter.[294] It is nevertheless still possible that the Jewish quarter of
the city ought to be looked for to south of the Agora, as here was
found the fragmentary Jewish lamp to be described below (pp.
234sq.), and another of similar type has since been recovered in the
Agora itself.[295]

It is natural to assume that the ancient "temple" referred to by
Procopius at Boreion in the south of the country, where the Jewish

---

[290] *ASAA* 39-40, 1961-2, p. 288, no. 166, fig. 88.
[291] *SEG* 18, 738; *Berytus*, 12, 1958, pp. 115-6, no. 8.
[292] *CPJ* III, no. 1442.
[293] *IEJ* 7, 1957, pp. 157 sqq.; ct. *Zion*, 19, 1954, p. 43, no. 15 (Heb.).
[294] R. Goodchild, *Kyrene und Apollonia*, pp. 163 sqq.
[295] Stucchi, *Cirene*, p. 163; *Agora di Cirene*, I, p. 277; tav. xlv, 5b. Slouschz,
My Travels in Libya (Heb., II, 227), saw a hill called Ḥoreb el-Yahud to
west of the city. According to the map of the route taken by him, however,
(*ibid.*, p. 230) this was southward, but all memory of the name appears to
have vanished in the district, and I was unable to identify the site.

inhabitants were forced to adopt Christianity by Justinian, was a synagogue. The building became a church. This community possessed a tradition that their "temple" was established in the time of King Solomon.[296]

Halls of Council and Assembly. As we have seen, the Berenice community possessed in the 1st century B.C. a place of assembly called an amphitheatre. We do not know if it was identical with the prayerhouse or near it, but it is natural to suppose from what was normal in the hellenistic world—and the Berenice Jews were profoundly assimilated to Greek culture, to judge by their inscriptions, their procedures and the amphitheatre itself—that the building stood in the vicinity of the place of prayer, and was even connected with it.[297]

9. The Jews of Cyrenaica in the Rural Areas

As most of the evidence is indirect, it may be well to sum up the grounds for supposing that a considerable section of the Jews of Cyrenaica were settled on the land outside the cities in the hellenistic and early Roman periods. Attention has already been drawn [298] to the close connection seen by Josephus between the Jewish settlement in the country and their settlement in Egypt, nor does papyrology leave room for doubt that a considerable portion of Egyptian Jewry lived on the countryside in the Ptolemaic and earlier Roman periods, engaged in agriculture and made a valuable contribution both to the armed forces of Egypt and to its military cultivators.[299] It has further been noted that the juridical situation in the Greek polis was such as to oblige immigrants who took up agriculture to settle on land outside the city territories, since the right of acquiring city-land was rarely granted to non-citizens. The Cyrenean prejudice against trade and the crafts throughout the hellenistic period, on the other hand, would have ensured that those Jews who acquired citizenship at the beginning of the Roman period would have been owners of land.

---

[296] See p. 131.

[297] Eg. the council-house of Miletus is near the Delpheion, that of Priene opposite the Temple of Zeus; the Bouleuterion in the Athenian agora in the 3rd century B.C. stood behind the temple of the Cybele.

[298] See principally the introduction to Chap. IV, pp. 131 sqq.

[299] For details, Tcherikover, *Jews in Egypt*, pp. 30-63; *HCJ*, pp. 334 sqq.; *CPJ* I, pp. 147 sqq.

Additional evidence of the residence of Jews in the rural areas of the country is furnished by the Greek expressions used in a number of sources to describe the Jewish community; for example, in the *Acts*: "the Jews who live in the districts of Libya about Cyrene" (καὶ τὰ μέρη τῆς Λιβύης τῆς κατὰ Κυρήνην).[300] This phrase is translated into Latin as "Libyae quae est circa Cyrenen", and is also found in Eusebius—καὶ προσέτι κατὰ Κυρήνην οἱ Ἰουδαῖοι.[301] We find a parallel expression in Josephus: καὶ ὅσους (sc. Ἰουδαίους) ἡ πρὸς Κυρήνην Λιβύη κατέσχεν,[302] This form clearly refers to the Jews outside the city of Cyrene, and that this was so is testified by the following examples, drawn from ancient literature and epigraphy and applying to Cyrenaica: Augustus calls the province of Cyrene in his edicts τῆι κατὰ τὴν Κυρήνη ἐπαρχήαι;[303] the Ptolemaic governor in charge of the Libyan tribal regions is described as ὁ Λιβυάρχης τῶν κατὰ Κυρήνην τόπων;[304] the inhabitants of the port of Apollonia term themselves Ἀπολλωνιᾶται κατὰ Κυρήνην;[305] and the Libyan tribes outside the territory of Cyrene are referred to in an inscription of the 1st century B.C. as τὰ κατὰ τὰν χώραν ἔθνεα.[306] A similar conclusion may be drawn from the appearance of the form Βερνικίς in the inscription of the Jewish community of that city in A.D. 56, since this form possesses a suffix which denotes the entire city-land. An isolated confirmation of the evidence relating to Cyrene comes from Severus of Ashmunein's Coptic *Lives of the Patriarchs of Alexandria*, which reports that the parents of the evangelist Mark were Jewish peasants from the neighbourhood of Cyrene.[307]

Our detailed examination of the remains of the Jewish community of Teucheira, dated between the 2nd century B.C. and the 2nd century A.D. (Ch. IV) concluded that the main nucleus of this group was composed of cleruchs or katoikoi settled here by the Ptolemies; their residence about the city is made probable by the information that the entire coastal plain between Teucheira and Bengazi lay waste and in need of resettlement after the revolt of

---

[300] *Acts*, 2:10.
[301] Eus., *HE*, IV, 2, 2,
[302] *Ant*. XVI, 6, 1 (160).
[303] *SEG* 9, 8, 36.
[304] Polyb. XV, 25, 12: Λιβυάρχην τῶν κατὰ Κυρήνην τόπων.
[305] *IG¹* II, 3407.
[306] *AA* 1962 (iii), p. 437, f. ii; and see here pp. 63-4 and p. 203, n. 3.
[307] Cited by Goodchild, *Kyr. u. Apoll.*, p. 31, n. 33.

115-117. Elsewhere (p. 170) we have assembled evidence concerning 'Ein Targhuna, and concluded that this was a settlement of Jewish military agricultural settlers. Greek epitaphs including Jewish names are also known at al-Bagga, on the coast east of Ptolemais,[308] At the other end of the country, in the Martuba area, is a second point, whose exact locality has not been identified, called Topos Magdalis (Τόπος Μαγδαλίς), recorded in a survey of lands and property of the late 2nd century A.D.[309] Papyrology provides evidence that settlements with similar names in Egypt were inhabited by immigrants from Syria, including Jews, in the Ptolemaic period and even earlier.[310] Several other indications confirm the impression that a Jewish village-population existed in eastern Cyrenaica. A Jewish gnostic cameo found at Regensburg bears several names, including the word Ἴαβοχ,[311] which appears to be the Ἰοββαχ recorded by Papyrus Vatican 11 (the property survey already mentioned) in the Martuba region,[312] and here was also located the Βασσαχέιως Παρατόμη,[313] which must be reflected in the name of the Jewish woman Βεῖσχα buried at Teucheira.[314]

The memory of another Jewish settlement of the Cyrenean countryside reaches us from an unexpected quarter. Its name, which is Semitic, tells us that it was in a rural area: this is the Καπφάροδος or Καπφάροδις referred to by Synesius at the end of the 4th century A.D.;[315] the name appears to conceal the Hebrew words "kefar ḥadash" (כפר חדש) or "new village".

Reports or unauthenticated information are to hand of other rural sites where Jewish finds have been made, and there is no point in listing them here.[316] But it were well to refer to the Jewish settle-

---

[308] Λιδ´ Τερτία Ἰώσητος (ἔτων) μ´ Ἰώσης (ἔτων) κε´. I am indebted to Miss Joyce Reynolds for information on this inscription and its text.

[309] Παρατομὴ Μαγδαλειτῶν: NV I, 35; IV, 12/15; Ptol. IV, 5: Μασαδαλίς.

[310] Jerem., 44:1; P. Würz. inv. 5; P. Ent., 23; Tcherikover, Jews in Egypt, pp. 14, 19, 22; CPJ I, p. 4, n. 12.

[311] CIJ I, 673, 13.

[312] NV VI, 28/30.

[313] Ibid.

[314] See above; SEG 9, 703, and cf. the destruction of the temple south of el-Dab'ah in Marmarica in the rebellion of 115-7—see p. 290.

[315] Synes., Ep. 6; Migne PG 66, col. 1544, vi, para. 169.

[316] Professor Slouschz saw menorot incised on rockcut tombs at Messa (K. Friedmann, Misc. Stud . . . Chajes, p. 47). Near Lamluda he recorded a Hebrew inscription "Simon Samuel" (op. cit., p. 47, no. 11); one of my Italian antiquities workers told me of the discovery of a Hebrew inscription at the same site, and showed me where it was found, but nothing is now to

ment of Iscina Locus Augusti Iudaeorum near Medinat es-Sultan,
west of Cyrenaica on the coast of the Syrtis; this place will be
discussed later, but it is relevant to mention, that considerable
signs of ancient field-boundaries [317] are to be seen there, and it
can hardly be doubted that this remote settlement supported itself
on agriculture.

Of some significance for our subject is the Jewish influence
alleged to have existed among the Libyan tribes mainly in the
Byzantine period and at the beginning of the Arab conquest. This
influence began long before the Byzantine epoch, and was not
one-sided, as appears from the evidence of the Teucheira tombs;
nor would it have been possible if Jews had not been dispersed over
the country's rural areas. It is therefore relevant to reiterate that
the evidence at Teucheira is in any case in favour of the association
of Jews with agricultural settlement. The indications of close
contact between Jews and Libyans are also traceable in the Barka
plain, in the view of some scholars; the earliest trace may be the
conversion of the Libyan name Aladdeir ('Αλάδδειρ), king at
Barka in the time of Arkesilaos III,[318] (his descendants being
resident in the city in the 3rd century B.C.),[319]—to Eleazar ('Ελεάζαρ) in the writings of the hellenistic writer Lobon.[320]

The French scholar Gautier noted [321] that the Berber tribes of
the 7th century were divided into the Bernes and the Botr, the
latter being the Zenata, who lived in the Aurez mountains, and
were attached, according to Ibn Khaldoun,[322] to Judaism. The
Jerwa and their renowned Queen Diḥiyah al-Cahina,[323] belonged to
the same group. The Botr had two sub-divisions, the Luata and
the Nafusah,[324] whose descendants still inhabit the caves of Jebel

---

be seen. G. Narducci claimed to have seen Jewish antiquities at Driana
(near the ancient Hadrianopolis) but could not remember their character.
Hypogaea exist in this vicinity, one with the inscription Λυκύ[ας], a very
common name among Jews in Cyrene. (*AJA* 17, 1913, p. 183, no. 70; at
Apollonia; *SEG* 9, 624 and *JHS* 28, 1908, p. 199, no. 36 at Teucheira; *Zion*,
19, 1954, p. 42, no. 7, at Cyrene; cf. Eus. *HE* IV, 2).

[317] Goodchild, *GJ* 118, 1952, p. 146.
[318] Herod. IV, 164, 4.
[319] *CIG* 5147; cf. *BMC*, pp. clxiv; clxxxi.
[320] Müller, *FHG*, III, para. 209.
[321] *Les siècles obscurs du Maghreb*, 1927, pp. 201 sqq.
[322] Ibn Khaldoun, *History of the Berbers*, trans. de Slane, 1852-6, I, p. 168.
[323] *Op. cit.*, I, p. 208.
[324] *Ibid.*, pp. 170 sq.; 226 sq.

a-Nefusah on the Syrtic coast.[325] The Luata on the other hand, were derived from the Barka region,[326] and Gautier [327] is of the opinion that the tribal federation of the Zenata (i.e. the Botr) and their attachment to Judaism, were formed in the time of Trajan. But we shall see later that the Judaism of the Botr tribes has been subjected to sharp and negative criticism.

Finally, any consideration of the evidence for Jewish rural settlement in Roman Cyrenaica, must take into account the Arab tradition of Jewish occupation at a number of country-sites now virtually abandoned. Traditions of this sort are associated with ʿEin-Shaḥat (Cyrene), Lamluda, Messa, Negharnes, al-Gubba and Gasr ibn-Igdem, all known to be ancient settlements.[328] The name Ḥirbet al-Yahud is also found at several rural sites: such are ʿEin Targhuna, Siret al-Daḥar al-Aḥmar on the Tocra pass; Al-Asgafa (east of Bengazi), and Lamluda. The name al-Yahudiyeh survives near Sauro north of Barka,[329] while between here and the sea the names Ras e-Sabbat and Kaf e-Sabbat occur.

That these traditions preserve a historical nucleus is demonstrated by examples outside Cyrenaica: one is Ḥirbet al-Yahud, ascribed by the Arabs to the fortress of Bethar in Judaea; [330] others are Tell al-Yehudiyeh in Egypt, attached to the fortified temple of Onias (Leontopolis) [331] and Gasr bint al-Yehudi, associated with the Egyptian fortress of Tahpanhes, where Jews lived at the time of the Prophet Jeremiah.[332] The degree of truth in the name-tradition is demonstrated in Cyrenaica itself at ʿEin Targhuna. Such traditions, however, may reflect more than one period, and some may have grown up after the hellenistic and Roman periods. Such a possibility applies, for example, to the local Jewish tradition which holds that al-Fayyidiyeh, south of Cyrene, was the Rephidim of the Book of Exodus (XI, 1); here an ancient Hebrew tombstone has been found, to be dated, it would seem, after the Byzantine epoch.[333] A similar tradition identifies ʿEin

---

[325] Gautier, op. cit., p. 204.

[326] Ibn Khaldoun, op. cit., p. 232; cf. ibid. Appendix, I, p. 301.

[327] Op. cit., p. 201.

[328] N. Slouschz, Hébréo-Phéniciens et Judéo-Berbères, 1908, p. 463.

[329] M. Avi-Yonah, Palestine and Near East Economic Magazine, 14 (i), p. 11.

[330] ZDPV 56, 1933, p. 180; plan xii.

[331] W. F. Petrie, Egypt and Israel, pp. 102 sq.

[332] Jerem. 43:8-9; Petrie, op. cit., p. 91.

[333] The inscription has been published, but not quite accurately, by Gray,

Mara in the eastern Jebel (the ancient village of Hydrax), with the place of the same name that occurs in Genesis XV, 23, and Messa with the Masah of Genesis, XVII, 7.[334] Even if the resemblance of later names with those of the Bible caused the identification,— and we are bound to ask why such Semitic names should be present there in the first place—the al-Fayyidiyeh tombstone shows that they reflect, in given cases, actual Jewish occupation at some period or other.

---

and stated erroneously to be from Cyrene. (*MUC* 1952, pp. 56-7). The stone is not earlier than the 12th or 13th century according to Gray. Al-Fayyidiyeh is still a meeting place of Beduin tribes. For traces of ancient settlement and ancient field-systems here, see Mühlhofer, *Spelealogica Cirenaica*, p. 15.

[334] Slouschz, *My Travels*, II, p. 221.

CHAPTER FIVE

THE BACKGROUND OF THE JEWISH REVOLT

The period of transition of Cyrenaica from Ptolemaic rule to a thoroughgoing Roman administration was marked by two events, an understanding of which is important to our theme. These events were the social conflict revealed by the rising of Nicocrates and the revolution of Arataphila on the one hand, and the transfer of the Ptolemaic royal lands to the Roman state on the other.

Following the civil war which ended with the inauguration of an aristocratic régime at Cyrene by Arataphila in the years between 91 and 82 B.C., a Jewish *stasis* broke out. The word "stasis" may denote either a rising on the part of the entire Jewish group, or conflict between one section of the Jewish community and the rest of it. As we have no details of the affair, any explanation must be in the sphere of conjecture, yet an examination of the general contemporary background may cast some light on its significance. As mentioned above, the decade in which the rising of Nicocrates broke out at Cyrene was a stormy one; in the year 88 B.C. a civil war was raging in the Egyptian Thebais, one of a series of revolts by the lower classes of the Egyptian populace, more especially the peasants, caused by the general conditions imposed by the Ptolemaic régime. The same year beheld the beginning of the war of Mithradates king of Pontus against Rome, a war accompanied by violent social conflict, risings of debtors to throw off the yoke of debt, and of slaves to free themselves from their masters. In Italy the embers of the Social War still flickered, while the struggle between the party of the wealthy and the Populares continued, sharpened by monetary crisis and widespread indebtedness. On the sea, an unprecedented proliferation of piracy was nurtured by the same social privations. An investigation of Cyrene's agrarian plight (Ch. III) has revealed that in the later 2nd century B.C. there were signs of agrarian crisis, and documents indicate a fall of agricultural production, while rural disturbances are deducible from the edicts of Euergetes II or Soter II.

It may be supposed that this crisis also furnished the conditions of the severe struggle between the Cyrenean aristocracy and the

broad strata of the people, which reached a stage of violence several
years after the end of Ptolemaic rule. The question is, did these
antagonisms find an echo among the Jewish community, when
Lucullus arrived in Cyrene? One aspect that may assist a solution
of the question is the fact that we hear faint reports of anti-Jewish
disorders in Alexandria in the same year.[1] Even if we are not in
a position to decide whether what occurred at Cyrene was a clash
between Jews and Greeks or between two Jewish factions, either
would fit the situation of civil strife and economic crisis in which
social ferment was apt to seek an outlet in inter-community hatred
as a substitute for class-hatred. But the synchronization of the
phenomenon in both places—each important as a Jewish centre—
possesses historical significance in so far as it proves the unity of
public mood and of the social setting in both cities, and, despite the
difficulties of communication over distances in those days, shows
that the use of analogy is permissible in order to understand
events in the various eastern Mediterranean centres of the period.
If then we face two possibilities—the hatred of gentiles for Jews, or
antagonisms within the Jewish group itself,—we may note that the
events in Alexandria are decisively in favour of the first interpretation, while Josephus' language derived from Strabo that "(Sulla)
sent Lucullus . . . against the stasis of our people . . . at Cyrene",[2]
supports it. If so, it is possible that the Jews had fallen out with
the aristocratic régime of Arataphila, meaning that the movement
was the work of the popular elements among the Jewish community.

The acute class antagonisms revealed in the last period of Ptolemaic rule and at the beginning of Cyrene's entry into the sphere
of Roman influence, find expression also in the juridical division
of the city as reported by Strabo (p. 176), and principally in the
separation of the peasantry (meaning probably the Libyans)

---

[1] Jordanes, *Romana*, 81 (Mommsen, *MGH* V, p. 9); *CAH* IX, p. 433, n. 1;
CPJ I, p. 25.

[2] Ap. Jos. *Ant.* XIV, 7, 2 (114): "The same Strabo testifies . . . that at
the time that Sulla crossed to Greece to wage war against Mithradates and
sent Lucullus against the rising (ἐπὶ τὴν στάσιν) of our people of whom
(which?) the world is (was?) full, he said" etc. (Vers. Lat.: . . . quia tempore
quo transiit Sulla in Hellada pugnaturus Mithradati Lucullum transmisse
fertur in Cyrenen civitatem propter nostrae gentis seditionem, quae totam
orbem complevit). The text of the sentence mentioning the *stasis* is corrupt,
(Niese, *Fl. Jos. Operae*, ad loc., III, 1955, p. 260), but I think that the word
ἐπί is decisive. The primary meaning of the word *seditio* in the Latin version
is "rebellion".

from the rest of the population. In considering this subject, we encounter the phenomenon of the alliance between Anabus, the Libyan king, with Arataphila and the Cyrenean aristocracy. Under the Ptolemies the Libyan tribes were controlled by a royal official, the Libyarch, but on the "liberation" of the cities by Rome those settled on the fringes of their territories, in so far as their lands were not included in the *ager publicus*, gained their freedom, and again became a political factor and an influence on security. A tangible expression of Anabus' alliance with the Pentapolis towns has in my view been found in a new inscription from Cyrene, published in 1962: [3] this commemorates the erection by Cyrene of the statue of one "Aiglanor son of Demetrius of Cyrene, one of the kinsmen of the late King Ptolemy, benefactor in the greatest matters both of his country and of the other cities and peoples round about the city-territory". This inscription was engraved after the death of Ptolemy Apion, and informs us that the political situation created by the end of royal rule was common to all the cities of the Pentapolis; it also reflects the rapprochement between their aristocracy and the Libyan tribes. Such a rapprochement had taken place once before in the 6th century B.C. when Arkesilaos II's brothers founded Barka jointly with the Libyans and formed an alliance with the local king, whose descendant, Aladdeir, still lived in the town in the hellenistic period. That step was in its time an attempt to maintain together with the Libyans the extensive economy based chiefly once real cultivation and the rearing of horses and cattle, as opposed to a more varied and intensive agriculture combining sheep-raising, silphium, arable farming, plantations and green crops. The alliance of Anabus and Arataphila was a political one, and would have obliged certain concessions in exchange for the aid rendered by Anabus to the Cyrenean nobility in their struggle. Accordingly it may be supposed that the Libyan tribes were awarded greater freedom of movement over the plateau, and this tendency was probably not contrary to the will of the large estate-owners who devoted their lands chiefly to stock-rearing and cereals. This hypothesis would offer an explanation for the Jewish stasis suppressed by Lucullus, for the new political settlement would have exposed the tenants of the royal land to the

---

[3] *AA* 1962, p. 437; from the Valley Street of Cyrene: Αἰγλάνορα Δαματρίω Κυραναίον τὸν συγγένη τῶ βασιλεύσαντος ἁμῶν Πτολεμαίω τὰ μέγιστα εὐεργήσαντα τὰν πατρίδα καὶ τὰς ἄλλας πόλιας καὶ τὰ κατὰ τὰν χώραν ἔθνεα Κυραναῖοι.

unrestrained depredations of the nomads, and have alienated them from the rule of the aristocrats of Cyrene.

Our analysis has shown that in the 2nd century, under the Ptolemies, the agricultural economy of the country had declined as a result of the systematic intensification of their policy of étatism, the ground thus being prepared for the conservative agricultural régime at the expense of the small and medium peasantry. If Lucullus on his visit to Cyrene in the year 88/6 cited Plato[4] (pp. 63-4) on the flourishing state of the city's inhabitants, he did not do so in order to draw attention to their prosperity at the time of his visit, but on the contrary—the philosopher's words were his preface to a statement in the opposite sense: "No man is harder to govern than the successful one, and none is easier to govern than he who has been brought low by fortune"—"And this it was (Plutarch concludes) that made the Cyreneans submit without resistance to the legislation of Lucullus." Thus, Lucullus' words confirm the depressed state of the city in this period.

A second economic factor influencing the life of the country was constituted by the royal lands, which had passed into the hands of the Roman Senate on the death of Ptolemy Apion in 96 B.C. It has already been stated (pp. 110-11) that these lands were extensive and evidence can be adduced for their existence near Cyrene, on the Jebel to east and west of the city, near Ptolemais, and on the southern slopes of the plateau. Further areas have been conjectured between Teucheira and Bengazi. The extent of these tracts is shown by the size of the standard unit mentioned by Hyginus in his account of their division.

What in effect were the *agri Apionis* which thus became *ager publicus*? Tenney Frank, in a lengthy enquiry,[5] endeavours to prove that the term *ager publicus* did not refer in the 1st century B.C. to all the lands of the provinces conquered by Rome, but meant the personal estates of the hellenistic monarchs in Asia and Sicily, and other tracts confiscated from rebellious cities or enemies (Sicily; the lands of Corinth and Carthage). In Asia, for example, they did not on this view include the βασιλικὴ γῆ, i.e. the crown lands, but only the personal domains of the Attalids. If Frank was right, can his doctrine be extended to Cyrenaica? We have seen that Euergetes II regarded the χώρα as entirely his,

---

[4] Plut., *Luc.* 2:4; Aelianus, *Var. hist.*, XII, 30, 5.
[5] *JRS* 17, 1927, pp. 141 sqq.

but this was almost certainly a purely political conception, and did not carry the meaning of personal ownership. But Cyrene differed from Asia and Sicily in one important aspect, namely, that here a transitional period intervened between the Roman assumption of control of the *agri Apionis* and the inclusion of the whole country in a province. In Asia and Sicily, by contrast, the separation of royal domains from crown land was possible because the Roman authority was imposed on these countries in their entirety by a single act. Had the Cyrenean lands outside the city-territories and the personal property of the kings not been annexed to one of these two categories when autonomy was granted to the towns, they would have remained "in the air", without administrative control. This reality therefore obliges an interpretation not consistent with Frank's view on other provinces. The arrival of silphium in the Roman treasury in 93 B.C.[6] agrees with our own interpretation.

One document may throw some light on the problem, namely, an inscription from the ancient village of Negharnes, east of Cyrene.[7] This settlement is situated on the northern edge of lands divided up by the Roman method of *limitatio*, which shows that they belonged to the estates of Ptolemy Apion and subsequently to the Roman *ager publicus*. The present buildings of Negharnes are mostly Byzantine, but there are hellenistic mausolea to west of the village, which stands near the northern scarp of the plateau, overlooking the Lusaita, where its inhabitants doubtless grew wheat on the fertile terra rossa. Negharnes was further directly linked by road with Apollonia, through which port its grain could be exported. The inscription concerned is dated in the 1st century before the present era; its surviving portion commemorates an act of the village council, composed of fifty-three πολιάνομοι, releasing one of its inhabitants from the village liturgies and labour service; the man so exempted is appointed honorary priest of Dionysus and receives permission to make his own estimate of his corn-contribution when registering with the relevant official (the σιτώνης). As the inscription was set up in the 1st century B.C., and reflects characteristically hellenistic administrative arrange-

---

[6] Plin., *HN* XIX, 3, 15 (140).
[7] *SEG* 9, 354; *DAI* II, Cir. i, no. 135. The Arabic name of the settlement preserves, I believe, the Greek name which appears in Ptolemy's *Geography* (IV, 4, 7) in this neighbourhood as Ἀρχίλη.

ments, probably we may perceive in them Ptolemaic conditions, even if the inscription was dedicated after Rome had taken over these lands in 96 B.C. The purchaser of the grain is a government official, and the grain concerned is evidently the ἀγοραστὸς σῖτος of Ptolemaic Egypt,[8] the *frumentum emptum* mentioned by Cicero in relation to Sicily.[9] The document permits its subject to sell more when the prices are good, and less when they are low. Clearly then, the community was permitted to release its members from certain duties because it bore a collective responsibility to supply an annual quota of corn to be purchased by the government. It is known that in Egypt the ἀγοραστὸς σῖτος was imposed on cleruchs and cultivators of γῆ ἐν ἀφέσει.[10] i.e. land awarded by the king, and theoretically reverting to him. Negharnes therefore was inhabited by this category of cultivator (cleruchs or katoikoi), or by peasants working γῆ ἐν ἀφέσει, and not by λαοὶ βασιλικοί, or peasants cultivating royal lands (βασιλικὴ γῆ) under contract and royal supervision.[11] The presence of katoikoi at Negharnes would indeed agree with the internal autonomy enjoyed by its inhabitants, expressed by their council, and by their freedom to impose liturgies and labour-service. If this supposition is correct, we must conclude that in the 1st century B.C., before Cyrene became part of a Roman province, Negharnes, inhabited by comfortable holders of land granted to them by the king, but not by inhabitants of his personal estates—nevertheless became part of the *ager publicus*. And if the Negharnes evidence is not regarded as convincing, because the land here was not βασιλικὴ γῆ but γῆ ἐν ἀφέσει, it will be recalled that in Egypt, whose influence on Cyrenaica was generally considerable at this period, crown domain was assimilated to the *ager publicus* (δημόσια γῆ) under Augustus.[12]

The evidence we possess, nevertheless, shows that not all the *ager publicus* of Cyrene remained in the hands of its previous inhabitants. Pliny says explicitly that most of the silphium was destroyed by the publicani who had leased its tracts for grazing sheep.[13] Cicero also speaks of the leasing of the same areas in

---

[8] *JEA* 6, 1920, p. 175; Rostovtzeff, *A Large Estate*, pp. 90 etc.; C. Préaux, *L'économie royale des Lagides*, 1939, p. 141.

[9] *In Verrem*, II, 3, 63.

[10] Rostovtzeff, *JEA* 6, 1920, p. 175; C. C. Edgar, *P. Zenon*, 59723.

[11] This was the situation, at least, in Egypt.

[12] Rostovtzeff, *Stud. z. Gesch. römischen Kolonates*, 1910, pp. 131, n. 1.

[13] (Silphium) publicani, qui pascua conducunt, maius ita lucrum sentientes, depopulantur pecorum pabulo.—Plin. *HN*, XIX, 3, 15 (39).

62 B.C.[14] The silphium had till then, apparently, been paid as tax to the government, while a pasture-tax (ἐννόμιον) had been exacted from the Libyans; the southern areas were now opened to direct exploitation by the publicani, and the Libyans would have been driven from them. The destruction of the silphium, begun in the 3rd century by the Libyans themselves, was thus repeated in different circumstances. The end of the process is not known with any certainty; until recently it was accepted that the silphium was now destroyed completely, but this view has been challenged by Capelle.[15] The expansion of the publicani over the southern Jebel at the expense of the Libyan tribes may nevertheless be seen as part of the background of the Roman campaigns between 20 B.C. and 2 B.C. But these phenomena also indicate an important general development, namely, the completion of the trend perceptible since the dissolution of the kingdom of Ptolemy Apion, and perhaps even since the 2nd century B.C.,—namely, the abandonment of intensive agriculture for a pastoral economy combined with extensive arable, involving a renewed spread of the livestock branch.

Shortage of money may have induced the Roman Senate to use the country's depressed and conflicted situation as a pretext for undertaking the government of Cyrenaica in its entirety in 75-74 B.C., and to include it within a province consisting of Crete and Cyrene.[16] In 67 B.C., at any rate, on the epigraphical evidence already sketched above (p. 65), Cnaeus Lentulus Marcellinus was forced to take various steps to reform the situation, and even if his work was bound up with the campaign against the pirates, the phenomenon of piracy cannot be separated from the general social crisis of the time, nor is it chance that in a fragmentary inscription of the same year,[17] apparently set up by a group of Roman businessmen to express their thanks to Marcellinus, robbers (κλῶποί) are referred to. A fragment from Sallust speaks of a renewal of civil strife before 75 B.C.;[18] a contemporary inscription [19] shows that settlers were being settled near Ptolemais on surveyed plots which had been evacuated by their previous tenants.

---

[14] de leg. ag. II, 19, 51.

[15] W. Capelle, RM² 97, 1954, pp. 185-6.

[16] Badian (JRS 55, 1965, pp. 119-20) is not certain that Cyrene was definitely under direct Roman rule before 63 B.C.; Oost (Clas. Phil., 58, 1965, p. 19) accepts the establishment of Roman government in 75-74 BC.

[17] Reynolds, JRS 52, 1962, p. 98, no. 4.

[18] Hist. II, frag. 43.

[19] Reynolds, loc. cit., pp. 99-100, no. 5.

It is not clear how soon the country recovered after 67. The country was certainly a Roman province by 63. Pompey, at all events, obtained large quantities of grain from Cyrenaica,[20] but the city was taken by storm during the Civil War, and as late as the year 7 B.C. a small group of Roman citizens was in control of the country's law courts, and retained its monopoly till Octavian took measures to end it. We do not know what the position was in other respects at Cyrene or in the other towns of the country. Things were not bad in all of them, since several important buil- ding-projects were in train at Cyrene in the 1st century B.C., and we have seen evidence that the city then possessed wealthy citizens with ample resources. But internal tension also existed.

The basis of the dispute between the city and its Jewish com- munity between the years 31-13 B.C. has been investigated (p. 183), and when the city's nomophylakes set up a dedication to Ὁμονοία, or concord, under Augustus,[21] this obviously hinted at a situation which was the opposite of unity. In A.D. 54, in Claudius' reign, a special commissioner (*legatus*) was sent to Cyrenaica by the Em- peror to enquire into the situation on the state lands, the *agri publici*.[22] The commissioner, Acilius Strabo, found that part of these tracts had been abandoned by their tenants and had for some considerable time (*diutina licentia*) been occupied by the neighbouring tenants or landholders.[23] Why had these tracts been vacated—the more so since they constituted a considerable part of the fertile lands of the country? Natural conditions dictated that the livestock rearing of the Roman publicani could not be restricted to the south of the country. Like all other members of the population engaged in this branch, they had to transfer their animals northward to the Plateau in the summer months, hence the lot of the *agri publici* on the Jebel resembled that of the *agri*

---

[20] Caes., *B. Civ.*, III, 5.

[21] *RAL*⁶ 1, 1925, p. 421, fig. 9, line 13.

[22] Tac., *Ann.* XIV, 18, 2.

[23] Tacitus here uses the words "proximus quisque possessor", an expres- sion also found in the professional surveyors' literature (eg. Hyg., *de cond. ag.* (Thulin) p. 79 (Lachmann, p. 116). The word *possessor* frequently means "tenant" (cf. Rostovtzeff, *Stud. Gesch. röm. Kol.*, pp. 317, 341), hence it may be conjectured that Tacitus had before him some official report of the episode concerned, and that other tenants of the *ager publicus* had invaded vacant lots. But it might be doubted whether Tacitus was here using the term in its exact juridical significance.

publici in the south.[24] The seasonal transhumance of the livestock placed the *conductores pascuum* in the rôle of the Libyans, and thus the alliance between the wealthy landowners of Cyrene and the Libyan tribes, renewed under Arataphila, was terminated or infringed; its final annulment was achieved by the Roman campaigns against the southern tribes between 20 B.C. and 2 B.C.

What was the effect of the publicani on the inhabitants of the *ager publicus* of the Plateau, we do not precisely know, and no direct echo of their situation has reached us. But it is hard to suppose that this meeting was to the advantage of the inhabitants, especially if the conductores charged with the division of the lands also collected the rents (*vectigalia*) from their tenants.[25] It can be assumed with certainty that the stock-grazing publicani, keen for quick profits (cf. Pliny's expression, *maius lucrum sentientes*), neither heeded the tenants' plots nor respected their boundaries. It also suggests that they were not merely concerned in the collection of the *scriptura* or in the purchase of wool, but were directly involved in the grazing of the flocks. In this struggle, the publicani were the stronger,[26] and we may believe that they were allied with the small group of Roman citizens who had seized control of the juries, and perverted the law to put Cyreneans to death. Augustus intervened in 7/6 B.C. to end this perversion of justice, also facilitating appeals on the part of the provincials against the administration's acts of extortion. Whatever Augustus' influence on the activity of most of the publican companies, however, the lessees of the state pastures continued to discharge their function.[27] We have no information of developments in this sphere in Cyrenaica, but it is clear that the exploitation of the state lands by publicani came to an end in the first half of the 1st century A.D., when these tracts had been abandoned by their previous tenants. We can only

---

[24] On flock transhumance, see C. Yeo, *Tr. Amer. Philol. Assoc.*, 79, 1948, pp. 275 sqq.; P. A. Brunt, *Italian Manpower*, 1971, pp. 371-3 sqq. with special regard to Luceria, Calabria and Apulia. He points out that here transhumance had been made practicable by the confiscation of land, and had rendered impossible the recovery of the population. Its practice was here closely bound up with the public lands, and with grain-production—a branch in which the large landowners of Cyrene were interested.

[25] Hyg., de *cond. agrorum* (Lachmann), 116; Rostovtzeff, *Gesch. der römischen Staatspacht*, 1904, pp. 422-6.

[26] ubi publicanus esset ibi aut ius publicum vanum aut libertatem sociis nullam esse—Liv. XLV, 18, 4.

[27] Rostovtzeff, *Staatspacht*, pp. 410-11; cf. *CIL* III, 1209, 1363; IX, 243.8

conjecture the causes, but it is difficult to avoid the simple conclusion that the extensive pastoral economy based on seasonal
transhumance had reached its peak in this period and had destroyed
the economy of the original tenants of the *ager publicus*. When
Acilius Strabo arrived to investigate the legal position of the state
lands in 54, they were in the hands of entirely new holders, the
Cyrènean proprietors whose property bordered on the *agri publici*.

Lucius Acilius Strabo came as judge and arbitrator (disceptator),[28] which means that a dispute over land ed rights had broken
out between two sides. Strabo's judgment that the land belonged
to the Roman state aroused the anger of the Cyreneans, and they
appealed to the Senate, who referred them to the Emperor Nero,
who had meantime acceeded. The Emperor confirmed Strabo's
finding, but as a concession left the Cyreneans with the land.
Thus, at least, Tacitus.[29] It may be asked, however, who were the
parties to this dispute: were they simply the Roman people versus
the Cyrenean occupiers, or was there a third party? Tacitus' use
of the term *disceptator*, meaning arbitrator, to describe Acilius'
rôle, implies that he came to adjust a dispute between two claimants; had he merely represented the Roman people, he himself
would have been an interested party, and the term *disceptator*
would have been inappropriate. Tacitus, however, was a man of
legal experience,[30] and hence the term must be taken seriously.
Ruggiero indeed,[31] thought that the other party was constituted
by the *publicani*, but this is unlikely, since they had apparently
abandoned their concessions on the *ager publicus* a long time before.
It is much more probable that the heirs of the previous tenants
were the claimants who challenged the rights of the Cyrenean
occupiers. Indeed, the most acceptable interpretation of an unclear account would be, that in the course of adjudicating their
claim Acilius found that the state was the rightful owner, and left
the State to assign the tenancies.[32]

---

[28] Tac., *Ann.* XIV, 18: missum disceptatorem a Claudio agrorum quos
etc.

[29] *Loc. cit.*: Nero, probata Strabonis sententia se nihilo minus subvenisse
sociis et ursurpata concedere scripsit.

[30] Plin., *Epp.* 2, 11; cf. Furneaux, *The Annals of Tacitus*, 1907, I, pp. 3-4.

[31] *L' arbitrato publico*, 1893, p. 345; cf. Oliverio, *DAI* II, Cir. i, pp.
128-23.

[32] A judicial dispute which is likely to throw light on the Cyrenean problem
is reflected in an inscription from the town of Aezani in Phrygia (*CIL* III,

These settlers had been placed in a serious position by the separation of the *agri Apionis* from the rest of the country's tracts in 96 B.C. Torn away from the administrative framework of the Ptolemaic state, which had till then ensured their rights, and furnished both legal and military protection, they remained defenseless before the oppression and profit-hunting of the *conductores*, and before the raids and trespassing of the Libyan tribes. If we read between the lines of Tacitus' account, we see that most of them had been driven from their farms some years before the arrival of Strabo to investigate their claims. It would seem very probable that these years beheld the creation of a landless and embittered agrarian proletariat. We have already sought to show that from the beginning of Ptolemaic rule in the territory, most of the new agricultural settlers, whether Jews or gentiles, had settled on the Ptolemaic royal lands, impelled both by the juridical and by the economic situation. The consequences of their plight will be examined below. Nero's decision, according to Tacitus, confirmed the state's ownership of the areas in dispute, but left the Cyrenean squatters where they were, that is, as state tenants.[33] If this was the case, then the former tenants remained landless.

Tacitus' account, however, can be compared with three other sources drawn respectively from epigraphy, from archaeology and from the professional literature of the Roman state-surveyors. The surveyor Hyginus, who lived under Trajan (98-117), describing the surveying and dividing up of the *agri Apionis* of Cyrenaica as an eye-witness, writes: "And there are here boundary

---

355; *OGIS* 502; F. F. Abbott, A. C. Johnson, *Municipal Administration in the Roman Empire*, 1926, pp. 403 sq., no. 82). The lands of the Temple of Zeus here had been appropriated by one of the Hellenistic rulers and divided out among cleruchs. Under Hadrian it was found that part of the tenants had enlarged their plots at the expense of others, and regarded their land as completely theirs. It appears that they owed rent both to the city of Aezani and to the emperor, hence, after a prolonged conflict (πολυχρόνιος μάχη), the city had appealed to the Roman governor, and the case ultimately came before the emperor himself. Hadrian, in his reply to the governor's communication, instructs, that if it proves impossible to ascertain the size of the original plots, the governor must find out the average size of similar plots in the neighbouring cities, and redraw the boundaries at Aezani accordingly. The tenants must pay vectigal (τέλος) to the city; the governor also sends instructions to the local procurator of the emperor to find surveyors to complete the enquiry, and the procurator replies that for this he needs experienced specialists (eos qui usu sint eorum periti).

[33] Oliverio (*loc. cit.*) thought that Nero forewent arrears of rent, but there is no evidence of this.

stones on which is inscribed the name of the Divine Vespasian, and these end with the words: these boundaries, seized by private individuals (Vespasian) restored to the Roman people." [34] Several of the said stones have actually been discovered, bearing inscriptions which witness the survey-work of Acilius Strabo and of an official who succeeded him, Quintus Paconius Agrippinus. Of the three known stones set up by Strabo,[35] one is from Gasr Targhuna, one from Marazig in the eastern Jebel, and the third from an unknown provenance. The first of them was erected in A.D. 54-56. Another belongs to Nero's reign, and the third is undatable, as only part of it remains. Their bilingual texts end with the words: ". . . (Nero) restored to the Roman people the boundaries seized by private individuals".[36] It is harder to interpret the four known boundary stones bearing the name of Paconius Agrippinus,[37] who came, like Acilius Strabo, as special imperial commissioner—this time for Vespasian (ἴδιος πρεσβευτής: *legatus*). All these stones were found at Cyrene, two on the north-east edge of the city, a third in the south-west of the Agora, and the fourth near the city's northern wall. The first three are dated to 71 and their text resembles that of Strabo's stones, showing that Hyginus' version is inaccurate, although its contents corresponds to reality: but no private boundary trespassers are mentioned, and the property restored to the Roman people by the Emperor through the agency of his commissioner Agrippinus is called Πτυλυμαῖον. Opinions differ on the meaning of this word: Ferri[38] identified the "Ptulumaion" with the Temple of Zeus on the eastern hill of Cyrene; Rostovtzeff[39] understood it as a temenos, probably a garden or grove; others have seen in these four stones evidence that the restoration of Apion's lands to the state continued, interpreting the word "Ptulumaion" as "Ptolemy's land".[40] Difficult as it is to decide, it may be said in favour of the last suggestion that the

---

[34] *de cond. ag.* 122-3: Lapides vero inscripti nomine divi Vespasiani sub clausula tali: occupati a privatis—P. R. restituit.

[35] *SEG* 9, 352; *DAI* II, Cir. i, p. 129, no. 137. The third, which I have seen personally, is fragmentary.

[36] Fines occupatos a privatis P.R. restituit-ὅρους δικαατεχομένους ὑπὸ, ἰδιωτῶν δημῷ ῾Ρωμαίων ἀποκατέστησεν.

[37] *DAI* II, Cir. ii, p. 133, no. 138; *NAMC* 2, 1916, pp. 165 sqq.; *SEG* 9, 165, 166, 167; *FA* 9, 1956, 3802 (p. 281).

[38] *Aegyptus* 4, 1918, p. 164.

[39] *SEHRE* p. 681, n. 64; cf. *SIG³* 463.

[40] Ghislanzoni, *NAMC* 2, p. 173; *CR*, p. 103 n.

first two stones were incised by different masons,[41] while the letter-style of all of them is more characteristic of field boundary-stones than of urban buildings or parks, and even more so the spelling of the word "Ptulumaion', which is decidedly Libyan.[42] It should further be remembered that the boundaries of ancient agricultural plots reach the very walls of Cyrene on all sides. A similar boundary-stone, dated in 72, was also set up opposite the west gate of Ptolemais, recording (in Latin and Greek) the restoration of a garden (κῆπος, hortus) to the Roman people by Vespasian through the agency of Paconius.[43] The significance of these Flavian inscriptions, therefore, lies not so much in the extensiveness of the areas restored, as in the evidence they afford of the aim of Vespasian and his sons to restore as much as possible crown property to state ownership and thereby to recover its revenues. Important in this respect is the evidence of Hyginus.[44] who states specifically that the boundary-stones he had seen were Vespasian's, meaning that in Agrippinus' time the systematic resurvey of the agri publici had begun. If indeed the grid was first laid out after the transfer of these areas to Rome in 96 B.C.—as Fabricius, for example, seems to have believed—[45] then the boundaries were now set out afresh under the supervision of Paconius Agrippinus.

The two sources just cited, Hyginus and the inscriptions, do not contradict Tacitus' account; but the redivision of the ager publicus should not be interpreted to mean that the Cyrenean "squatters" remained on their plots undisturbed in accordance with Nero's permissive decision. The resurvey meant a redivision of the areas, and this operation was apparently an extensive one; it was therefore the expression of a stubborn determination to settle the affairs of the statelands of Cyrenaica for good and all, since the surveying was still going on in the reign of Trajan, on the evidence of the surveyor Hyginus, who worked in Cyrenaica personally in the examination of the said boundaries.[46] In the late republican and early imperial period limitatio was used chiefly to divide out lands

---

[41] Ghislanzoni, loc. cit.

[42] Cf. NAMC 2, p. 173, 177 n.; SEG 9, 166.

[45] DAI II, Cir. i, pp. 132-3, no. 138; SEG 9, 360.

[44] Loc. cit.

[45] PW XXV, 1926, sv. Limitatio, col. 674: The use of Ptolemaic units of measurement and Hyginus' language (lapides vero divi Vespasiani) perhaps point to the earlier date.

[46] Neque hoc praetermittam, quod in provincia Cyrenensium conperi . . .

assigned to military colonies or public land acquired by conquest. In the latter period it also seems to have been found useful for adjusting the rights of new Roman settlers in conquered provinces with indigenous native tribes (Numidia, Pannonia).[47] These considerations may assist us to understand the resurvey of the Cyrenaican *ager publicus* under the Flavians and Trajan; but it is not clear whether the Greek units of measurement used in the Cyrenaican survey should be taken to prove a Roman method applied by a hellenistic state, or whether the project originated when the royal lands were taken over by Rome. Beside the purpose of adjustment between inhabitants and new settlers evident in the arrangements of the early Empire, the renewed survey in Cyrenaica served two further purposes: it reregularized the payment of rents and taxes by the settlers, and thus renewed the revenues of the treasury; it also restored the tracts to proper cultivation.

There is no doubt that agriculturally *limitatio* acted more particularly in the Mediterranean area, as a framework for the cereal branch, and secondarily for the plantation economy. This is proved beyond all doubt by the air-photographs in Africa and Italian Apulia, where traces of the plantations are seen among the fields.[48] The Flavian revision of the field-boundaries of Cyrenaica must therefore be seen as the first renewal of mixed farming and intensive cultivation in the territory.

---

[47] For Limitatio (centuriation) see Blume, Lachmann, Rudorff, *Die Schrifte der römischen Feldmesser*, 1848; A. Schulten, *BJ* 103, 1894, pp. 12-41; W. Barthel, *ib.* 120, 1911, pp. 39-125; *PW* XXV, 1926, sv. Limitatio, (Fabricius); J. P. S. Bradford, *Antiq.* 21, 1947, pp. 197 sqq.; 23, 1949, pp. 65 sqq.; C. E. Stevens, *Antiq.* 32, 1958, pp. 25 sqq.; Ministère des travaux publiques (Tunisie), *Atlas des centuriations romaines de Tunisie*, 1954; J. P. S. Bradford, *Ancient Landscapes*, 1957, Ch. iv, pp. 145 sqq.; R. Chevallier, *BCH*, 82, 1958, p. 636; *id. Hommages à Albert Grenier*, ed. Renard, 1962, (Collections Latomus, 58), pp. 403 sqq.; Notes sur trois centuriations romaines, Bononia, Ammaedara, Vienna; Bibliothèque générale de l'école pratique des hautes études, 6, *Colloque international d'archéologie aérienne*, 1964: M. Guy, L'apport de la photographie aérienne a l'étude de la colonisation antique de la Province de Narbonnaise, pp. 117 sqq.; Gymnasium, Beih. 7: *Germania Romana*, III: *Römisches Leben auf Germanischem Boden*, ed. H. Hinz, 1970, pp. 26-42, Die Landwirtschaftliche Grundlage der Villae Rusticae, with extensive further literature; O. A. W. Dilke, *The Roman Landsurveyors*, 1972.

[48] For areas of Limitatio in Africa in which the tree pits of the olive-plantations are clearly visible, Bradford, *Ancient Landscapes*, pl. 49, a-b, and p. 204.

The fact that the revision of the survey of the Cyrenaican *ager publicus* continued, even with intermissions, over half a century, shows that this was not simply a re-marking of boundaries. The field-divisions still traceable in the Safsaf district, for instance, contain farmsteads, and there is evidence of the active clearance of new areas.

The Roman method of division also possessed advantages from an agrotechnical point of view, since the definition of the plots contributed to the checking of soil-erosion, to the clearing of stones, to drainage and to protection against wind-erosion.[49] Administratively, the correction of the boundaries of the *ager publicus* in Cyrenaica was only one of a number of similar activities conducted on the initiative of Vespasian and his Flavian successors, which included the institution of offices to administer the large imperial estates of Africa,[50] the merging in Egypt of the crown-domains with the *ager publicus* and the Egyptian temple-lands,[51] the surveying and organization of the *agri publici* of Apulia and Calabria[52], and the restoration of the irregular fringe-areas of the centuriated tracts (*subseciva*) to state-ownership.[53]

The time has come to examine the influence of the present process upon the Jewish community of Cyrenaica. A growth of the number of Jews in the country between the 1st century B.C. and the 1st century of the common era is indicated by the tombs of Teucheira and by the three Jewish inscriptions at Berenice, also by what Josephus reports of Cyrenean Jewry as a whole.[54] It is clear that their number was large in the city of Cyrene at the time of Lucullus' visit, when they were already a political factor, and the same inference may be drawn from their clash with the city over the despatch of the half-sheqel tax to Jerusalem between 31 and 13 B.C. At both Berenice and Cyrene the community was able to elaborate and beautify its public buildings during the 1st century B.C. The influence of the comfortable and wealthy city-elements seems to have grown in the second half of the century, since by 7-6 B.C. some Jews had attained citizen-status in the Greek polis

---

[49] Bradford, *ibid.*, pp. 154, 203.
[50] The clearest sketch of this development is still that of F. Pelham, *Essays in Roman History*, 1911, pp. 275 sqq.
[51] Rostovtzeff, *Kolonat*, p. 328.
[52] Blume et al., *Die Schrifte*, pp. 211, 261.
[53] Hyg., *de gen. controv.*, Lachmann, p. 133.
[54] *Ant.* XIV, 7, 2 (116).

of Cyrene, and by 13-12 B.C. the same had occurred at Ptolemais. Their community's ties with the Jewish homeland, more especially with Jerusalem, had also been drawn closer in the last century before and in the first century of the common era; this is shown by the tombs of Cyrenean Jews discovered in Jerusalem in 1941. Here eleven ossuaries of Jews with Cyrenean names were found by Sukenik in a rockcut tomb in the Qidron Valley,[55] while another ossuary from the tombs of Dominus Flevit, dug by Bagatti and Milik, bore the name of a Cyrenean.[56] The first group was accompanied by pottery and lamps of the 1st century of the current era, the second by coins from the Hasmonean period (from c. 135 B.C.) down to A.D. 16. This evidence may be connected with the New Testament report [57] of a synagogue in Jerusalem owned by Cyrenean Jews, which existed a short time after the death of Jesus, and of the presence in Jerusalem of Simon of Cyrene, who carried the cross.[58]

Two documents of Cyrenean Jewry belong to the first third of the 1st century A.D., namely, the resolution of the Jews of Berenice in honour of the Roman official M. Tittius in A.D. 24/5, and the inscription recording the mission of Ittalammon son of Apellas and Simon son of Simon to Lanuvium in an unknown year, apparently in the first decades of the century. These two documents have been discussed, (pp. 146 sqq.; 167 sqq.) and on neither can a firm conclusion be reached. If we accept the view that the Lanuvium

---

[55] N. Avigad, *IEJ* 12, 1962, pp. 1 sqq: A depository of inscribed ossuaries in the Kidron Valley. Professor Avigad decided for the Cyrenean origin of the people buried here on the strength of the words "Alexander the *QRNYT*" (sic) incised on one of the ossuaries (no. 8), and of the general composition of the names, most of which are to be found in the onomasticon of Cyrenean Jews. To these indications another may be added, namely the spelling of the word Πτυλιμαϊκή (sic) on no. 7a, which is peculiar to Cyrene, where the upsilon frequently takes the place of the omicron—cf. here p. 213. In connection with relations between Judaea and Cyrene, we may mention the names of the proselyte Batti ben Tebbi, (Tobiah) the slave of the younger Rabban Gamliel (*Qiddushin*, 70b). Batti may be a form of the Cyrenean "Battus", cf. 'Azariah di Fano's remark concerning this proselyte, that he was derived from Ham. The name Tobiah is found among the names of the Jews of Teucheira (Gray, *MUC*, no. 24), and cf. Βαρθύβας, which occurs four times on the Cyrene stele *QAL* 4, 1961, p. 20, nos. 7, 34, 37, 47 (A.D. 3/4).

[56] P. B. Bagatti, J. T. Milik, *Gli Scavi del "Dominus Flevit"*, I, 1955, p. 81, no. 9, Vanno 74, Oss. 10.

[57] *Acts*, 10:9.

[58] *Matt.* 27:32; cf. *Acts* 3:1 etc.: Λούκιος ὁ Κυρηναῖος.

inscription was set up by a delegation in the name of Ptolemais, we must see this as evidence that the Ptolemais community had then reached such a measure of influence that the polis found it profitable to send two of its Jewish citizens to prosecute its affairs, apparently a claim for the recovery of money from the Roman authorities. But if we interpret the inscription as belonging to the tenants of the *ager publicus*, the former *agri Apionis* (and I think the language of the document supports this interpretation), we shall discover in the text a common element with the Berenice stele of A.D. 24-25, which expresses gratitude to M. Tittius who came to Cyrenaica "on public affairs" (ἐπὶ τῶν δημοσίων πραγμάτων), an expression which could be interpreted to mean "on affairs of the *ager publicus*".

If then our analysis of the situation of the tenants on the country's public lands in these years is correct, involving their expulsion by the spread of the pastoral economy managed by the publicani, and if we are justified in our belief that many of the tenants were Jews,—then the Berenice and Lanuvium documents may be seen as expressions of the Jewish community's economic struggle against the Roman contractors on the one hand, and against the private landowners who had replaced the Roman contractors on the other. An analysis of the agrarian development of the Cyrenean *ager publicus* in the first half of the 1st century A.D. obliges us to suppose that the activity of the Roman publicani on those tracts and their seizure by the Cyreneans themselves, brought into existence a landless agrarian proletariat which included a considerable Jewish element. We do not know whether the Jewish wealthy of the Pentapolis came to the assistance of their brethren. The honorary inscription dedicated to M. Tittius by the Jewish politeuma of Berenice looks like an act of the well-to-do leaders of the community, and its text can be interpreted to mean that the dedicators had a tangible interest in the state-lands. It would be less natural for the propertied group to be on the side of the Roman publicani and the *conductores*; that they would have supported the oppressed tenants and peasantry is nevertheless uncertain. But the Lanuvium inscription would appear to mean this, if we agree to see in it evidence for a delegation on behalf of the tenants of the *agri Apionis*. It is likely enough that differing attitudes were held concurrently among the wealthier members of the community. One thing at any rate is made very clear by this study—namely, the sharp cleavage prevailing in this period between the inhabitants of the cities and the country population, particularly that living outside the city territories (ἡ χώρα). The situation is reflected by Strabo (p. 176) and is prominent in most phases of the country's history from the Ptolemaic conquest onward.

One event that belongs to this period, between the years 60 and 70, might have thrown some light on the Jewish position in Cyrenaica had we possessed details: this is the fate of the High Priest Ishmael ben Phiabi, who was put to death at Cyrene between the above dates.[59] Ishmael was apparently appointed High Priest by the Roman procurator Porcius Festus between the years 61-64; [60] he appears to have been of Egyptian origin. Something is known of his personality from Josephus [61] and from rabbinical literature.[62] He conducted an aggressive policy against Agrippa II and the Roman procurator, expressed by the erection of a wall between the Temple and the royal palace, and headed a delegation to Rome to state his case in the dispute before the Emperor himself. In respect of internal Jewish problems he was both masterful and unscrupulous, gathering about himself a gang of roughs to manhandle his opponents in Jerusalem, and depriving the lesser priests of their dues by sending his slaves to the threshing floors to seize their tithes. After his collision with Agrippa and the procurator Festus over the high wall he had built to screen the Temple service, (61-64), Ishmael arrived in Rome at the head of eleven Jerusalem notables, and with the aid of the Empress Poppaea Sabina successfully gained Nero's support for his case, but was detained by Poppaea in Rome when his colleagues left to return to Judaea.[63]

This is the end of Josephus' account, and we do not know how or why Ishmael found his way to Cyrene. One thing however is clear: he died by the sword of the Roman administration, for decapitation was a pronouncedly Roman form of execution.[64] His general outlook, indeed, bore no resemblance to that of the Zealots, yet obviously the appearance of so stormy a personality among the Jews of Cyrene not long before the outbreak of the great rebellion in Judaea, could not but evoke strong reactions and a sharpening

---

[59] Jos., *BJ* VI, 2, 2 (114).
[60] *Ant.* XVIII, 2, 2 (34).
[61] *Ant.* XX, 8, 8; 8, 11 (180-1, 194-6).
[62] B. *Pes.* 57a.
[63] *Ant.* XVIII, 8, 11 (195).
[64] *DS* sv. Poena, pp. 539-40.

of antagonisms within the Jewish community. A rapprochement between the leaders of the community and the Cyrenean aristocracy precisely in the 'sixties, was expressed by the appointment of Eleazar son of Jason to the post of nomophylax in 61 (pp. 178 sqq). Eleazar does not, indeed, appear to have hidden his Jewish identity, but the members of his hellenizing group had been educated in the Greek gymnasia and did not hesitate to permit their names to be engraved on ephebe steles dedicated to the gods Hermes and Heracles, and the same applied to a parallel Jewish group at Ptolemais. Eleazar's name, moreover, was listed on an inscription which opened with the names of the high priests of Apollo. Probably the years of the 'sixties saw the creation of a deep rift between this group and the broader sections of the Jewish population, both in the town and the country. It is hard to imagine the High Priest Ishmael as an ally of the Sicarian Jonathan the Weaver on the one hand, or of the communal leaders who informed the Roman government of Jonathan on the other; or yet that he would have given aid to the Jewish peasants. He must then have been isolated in the politics of the Jewish society at Cyrene, yet his presence could have created strong reactions, deepening conflicts and widening cleavages. Probably he met his end in the events of the year 73 yet to be described, falling victim to Roman suspicion.

Meanwhile the Roman activity designed to settle the problem of the *ager publicus* went forward. Paconius Agrippinus is known to have been still active in this sphere in 75,[65] and Hyginus was in Cyrenaica under Trajan (i.e. after 98) measuring the same lands. Probably not a few Jews were interested in profiting from the reform to return to the plots from which their fathers had been evicted years before, and if the settlement was carried out at the expense of Cyrenean squatters by Vespasian's decision, this would have exacerbated relations between Greeks and Jews. But here a new factor intervened—the prolonged and growing tension in Judaea, which ended in A.D. 66 with the great explosion in Jerusalem and a bloody clash between Jews and Greeks first at Caesarea, then in the Greek cities of Judaea and Syria, and in Alexandria, which finally brought about the outbreak of trouble in Cyrene.

The year 73 beheld a further event whose direct influence is hard to assess, but which certainly did not improve the attitude of

---

[65] *SEG* 9, 360.

most of the Jews to the Roman power: This was the imposition of the penal Ἰουδαικὸν τέλεσμα (Jewish tax), first exacted in Judaea the same year; [66] in Egypt it was paid in the year 72-73.[67]

We may distinguish, hypothetically, between three groups among Cyrenean Jewry at this moment: those involved in the affairs of the cities and who stood close to their authorities; a broader group, for the most part now nationally aroused by the events in Judaea, and the broad populace, not a few of whom were a landless proletariat concentrated in the towns or scattered in the lesser settlements and on the fringes of the agricultural areas; the plight of this group may well be reflected in the tombs of Teucheira. This third group, the ἄποροι, or indigent, made its contribution to the events of 73, when the Sicarian Jonathan the Weaver fled to Cyrene.[68]

If Josephus' account can be trusted, two outstanding points are to be discussed in the episode connected with him. First, that the movement which he led was not restricted to the city of Cyrene, as according to Josephus' words "the Sicarian madness infected the cities like a plague;" [69] second, that his initial acts did not assume the form of an armed rising, but were an attempt to lead two thousand of the poorer Jews towards the desert, where he promised to show them signs and wonders. The Jewish wealthy did not hesitate to inform the Roman administration, which appears not to have noticed what was happening, of the movement, and the proconsul Catullus [70] despatched cavalry and infantry to disperse the participants. Most of the unarmed mob was cut down; the remnant was captured. Jonathan was caught after a prolonged chase. Whereupon, whether in despair or inspired by the class-hatred which was so prominent a feature of the several contemporary Jewish activist currents, he accused various Jews among the wealthier of the country of supporting the movement. The first objects of his charges were one Alexander, with whom he

---

[66] Jos., *BJ* VII, 6, 6 (218).

[67] *CPJ* I, 1957, p. 80.

[68] Jos., *Vita*, 76 (424); *BJ* VII, 11, 1 (437) sq.

[69] Ἥψατο δὲ καὶ τῶν περὶ Κυρήνην ἡ τῶν σικαρίων ἀπόνοια καθάπερ νόσος. Cf. P. Lon. (*CPJ*, no. 153), 1912, 98-100; εἰ δὲ μή, πάντα τρόπον αὐτοὺς ἐπεξελεύσομαι καθάπερ κοινὴν τεῖνα τῆς οἰκουμένης νόσον ἐξεγείροντας.

[70] For the identity of this governor see Ritterling, *JRS* 17, 1927, p. 29: he was L. Valerius Catullus Messalinus, consul for 73 (*PW* XIV, 1948, col. 2411, sv. Valerius no. 127). Under Domitian he was a member of the emperor's council and much feared as an informer.

(or the governor) appears to have clashed previously, and his wife Berenice, and they were put to death by Catullus. Their execution was followed by the infliction of the death penalty on several thousand of the richer Jews of Cyrenaica—or three thousand according to one of Josephus' versions. "And this," concludes the historian, "he (Catullus) thought could be done without danger, because he had confiscated their property to the credit of the imperial exchequer." [71] He then proceeded to impel Jonathan to extend his charges to the leaders of the Jewish communities in Alexandria and Rome, among those accused being Flavius Josephus himself, whom Jonathan charged with furnishing weapons and money to the alleged conspirators.[72] These people, however, were cleared by Vespasian after a personal investigation, and Jonathan was sentenced to death by burning.

Critical examination of the above story, as related by Josephus, raises several problems, not all of which are soluble. Klausner long ago remarked [73] that the term "Sicarian" applied to Jonathan hardly accords with his behaviour, namely, the leading of an unarmed mob towards the desert on the promise of showing them signs and wonders. The Sicarians generally believed in armed insurrection against Rome and their other enemies, whereas "signs and wonders" belong to the sort of action ascribed in Judaea, in the years before the great rebellion, to "the Egyptian prophet," who led 30,000 people from the desert to the Mount of Olives with the purpose of capturing Jerusalem by performing miracles,[74] and to one Theudas, who led a large mob to the Jordan in order to take them to the desert,[75] and was killed by the procurator Fadus. The contradiction between the acts of Jonathan and his title of "Sicarian" can indeed be resolved, and to this we shall return. But first another question arises: Why did the Roman authorities fail to notice Jonathan's departure at the head of two thousand Jews in the direction of the desert? The answer might be that they had left the towns secretly, in small groups, making for a common meeting place, yet the whole action rather suggests an excited assembly and a mass-march under the influence of Jonathan's

---

[71] καὶ ταῦτα πράττειν ἐνόμιζεν ἀσφάλως, ὅτι τὰς οὐσίας αὐτῶν εἰς τὰς τοῦ Καισάρος προσόδους ἀνελάμβανεν.

[72] Jos., *Vita*, 76 (424).

[73] J. Klausner, *Hist. of the Second Temple*, V, 1951, p. 168, note 5 (Hebrew).

[74] *BJ* II, 13, 5 (261-3); cf. *Acts* 21:38; Eus., *HE* II, 21.

[75] *Ant.* XX, 5, 1 (97-8).

personality. The explanation is rather to be sought elsewhere; that the assembly took place not in the city, but in the rural area.[76]

Another question forces itself upon the enquirer; why did Catullus believe that there was no danger in putting to death wealthy Jews since he had confiscated their property to the treasury? It is easy to connect this remark with the avarice and covetousness of Vespasian; it is known that the new emperor faced an empty treasury at the end of the civil war, hence his severity in the collection of taxes and in the augmentation of revenue,[77] nor are anecdotes lacking of his greed.[78] Suetonius accuses him of promoting corrupt officials so that he could condemn the wealthier ones, and it was said of him that he then wrung them out like sponges.[79] On the other hand Suetonius writes that "no innocent person was ever punished except in his absence, because he did not know of it, against his will, or because he had been deceived." [80] Suetonius' two statements are contradictory, and the first accords better with the conduct of Catullus. Yet even if we assume that it is correct, Josephus would not have admitted the reality of this vicious characteristic on the part of the patron to whom he owed his life. The facts remain to carry their own condemnation.

Catullus' execution of the Jewish aristocracy of Cyrene can indeed be interpreted in the light of the situation prevailing at the time with regard to the Jewry of the Empire as a whole and of Cyrene in particular. In Judaea the last embers of rebellion had only just been stamped out, while violent reactions had occurred also among Alexandrian Jewry.[81] No one knew where new reactions might appear, and the nervousness of the authorities in those provincial centres where Jews were numerous is understandable. The destruction of the Temple made it natural to anticipate in-

---

[76] Some confirmation of this suggestion is perhaps to be found in the wording of Josephus, who writes: "After he (sc. Jonathan) had convinced two-thousand of the ἐγχώριοι". The last word has two meanings, viz. "local people", and "country-people".

[77] Suet., *Vesp.*, 16.

[78] Sola est, in qua merito culpetur, pecuniae cupiditas—*Ibid.*

[79] *Ibid.*, 16: Creditur etiam procuratorum rapacissimum quemque ad ampliora officia ex industria solitum promovere, quo locupletiores mox condemnaret; quibus quidem volgo pro spongiis dicebatur uti, quod quasi et siccos madefaceret et exprimerit umentis.

[80] *Vesp.* 15: Non temere quis punitus insons reperiatur nisi absente eo et ignaro aut certe invito atque decepto.

[81] Jos., *BJ* VIII, 10, 1 (407).

surrectionary conspiracies in every Jewish community, and Jonathan may not have been isolated in his revolutionary plans. At Cyrene, in addition, socially explosive material had accumulated in the form of a landless proletariat on the one hand, and in the discontent of the landowners who held themselves to be injured by the new regulation of the *ager publicus* on the other. The confiscation of the land of Jewish proprietors would have been an "ideal" solution in such a complex situation, the more so if they were accused of fostering sedition against the Emperor.[82] As a number of the condemned Jews were citizens of the city (or cities), no small part of their possessions would have been landed property, which now passed to the imperial fiscus. Catullus, according to Josephus, was not tried or punished by Vespasian, a fact which appears to prove the latter's concurrence with the judicial murder and with the spoliation of the possessions of the accused. In defence of Vespasian it can only be said that the punishment of a governor at this juncture, when the Jewish insurrection had just ended and the Flavian dynasty was barely consolidated in power, would not have been popular among the groups about the Imperator. Whatever the case, the facts served to emphasize the cynical attitude to a perversion of justice affected by political considerations. The most moderate of the Cyrenean Jews was bound to realize clearly that from now on the Jews were outside the law. A boundary-stone found below the Jebel escarpment 500 metres south of the modern townlet of Susa, which impinges on Apollonia, records the acquisition and leasing of two farms covering $23\frac{1}{2}$ medimnia (about $25\frac{1}{2}$ iugera) of land by the city of Apollonia.[83] The transaction was carried out with the sanction of the Emperor Vespasian by the provincial governor C. Arinius Modestus, who was discharging a second term of governorship, two local men acting as guarantors. Arinius' prolonged term was probably necessitated by the disturbances of 73; the acquisition and leasing of the land—presumably state property, may well have been a consequence of the confiscations of Jewish property by Flavius Catullus.

It has already been observed that an apparent contradiction exists between Jonathan's description as a "Sicarian" and his conduct as a prophet and revealer of signs and wonders. There can

---

[82] It is interesting that Josephus' words can be interpreted to mean that the property had been confiscated before the execution of its owners.

[83] *Lib. Ant.*, 2, 1965, pp. 103 sqq.

be no doubt, however, that the Zealot aspirants to the Messianic kingdom in the last years before the destruction of the Second Temple, included two principal currents, one of which saw the road to the achievement of its aim in military action and political organization, while the other sought realization in the anticipation of miracles and wonders to be performed by the Almighty through the instrumentality of men of particular charisma. To the second current doubtless belonged the Egyptian prophet and Theudas, whose acts are described by Josephus. But there was a close connection between the two currents, and there was also a group or trend that combined both aspirations. This group is described by Josephus [84] after he has described the Sicarii: "Additional to these men of blood was another group, evil men, whose hands were clean of blood, but were themselves even more wanton in heart, since they, no less than the assassins, destroyed the peace of the city. For themselves misled, they misled others, and pretending to Divine inspiration, engaged in revolution and revolt, influencing the multitude to madness, leading them to the desert and claiming that there God would reveal to them omens of liberation". The Qumran scrolls have now proved to us the activist revolutionary content of the sect's aims—more particularly the *Scroll of the War of the Sons of Light with the Sons of Darkness*.[85] This document appears to belong to a period between the 1st century B.C. and A.D. 70, and very probably, in Yadin's opinion, to the Roman period, i.e., between 64 B.C. and the latter date. Its contents are the definition of the aims and phases of the war to be waged by Israel against the nations on the final day in order to attain complete redemption. It drafts the regulations and the régime to prevail among the combatants, describes the organizational structure and armament of their army, its array and tactics. As Devir has observed,[86] the desert performed an important function in Jewish history, as a symbol and source of religious and political inspiration, in which divers trends and individuals in Judaism saw a place of devotion and solitary retreat, where the spiritual powers could be renewed and purified, where profounder contact with God could

---

[84] *BJ* II, 13, 4 (258-9).

[85] Y. Yadin. *The Scroll of the War of the Sons of Light with the Sons of Darkness*, 1957.

[86] Y. Devir, *Bar Kokhba, the Man and the Messiah and the Dead Sea Scrolls*, 1964, especially Chapter II: "The Desert as a place of inspiration throughout the generations" (Heb.).

be attained. The desert symbolized the furnace in which the nation had been annealed, the heroic cradle of its unsullied youth, and the place of creation of its law of righteousness. For this reason the men of the Qumran sect saw their sojourn in the desert as a stage of spiritual and physical preparation for the final struggle which was to bring about the liberation of Israel and the redemption of mankind.

That they were not alone in their outlook on the function of the desert, is shown by the appearance of the idea in various forms over centuries of Jewish life [87] and by the "exodus to the Desert' of which we hear both in Judaea and in Cyrenaica. Knowledge of the aims of the Qumran Sect enables us to reconcile the apparent contradiction between the character and acts of Jonathan the Weaver. The currents and sects of the period also included men in whom the two ideas were associated: sojourn in the desert as a place of preparation, physical and spiritual, for the messianic war, the warlike aim being the way to complete redemption. The same conclusion has been reached by Professor Y. M. Grinz,[88] who identifies the "prophets of the desert" with the aims embodied in the *Scroll of the War of the Sons of Light with the Sons of Darkness.* The two principal ideas of this current are such as to explain Jonathan's programme and enable us to divide it into two phases: the assembly of the rebellious for preparation in the desert, and, subsequently, the war itself. Jonathan did not survive the first phase.

Does the study of the Libyan tribes enable us to add to a reconstruction of the events under discussion? The opinion of Gautier has already been cited, that the federation of the judaizing tribes of Algeria, the Zenata, took its origin in Cyrenaica at the time of the Jewish rising under Trajan. On the other hand the period of the most rapid spread of Judaism among the tribes of the Maghreb is placed by Gautier in the Severan epoch, when the camel-riding tribes came into being after the nomads had been thrust into the desert by the Roman administration. This view has been criticized

---

[87] Compare the Rechabites, the sojourn of various prophets in the desert, the flight of the Maccabean brothers to the wilderness and similar. See further M. Hengel, *Die Zeloten*, 1961, pp. 225 sqq.; W. R. Farmer, *Maccabees, Zealots and Josephus*, 1956, pp. 116 sqq.

[88] *Studies in the Dead Sea Scrolls* (ed. Yadin, Rabin), 1961, pp. 19 sqq.: "The date and authorship of the Scroll of Light and Darkness."

by Julien and Marçais,[89] who doubt the exclusively nomadic character of the Botr tribal group constituting the Zenata. Albertini [90] dates the judaization of certain Berber tribes and their expansion from Tripolitania to the Saharan oases, to the end of the 1st century A.D. Simon,[91] for his part, sees the first point of contact between the western Berbers and Judaism in the great Jewish Rebellion of 66-70. If the opinion is correct that the origin of the Botr tribes was in Cyrenaica, it is clear that they moved westward to Tripolitania and the Maghreb after the First Revolt on account of their attachment to Judaism, and this would support the view that their association with Judaism began before the time of Trajan. Simon writes of this conclusion,[92] that the circumstances of the rebellion under Trajan imply "the presence, on the fringes of the hellenized Jewish communities, on the desert borders of the province (i.e. Cyrenaica), of important Palestinian Jewish elements, doubtless of Zealot spirit and origin, part of whom flowed, as time went on, to the Saharah, while others sought refuge in the direction of the Maghreb plateau."

But unfortunately it now seems that the information concerning the judaizing Berber tribes alleged to have existed before the Arab invasion is less proven than it appeared to be some years ago. In 1963 Professor H. Z. Hirschberg published a detailed enquiry containing a systematic criticism of the sources of this information,[93] showing that the first report of the phenomenon is not older than the Middle Ages. The main source is Ibn Khaldoun, but his statement concerning the Judaism of the tribes concerned in Tripolitania and the Maghreb is less confident than would appear to the reader from the French translation of de Slane.[94] Most of the stories of Jewish influence on the Berber tribes, moreover, originated, as Hirschberg shows, not earlier than the 12th century, as a result of the contemporary spread of Jewish communities over north Africa; they also stem from tales of the Lost Ten Tribes, and above

---

[89] W. Marçais, *Rev. critique d'histoire et de la littérature*, 1929, p. 260; C. A. Julien, *Hist. de l'Afr. du nord*, II, 1952, pp. 22-4.

[90] *L'empire romain*[3], 1939, p. 165.

[91] M. Simon, Le Judaïsme berbère dans l'Afrique ancienne, ap. *Recherches d'hist. Judéo-Chrétienne*, 1962, p. 69.

[92] *Loc. cit.*, p. 69.

[93] *Jour. of African Hist.*, 4, 1963, pp. 313 sqq.: The problem of the Judaized Berbers.

[94] See Hirschberg, *loc. cit.*, p. 317, note 8.

all from the ethnic and religious assimilation, forced or voluntary, of Jews to the Moslem population. Despite all this, Hirschberg sums up the discussion by saying: [95] "the possibility of Jewish influence on the Berbers, and even Judaizing by certain Berber groups, should not be ruled out. That influence may have obtained not only in the pre-Islamic period, but also in the days of Arab rule." There survive, indeed, several fragments of evidence of such influence in the pre-Arab period. The epigraphical material at Teucheira speaks in clear language of reciprocal influence between the two elements in the 1st century B.C., and similar hints appear in eastern Cyrenaica and at Ptolemais; [96] we have also noticed signs of contact between Jews and Libyans at Barka. [97] Even if the tribes of the Nafusa and the other tribes of Cyrenaican origin did not really Judaize, Jewish settlement on the Syrtic Gulf is very ancient, and we shall shortly see evidence that the Jews continued to enter that area in the 1st century A.D. This study has also made it clear that the physiographic conditions of Cyrenaica, as well as its agrarian development, associated the Jews and the Libyan tribes in a common plight.

Jewish literature early reveals an interest in Libyan origins, and claims that they are kindred to the Jews because they are descended from the Canaanites who had been expelled from their country by Joshua. This idea is expressed in the *Book of Jubilees*, composed a short time before the beginning of the Christian era; [98] the same information, cited by Flavius Josephus, [99] derives from Cleudamos, also known as Malchus, a Jewish or Samaritan historian who appears to have written in the 2nd century B.C. The tradition, then, originated not later than in the same century; it is further quoted by King Juba in his work. [100] Yoḥanan Lewy on the other hand, [101] argues that belief in the Canaanite origin of the African natives arose from the dispute between the Jews and Phoenicians over the ownership of Eretz Yisrael, which flared up following the

---

[95] *Ibid.*, p. 338.

[96] In eastern Cyrenaica, the name Βεῖσχα (see here p. 290); at Ptolemais the name Itthalammon son of Apella (p. 168).

[97] Aladdeir—Ele'azar, see here p. 198, note.

[98] Simon, *Le Judaïsme* etc., *loc. cit.* (note 91), p. 40.

[99] *Ant.* I, 15 (239-241).

[100] Jacoby, *FGH*, II, frag. 123.

[101] *Worlds Meet: Studies in the Situation of Jewry in the Greek and Roman World*, 1960, pp. 60 sqq. (Heb.).

Maccabean conquests, and was influenced by Greek legal conceptions. If Lewy was right, then the tradition on the Canaanite
origins relates not to the Libyans but to the Phoenicians. This
view, however, evokes two questions: Why was the tradition of
Canaanite origin also accepted by the Jews, precisely in connection
with Africa; and how did it become popular among the simple
people of the African countryside? [102] If these ideas were known
to the Phoenicians, who used them as propaganda against the
Jews, such propaganda was apt to be useful to both sides, and in
Africa it could be turned to the advantage of the latter. The very
use of such propaganda by non-Jews beyond the frontiers of Eretz
Yisrael means that Jewish counter-influence existed. Professor
Y. Guttman, indeed,[103] has noticed an interesting element in later
Jewish hellenistic literature which constitutes valid evidence of a
rapprochement between Jews and Libyans in the 1st century
A.D. This is to be found in the surviving portions of the Greek
tragedy of Ezekiel, written in Egypt in the 1st century A.D., on
the subject of the Exodus.[104] It is superfluous to remark that the
theme was not one likely to appeal to Egyptians; more important,
it transfers the encounter of Moses with the Midianites and his
subsequent friendship with them to the Libyans of the Western
Desert. As Josephus recorded that Eophren, who conquered
Libya, was descended from Madian son of Abraham, Ezekiel must
have read an allied source, perhaps Cleodamus,[105] and it becomes
clear that this genealogy was being used by the Jews as propaganda
among the Libyans at least as early as the 1st century of the
present era.

If this was so, whether or not Simon's conjecture on Jewish
expansion in this period is right, his idea of the concentration of
rebellious elements in the desert borders is extremely likely, and
helps us to understand the episode of Jonathan the Weaver, the
more so in the light of the knowledge provided by the *War Scroll*.
Josephus states explicitly that "the Zealot madness' was not
restricted to one city of Cyrenaica, hence it is clear that Jonathan
was not isolated in his activity and that the ferment did not die

---

[102] Augustini *Ep. ad Rom. expos. inchoata*, c. 13,—*PL*, Migne, 35, p. 2096.
[103] Y. Guttman, *Jewish Hellenistic Literature*, II, 1963, pp. 9-69; 68
(Heb.).
[104] Clemens Alex.; *Stromata*, I, 23, 155-6; *PG* 8, cols. 901-3.
[105] *Ant.* I, 15 (238-9); cf. *ibid.* 240.

down with the massacre of two thousand Jews and the execution of Jonathan. The pressure of the renewed intensification of agriculture which spread over the plateau hand-in-hand with the revision of property boundaries (the *limitatio*), displaced a growing number of Libyans, driving them to the desert fringes, which became the seed beds of the rebellion which was to break out in the reign of Trajan; here was created and forged the religious covenant between the Jewish zealots and the Berber tribes of the south.[106]

Both Jewish tradition and Roman geographical sources add certain information which tends to support the view that the Jews

---

[106] The analogy that suggests itself is the settlement of Ḥirbet Qumran. As to Cyrenaica itself, a historical parallel might be seen in the function of the "Zawiet" or settlements of the Order of the Sanusi during the war conducted by the Libyans against the Italian government in 1912-1931. The more important of these settlements were on the margin of the desert and also in the oases linked by the caravan routes. They were supported by contributions from the tribes and by trade; some of their supplies came from the occupied regions. It is important to emphasize that their existence was rendered possible by tribal support and by supplies from without. It should also be remembered that the Sanusis were first and foremost a movement of the countryside. The rebel forces that fought the Italians and found their leadership in the Order, were supported by an underground of the inhabitants of the Plateau, who were outwardly reconciled to Italian rule. From these they derived arms and manpower; among them they rested and recovered from their wounds. (For an account of these circumstances, see E. Evans Pritchard, *The Sanusi of Cyrenaica*, 1949, pp. 50 sqq.). This analogy informs us that a rebellion organized on the desert margin, particularly in ancient times, and probably without the aid of the camel, which only appeared west of the Nile valley at the end of the 2nd century A.D., required the cooperation of the tribes inhabiting the desert margins and of the settled population of the fertile areas. Yet for all the suggestive value of the analogy concerned, any conclusion based on such vis-à-vis the character of the development of the Jewish rising in Cyrenaica, remains conjectural in the absence of archaeological research on the relevant desert margins. Nor should it be forgotten that Roman garrisons were stationed at several keypoints of the desert such as the Oases of el-Behneseh, Ḥargiyeh and ed-Daḥliyeh. (For details, see J. Lesquier, *L'armée romaine de l'Égypte*, 1918, II, pp. 412-17). The period of the occupation of some of these stations is unknown, but 1st-century inscriptions are known at el-Daḥliyeh and el-Ḥargiyeh; an inscription of Trajan's time has been found near the latter oasis. (AD 107). A Roman fortlet at Nedurah, between the above two oases, was built under Hadrian or Antoninus Pius, and Gasr az-Zayyin south of el-Ḥargiyeh, was restored in 157. Important *in pari materia* is the inscription from the fortified temple at Kissos, (Gasr ed-Dush) in the Ḥargiyeh oasis, which records the building of its pylon in 116, and the completion of the work between April and May of that year (*OGIS* 677—Λιθ′ Αὐτοκράτορος Τραιανοῦ Πάχων α′, and cf. *JRS* 21, 1931, p. 6). The absence here of the title "Parthicus" is explained by Longden (*ibid.*) as owing to the Jewish revolt, which had interfered with the transmission of news along the desert routes.

in the period were being pushed westward and southward. The
Jews of the Syrtis retain a tradition that one of Titus' commanders,
named Pangor, settled 30,000 Jews in that country.[107] This tradition should apparently be connected with the story in a fragmentary mediaeval manuscript, perhaps derived from the Chronicle of
Yeraḥmeel, who wrote in the 12th century and used various
classical and Jewish sources, concerning the settlement of 30,000
exiles from Jerusalem by Titus' commander, Pangor, in Carthage.[108]
It is interesting that the name of "Pangor" contains four letters of
the names Paconius Agrippinus in their correct order. Moreover,
the historical nucleus of this tradition may be reflected in the
Roman settlement of Iscina Locus Iudaeorum Augusti, situated on
the Syrtic coast in eastern Tripolitania, some 80 kilometres west
of the frontier between Cyrenaica and Numidia. The place appears
under its full name only in the *Tabula Peutingeriana*,[109] in the 4th
century; as Iscina in the *Itinerarium Antonini* (3rd century A.D.),[110]
and in Ptolemy's *Geography* (mid-2nd century A.D.).[111] In sources
of the 4th and 1st centuries B.C. the same locality is marked
as Charax.[112] It is therefore probable that Iscina was founded
between the 1st century B.C. and the middle of the 2nd century
A.D.[113] There is indeed additional evidence suggesting that Iscina
was founded in the Flavian period. The name "Locus Augusti"
is a clear indication that the settlement originated on imperial
land and was never a municipium or a colony. A number of sources
preserve cases of the founding of settlements, generally without
municipal status, by the personal initiative of the first Flavian
Emperor: to this class belonged the colony of Flaviopolis, preceded by a Claudian settlement in Thrace, whence it was removed
to Asia by Vespasian;[114] a similar settlement founded by Vespasian

---

107 N. Slouschz, *The Jewish Dispersion of North Africa*, 1946, p. 29. (Heb.).

108 A. Neubauer, *Mediaeval Jewish Chronicles*, I, 1887, p. 190—*Mid.
Lam. I*, 31; *Sepher le-Yuḥsin le-R.A. Zakkut*.

109 K. Miller, 1962, VIII, 1; cf. p. 15.

110 65.1.

111 IV, 3, 11.

112 *Stadiasmus* (Müller), 87; Strabo, XVII, 3, 20 (836).

113 The catacomb epitaph at Rome (*CIJ* I, 7) recording a grammateus of
the Σεκηνοί, has been thought to refer to Iscina, but this is far from certain
(cf. H. J. Leon, *The Jews of Ancient Rome*, 1960, pp. 149-51). For a new
suggestion, that the reference is to the island of Sikinos in the Aegean, see
now Applebaum, *The Jewish People in the First Century*, II, 1977, p. 720.

114 T. Mommsen, *Provinces of the Roman Empire*, I, 1909, pp. 306-7, n. 1;
JRS 3, 1913, p. 120; Plin, *HN*, IV, 11, 47.

in Samos;[115] tracts near Panormus in Sicily allocated for the settlement of discharged troops and of members of Vespasian's own household (i.e. slaves);[116] and land assigned by the same Emperor to tenants and members of his household at Abella in Campania.[117] On the basis of these examples, we may follow Monceaux's suggestion [118] that Iscina was established by Vespasian (or Titus) for Jewish slaves transferred as prisoners of war from Judaea, or for Jews from Cyrenaica who no longer found a place there or were suspected of seditious activity.[119] It is inherently likely that both elements were represented at Iscina.

The name *locus* is defined by Ulpian [120] as part of an agricultural estate (*fundus*), and in the texts of agrarian laws frequently appears as a term designating rural property (*ager, locus, aedificium*);[121] in the south of France more especially the term indicates an agricultural settlement, and in one case at least, the centre of a large estate.[122] In Britain, however, and in some regions of the Danube basin, the *loci* were points near the frontier regions where fairs were held by the natives at fixed times under the supervision of the authorities and with its permission,[123] These points were generally also cult-centres, hence it is very possible that Locus Iscina was a place of meeting for the Jewish inhabitants of a number of local settlements at festivals and on appointed days. It is at any rate clear from the Roman name, that the settlement stood on imperial land, and was essentially agricultural, although it is not impossible that it was meant also as the site of a fair at fixed times. The modern name of the place, Medinet es-Sultan, still preserves the memory of imperial ownership.

---

[115] *IGR* IV, 991. 992.

[116] *Schriften der römischen Feldmesser*, p. 211.

[117] *Ibid., Liber coloniarum*, I, p. 230.

[118] *RétJ*, 44, 1902, p. 7; A. Merigli, *La Tripolitania antica*, I, 1940, p. 212 n.: "Non è improbabile che fomentassero la rivolta (sc. dei Nasamones) gli Ebrei immigrati nella Sirtica in seguito alla repressione della sommossa scoppiato in Cirenaica l'anno 72 d. Chr."

[119] Cf. in the same period the settlement by Vespasian of opponents of the great revolt at Yavneh, which was an imperial estate (B. *Gitt.* 56b; Jos. *BJ* IV, 81 (444); *Ant. XVIII*, 2, 2 (31).

[120] Ulp. *Dig.* L, 16, 27 (Mommsen, *CIC*, I, 910).

[121] Bruns, *Fontes Iuris. Rom.* 1, no. 11 (111 BC).

[122] A. Grenier, *Manuel d'archéologie gallo-romaine*, VI, ii, 1936, pp. 730-32; *CIL* XII, 1524.

[123] I. A. Richmond in *Archaeologia*, 93, 1959, p. 15; cf. *Cosmographus Ravennas*, (Schnetz) paras. 228-35—*ibid.* p. 19.

As we have seen, Jewish settlement in the Syrtis region had begun in the hellenistic period, and perhaps even earlier. But Iscina is not the only evidence of Jewish migration to this shore in the Roman imperial period. A cemetery of the 4th century A.D. discovered at Syrtis itself, included inter alia a number of tombstones with pronouncedly Jewish names, some bearing the imperial family names.[124] Bertoccini remarked of this discovery: "We have here slaves or tenants, most of them Jews, employed in the maintenance and working of the imperial estates which were numerous in Tripolitania." [125] It may well be that this settlement began in the Flavian period, and that the nearby Roman station of Praesidium, whose site is known by the Arabs as "Yehudiyeh", was founded about the same time.[126]

The year 73 saw the annihilation of the Jewish aristocracy of Cyrenaica, and the disappearance of the mediating factor between the Greek population and the Jewish community. This had doubtless included the most hellenized element of local Jewry, meaning the more "moderate" among them in all that concerned national and economic problems. The Jews of Cyrenaica thus remained leaderless, and the way was open for the revolutionary activists. They were aided by the social situations for our analysis indicates the presence among the Jews of a considerable number of landless peasantry, and it may be supposed that these elements were an object of propaganda the aim of which is represented by the acts of Jonathan the Weaver and described in the *War Scroll* of the Dead Sea sect.

It is impossible to say whether a Jewish rural population remained in Cyrenaica at this time. But in so far as Jewish tenants or subtenants remained on the *ager publicus*, something might be learnt of their plight from evidence on the attitude of Trajan's government to the Jewish tenants on the land of Eretz Yisrael. This can be derived from several Midrashim which relate to the predicament of Jewish tenants on confiscated land in Judaea in the same period.[127] Vespasian had confiscated much of the country's land at the end of the War of the Destruction.[128] Much of this ap-

---

[124] *AI* 2, p. 200.
[125] *Loc. cit.*
[126] P. J. Mesnage, *Le Christianisme en Afrique*, 1914, p. 11.
[127] See Applebaum, *Prologomena to the Study of the Second Jewish Revolt*, (132-5), 1976, pp. 10-12.
[128] Jos., *BJ* VII, 6, 6 (216-7); not *ager publicus*, as stated by Alon, *Hist.*

pears in the records as subject to holders who are called Matziqim (מציקים).[129] who oppress and harass the Jewish cultivators. These are not *conductores*, or state lessees, since they can sell their holdings; it is clear from a Midrash [130] that they included various elements from the Roman aristocracy to ex-soldiers, or their agents, who had received their lands in grant from the Emperor. *Midrash Siphri de-bei-Rav* [131] surveys all the regions of the country in which these holders are active, writing *inter alia*: "and the Negev, meaning that He showed him the South enjoying its calm, then showed it to him again with Matziqim holding it . . . the City of Palms (Jericho) . . . unto Zoar, these are the Matziqim of Israel." *Midrash Tannaim* speaks in similar language: [132] ". . . the Negev . . . unto Zoar, where He showed him the place, Matzirei Yisrael (= Matziquei Yisrael)".

The two extracts cited inform us that there were Matziqim in the northern Negev, or the Darom, also in Zoar at the south end of the Dead Sea. These midrashim are not later than the 2nd century of the common era, but the reference to lands at Zoar which are in the hands of Roman owners cannot precede Trajan's annexation of the Province of Arabia in A.D. 106/7.[133] It may therefore be deduced that Vespasian's original policy towards Jewish cultivators in Judaea had not changed under Trajan twenty or thirty years later.

We have no actual evidence that Trajan discriminated against the Jews of the Diaspora before the revolt of 115, just as there is no information that his predecessors had done so as a result of events in Judaea, if we except the imposition of the Jewish tax. But in Cyrenaica in 73 an abnormal situation had developed. The weal-

---

of the Jews of Eretz Yisrael in the Period of the Mishnah and the Talmud, I, 1954, p. 97 (Heb.), unless we are prepared to accept the fine legal distinction drawn by Baldacci, *PP* 24, 1969, pp. 363 sqq., between the emperors' *patrimonium* and previous royal property administered by the emperors for the Roman people.

[129] A. Büchler, *Der galiläische Amhaares*, 1906, pp. 36 sq.; S. Klein, *Palästinensische Studien*, I, 1923, pp. 10 sqq.; Alon, *op. cit.*, p. 37; Applebaum, *Prologomena, loc. cit.* (n. 127).

[130] *Mid. Tannaim* (Hoffmann), pp. 224, 317; the full evidence will be found in Applebaum, *Prologomena* (n.117), pp. 10-11; *id., Aufstieg und Niedergang der römischen Welt*, II, 8: The countryside as a political and economic factor 1979, pp. 289-94.

[131] Friedmann, 352, p. 149.

[132] Hoffmann, p. 224.

[133] *IEJ* 12, 1962, p. 258; *CIL* III, 4-5; Supp. 14149; Dessau, *ILS*, 5834.

thier Jews had been put to death and their property sequestrated, while the rest of the community had manifested signs of ferment and rebellion. And if in the process of the reorganization of tenures, which lasted down to Trajan's reign, problems occurred involving Jewish tenants or their settlement, it is not hard to imagine what attitude they encountered on the part of the representatives of the imperial government.[134]

In proportion as the outbreak of the Jewish rebellion draws nearer, the evidence diminishes which might throw light on the immediate circumstances of its outbreak.[135] But since the Second World War archaeology has made one important contribution to an understanding of the general background. In 1949 the late Colonel J. Baradez published his important book on the Roman frontier-system of Numidia,[136] containing details of his explorations by air-photography of a hitherto relatively unknown Roman fortified system. These fortifications surround the Aurez Mountains on the west and south; inscriptions evidence that they were first organized under Trajan or Hadrian,[137] and the line is closely bound up with planned areas of cultivation and with installations for storage of runoff and its direction to the fields, in other words, with an extensive and systematic scheme of agricultural settlement. This undertaking may be interpreted to mean that its purpose was to pin down the nomadic tribes of Numidia, to settle them in fixed agriculture and thus to put an end permanently to their seasonal movement backward and forward between the desert fringes and the cultivated areas. The significance of this impressive undertaking is, that in the reign of Trajan the problem of the relation between the Libyan tribes inhabiting the desert borders and the permanently settled population of the Roman provinces of Africa had reached a crisis.

Another archaeological discovery illumines the darkness shrouding the outbreak of the rebellion. This is part of a clay lamp al-

---

[134] Cf. Aurelius Victor, *Epit. de Caes.*, 42.21: cuius (sc. Traianus) procuratores cum provincias calumniis agitarent . . .

[135] The rebellion of the Nasamones noted here in n. 118 (A.D. 85—Jos., *BJ* II, 16, 4 (381); Eus., *Chron.*, ann. 2101) may well have been a symptom of what was to occur in the area at a later date. See here n. 118.

[136] *Fossatum Africae: Recherches aériennes de l'organisation des confins sahariens à l'époque romaine*, 1949.

[137] Baradez, *op. cit.*, pp. 100-104; 359-63; *The Congress of Roman Frontier Studies*, 1949, ed. Birley, 1952, pp. 18-19.

ready alluded to (p. 194),[138] found at Cyrene in the area east of the Acropolis and south of the Agora. Another similar example, also fragmentary, was subsequently found in the Agora itself, alongside the foundation of Temple E6.[139] Less than half the first lamp remains, but this is sufficient to show that its diameter was as much as 9.3 cm. The lamp is covered with a burnished maroon slip, its upper face being surrounded by a moulding and an ovolo frieze; within this is figured a seven-branched candlestick (menorah), and to its right appears an unidentifiable object, possibly a palm-branch. The menorah evidently occupied only part of the face, and what filled the remainder of the surface can only be conjectured. The filling hole must have been small. The type belongs to the second half of the 1st century and to the 2nd century, A.D., and is one of the commonest in this period, being known in Asia Minor, Italy, Egypt, Africa, Gaul, Greece and Eretz Yisrael.[140] The excavations carried out at Teucheira in 1954 proved that this type of lamp was also manufactured in Cyrenaica; the rubbish dump of a pottery kiln was found in the Jewish cemetery to the west of the town, and in this similar lamps had been fired, as shown by the presence of the same type.[141] The figures on those found were chiefly pagan deities (Astarte, Ganymede, Erotes), also gladiators and an erotic scene; only one decorative motif, a rosette, could have been acceptable to Jews. A number of examples of this type are known from Cyrene,[142] including one which had been spoilt in the firing,[143] providing additional evidence of local manufacture. Similar lamps have been found at Gerasa in Transjordan, among remains of a potter's workshop turning out lamps and figurines, the finds belonging in the main to the reign of Trajan.[144] Of the examples of this type from Gerasa, numbers 134-6 included figures

---

[138] *IEJ* 7, 1957, pp. 157 sqq.; *Eretz Yisrael* (Narkis Memorial Volume), 6, 1960, pp. 73 sqq. (Heb.-Eng. résumé).

[139] Stucchi, *Cirene*, 1957-66, 1967, p. 163; *L'agora de Cirene*, 1965, I, pp. 217, 237.

[140] O. Bronner, *Corinth IV*, (ii), 1930, Terracotta Lamps, pl. x, xii, Types xxv, xxvii, and pp. 83, 90, 182; H. B. Walters, *Catalogue of Greek and Roman Lamps in the British Museum*, 1914, eg. no. 787; cf. H. Goldman, *Excavations at Gozlu Kule, Tarsus*, I, 1950, p. 115, Group xvi, Class B, no. 203.

[141] G. R. Wright, Excavations at Tocra, *PEJ* 1963, pp. 28 sqq.

[142] Walters, *op. cit.*, nos. 1059, 1125.

[143] *Ibid.* 1065.

[144] J. Iliffe, *Imperial Art in Transjordan*, QDAP, 11, 1945, pp. 1-26, pl. viii-ix, nos. 134-6, 114-5.

of pagan deities, and one bore the figure of the ram of Jupiter Ammon and palmleaves: the appearance of the ram proves that this lamp did not precede the transfer of the legion III Cyrenaica to the province of Arabia about the year 128.[145]

All the above finds carried pagan decoration, and no other examples of the type are recorded to the best of my knowledge, with the figure of the menorah. All other known clay lamps bearing the menorah-symbol belong, on the view till recently accepted, to the late Roman or to the Byzantine period; they have been classi-fied by Reifenberg,[146] who dated them not earlier than the 3rd century A.D., the overwhelming majority of them being of the 4th century or later. (On new evidence from Judaea, see p. 240). It is further generally agreed that the menorah as a decorative motif in Jewish art does not precede the destruction of the Second Temple, and even if some exceptional cases are known,[147] there is little doubt that it became common chiefly after the year 70. This is confirmed at Teucheira, where the latest datable Jewish tomb belongs to the year 94 (see pp. 154 sqq), and symbols are virtually lacking, only two examples of the menorah being known.[148] This is precisely what we should expect in a cemetery most of whose burials belong to the period before 70, on the assumption that the menorah became common on graves after that year. The Cyrene lamps with menorah motif, therefore, were probably made after the Destruction, and obviously cannot be later than the years 115-117, when the country's Jewish community was annihilated. If these deductions are correct, the present lamp-type is the oldest known which bears the figure of the menorah-symbol.

The figure of the seven-branched candlestick appears in Cyrenaica at two places in very unusual circumstances. The first is at 'Ein Targhuna, where it is cut deeply into a Roman road leading to Ḥirbet al-Yahud (on this site, see p. 170 sqq.). What is the meaning of a menorah incised in so extraordinary a position? The second

---

[145] H. M. D. Parker, *The Roman Legions*[2], 1958, p. 162. But see now Keppie, *Latomus*, 32, 1973, p. 862.

[146] A. Reinfenberg, Jüdische Lampen, *JPOS* 16, 1936, pp. 166-79.

[147] On coins of Antigonus Matthias, (40-37 B.C.), and on the walls of the Jewish rockcut tomb in Alfasi Street, western Jerusalem (*IEJ* 6, 1956, pp. 127-8). The finds in the tomb were dated between the 2nd century BC and the 1st century AD, and nothing was found later than the reign of Tiberius.

[148] *PEJ* 1963, p. 54—"Tomb A"; *Bull. Amer. Arch. Inst.* 2, 1911, p. 57, pl. ii.

instance may assist an answer. It is located at Ptolemais, where the figure is seen cut on the north wall of the south tower guarding the western city gate. The latter was built by Comanus, minister of Euergetes II, in about 158 B.C., and the same wall exhibits other incised inscriptions made by Greeks, apparently soldiers of the garrison.[149] The menorah is so inappropriate to what surrounds it that it may be interpreted as a challenge, and after A.D. 70 it would only be attributed to the revolt of Trajan's time. An aggressive act like the cutting of a menorah [150] in a public place can only possess the significance of defiance or victory. We are thus reminded of the formula inscribed on two milestones of Hadrian from Cyrene and its vicinity: "The Emperor Hadrian (with all his routine titles) restored the road which had been overturned and broken up (*eversa et corrupta*) in the Jewish revolt." [151] A paved road can be overturned and broken up; this cannot be done to a rockcut road, but Jewish victory can be expressed in relation to it by cutting the menorah symbol in its surface.[152] The conclusion is, that the menorah became for the Jews of Cyrene in the years 115-117 a political symbol and a sign of defiance and revolt. This conclusion harmonizes with the origin of lamps bearing the menorah figure in Cyrenaica, and if this suggestion is correct, Cyrenaica may be regarded as one of the points of diffusion of that symbol as a decorative motif on Jewish objects and buildings after the destruction of the Second Temple.

Several facts can be adduced concerning the function of this and similar types of lamp in the early Roman Empire. The decorative motifs on them are many and various, but we may notice among them the appearance of the figure of the Goddess of Victory,[153] of victors of a horse-race with their horse,[154] and the oakleaf wreath (*corona civica*), symbolizing valour.[155] Very popular and well

---

[149] *DAI* I, Cir. i, 1933, p. 169.

[150] Cf. *Zion*, 19, 1959, p. 26, n. 16. (Heb.).

[151] *SEG* 9, 252; *JRS* 40, 1950, p. 89, D/4.

[152] The confrontation of a menorah with the inscription "Victoria Augusta" among the rock cuttings in Wadi Umm Sidera in south Sinai (Rothenberg, in *Roman Frontier Studies* 1967, 1971, p. 221, fig. 109) might well belong to the time of Trajan. For the development of the imperial Victory cult in his reign, see J. Beaujeu, *La religion romaine à l'apogée de l'empire*, I, 1955, pp. 58-64.

[153] Walters, *op. cit.*, no. 780.

[154] *Ibid.*, no. 788.

[155] *Ibid.*, no. 1016.

known is the lamp bearing the new year greeting *annum novum, faustum, felicem*, accompanied by the figure of the Goddess of Victory.[156] Fragmentary examples of such found at Petra were incised with the addition word "Shalom" (peace) in Nabataean characters.[157] Cases are also known in which lamps served as propaganda in the Roman world; such were the lamps inscribed *Genio Populi Romani Feliciter* (in the form of the abbreviation *GPRF*),[158] or *Ob cives servatos*.[159] In several instances these inscriptions occurred on a round shield (*clipeus*) supported by the figure of the Victory Goddess appearing in much the same form as on the new year lamps. Others of this type carry the letters *S(enatus) C(onsulto)*,[160] evidencing that they were manufactured officially under state auspices. The date of the general type of the "Victory lamps" is in the reigns of Augustus and his successors,[161] while the inscription *Ob cives servatos* connects them with the coins inscribed with the same words. These were first struck by Augustus to commemorate his successful campaign in Spain in 27 B.C.; they appear again on coins of 19 B.C. to celebrate the recovery of the Roman military standards from Parthia.[162] The inscription is again encountered on coins of Vespasian, on which it surrounds an oak leaf wreath, symbol of victorious courage.[163] There can be little doubt, therefore, that certain types of "Victory Lamps" resembling typologically the Cyrenean specimen under discussion, were used for purposes of state propaganda, and on two occasions one of these inscriptions marked successes on the eastern front of the Empire.

Very interesting is the function assigned to a lamp found in Campania,[164] which belongs to the same type as the example from Cyrene. Its shape is similar, but the decorative motifs around the inner circle of the face are divided into pointed leaves .The face of the lamp shows the figure of a seated goddess, winged and hel-

---

[156] Walters, *op. cit.*, no. 780; Dessau, *ILS* 8613.

[157] Hammond, *BASOR*, 146, 1957, pp. 10-13.

[158] Dressel, *CIL* XV, p. 784; 6194-6220.

[159] Walters, *op. cit.*, nos. 649-652; Dressel, *ibid.*, p. 786.

[160] S. Loeschke, *Katalog der Lampen aus Vindonissa*, 1919, no. 386.

[161] See n. 156.

[162] For both groups of coins see C. H. V. Sutherland, *Coinage in Roman Imperial Policy*, 31 *B.C.*—68 *A.D.*, 1951, pp. 37, 47.

[163] H. Cohen, *Description historique des Monnaies Impériales*, 1880, I, no. 275 (Vespasian, p. 388).

[164] A. Héron de Villefosse, *Monuments Piot*, V, 1889 sqq., pp. 180 sqq., fig. 44; M. Rostovtzeff, *SEHRE*, 1957, pl. xviii, 2 and p. 132.

meted, who symbolizes, it would seem, both Rome and Victory. She is pouring a libation onto an altar before her, and is surrounded by symbols of the Empire's more important cults; the eagle of Jupiter, the dolphin of Neptune, the hawk of Horus, the club of Heracles, the sistrum of Isis, the lyre of Apollo, the pincers of Vulcan, the caduceus of Mercury and the torch of Demeter. A central place is occupied by the corn-ear, pomegranate, cymbals and raven of the Great Mother (Magna Mater) of Asia, also by a sacred standard combining the sun and the moon, the symbols of the deities of Asia and Syria alike. It is probable enough that this lamp originated in the east, and that its purpose was to emphasize the unity of the Empire's cults under the leadership of Rome. A group of figures which resembles the above in every respect is represented on a circular lamp found at Rome; [165] the lamp-face here being defined, not by leaf motifs, but by simple mouldings. This specimen has sixteen nozzles. Parallel in function and content are two earthenware medallions from Italy, today in the Museum of Mediterranean Archaeology at Nir David, Israel; they bear a number of religious symbols, including the caduceus, the trident, the pincers, the sun-wheel, the moon, the double cornucopeia, the sceptre, the thunderbolt and the cymbals. Another example of lamp propaganda is represented by the specimen found at Gerasa already referred to, bearing the figure of Zeus Ammon. The third legion "Cyrenaica" was transferred to Arabia somewhere about 128, and as the worship of Ammon in Eretz Yisrael was in the main confined to the military and originated there with the same legion,[166] this find must be later than most of the other objects from the same workshop, and it may be supposed that it reflects propaganda conducted to spread the cult of Ammon for political purposes.

It has also been remarked that the Cyrenean lamp is of unusual size, and the menorah on it constituted only a small part of the decoration occupying the upper surface. What constituted the

---

[165] H. Th. Bossert, *Geschichte des Kunstgewerbes*, IV, 1930, p. 275. The lamp is the work of the potter Primus, who worked in Greece in the 1st and 2nd centuries of the present era, although he came from Italy. (O. Bronneer, *Corinth* IV, 1930, ii, p. 97; *CIL* XV, 6684, 6784; Loeschke, *op. cit.*, p. 248; Walters, *op. cit.*, p. xxxvi). The lamp with face surrounded with leaf-motifs is among his products. One of his lamps, of 2nd-century date, bears the figure of Zeus enthroned (Walters, *op. cit.*, no. 1204).

[166] D. Sourdel, *Les cultes de Hauran à l'époque romaine*, 1952, pp. 89 sqq.

rest of it? As we have been able to determine which types of gentile lamp were the prototypes of the Jewish example, a conjecture may be hazarded. The gentile examples, some of which were circulated at the instance of the government itself, laid stress on the idea of victory, figuring the Roman goddess of Victory or a similar deity (such as Zeus) as victor, or the Roman Victory as leader and unifier of the Empire's cults; this motif takes the form of Victorious Rome surrounded by the symbols of those same cults.

The Cyrene lamp is the Jewish response to this iconic propaganda, hence it may be supposed that it too represented a group of symbols emphasizing—as against the unity of the pagan worship concentrated about the Roman victory—the unity of Judaism about the One God.[167] It is clear from the angle of the menorah-figure and from its relation to the object by it, that it was not one of a pair of candlesticks flanking a central figure, as often seen in a later period on Jewish lamps, frescos, sculptures, glassware and mosaics. It apparently occupied a central position over other symbols. It may be conjectured that these symbols were ranged round one central object, and if this was a symbol of God, it could only have taken the form of the Temple or the Ark of the Covenant. It is probable enough that the other symbols were of the type appearing on later Jewish lamps and more especially on the "Gold Glass" bowls [168] which have been found chiefly at Rome and Cologne. These are the lulab, etrog, and incense shovel, the cruse of oil and the other vessels of the Temple service. On the other hand the menorah figure seems to have been emphasized, despite its relative smallness.

The Cyrene lamp, then, may be interpreted as interesting evidence of the "cold war" between pagan worship and Judaism in the period preceding the revolt against Trajan in the years 115-117. This hypothesis finds some support in the distribution of a decorated Jewish lamp-type bearing the menorah symbol in the Hebron—Beth-Govrin—Gaza area of Judaea.[169] Typologically these lamps are Herodian, but are known to have lasted down to the time of the

---

[167] Cf. R. Yoḥanan's statement (*Meg.* 13a): "Every man who rejects idolatry may be termed a Jew".

[168] R. Vopel, *Die Altkristliche Goldgläser*, 1889; F. Neuberg, *Glass in Antiquity*, 1949, pp. 49 sqq.; E. R. Goodenough, *Jewish Symbols in the Greco-Roman Period*, II, 1953, pp. 108 sqq.

[169] V. Sussmann, *Ornamental Jewish Oil Lamps*, 1972, (Heb.), pp. 32-3.

Second Revolt (132-135), while the widespread use of the menorah as a decorative symbol does not generally precede the year 70 (above). It is probably significant, therefore, that the distribution of these lamps coincides with one of the focal areas of the Second Revolt. The Cyrene lamp shows, moreover, that the struggle was being conducted in the urban centres of Cyrenaica, and that the preparation for the violent outbreak which took place in Trajan's reign, if it was based on the countryside and on the fringes of the desert, was not restricted to it.

CHAPTER SIX

THE CYRENEAN REBELLION AND
THE ZEALOT MOVEMENT

The destruction of the Second Temple in the year 70 did little
to alter the basic status of Judaism in the Roman Empire, for this
was determined not by a general legislative act but by the policy
of the Emperors and the laws of the Greek cities of the eastern
Mediterranean.[1] If a written political treaty had previously existed
between the Roman Senate and the Jewish nation in Judaea, this
now ceased to be valid,[2] and we must assume that the Jews of
Judaea now became *dediticii*, meaning, a conquered people without
internal autonomous rights or external representation. But one
grave discriminatory measure was imposed upon the Jews in
all provinces of the Empire, namely, the diversion of the half-
sheqel contribution till then paid to the Temple of Jerusalem, to a
Fiscus Iudaicus to be devoted to the cult of Jupiter Capitolinus.
An additional contribution (ἀπαρχή) was also imposed upon them.[3]
In the words of Baron,[4] "for the first time, the Jews of the whole
empire became a special source of revenue. Here was born the idea
of the Jew as a specific tax-payer, to play so important a rôle in
later fiscal history."

The struggle between Jews and gentiles had indeed been growing
steadily during the 1st century of the common era. The resistance of
the Greek cities to Jewish influence had begun as early as in the
middle of the 2nd century B.C. with the collision between Antiochus
IV and the Hasmoneans, while in Egypt there grew up contemporarily an anti-Semitic propaganda literature and a Jewish
literature of counter-propaganda.[5] This continued antagonism

---

[1] J. Juster, *Les Juifs dans l'empire romain*, I, 1914, pp. 223-4.

[2] Cf. Juster, *op. cit.*, I, p. 226. Juster saw the source of Jewish rights
throughout the Empire in a political treaty, and accordingly believed that
such a treaty remained uncancelled. For the difficulties affecting Juster's
view, see Applebaum, *The Jewish People in the First Century*, edd. Safrai,
Stern, I, 1974, pp. 456-7.

[3] H. I. Bell, *Juden und Griechen in römischen Alexandrien*, 1925, p. 33;
Appian, *Syr.*, 50.

[4] *SRHJ* II², 1952, p. 106.

[5] *SRHJ* I², pp. 188 sqq.; *CAH* IX, p. 433.

found expression in the attempt of the hellenic cities to abolish the autonomous rights of their Jewish communities, whose confirmation was demanded and implemented by Rome (thus in Ephesus, Alexandria, Tralles, Laodicea, Miletus and Cyrene itself)[6] Closely associated with this conflict was the continual refusal of the Greek towns to admit a status of equality between their own urban organizations and the Jewish politeumata existent in their midst. The prevailing Jewish attitude seems to have been to demand recognition of such equality, whereas the Greeks desired to impose the supremacy of their city government upon all Jews and other non-citizens resident within the city's territory.

This struggle however did not persist with equal intensity in every place. We have no record of it in Asia Minor after the beginning of the 1st century of the present era.[7] Yet it is clear from events at the time of the outbreak of the Jewish revolt of 66, that hatred for the Jews burned strongly among most of the Greek populations of the Syrian cities, and no less among the Greeks of Alexandria by Egypt.[8]

The Greeks justified their attitude by pointing to the non-participation of Jews in their cults, to their missionary activity, to their self-seclusion from gentile society and (in Alexandria) to their attacks upon the city's gymnasia. Greek hatred found expression, more particularly in Alexandria, in fierce and bloody intercommunal collisions such as occurred in the reign of Gaius, Claudius and Nero. Some scholars have further found as a cause of Greek hatred for the Jews in Egypt the factor of economic competition, and it has been stated that the Egyptian grain trade and transport branch were the monopoly of Roman and Jewish groups in the imperial period.[9] This alleged factor, added to the Roman government's defence of Jewish rights, it has been claimed, diverted against the Jews the hatred which the Greeks and Egyptians feared to express openly against the imperial rulers. I do not think however, that there is sufficient evidence of the real part played

---

[6] U. Kahrstedt, *Kulturgeschichte der römischen Kaiserzeit*[2], 1958, p. 389; Juster, *op. cit.*, I, p. 218, n. 3.

[7] Kahrstedt, *ibid.*, p. 387.

[8] The picture was not uniform. We may record fraternal relationships at a critical testing time at Gerasa in Transjordan (Jos., *BJ* II, 18, 5 (479-80)) and at Scythopolis-Beth Shean (*BJ* II, 18, 3-466), yet the latter episode also demonstrates the lack of stability of such relationships.

[9] Milne, *JRS* 17, 1927, p. 6.

by the Jews of Egypt in the country's trade in this period, to enable a decision on this question to be made,[10] but the study of the so-called *Acts of the Pagan Martyrs* [11] shows that there is a measure of truth in the idea of a "transference" of hatred, since the *Acts* frequently exhibit a desire to discredit the Roman administration by claiming it to be the ally of the Jews, also to discredit the Jews by pointing to their connections with the administration. The Jews indeed, like every minority, were interested in stable government, hence their leadership inclined to support, first the Ptolemies, later the Roman régime.

These factors, notwithstanding, were superficial, compared with one basic characteristic deeply inherent in Judaism, namely, the close identity between the Jew's religious consciousness and his ethnic-national awareness. The decline of the religion of the city-state in the hellenistic period had caused a growing separation between the Greek community's religion and the religion of the individual. The taboos bound up with the purity and destiny of the city, which had imposed certain cultic rites upon the community and certain restrictions upon the behaviour of its citizens, retreated before rationalism and the growth of larger political entities. The cults of the rulers of the hellenistic states and their successors, the emperors, were mere political instruments (albeit successful ones), and religious experience was relegated to the sphere of the individual, who now sought an answer to his spiritual needs in the philosophical schools or in the collective experience of the mystery cults. The attention of the individual turned to problems of personal moral behaviour, while the masses sought satisfaction and an outlet for their emotions in new symbologies. Throughout the Empire no single major group existed to advocate a conscious ethical code operable both in individual life and equally in politics—with the exception of the Jews. Some cultured and conscientious Roman officials believed, doubtless, in Rome's

---

[10] For Jewish merchants in Alexandria, see Tcherikover, *The Jews in Egypt*, pp. 63-6; *CPJ* I, pp. 49-50; Applebaum, *The Jewish People in the First Century*, II, 1977, pp. 706-7; and cf. *Tell Edfou* I, 1957, no. 141; P. Oxy. 276,—Jews engaged in grain transport. But the share of the Jewish ἔμποροι and ναύκληροι in the corn trade remains conjectural; Josephus (C. *Ap.*, II, 5 (64) attributes to them a part in the *administratio tritici*, but I would regard this as an exaggeration, and in any case what there was, was abolished by Augustus (*ibid.*).

[11] *CPJ* II, nos. 154-9.

civilizing mission and in the Stoic doctrine which saw in them the servants of humanity, but the character of their task and their class derivation restricted the realization of their outlook.[12] Only from Trajan's day were emperors chosen who were faithful to such conceptions and strove to carry them out. Yet it was precisely the first two of these, Trajan and Hadrian, in whose reigns the most violent conflicts between Rome and the Jews occurred. The Greek Cynic agitator might seek, indeed, to fan the spark of liberty among the populace of the eastern Mediterranean,[13] but the disappearance of the Greek polis as a political factor robbed it of its moral content and uprooted the social tradition capable of serving as the basis of a community wishing to realize its teaching. It was, in fact, Cynic influence that appears to have contributed in Alexandria to anti-Semitic violence.

The Jews, on the other hand, presented the unique synthesis of an ethnic unit with a geographical centre and a specific code of conduct based on a coordinated philosophy. There was no distinction amongst them between the religious and the secular, which sprang from a common source.[14] In other communities social evolution from a tribal structure had caused the separation of law from religious experience; the Jews had achieved a certain continuity of evolution which preserved the unity of the personal ethical (the prophetic) and legalist currents, and made them identical with a definite ethnic group. It was this peculiar complex which formed in the ancient world (as it does today) the source of confusion and misunderstanding among non-Jews. For the gentile of the hellenistic period and the Roman Empire, religion was a matter for the individual or an expression of loyalty to the state; he could not understand the unity of a religious-ethical group and an ethnic entity, and frequently feared it. The Jew felt his ethical code and ethnic identity to be inseparable; the effective application of the first was ensured by the preservation of the second, and this made

---

[12] "The Stoic teaching, indeed", writes Syme (*The Roman Revolution*, 1952, p. 57) "was nothing more than a corroboration and theoretical defence of certain traditional virtues of the governing class in an aristocratic and republican state."

[13] On the question of the Cynic opposition and the Stoic current in the Flavian period and their influence in the cities of the eastern provinces, see Rostovtzeff, *SEHRE*, 1957, pp. 114 sqq.; cf. Applebaum, *Studia Classica Israelica*, I, 1974, pp. 119-23.

[14] M. Hengel, *Die Zeloten*, 1961, pp. 97-8.

him a force in gentile society—a group individuality in an empire
that possessed, otherwise, an almost unlimited power of cosmopolitan absorption. It might be true to say that Judaism was the only
fully-fledged nationalism of the ancient world. Thus the Jewish
fusion of group identity and ethical code has widespread reper-
cussions when the Jewish diaspora began to expand; it became a
missionary force that made numerous converts. Although border-
line groups of half-proselytes arose, full proselytes inevitably became assimilated to the Jewish community: the Jews presented in
the diaspora the anomaly of a persistent sub-nation, active and
distinct. That their "exclusiveness" alienated the gentile is, however, unconvincing, since their widespread proselytizing activity
could never have been carried on had they maintained it. Nor are
proofs lacking of active assimilation by Jews to the gentile world,
whether internally or externally. Hellenistic Jewry sought various
compromises with its environment, and tried to make itself comprehensible to the non-Jew; there is no doubt that the wealthy
Jewish upper class saw no contradiction between loyalty to the
Ptolemies or the Caesars, and loyalty to Judaism; this is amply
evidenced by the *Aristeas Letter*, by the attitude and apology of
Josephus, by the conduct of the House of Herod and the Jewish
groups which deserted to Rome during the war of 66-73, or by the
behaviour of the Jewish upper class of Alexandria and Cyrene in
the years 70-73. But the Jewish fate was not to be decided either
by these or by the assimilated elements; the gentile was quicker
than many Jews to reject the reconcilability between a nation-
religion imposing a complete way of life, and the demand for complete equality of status on the part of its adherents living in alien
communities. The Jewish nation-religion was ultimately unreali-
zable except on its own soil. Not Jewish "exclusiveness" (a historical anachronism in this period) alienated the Greeks, but Jewish
difference.

In the fact of Jewish difference the Greek and Roman world
encountered a phenomenon which it did not understand and to
which it ultimately reacted with hostility; the active Jewish social
offensive further increased this hatred. In contradiction to this
reality stood the generally moderate policy of most of the emperors
towards the Jews until Hadrian's time. The reason for this moderation, expressed in the defence of Jewish internal rights throughout
the Empire, was not connected with any sympathy for Jewish

doctrine or for the Jewish people. The populous diaspora communities, their distribution on both sides of the eastern frontier, and the military potential ascribed to oriental Jewry by the Roman commanders, combined to deter Rome from provoking Jewish hostility so long as this could be avoided. Even Vespasian, after his victory in Judaea, did not abolish the rights of Diaspora Jewry, and Hadrian was the only emperor who attempted to root out Judaism by prohibiting the performance of its fundamental commandments. But concomitantly with Vespasian's imposition of the discriminatory Jewish tax, two warning notes are heard in the first century. Claudius, in confirming the internal communal rights of the Jews of Alexandria, warns them not to encourage the arrival of additional Jews in the city, lest he be compelled to take measures against them "as those provoking a general sickness throughout the world" (καθάπερ κοινόν τεινα τῆς οἰκουμένης νόσον ἐξεγείροντας).[15] Domitian, although he did not infringe Jewish rights, took aggressive steps against judaization among the Roman aristocracy.[16] The conception of Jews, therefore, as authors of an "international conspiracy", as a nuisance and an anomaly which might be tolerated but could become intolerable, because they were the agents of a world-wide disease, was near to Claudius, and Domitian saw in the diffusion of Jewish ideas in Roman society a danger to the Empire's established order.

The situation leading to Domitian's murder in 96 was indeed closely bound up with the impact of Judaism on Roman society. Its occasion was the execution of Flavius Clemens, Domitian's close kinsman, for judaization. It came as the culmination of the Emperor's widespread persecution of members of the senatorial order, in which the charge of judaizing frequently figured. Both Dio Cassius and Epictetus, himself the slave of a high equestrian official who probably had Jewish contacts, testify to the widespread influence of Judaism in contemporary Roman society, and Epictetus [17] describes clearly the intense struggle for influence throughout the Empire between the Syrian, Egyptian

---

[15] *CPJ* II, no. 153, 99-100. Cf. Oros. VII, 27, 6: tertia sub Traiano plaga Iudaeos excitavit; *Acta Isid.* (P. Berol. 8877 = *CPJ* II, no. 156c; 21-4: [σοὶ δὲ] 'Αγρίππα πρὸς ἃ εἰση[γεῖ περὶ 'Ιου[δαίων] ἀντικαταστήσομαι. ἐν-κ[αλῶ αὐτοῖς [ὅτι κ]αὶ ὅλην τὴν οἰκουμένην [ἐπιχειροῦσιν ταράσ]σειν. (Musurillo, *APM*, 1954, iv, p. 23).

[16] Dio LXVII, 14.

[17] Arrian, *Epictetus*, 2.9.19-22.

and Jewish cults. The opposition to Domitian's absolutism on the part of the Stoic and Cynic philosophers of the time was considerable, and probably constituted a far more serious factor than historians have appreciated, while Epictetus, who constituted a link between them and the influential circles that suffered from his tyranny, was fully cognizant of the determined stand of the Jewish revolutionaries against imperial oppression.[18] In the years following the destruction of the Second Temple, in fact, Judaism became closely associated with the protest of the Roman upper classes against Domitian's repressive rule.[19] It was Domitian who not only converted the collection of the Jewish tax into an aggressive hunt for secret judaizers, but also investigated collateral descendants of Jesus whom he suspected of messianic aspirations. How far conservative senatorial groups continued to see in Judaism, even after Domitian's death, a threat to the moral order, is revealed by Tacitus' anti-Semitic travesty of Jewish history in the *Histories* (V, 1-13), the more scandalous and calculated because Tacitus was certainly better informed on Jewish character and beliefs than his text could convey.[20] Yet the apprehensions of these circles were not exaggerated, as time was to show.

Why did Domitian and Tacitus see in the spread of Judaism a peril to Roman society? The key to the matter is to be sought, I think, in the nature of the revolutionary movement as it had been manifested in the years before the rebellion of 66-73 and during the rebellion itself. The wealthy Jewish upper class, the Sadducee priests, the landowners and the Jewish aristocracy of Alexandria, Cyrene and the other cities of the eastern Empire, distinguishing between Jewish religious morality and questions of social and political behaviour, compromised with Rome. The Pharisees, for their part, as the spiritual heirs of the prophets and the Ḥassidim, determined to maintain a consistent and compact religious moral outlook, persistently demanded a society built on justice and righteousness, regarding social justice as obligating the Jewish people as a group; hence they found it impossible to reconcile their demands either with idolatry or with Roman economic oppres-

---

[18] *Ibid.* 4, 7, 6.
[19] See Applebaum (n. 13), pp. 116 sq.
[20] See Y. Lewi, *Worlds Meet*, 1960, pp. 115 sqq.

sion.[21] The extreme activist current went further still, refusing to recognize a régime not built on justice, whether it was the Zaddokite priesthood or the Roman power. This outlook brought them logically to direct action against Rome and the Jewish ruling stratum equally.

It is necessary here to pause a moment to consider the connotation of the word "Zealot". The term has inevitably, though incorrectly, been used by various historians as an overall term applying to all the radical and extremist groups active before and during the Jewish rebellion which led to the destruction of the Temple in 70. In effect, examination of the sources,[21A] confused as their evidence is, shows that the word "Zealot", though applied prior to the revolt to a general political-religious type originating in the Maccabean period, was attached almost exclusively during the revolt itself to the extremist, largely peasant, party, in Jerusalem. The architypal organized group which crystallized in the first decade of the century about the figure of Judah of Gamala (or Galilee), and which appears to have laid the foundation of the ideology which influenced in greater or lesser degree the subsequent revolutionary groups emerging during the rebellion of 66-73—was known to Josephus as the Sicarii. This party took a major part in expelling the Roman forces from Jerusalem, but ceased to be centrally active after the murder of its leader Menahem, and retired to Masada, where it met its end in the year 73. The politically distinct groups which crystallized outside Jerusalem under the respective leaderships of Yoḥanan of Gush Ḥalav (John of Gischala) and Ele'azar son of Simon, were in Jerusalem grouped under the name of Zealots. The group led by Judah of Galilee—which appears to have had a predecessor in the "bandits" led by Hezekiah, probably Judah's father, who was put to death by Herod in 47 B.C.— possessed an ideology which probably influenced the remaining activist parties that emerged shortly after the outbreak of the revolt of 66. This has been summarized by Hengel[22] under the following heads: 1) a refusal to acknowledge any sovereignty but that of God; 2) a devotion to the idea of liberty as expressed historically in the Exodus from Egypt and in the Jewish com-

---

[21] For denouncements of Roman oppression and exploitation, cf. the words of Rabban Gamliel (*Avot de-R. Nathan*, 28d) and the famous conversation between R. Judah and R. Simon (B. *Shab.* 33b).

[21A] Cf. especially Morton Smith, *Harvard Theological Review*, 64, 1971, pp. 1 sqq.

[22] Hengel, *Die Zeloten*, pp. 93-146.

mandments; 3) the belief that God would aid them in the struggle
for their aims only in so far as they were ready to be active in it; 4)
resistance to the Roman census as a preparation for the imposition
of taxes, arising out of the Jewish prohibition to number the
people, and out of the principle that the earth belonged to God,
while the imposition of the Roman land-tax (*tributum soli*) implied
a recognition that it belonged to Caesar.[23] 5) The zeal for the
Law, exemplified in various ways in Jewish history, obligates to
personal and direct action against its transgressors. Guignebert
summed up effectively the general aim of this ideology when he
wrote: [24] "The ideal of the Zealots was a Jewish commonwealth
with God as its president and the Law as its constitution". Such
an ideal, a fusion on the one hand of Jewish religion and morality,
which rejected any political régime except the Law and its ethics,
and on the other of Jewish ethnic and collective compactness—
amounted to a revolutionary factor which the Roman Empire
could not afford to tolerate. The final trial of arms between the
two forces was inevitable.

The fall of Masada put an end for the time being to the extremist
movement in Eretz Yisrael as an organized force. The destruction
of the Temple terminated the rule of the priesthood and the Sadducee aristocracy. The leadership in Judaea now passed to the
scholars, whose intellectual direction was Pharasaic; they set about
crystallizing national institutions about a body that ruled by
moral force with the consent and will of the community, its authority being based on the social system of scholarly rulings known as
the halakhah. Most of the new leaders held moderate views, and if
they viewed Rome without illusions, saw no prospects in struggling
against her. The revolutionary remnants doubtless regarded them
as traitors and collaborationists, but no one could accuse them of
lack of devotion either to the Law, or to the people. The position of
the Diaspora communities, however, was different. There the
wealthy had collaborated with the Roman government to stifle

---

[23] Hengel, indeed, (*ib.* p. 137) was probably in error in assuming that all
provincial lands were regarded as *ager publicus* when they were conquered.
Many jurists, at any rate, do not see the imposition of *tributum soli* as indicating a claim of proprietorship before Claudius' reign. For the discussion,
cf. here n. 128 to Chap. V; fundamental are T. Frank, *JRS* 17, 1927, pp.
141 sqq.; A. H. M. Jones, *JRS* 31, 1941, pp. 26-31 = *id. Studies in Roman
Government and Law*, 1960, pp. 143 sqq.
[24] *The Jewish World in the Time of Jesus*, (Eng. trans.), 1939, p. 40.

the extremist risings at their beginning. But the psychological blow inflicted on entire Jewry, without distinction of class or outlook, by the destruction of the Temple, could not be effaced. If a party seeking some compromise with hellenism had existed in Egypt, it encountered final defeat under Claudius, whose rescript in 41 had emphasized to the Alexandrian Jewish community that they lived in a city not theirs from which they must make no further demands.[25] The widespread and horrifying pogrom of 66, and the longdrawn tension between Jews and Greeks in the Egyptian capital and in other Greek cities, were apt ultimately to impel many Jews to ask whether a modus vivendi with the gentile world could now be achieved, or whether a final battle was needed to settle the issue for good. Among the messianic section, moreover, so strong was the belief that the "final day" and the rule of the Messiah were coming in their own time,[26] that their survivors could not but see the destruction of the Temple as "the pangs of the Messiah", and the Jewish defeat as a sign that redemption was at hand.

The idea of a final decision had indeed been long current among the Jewish people. It already appears in the Third Book of the *Sibylline Oracles* in the middle of the 2nd century B.C.[27] and forms the focus of the messianic idea throughout the 1st and 2nd centuries of the current era.[28] Its various forms cannot be detailed here. The profound faith in the Jewish moral mission and in the ultimate victory of justice impelled the oppressed nation to believe that its suffering heralded the final destruction of the criminal government, the day of judgment of humanity and the "reform of the world after the fashion of the kingdom of God." Contemporary literature expresses this belief along common lines. The end will be heralded by terrible natural catastrophes and wars amongst the nations; a messiah will appear to smite his enemies and the oppressors of Israel; he will inaugurate a kingdom of justice and plenty, will gather the exiles of Israel unto their land (according to certain

---

[25] This defeat found expression in Claudius' final decision recorded in *CPJ* II, no. 153.

[26] Hengel, *op. cit.*, p. 316.

[27] Schürer, *GJV*, III, 1909, pp. 555-92; *PW* II² (IV), 1923, cols. 2117 sqq. sv. Sibyllinische Orakel (Rezach); R. H. Pfeiffer, *A History of New Testament Times*, 1949, pp. 226 sqq.

[28] Klausner, *The Messianic Idea in Israel*, 1950, passim, and especially pp. 199, 213 sq. (Hebrew).

versions), and before or after this, will come the resurrection of the dead and the judgment of humanity.

The degree of seriousness with which the emperors regarded the possibility of such a movement, is demonstrated by the interrogations of the alleged surviving members of the House of David conducted by Domitian and Trajan; [29] Trajan, moreover, appears to have put to death those related to the family in 107.[30] The idea of the overthrow of Rome had been popular among the Jews ever since Sulla's time,[31] and during the war of 66-73 the belief was rife that Judaea would conquer the world.[32] The extremist Sicarian ideology, vocal since the foundation of the sect by Judah of Galilee, inspired the activists with the belief that only personal action would earn Divine assistance and complete redemption.[33] Hence not merely did the defeat of the Great Rebellion not allay the storm, or induce resignation in accordance with the Pharisaic belief in a future life which would compensate the sufferings of thepresent world, but, on the contrary, it induced the readiness for immediate action and a renewed assault upon the hated Roman power throughout the Diaspora. More particularly in this period, (cf. p. 228) the very destruction of Jerusalem promoted a greater disposition to proselytism among a wide circle of the Roman populace, nor is this mood explicable except by an assumption that the situation was interpreted to mean that redemption was imminent.

The echo of this conviction is to be heard in Jewish works written immediately before the Diaspora rising, nor can it be doubted that their study has something to teach us of the aims of the movement, The principal sources are four: the fourth and fifth books of the *Sybylline Oracles*, the *Second* (also called the *Fourth*) *Book of Ezra* and the *Vision of Baruch*.[34]

The fourth book of the *Sibylline Oracles* is generally thought to have been completed about 80 C.E., the fifth book in the reign of Domitian, but with later additions under Hadrian which in-

---

[29] Hegesippus ap. Eus., *HE*, III, 20 (5), 32.

[30] *Ibid.*, 32 (3).

[31] *Or. Sib.* II, 178-89.

[32] Tac., *Hist.* V, 13; Jos., *BJ* VII, 5, 3 (312); H. Fuchs, *Der geistige Widerstand gegen Rom in der antiken Welt*, 1938, p. 62, n. 77.

[33] Jos., *Ant.* XVIII, 1, 1 (5).

[34] C. C. Torrey, *The Apocryphal Literature*³, 1948, pp. 116 sqq., 123 sqq.; R. H. Pfeiffer, *Hist. NT Times*, pp. 81 sqq.; 226; Schurer, *GJV*, 1909, III, pp. 305, 325, 327, 555-92; Klausner, *The Messianic Idea*, pp. 191, 201, 213.

clude several references to the diaspora rebellion of 115-117. The *Second Book of Ezra* was redacted at the end of the 1st century of the current era, or at the beginning of the 2nd, while the *Vision of Baruch* assumed its present form at the beginning of the 2nd century.

The fourth book of the *Sibylline Oracles* was composed, in the opinion of scholars, by a Jew of Asia Minor or Eretz Yisrael; it is imbued with profound religious feeling, and expresses throughout its author's pain at the destruction of the Temple. The book preaches faith in one God and the moral life, prophesying the destruction of sinful gentile society, and listing a long list of cities doomed to punishment; finally it describes the resurrection of the dead and the day of judgment. It further predicts the return of Nero from over the Euphrates, that is, from Parthia.

That part of the fifth book of the *Sibylline Oracles* composed before the revolt, of 115-117 is the work of an Egyptian Jew. It alternates praise of the Torah with expressions of hatred for Rome and with apocalyptic visions. It foresees the return of Nero with the aid of the Parthians and accompanied by frightful natural catastrophies, the conquest of Eretz Yisrael and the Temple by the Jewish people. It describes the coming and deeds of the sacred ruler, who will burn down cities and slay the wicked. In the catalogue of the numerous cities doomed to destruction by the author, Memphis, Salamis of Cyprus, Barka, Cyrene and Teucheira appear.

The *Second Ezra*, on the other hand, sets forth the foundations of the Jewish faith, dwelling more especially on the peculiar value of the Jewish people and its perpetuation. The author struggles with the problem of the sufferings of the righteous, but announces that the end is near and will not be delayed; the community of sinners is condemned to extinction and only a few will be redeemed. Violent hatred for Rome is expressed in the vision of the eagle; the symbol of the Empire, whose doom is pronounced by the lion, the symbol of the Messiah, for—

"Thou hast ruled the world with much fear. . .
Thou hast harassed the humble
And oppressed the peacemakers.
Thou hast hated the righteous
And loved the sons of falsehood,
Thou hast destroyed the citadel of the fruitful." [35]

---

[35] Ap. R. H. Charles, *Apocrypha and Pseudepigrapha of the Old Testament*, 1913, (Box), XI, 40-43.

The concluding chapters of the poem describe the new Jerusalem which will arise in the days of the Messiah and will flourish four hundred years, when foes have been annihilated and the Ten Tribes have returned to Eretz Yisrael. It should be noted that this chapter (11-12) is also the latest in the work, added by the last redactor between the years 100-120 C.E. Box dates it to 120 approximately,[36] but I see no reason for not dating it in the time of Trajan.

The *Vision of Baruch* also sees the messianic kingdom as a temporal kingdom of this world, unlike the writers prior to the 1st century B.C., who envisage it as an everlasting empire.[37] Although the messianic rule is to put an end to the corruption of human society, the poet wrestles with bitter doubts over the meaning of human existence. Among the signs foretelling the coming of the Messiah he numbers earthquakes (27, 7-9). He tells a beautiful parable of the destruction of Rome and the rebirth of the Jewish people—the burning of the cypress and the springing of the vine: "And I beheld the cypress burning, and the vine growing, it and all around it, and the valley was filled with unfading flowers. And I awoke, and rose." [38]

The peoples which have not oppressed Israel will find pardon, but the oppressors will be trampled under foot. Chapters 78-87 describe a letter sent to the nine and a half Israelite tribes in Assyria, announcing to them the Destruction of the Temple, arousing their hopes and loyalty to the Law, warning them that "the time is very near". A letter to the two tribes in Babylon is also referred to but not quoted by the author.

It is an interesting question, how far the above writings reflect the extremist ideology of the Sicarii, the Zealots and their allied currents. The expectation of the messianic coming, the rejection of Roman rule and the aspiration to a régime of justice, are certainly a continuation of the general ideology to which the extremist elements of 66-73 were party. But it must also be asked whether in confirmation of the same trend we can trace in the ideology of these works a class orientation hostile to the wealthy.

The only expression in the *Vision of Baruch* suggesting a class

---

[36] Ap. Charles, *op. cit.*, p. 552; Pfeiffer too (*Hist. NT Times*, p. 84) believes that the text was supplemented and emended after the reign of Domitian.

[37] Charles, *op. cit.*, p. 478.

[38] *Ibid.*, xxxvi-xxxvii (p. 500).

orientation is not in favour of the poor. In Chapter 70 the poem numbers among the horrors of the period before the messianic coming a situation in which "the poor shall enjoy abundance beyond the measure of the rich"; yet in Chapter 74 we encounter an emphasis on the ideas of labour and plenty:

"And it shall come to pass in those days that the
harvesters shall not weary,
Nor those that build,
For their toils shall advance swiftly of themselves,
With those who engage in them in much tranquillity."

In the fourth book of the *Sibylline Oracles* the absence of the pronounced views in favour of social equality to be found in the third book, (mid-2nd century B.C.E.) and in the fourteenth (4th century C.E.) is conspicuous. But a denunciation of wealth is found in the fifth book (line 405) and lines 416-17 foretell that the Messiah will restore to all righteous men the wealth which the wicked have taken from them.

The literature which reflects the ideas of the generation before the revolt, then, possesses no one uniform direction with regard to class questions, and this, I think corresponds to the reality reflected in what information we possess of the various extremist currents. The revolutionaries burned the records office at Jerusalem at the outbreak of the revolt,[39] not merely because it contained deeds of property drafted in contravention of the principle that the land belonged to God,[40] but because, as Josephus wrote explicitly, "they rejoiced to destroy the loan-records and to prevent the payment of debts, in order to gain the support of the multitude of debtors and to incite the poor to revolt without fear against the rich." The Zealots further demand the appointment of a High Priest by lot and elevate a simple peasant to this office.[41] The followers of Bar Giora destroy the houses of wealthy landowners[42] and liberate slaves.[43] On the other hand we do not hear of any "left" revolutionary tendencies on the part of Yoḥanan of Gush-ḥalav (Gischala), nor is it clear if the disciples of Judah of Galilee and his son Menahem fostered ideas of this sort. It is a fact, at any rate, that while

---

[39] Jos., *BJ* II, 17, 6 (427).
[40] *Die Zeloten*, p. 136.
[41] Jos., *BJ* IV, 3, 8 (155).
[42] *BJ* II, 22, 2 (652).
[43] *BJ* IV, 9, 3 (508).

they were at Masada after the outbreak of the war and the death of Menahem, they found no common ground with Simon bar Giora, and ultimately the two groups parted from one another.[44] The question of the degree of community of ideas between the Sicarii of Masada and the "Serah ha-Yahad" of Hirbet Qumran also awaits its final clarification. The revolutionary messianism of the latter is no longer to be doubted, since the discovery of the "Scroll of the War of the Sons of Light with the Sons of Darkness",[45] nor is the scroll's military character open to allegorical interpretation.[46] It is further probable that the organization led a life based on the principles of collectivism,[47] but this would be more credible if we could accept the identity of the Yahad with the Essenes [48], which is far from proven and may be a fallacy.[49]

We may sum up by stating, that the "leftist" class content of the revolutionary groups of 66-73 was not common to all currents, hence it is not clearly reflected in the Jewish literature which expresses the extremist mood in the years before the outbreak of the diaspora rising under Trajan. But we may conclude from the same literature, that the revolutionary spirit did not die down among Jewry in the years after the destruction of the Temple. Josephus wrote in the year 93 C.E. or thereabouts [50] that the behaviour of the Zealots and Sicarii was known to all; in the same period Epictetus mentions the Jewish revolutionaries' resistance to tyranny and their faith in the exclusive kingship of the Almighty.[51] This being the case, was the spirit at work in organized form as the main factor in the revolt of the Diaspora?

---

[44] *BJ* IV, 9, 3 (503-5).

[45] See Chap. V, n. 85.

[46] Millar Burrows, *More Light on the Dead Sea Scrolls*, 1958, p. 394, "The Rule of the Congregation", col. i, para. 3.

[47] Millar Burrows, *The Dead Sea Scrolls of Saint Mark*, II, 1951, pl. i.

[48] For a bibliography of the controversy, (to 1967), see Brandon, *Jesus and the Zealots*, 1967, pp. 61-2.

[49] Perhaps a distinction ought to be made between the purely "internal" socialism of the Essenes, which possessed a "kibbutzic" significance, and the political revolutionary trend of Bar Giora's men and those that thought like them. Yet it may be doubted whether in that period such a distinction existed. For the social equalitarian trend in contemporary Judaism, cf. *Pirqei Avot*, V, 13.

[50] *Ant.* XVIII, 1, 6 (24).

[51] Arrian, *Diss.*, 4, 7, 6. Yet for doubts that Epictetus means the Galilean revolutionaries, see M. Stern, *Greek and Latin Authors on Jews and Judaism*, I, 1974, p. 541, n.

Josephus' information leaves no doubt that Sicarian refugees reached both Alexandria and Cyrene after 70 with the aim of rousing the Jewish masses to revolt.[52] We hear from the same source of the "Egyptian prophet" who had entered Judaea in the years 56-58 in order to incite the people.[53] This man was one of the "desert prophets" and "seers" (γόητες) who have already been discussed, and whose affinity with the revolutionaries is clear. It follows that at this period a like movement existed also in Egypt. Tcherikover and Fuks have indeed concluded from the course of events there in the 1st century C.E. and from literary evidence, that the revolutionary movement grew and spread among Egyptian Jewry, more particularly among the Jews of Alexandria, under the influence of Judaea and of its revolutionary movement.[54] The blow dealt to the Alexandrian Jews in 66 and the destruction of the Temple undermined the position of the peace party and transferred the initiative to the extremists. The aristocratic leadership was nevertheless able to arrest the incitement of elements from Judaea after 70,[55] and after the initial failure of an organized minority in 115 the remaining Jewish majority in the city seems to have been the victim of attack rather than the attacker; the focus of the rebellion passed to the rural areas outside Alexandria (see below p. 266). Lesquier indeed stated that the revolt in Egypt bore "a prominently rural character",[56] and Yeivin [57] concluded from an analysis of the evidence that most of the inhabitants of the towns of Judaea and Galilee remained indifferent to the rising of 66-73, and that the active element was the peasantry.[58] Hengel also emphasizes the withdrawal of the revolutionary groups from city-life.[59] If this was so, the violence of the revolutionary movement among the Jews of the Egyptian countryside in Trajan's reign is apt to support the view that the influence at work came from the Sicarian, Zealot and other activist groups of Judaea.

---

[52] *BJ* VII, 10, 1 (407) sq.; VII, 11, 1 (437) sq.

[53] *BJ* II, 13, 15 (261-3).

[54] *CPJ* I, 68,

[55] *BJ* VII, 10, 1 (412).

[56] *L'armée romaine en Égypte*, p. 24: "son charactère rurale et fortement marqué."

[57] *The War of Bar Kokhba*², pp. 22-3.

[58] Rostovtzeff, *SEHRE*¹, p. 664, n. 32: "the national movement in Palestine, which was based almost wholly on the religious fanaticism and economic oppression of the peasants."

[59] *Op. cit.*, p. 198.

We have already seen that the nature of the activity of Jonathan the Weaver in Cyrene in 73 forms a link between the contemporary Sicarian movement in Judaea and the origins of the rising in Cyrene. In his action of leading 2,000 Jews into the desert, Jonathan resembled the "desert prophets" of Judaea before the great revolt, and in this reveals an affinity with the ideas and aims expressed in the literature of Ḥirbet Qumran—organized life in the desert for the purpose of spiritual and military preparation for the final messianic war. The finding of fragments of the Qumran literature at Masada [60] is suggestive in this respect, for it indicates contact between the Yaḥad and the Sicarii of Eleazar ben Yair, if nothing more, and Josephus explicitly calls Jonathan a Sicarian.

The revolutionary movement which broke out under Trajan reveals three additional features closely associated with the Judaean extremist groups. These are: (a) the aggressive activism of the movement; (b) the character of its leadership; (c) the attitude of the insurgents towards all manifestations of idolatry, such as temples, altars and images.

The first characteristic requires little emphasis: the gentile sources stress the suddenness of the rising in Cyrene and in Egypt, where the Jews fell upon the Greeks, rising "with an incredible fury and all at once, .. as if smitten with madness," (ὥσπερ ὑπὸ πνεύματος δεινοῦ—[61] quasi rabie efferati); [62] "suddenly and all impelled by rage" (repentino omnes calore permoti); [63] and if there is some doubt who were the first aggressors in Alexandria,[64] it would nevertheless appear that the Jews began the attack in Cyprus. The large number of casualties among the gentiles in Cyprus and Cyrene (even if Dio's figures are exaggerated) indicates the fury of the Jewish attack and evidences the element of surprise involved. The implication is that this was a movement initiated by the insurgents according to a prepared plan. The scale and systematic character of the destruction at Cyrene also witness to the

---

[60] Yadin, *Masada, The First Season of Excavations*, 1963-1964 (1965), pp. 103-15.

[61] Eus., *HE* IV, 2, 2.

[62] Oros. VII, 12.

[63] Oros. VII, 12, 6.

[64] A battle (μάχη) took place between Jews and Greeks in Alexandria in October, 115, and in this the Jews were the attackers (*M. Boissacq*, 1937, pp. 159 sqq.; Tcherikover, *Jews in Egypt*², p. 167), but this clash probably preceded the actual revolt—see here below, pp. 266 sq.

organized character of the movement, and to its prior preparation.[65]

The rising in Cyprus was headed by a leader named Artemion
('Ἀρτεμίων),[66] while the leader of the rebels of Cyrene is given one
name by Eusebius, another by Dio.[67] Dio calls him Andreas,
Eusebius—Lucuas, and there is no certainty if one man is meant,
or two. It is however a fact, that each historian had heard of one
leader only. Eusebius calls Lucuas "their (i.e. the Jews') king".[68]
Eutychius ibn Batrik,[69] whether or not he derived the information
from Eusebius, writes that the Jews returned to Jerusalem in
Trajan's reign and crowned a king there. The monarchical or one-
man leadership characterizes the Jewish revolutionary groups of
66-73, and if this phenomenon can be explained by the need for a
single commander in a warlike situation, this is inadequate as an
explanation regarding the Sicarian movement headed by Judah
of Galilee, whose leadership descended hereditarily through three
generations. Judah's place was taken by his sons Simon and Jacob,
their's by Menahem, and Menahem was succeeded by his nephew
Eleʿazar ben Yair.[70] It may be supposed, therefore, that those
men enjoyed the reputation of a hereditary charisma; furthermore,
Judah, Simon [71] and Menahem are all alleged to have aspired
to royal status.[72] The tendency to hereditary leadership was
characteristic, it seems, and perhaps peculiar, to a given current or
perhaps to several currents of the revolutionary movement, and
appears also to have been manifested by the rebels of Cyrene in
Trajan's time. It is not irrelevant to recall that a similar hereditary
leadership of the descendants of Jesus, persisted in the early
Christian community in Eretz Yisrael, and this was probably one
of the factors which drew upon them the suspicions of Domitian
and Trajan (see above, p. 248).

The uncompromising attitude of the Jewish rebels of Cyrene to
idolatry is reflected in the clearest possible fashion by the archaeological testimony. The evidence of the systematic destruction of

---

[65] On these details, see Chapter VII.
[66] Dio LXVIII, 32.
[67] Eus. IV, 2, 4; Dio LXVIII, 32.
[68] Eus. IV, 2, 4.
[69] PO III, p. 986.
[70] Jos., BJ II, 17, 9 (447).
[71] Jos., BJ II, 55; Tac., Hist., V, 9.
[72] BJ, loc. cit. (444): "He had gone up in state to pay his devotions,
arrayed in royal robes." (ἐσθῆτί τε βασιλικῇ κεκοσμημένος).

buildings, and especially of temples, during the revolt, is clear and prominent at Cyrene and has left not inconsiderable traces at other places in Libya,[73] and to some extent in Alexandria and Cyprus. This extremist attitude to images as an expression of idolatry is associated in Eretz Yisrael more especially with the opponents of the Herodian dynasty and of Rome, from the time of the conquest of Judaea by Pompey. Examples are the tearing down of the eagle figure from the façade of the Temple under Herod,[74] the resistance to the introduction of the Roman military standards into Jerusalem under Pontius Pilate,[75] and the destruct-tion at Tiberias of the palace of Antipas, adorned with animal figures, after the outbreak of the Great Rebellion in Galilee.[76] It can hardly be doubted, from Josephus' accounts, that the first and last actions were the fruit of the influence of the extremist revolutionary groups such as the Sicarii and the Zealots, if not actually carried out by them.

In short the insurrectionary movement at Cyrene and elsewhere in the reign of Trajan reveals some of the features most charac-teristic of the current collectively (and in a sense erroneously) known as the Zealots; the influence of the same trend is visible in the rising in Egypt as well. The spirit of the movement was messianic, its aim the liquidation of the Roman régime and the setting up of a new Jewish commonwealth, whose task was to inaugurate the messianic era.

---

[73] See Chapter VII.
[74] *Ant.* XVII, 6, 2 (149) sqq.; *BJ* I, 32, 2 (648).
[75] *Ant.* XVIII, 3, 1 (55); *BJ* II, 9, 2-3 (169-72).
[76] Jos., *Vita*, XII, (66-7).

CHAPTER SEVEN

THE WAR

1. TRAJAN AND THE EMPIRE

It is the view of some historians that Trajan's attack on Parthia in 114 was not inevitable; Roman control of Armenia was not necessary to ensure her military position and although Parthia was a nuisance at most times and hostile at others, quick to complain of the actions of a governor of Syria,[1] or to support a false Nero,[2] she was neither united within nor ready for real war.[3] But this need not mean that there was no real clash of interests. Rostovtzeff has pointed out that an independent Armenia was acceptable to neither side; herself a potential aggressor, as a Roman protectorate she threatened Mesopotamia, while under Parthian influence she furnished access to the Black Sea states, to Asia Minor and to the hostile Sarmatians.[4] Nor did complete calm prevail in the eastern provinces. The mood of Judaea during the Jewish revolt will be gauged presently. The very annexation of "Provincia Arabia" to the Empire lights up the real situation. Only Rostovtzeff manifested, albeit obliquely, some understanding of the significance of this operation, remarking,[5] with reference to the hellenistic period, that "Palestine, a country organized from very ancient times, and now in a recalcitrant mood, they (the Ptolemies) surrounded with a screen of fortified cities of the Greek type." The liquidation of the client kingdom of Nabataea and the establishment of the new province of Arabia, then, may have had three objects: the control of the trade routes over the Negev between Arabia and Gaza and between Arabia and Damascus along the line of the present railway to Mecca; the protection of the frontiers of Syria and Judaea against the raids of desert tribes, including the Arabs; and the containing of Judaea, still fermenting and recalcitrant, within a military zone designed to cut her off com-

---

[1] Suidas, sv. ἐπίκλημα; cf. Longden, *JRS* 21, 1931, pp. 12 sq.
[2] Suet., *Nero*, 57, 2.
[3] Syme, *Tacitus*, 1958, I, 238.
[4] *CAH* XI, 1954, pp. 104 sqq.
[5] *SEHHW*, I, p. 346.

pletely from influences outside the Empire—whether from Parthian
intervention or from direct contact with Babylonian Jewry.[6]
Syme has observed [7] that Q. Pompeius Falco, governor of Cilicia
and Pamphylia under Trajan, passed on in an unusual manner to a
second praetorian governorship of Judaea. He reached the consulate in 108, hence his second praetorian post fell in 106/7, a short
time after the acquisition of the new province. Pompeius had
served in Judaea previously and taken part in the Dacian War,
hence it is to be suspected that he was transferred to Judaea for a
second term owing to some unrest then prevailing there. A recently
published inscription from Ephesus [8] throws some additional
light on events in Judaea during Pompeius' second governorship.
This is a dedication made in 123/4 by two delegates of the Samaritan city of Flavia Neapolis in honour of Pompeius, who is here
called Saviour and Benefactor (σωτῆρα καὶ εὐεργέτην). It would
seem reasonable to connect the events implied by this text with
the year 107, and to believe that Neapolis stood in some danger
during the disturbances which then took place. It is further known
that 'Avdat in the Negev suffered destruction and abandonment
shortly after the year 128, due, in all probability, to the penetration of new nomadic elements from the east; [9] whether this trouble
had begun some years before we do not yet know. At Mampsis
occupation appears to have ceased about 130.[10]

The closing off of Judaea by fortified zones was nevertheless
such as to secure quiet in that province, and it shows that Trajan
was not blind to the prospects of a Jewish outbreak in his rear
when he attacked Parthia. The said fortifications were along the
via Traiana, which extended from Hauran to the Red Sea. Trajan
indeed had received a training thoroughly conducive to an understanding of the political and military problems of Syria and Judaea.

---

[6] Much light on this consideration is shed, in my opinion, by certain
phenomena of the 3rd century, which may be regarded as valid also in the
time of Trajan. I refer to the messianic aspirations expressed in the frescos of
the synagogue at Dura Europos (see here p. 322), and the words of *Lam.
Rabba*, (I, 43): "If you see a Persian horse tied up in Israel, expect the
footsteps of the Messiah."

[7] Syme, *Tacitus*, I, p. 222, n. 5; *ILS* 1035.

[8] *AE* 1972 (1975), p. 178, no. 577; cf. Applebaum, *Prolegomena to the
Study of the Second Jewish Revolt*, 1976, p. 77, n. 149a.

[9] A. Negev, *PEQ* 1966, p. 96; *IEJ* 13, 1963, p. 121; 17, 1967, p. 46. For
doubts and criticisms, Bowersock, *JRS* 61, 1971, p. 225.

[10] *IEJ* 17, 1967, p. 54.

His father M. Ulpius Traianus had served under Vespasian as commander of the Tenth Legion in the Jewish War, and had subjugated the areas across the Jordan.[11] In 73 or 74, after discharging the consulate, he had been appointed governor of Syria,[12] and had silenced Parthian threats of war by a concentration of forces on the frontier.[13] According to one view, he "may have been Vespasian's principal agent in the ordering of the whole frontier and its defences from the Armenian mountains to the desert of Arabia".[14] Trajan, then, was in a position to learn about the Jewish problem, the nature of the Parthian question and the provinces connected with both.[15] He himself had served as *tribunus militum* in the Syrian army, and was thus acquainted with the region of the Euphrates [16] For this reason he would have regarded the Jews essentially with the eyes of a soldier; [17] it is doubtful if he was an anti-Semite in the accepted sense, but it is likely that he gauged them as potential, if not actual, enemies, and participated in the attitude of contempt for Judaism which was hereditary among the majority of the Roman aristocracy. But as a military man he may have estimated (and even overestimated) the military strength of the Jews of Eretz Yisrael, and underestimated the military potentialities of the Jews of the Diaspora.

There are contradictory traditions concerning the attitude of Trajan's family to the Jews. The so-called *Acts of the Pagan Martyrs*,[18] which present a satirical account both anti-Roman and anti-Semitic, make Trajan's wife Plotina a supporter of the Jews, and one of the participants in the episode, an Alexandrian, alleges that Trajan's council of state is full of "sacrilegious Jews" (τὸ συνέδριόν σου ἐπλήσθη τῶν ἀνοσίων Ἰουδαίων). Scholars differ on the truth of this allegation, but Musurillo has remarked [19] that several

---

[11] *BJ* IV, 8, 1 (450).

[12] *ILS* 8970.

[13] Plin. *Paneg.*, 14, 1; Aur. Victor, *Epit.* 9, 12; *De Caes.*, 9, 10; cf. *CAH* XI, 1936, p. 143.

[14] Syme, *Tacitus*, I, 31.

[15] Cf. Pliny on Trajan (*Paneg.* 25): Cognovisti per stipendia decem mores gentium, regionum situs, opportunitates locorum et diversam aquarum caelique temperiem, ut patrios fontes patriumque sidus ferre consuesti.

[16] Plin. *Paneg.*, 14, 1.

[17] His council was mainly composed of "the heads of the military oligarchy" (Syme, *Tacitus*, p. 231). He was first and foremost "the candidate of the generals."

[18] P. Oxy. 1242; cf. H. A. Musurillo, *APM*, 1954, pp. 162 sq.

[19] *APM*, pp. 168 sqq.

"court Jews" and prominent renegades, such as the descendants of Tiberius Alexander and Herod, perhaps Josephus himself, and some aristocratic Roman proselytes, may have served on Trajan's council or have been invited to its sessions to advise on the Jewish problem. On the other hand, the relevant papyrus, P. Oxy. 1242, in its present version is regarded as of late 2nd century date, and the allegation of Jewish participation in the imperial council may really be directed, not to Trajan but to one of the Severan emperors, among whom Caracalla and Severus Alexander were well known for their favourable attitude to the Jews.[20]

A contrary tradition is to be found in the Jerusalem Talmud, which says: [21] "In the days of Troginus the wicked, a son was born to him on the ninth of Av, and (the Jews) fasted; his daughter died on Hannuqah and they lit candles. His wife sent to him and said: Before you conquer the barbarians, come and conquer the Jews who have rebelled against you." This tradition follows the account of the famous synagogue of Alexandria, and is succeeded by the description of the extermination of Egyptian Jewry in Trajan's reign. As Plotina never bore either sons or daughters, the story cannot be seen as historical in its details, but if it contains a grain of truth, it possibly reflects a popular view, that some change of attitude to the Jews had taken place in imperial circles immediately before the outbreak of the revolt. If Trajan was careful to check petticoat influence among his immediate entourage,[22] Plotina nevertheless exercized considerable influence,[23] nor must her rôle in the elevation of Hadrian to the imperial throne after her husband's death be forgotten. It may therefore be said in conclusion, that Trajan saw the Jews chiefly from a military point of view, as the problem of a people situated on the border of the Empire, and in the light of the experiences of his father and his own experiences in Syria and Judaea. If any change occurred in his attitude to the Jews which hastened the outbreak of the rebellion, it must have come as the result of a decision to their disadvantage taken after the beginning of his Parthian war in 114.

---

[20] *Dig.* 50, 2, 3, 3; Hieron., *In Dan.* 11:34-5—*PL* 25, p. 595, para. 717; cf. *Hist. Aug., Carac.*, I, 6; *Sev. Alex.* XXII, 4: Momigliano, *Bib. Zeitschr.*, 1934, p. 406.

[21] Jer., *Sukk.* V, 1, 55b; cf. *Mid. Lam. Rabba*, I, 16.

[22] Syme, *Tacitus*, I, p. 232.

[23] Syme, *loc. cit.*,; cf. Aur. Victor, *Epit. de Caes.*, 42, 21.

2. CHRONOLOGY

The chain of events in Egypt has been fully investigated by a number of scholars,[24] nor is there need within the limits of the present work to do other than repeat their conclusions, sum up briefly the course of events against the background of the rising as a whole, and discuss several special questions. The information on the rising in Cyprus is slight, but a few archaeological scraps have accumulated in recent years to enlarge our knowledge. The archaeological evidence on the revolt is plentiful in Cyrene, in Egypt it is chiefly papyrological, while most of it in Eretz Yisrael and Mesopotamia is literary and involves difficult problems.

First let us survey briefly the order of events according to Eusebius and Dio Cassius. The Jews in Egypt and Cyrene attacked their Greek neighbours with sudden fury and slew many of them. These events were repeated in Cyprus, where the rebels were led by one Artemion. In the following year the Jews of Cyrenaica invaded Egypt under the leadership of their "king" Lucuas, and at first defeated the Greeks, who fleeing to Alexandria wreaked their vengeance on the Jews of the city. The Jews under Lucuas meanwhile ravaged and destroyed the country districts, until Trajan's marshal Marcius Turbo arrived with strong forces, and exterminated the insurgents after numerous and prolonged combats. The Jews of Cyprus were also wiped out, and a decree was passed that no Jew should in future set foot on the island on pain of death. In Mesopotamia, anticipating a Jewish rising, Trajan ordered Lusius Quietus to slay many of the Jews resident there, then appointed him governor of Judaea. This is the sum of the account to be derived from Greek literature; it can be supplemented here and there by details from other and parallel sources.

Two questions arise at the outset: 1) the date of the outbreak of the revolt; 2) did the rising in any one province precede the outbreaks in the rest?

The views of scholars on the year of the outbreak differed till comparatively recently.[25] Schürer assumed it took place in 115 on

---

[24] Tcherikover, *Jews in Egypt*, Chap. 6; Tcherikover, Fuks, *CPJ* I, pp. 86-93; Fuks, *JRS* 51, 1961, pp. 98 sq.; *Zion*, 22, 1957, pp. 1 sqq.; *Aegyptus*, 33, 1953, pp. 131 sqq.

[25] For the various views, Schürer, *GJV*, I, 1901, p. 663, n. 46; Vermes and Millar, *Hist. of the Jewish People*, I, 1973, p. 530. Of recent scholars, Longden (*JRS* 21, 1931, pp. 6-7), Alon (*Hist. of the Jewish People*, I, p. 237), Tcherikover

the authority of Eusebius; [26] Fuks accepts that year as the date of
the outbreak in Egypt,[27] also dating its beginning in the first
months of 115 on the evidence of the papyrus containing the edict
of Rutilius Lupus, then governor of Egypt,[28] dated on the 13th
October 115. This document mentions a hand-to-hand combat
(μάχη) which had taken place previously between Romans and
Jews in Alexandria, also acts of violence perpetrated by Greeks
and their slaves subsequent to the episode but in continuation of it.
A special judge has arrived from Rome to investigate the offences,
and in the meantime the Prefect warns the Jews not to disturb the
peace of the capital. The conclusion to be drawn from this information is, that the rebellion broke out in early 115, more especially
(Fuks' view) [29] because the rising in Cyrene had preceded that in
Alexandria. But the principal sources on which this opinion depends [30] do not state with any clarity that the Jews of Cyrene
initiated the revolt. Eusebius says: "The Jews were exterminated
in Libya and Cyrene, in Egypt, Alexandria and the Thebais when
they were fighting with the Hellenes dwelling with them." The
distinction made here between Libya and Cyrene is very interesting,
and shows that the two were not identical. In the Latin version
Libya is mentioned first, then come Egypt, Alexandria, Cyrene
and Thebais in that order.[31] Dio Cassius, having described the
rising in Cyrene and the Jewish atrocities there, continues: "and
in Egypt they did many similar things." Hence the order of events
is far from clear, and the other passages cited in this context,
namely, the Armenian version of Eusebius,[32] Jerome and Syncellus,

---

(*Jews* in *Egypt²*, p. 161), Romanelli, *CR*, p. 113 n.) and Fuks (*JRS* 51,
1961, p. 100) date the rising to 115; Fuks places the outbreak at the beginning of the year. F. A. Lepper (*Trajan's Parthian War*, 1948, pp. 91-2)
came to no final conclusion. Vermes and Millar (*l.c.*) are for 115.

[26] Eus., *HE* IV, 1: And now as the Emperor entered the eighteenth year
(of his reign) another Jewish rising began etc.

[27] *Zion*, 22, p. 2. (Heb.).

[28] *Mél. Boissacque*, I, 1937, pp. 159 sqq.; *Zion, ibid.*; *JRS* 51, 1961, p.
100; *CPJ* I, no. 435.

[29] *JRS* 51, p. 100.

[30] Eus., *Chron.* II (Migne), 19, p. 554; Dio LXVIII, 32.

[31] Eus., *Chron.* II, *loc. cit.*: Ἰουδαῖοι κατὰ Λιβύην καὶ Κυρήνην καὶ Αἴγυπτον
καὶ Ἀλεξανδρίαν καὶ Θηβαΐδα πολεμήσαντες πρὸς τοὺς συνοικοῦντας Ἕλληνας,
διεφθαρέντας. Iudaei qui in Libya erant, adversum cohabitatores suos alieni-
genas dimicant. Similiter in Aegypto et in Alexandria. Apud Cyrenem
quoque et in Thebaide magna seditione contendunt.

[32] *Vers. Arm.*, II, 164.

depend on Eusebius' *Chronicon*. It is indeed possible that the movement first broke out in Cyrenaica, but the authority for such a view is not to be found in the historians but in the interpretation of the papyrological document associated with Rutilius Lupus. The entire atmosphere reflected in this papyrus, and in those connected with the same events [33] is not that of the rebellion itself. The battle between the Jews and Romans in the city seems to have been an isolated occurrence, and the acts of retaliation of the Greeks through slaves or in order to free them, did not affect many people. Their character is rather than of intercommunal street-rioting of the type long known in Alexandria; it was not in this sort of conflict that the Great Synagogue of Alexandria, the Temple of Nemesis and the Serapeium were destroyed. Even if the "battle" which formed the subject of Lupus' proclamation was the result of an attack planned by the Jews, and hence, very probably, of organized activists, it was not part of the actual war, since the Prefect's words are appropriate to a time before the rebellion had begun or had spread from Cyrene to the rural districts of Egypt and had broken out in Cyprus. The attitude to the Jews is still moderate and judicial, and the verdict of a judge sent by Trajan to investigate the incidents is awaited. It is clear that no "war psychosis" had yet developed and that control of events had not yet been lost by the authorities. A rising had broken out against the Roman government, and had been immediately suppressed.

In the light of this conclusion it may be deduced that the movement began in Cyrene, and an attempt at organized rebellion had already been made in Alexandria which failed because it did not include most of the Jews of the city, had been quickly isolated, and suppressed by the Roman government. Only in the course of a year, in 116, according to Eusebius, did the war spread to Egypt, evidently on the arrival of the Jews of Cyrene under their leader Lucuas.[34]

We have no absolute evidence concerning the time of the outbreak of the rebellion in Cyrene.[35] Eusebius' words leave no room

---

[33] *CPJ* II, nos. 158a-b.

[34] "And having extended the rebellion on a large scale, the following year they waged a considerable war. . . but in the city (sc. Alexandria) the Jews were hunted down and slain. And as the Jews of Cyrene had lost their allies, they ravaged the country areas of Egypt under the leadership of Lucuas."

[35] A Jewish epitaph from Teucheira dicussed in *Zion*, 22, 1957, pp. 84-5;

for doubt that the Cyrenean Jews reached Egypt only in 116, nor
should it be forgotten that the ostraka used as receipts for the Jewish
tax (τὸ 'Ιουδαϊκὸν τέλεσμα) at Edfu (Tell Tevet = Apollinopolis
Magna) cease in that year, and are not renewed until the years
161-5.[36] On the other hand it is clear according to Eusebius' account that fighting was going on in Egypt in the autumn of 115,
as is shown, for instance by P. Giessen 19 (see p. 315). This being so,
it seems probable that the rising broke out in Cyrene in 115, and in
Egypt between October 115 (when Lupus' proclamation was
issued) and the beginning of 116.

A conclusion in favour of a date earlier in the year 115 for the
outbreak in Cyrene, i.e. in agreement with Eusebius' date (at the
beginning of Trajan's eighteenth year) is Longden's,[37] who dates
the destructive earthquake at Antioch which devastated the city
and cost numerous lives,[38] to the opening of 115. The said earthquake also seriously damaged Rhodes and the cities of Asia Minor.
Trajan, who had meanwhile returned to Antioch from the Parthian
War, was slightly injured in the disaster, and one of the year's
consuls was killed, an event which enabled the precise dating of
the event. The numerous passages of the *Sibylline Oracles* which
repeat prophecies of similar natural cataclysms which are to herald
the advent of the Messiah, and the fact that Antioch was among
the cities designated for destruction,[39] as well as the personal
presence of the Emperor on the scene of the catastrophe—all
these evoke the possibility that the event was a signal for revolt
among the Jews of the east.[40] Against this attractive conjecture it
can however be claimed that the time elapsing between an outbreak
at Cyrene at the beginning of 115 and Lucuas' invasion of Egypt in
early 116, is too long, as this period of twelve months would have

SH 7, 1961, p. 32 and n. 26, appeared to show that there were still Jews at
Teucheira in the year 116, but has now been reread by Miss Joyce Reynolds
to date many years earlier (*SEG* 16, 887).

[36] Tcherikover, *Qedem*, I, 1942, pp. 82 sqq. (Hebrew).

[37] *JRS* 21, 1931, pp. 2-6; cf. *CAH* XI, 1936, pp. 858-9. Longden dated
the event to the beginning of 115 despite Malalas' information and in accordance with Xiphilinus, on the evidence of the death in the earthquake of the
consul M. Pedo Vergilianus, whose name disappears from the inscriptions at
the beginning of that year (*JRS* 21, p. 4).

[38] Iudaei ... toto orbe saevierunt absque magnis multarum urbium
ruinis, quae crebri terrae motus isdem temporibus subruerunt.

[39] IV, 140-43.

[40] As suggested by G. Riccioti, *The History of Israel*, II, 1955, p. 449.

given the Romans time to concentrate forces from a distance for a
counterattack on the Cyrenean Jews before they left the country.
This strategic consideration appears to be decisive, and it seems
better to place the date of the Cyrene outbreak in the middle of 115
at earliest, at least till more definite evidence is forthcoming.

We have no more exact information on the date of the attack in
Cyprus, but an inscription at Soli deserves attention. This records
the setting up of a statue of Trajan not later than August of 117.[41]
This makes it difficult to believe that the *tumultus* on the island
was suppressed later than 116 or at the beginning of 117. An extreme
terminus ad quem for the suppression of the rising is furnished by
an inscription dedicated at Beyruth to Gaius Valerius Rufus,
commander of a *vexillatio* (detachment) of the VII legion Claudia,
which had operated in Cyprus to suppress the revolt.[42] This dedication was set up shortly after August, 117. As Valerius managed to
hold another military post after the Cypriot operation, and the
inscription was put up during the discharge of a third civilian duty
when Hadrian had already ascended the imperial throne, his command in the island is likely to have belonged to 116. It is further
worthy of note that Hadrian personally dedicated a statue in honour of the deceased Trajan at Curium in 117 or 118.[43] As the
Emperor, then, seems to have come to Cyprus during the rebellion
(see p. 269) and was again in Antioch in August, 117, the statue
must have been erected in August of the same year immediately
after Trajan's death.

The chronology of the events connected with the rising in Judaea
and Mesopotamia will be discussed when we come to treat of those
countries.

3. THE ARCHAEOLOGICAL EVIDENCE FOR THE EXTENT OF THE
REVOLT

i. *Cyrenaica*

Cyrene

The effect of the Jewish rebellion in Cyrene is recorded in three
forms: a) the written sources, i.e. in the ancient historians and in
documents epigraphical and papyrological; b) by the archaeological
remains, i.e. in buildings which exhibit signs of destruction at the

---

[41] *Opuscula Archeologica*, VI, 1950, p. 32, no. 16; cf. *Zion*, 19, p. 39.
[42] *CRAI* 1912, pp. 249-56.
[43] *SEG* 20, 157 = *AJA* 65, 1961, 124/5.

time of the revolt or of rehabilitation after it. Sometimes this type
of evidence supplements the epigraphical testimony; c) in administrative or topographical changes (e.g. the foundation of new
settlements) seen after the rising. These changes are evidenced both
by epigraphy and by literature.

Most of the evidence of the first two categories is concentrated
at present at the city of Cyrene, firstly because archaeological
excavation here has been carried out on a scale far exceeding that in
the other towns of the country; secondly, because excavation here
has penetrated to the city's earliest strata. It is further probable
that the Jewish population of Cyrene or its vicinity was immeasur-
ably larger than the Jewish population of the other towns of Cyrenaica, hence the destruction there was more thorough and extensive. But this assumption remains hypothetical so long as excavation
has not been carried out on a larger scale and to a greater depth
in such centres as Ptolemais, Teucheira and Berenice.

Orosius writes: [44] "(the Jews) waged war on the inhabitants
throughout Libya in the most savage fashion, and to such an
extent was the country wasted that its cultivators having been
slain, its land would have remained utterly depopulated, had not
the Emperor Hadrian gathered settlers from other places and sent
them thither, for the inhabitants had been wiped out."

This information is especially useful because it suggests that not
only urban centres but also villages were destroyed by the insurgents. The report is supplemented by an important inscription
from Attaleia in Asia Minor, which informs us of a camp prefect
entrusted by Trajan with the settlement of 3,000 discharged legion-
aries in Cyrenaica.[45] Part of the maritime plain between Teucheira
and Bengazi was resettled by the establishment of a new town at
Hadrianopolis [46] known to have been located at Sidi Ibrahim
al-Ghamari to north-east of Driana.[47] Teucheira and Cyrene each
received, some time in the 4th century or earlier, the title of
colonia.[48] Two other Greek names in Cyrenaica, which appear in

---

[44] VII, 12, 6: per totam Libyam (Iudaei) adversus incolas atrocissima
bella... gesserunt: quae adeo tunc interfectis cultoribus desolata est, ut,
nisi postea Hadrianus imperator collectis illuc aliunde colonias deduxisset,
vacua penitus terra abraso habitatore mansisset.

[45] *Türk Tarih Belletin*, 11, 1947, pp. 101-4, no. 19. Cf. Tac. *Ann*. XIV, 27,
4 on the settlement of legionary veterans together with their officers.

[46] *Tabula Peutingeriana*, (Miller), VIII, 4.

[47] R. G. Goodchild, *GJ* 118, 1952, p. 152.

[48] *Tab. Peut.*, VIII, 4, 5.

post-Trajanic sources—Neapolis [49] and Kainopolis,[50] may relate, according to their meaning ("new town") to the work of rehabilitation after the rebellion. Kainopolis lay between Cyrene and Ptolemais, and Neapolis was apparently the settlement mentioned and described in Vatican Papyrus no. 11,[51] which dates from the late 2nd century (A.D. 191), being the record of a census of property and land carried out at that time. Neapolis was in the east of the country, in the Martuba region. The papyrus records a considerable number of "vacant plots" (ψιλοὶ τόποι) in the vicinity of the town itself, which was clearly still being built at the time of the survey. Oh the other hand the papyrus does not record many signs of devastation in the rest of the region, nor are such to be expected seventy-four years after the end of the rebellion. We know, however, that Jews had lived in eastern Cyrenaica, as indicated by the name Magdalis, by the Jewish name Beischa, connected with the region (sup. p. 150), and by the local names appearing on a Jewish-Gnostic amulet found at Regensburg.[52] Accordingly the evidence for the destruction of a small Roman temple 35 kilometres from ed-Dab'aa in the 2nd century, ascribed by its excavators to the Jews in Trajan's time,[11] need not surprise us.

The *Geography* of Claudius Ptolemy, completed in the middle of the 2nd century, contains a list of the administrative districts (νομοί) of Egypt which is accurate and agrees with the evidence of coins struck at the end of the same century.[54] The *Geography* places the eastern frontier of Cyrenaica at Derna,[55] an arrangement unknown to Strabo [56] and Pliny [57] in the 1st century, and while recording the district of Marmarica east of Derna, lists it separately from the other Egyptian nomes. This would show that the moving of the frontier and the transfer of Marmarica to Egypt were new changes when Ptolemy edited the last version of his work. It follows that Marmarica was separated from Cyrenaica round about

---

[49] Cf. *NV* IX, 24/5 sqq.; *Chor. Ravennas*, 137, 13, 354, 1.
[50] Cenopolis (Καινόπολις)—Ptol. IV, 6, 7.
[51] See above, n. 49.
[52] *CIJ* I, 673; cf. *Zion*, 19, p. 26, n. 29.
[53] *JEA* 17, 1931, pp. 81 sqq.; and see below, p. 000.
[54] *CERP*, p. 498.
[55] IV, 4, 4.
[56] XVII, 3, 22 (838).
[57] *HN* V, 5 (5).

150, to which time would also belong Ptolemy's information on Cyrenaica as a whole. But before the end of the century the eastern frontier had again been moved westward to a point between Limniades (Lamludah) and Cyrene.[58]

In accordance with the mid-2nd century date of Ptolemy's information, the building of Neapolis and Kainopolis had begun before that time, and excavation showed that similar work at Balagrae (called by Ptolemy Φαλάκραι), now Zawia Beida, belongs to the Antonine period.[59] Restoration work in the rural area, therefore, appears to have encountered such difficulties that the area of the province east of Derna was transferred to the Marmarican district of Egypt in the middle of the 2nd century, in order to relieve Cyrenaica financially. Even this alleviation apparently failed to solve the problem, so an additional region of eastern Cyrenaica was handed over to Egypt in the second half of the century.

The milestones found along the road between Cyrene and Apollonia also reflect the destructive work of the Jews in the rural areas. One of them, belonging to the time of Claudius, was found to have been deliberately damaged, the injury being attributed by Ghislanzoni to the rebels.[60] To the evidence of the devastation of the Cyrenean countryside should perhaps be added one other detail, in relation to Messa, a rural settlement 25 kilometres west of Cyrene. A new bathhouse was built among a group of houses within this village area at Siret el-Jenein at the end of the 2nd century.

The evidence in the city of Cyrene itself must now be surveyed.* We may begin with a summary of the inscriptions which refer to the rebellion (tumultus) [61] explicitly. These are (i): the rebuilding tablet in the baths of the Sanctuary of Apollo,[62] which records the restoration by Hadrian of "the baths with the porticoes, ball-courts and other neighbouring buildings, which were destroyed and burnt down in the Jewish revolt" (balnea cum porticibus et sphaeristeriis ceterisque adiacentibus quae tumultu Iudaico diruta et exusta erant); (ii) a Hadrianic milestone found on the road going down from

---

[58] P. Romanelli, Rendic. Pontif. Accademia Romana di Archeologia, 16, 1940, pp. 215 sqq.

[59] RAL 17, 1918, p. 356; AA 74, 1959, cols. 326 sqq.

[60] NAMC 2, 1916, p. 66. On another stone of Hadrian's reign, see below.

[61] On the meaning of the word tumultus, see below, p. 302.

[62] AI 1, 1927, p. 321.

* See end-map 6.

Cyrene to its port of Apollonia; it dated to 118-119, and commemorated the repair of the road "which had been overturned and
smashed up in the Jewish revolt" (*quae tumultu Iudaico eversa et
corrupta est*); [63] (iii) similar expressions are found on a milestone of
Hadrian's reign within the city, east of the baths; [64] (iv) a similar
formula to that of the baths inscription probably appeared on the
tablet commemorating the rebuilding of the Temple of Hecate in
the Sanctuary under Hadrian: "(Hadrian) ordered the restoration
on behalf of the city of Cyrene of the temple des[troyed] and
[burnt down in] the Jewish revolt" [65] (*quod tumultu Iudaico
di[rutum] et [exustum erat]*). A parallel formula can be inferred from
the remains of the Greek text, itself incomplete, reading: ἐν τῶι
ταράχωι 'I]ουδαικῶι κ[εκαυμένου καὶ πεπορθημένου τὴ]ν ἀποκατάστασ
[ιν προσέταξε]; (v) the *tumultus Iudaicus* is also the subject of the
fragments of an inscription found near the Caesareum of Cyrene in
the south-east of the city,[66] and a like formula can be restored
(vi) from fragments of another inscription of Hadrian's reign from
the same building.[67] The Greek version of the expression *tumultus
Iudaicus* apparently is to be sought in what remains of the rebuilding inscription in the Temple of Zeus in the north-east of the
city.[68] The proposed restoration is "(The) city and metropolis
of Cyrene (erected) the temple of Zeus . . . which had been overthrown in the Jew[ish revolt] ([ἁ] πόλις [ἁ Κυ]ρανάων ἁ μητρόπολις
τὸν [ναὸν] τῶ [Διὸς . . . [κα]τ [αβλ]ηθέντα τοῖ 'Ιουδ[αικοῖ ταράχοι . . .].

For the purposes of a more detailed survey the evidence of
destruction wrought by the rebellion can be divided into four
sections, according to the areas of the city exposed by archaeological excavation, these being: 1) The Sanctuary of Apollo and the
Acropolis; 2) the Agora; 3) the Caesareum and its adjacent buildings; 4) the Temple of Zeus.

In the city's sanctuary the baths destroyed in the *tumultus* have
been mentioned. This inscription contains the important words
ceterisque adiacentibus, which relate, *inter alia*, to the Temple of the
Dioscuri, near the south-western corner of the baths, and to the
Temple of Pluto near the Roman Propylaea to south of them. The

---

[63] *AI* 1, p. 318; *SEG* 9, 252.
[64] *JRS* 40, 1950, p. 89, D4.
[65] *AI* 2, 1928, pp. 118-9; *SEG* 9, 168.
[66] *JRS* 40, p. 89, D3.
[67] M. Smallwood, *JRS* 42, 1952, pp. 37 sqq.; cf. 40, p. 89.
[68] *PBSR* 26, 1958, pp. 31-3.

northern gate of the city, the west part of which has been disclosed, and is connected with the north wing of the rebuilt baths, was also restored at this time.

The structure of the Temple of the Dioscuri embodies three periods, the second of which ended with a conflagration. The third involved a reconstruction in white marble. The two statues of the Dioscuri discovered in the baths and to north of them, also made of white marble,[69] belong to the end of the 2nd century A.D.; their dedicatory inscription is contemporary.[70] The rebuilding of the nearby Propylaea (or, to give it its recorded name, the Prothura), is mentioned in an inscription cut on the structure;[71] this takes the form of an interesting Greek verse-dedication in which (if its restoration is correct) an echo is heard of the psychological impact of the revolt upon the Greeks. A clay layer found beneath the level of the lowest course of the structure, covered débris from the time of the revolt.[72] One of the columns of the nearby Temple of Pluto bore an inscription of the priest Claudius Tiberius Theophrastus cut in letters of the end of the 2nd century of the present era.[73]

North of the baths, at the foot of the wall retaining the terrace of the Sanctuary, were found the remains of burnt buildings which were, in the view of the Italian excavators, casualties of the revolt.[74] The statues adorning the frigidarium of the baths also exhibited signs of repair, explained by Ghislanzoni as necessitated by damage inflicted during the rising.[75]

Reference has been made to the destruction of the Temple of Hecate, which stood between the baths and the Temple of Artemis to westward.

Several indications prove the destruction of the Temple of Apollo during the revolt.[76] In the 4th century B.C. the archaic temple had been surrounded by a crepis and a colonnade higher than the one which had preceded them;[77] in the building's third phase, in the 1st century B.C., the floor of the naos had been

---

[69] *AI* 3, 1930, pp. 161-4.
[70] *AI* 3, p. 210; *SEG* 9, 190.
[71] *AI* 3, pp. 193-6; *SEG* 9, 190.
[72] *AI* 3, p. 196.
[73] *SEG* 9, 186.
[74] *AI* 1, p. 155.
[75] *NAMC* 2, p. 12.
[76] Pernier, *TA* pp. 101 sqq.; 138 sqq.; S. Stucchi, *QAL* 4, 1961, pp. 71 sqq.
[77] *TA* pp. 71 sqq.; 75.

raised to the height of the crepis, and redivided into cella and adytum.[78] In the fourth phase, which belonged, as will appear, to the period after the Jewish revolt, a hasty work of restoration was initiated. First the naos only was reconditioned, and the repairs dragged on throughout the 2nd century, much use being made of old architectural features. A new pedestal for the image of Apollo was erected in the inner room of the naos; the columns of the peristasis were restored on the crepis itself, and fragments of the columns of the second phase were found in various nearby buildings, including the Temples of Apollo Nymphagetes, of Artemis and of Isis, the structures of which were rehabilitated in the course of the 2nd century. Roman lamps, including one of the 2nd century, were among the objects discovered beneath the columns of the archaic temple of Apollo, which were used in the structure of its fourth phase; a large quantity of ash and other signs of burning were found beneath the Phase IV naos floor. In this conflagration the naos of Phase III and its surrounding colonnade collapsed to ground-level, and the archaic building was destroyed completely. An inscription of the year 181 [79] was found incorporated in the structure of Naos IV, from which a statue of Hadrian was also recovered.[80] A stele of white marble had further been set up on the east of the entrance to the naos; this carried a number of inscriptions of priests of Apollo—among them being four lines of verse,[81] which may be translated as follows: "First, O Phoebus, Battus Aristoteles, sent from Thera, built thy house; and now Aristoteles erected the temple, thrown down to earth by war, to Apollo with reverence." This verse-inscription belongs to the end of the 2nd century A.D. Another inscription [82] from the naos, dated to 181, was dedicated by two priests of Aristoteles' family, who say explicitly that the Temple "rose and was consecrated" (ἐγένετο καὶ ἀφ[ιερώσθη]) in that year. The inscription cut on the architrave of the Temple to record the part of one M. Domitius in the reconstruction of the Temple, however, is later and

---

[78] We here follow the reanalysis of Stucchi (see n. 76), which emends the conclusions of Pernier.

[79] *AI* 1, pp. 142-3; *TA* p. 140.

[80] *SP* no. 63, p. 42.

[81] S. Ferri, *Contributi di Cirene alla storia della religione greca*, 1923, p. 5; *SEG* 9, 189.

[82] Ferri, *Contrib.*, p. 4/5, no. 3; *SEG* 9, 173.

belongs to the beginning of the 3rd century.[83] Inscriptions executed
by citizens who contributed columns to the outer peristasis of the
building are of the same period.[84]

Investigation has revealed three building periods in the Temple
of Artemis, which was situated to the north of the Temple of
Apollo. In the third, a portico was added to the front of the second-
period shrine, the new structure embodying within it various
fragments from destroyed buildings. Its columns possessed Ionic
bases and Doric capitals, in this resembling the columns of the
façade of the shrine of Hadrian and Antoninus Pius on the south
side of the Agora (p. 280). The third Temple of Artemis embodied
architectural members from the Temple of Apollo in its third
phase, destroyed in the Jewish revolt. It was thus evident that the
second temple of Artemis suffered damage in the same revolt, and
that its third phase was a 2nd-century restoration.[85]

East of this temple was found an incomplete inscription recording
the repair of a naos and portico under Hadrian.[86] Some scholars have
restored the text to relate to the Temple of Artemis, but the architectural details are such as to make the attribution uncertain.[87]

Some buildings, most of which extend along the southern limit
of the Sanctuary, were repaired or rebuilt at the end of the 2nd
century or at the beginning of the 3rd, and it was formerly not clear
whether this work was the consequence of the Jewish revolt or
not, the more so since Pesce saw the restoration of the Temple of
Zeus in the late Antonine period as the result of an earthquake.[88]
But since the subsequent British investigations have proved that
this too was due to the revolt and continued to the end of the 2nd
century, there is no longer reason to doubt that the repairs in the
Sanctuary also related to damage inflicted by the Jews. The buildings concerned include part of the baths, more especially the
calidarium, which was rebuilt towards the end of the 2nd century
according to the style of the mosaic floor associated with it in the
north-east; the same applies to the washbasins (labra) dedicated
by Claudius Jason Magnus, who renewed other structures in the

---

[83] SEG 9, 173.
[84] AI 1, p. 145; TA p. 112.
[85] AI 4, 1931, pp. 173 sqq.
[86] AI 4, pp. 212 sq.; SP, p. 117, no. 33; Ferri, Contrib., pp. 5/7; SEG 9, 171.
[87] The doubt arises with regard to the architectural style of the architrave
carrying the inscription.
[88] BCH 71-72, pp. 349 sqq.

Sanctuary between the years 176-180. The mosaic pavement of the frigidarium resembles others in the so-called "house of Jason Magnus" near the Agora,[89] also the pavement of the shrine of Hadrian and Antoninus Pius in the Agora itself, dedicated in 138. The mosaic associated with the frigidarium on the north-east likewise finds a parallel in "the house of Jason". It should however be stated that following the completion of the excavation of the latter complex, Stucchi[90], concluded that the earlier mosaics in the Bath [91] belonged to the Hadrianic restoration, and resembled the mosaic in the atrium of Jason's house. This would not, however, alter the fact that the reconditioning of the baths continued well into the lifetime of Jason himself, whose *floruit* was in the second part of the century.[92]

The small shrine of Apollo Ktistes ("the Founder"), situated south of the altar of Apollo, was restored between 176 and 180, according to its inscription, by Claudius Jason Magnus, then eponymous priest.[93] The temple of Apollo Nymphagetes, west of this, was re-erected by Tiberius Claudius Battus under M. Aurelius, in the governorship of Numisius Marcellinus; [94] the temple of Isis, south-west of the Temple of Apollo, on the other hand, was built by Hadrian, according to an unpublished inscription,[95] and rebuilt under M. Aurelius by Battus according to the inscription cut on one of the columns of its façade.[96]

The pool before the Spring of Apollo was purified in the year 68, as recorded by the inscription on its floor.[97] Near this inscription is a second, later in date, stylistically of the late 2nd century or the beginning of the 3rd; it apparently records another purification performed by one P[o]plius Serapion.[98] The spring to the east of the *triclinium* near the spring is sheltered by a portico of cippolino

---

[89] On this building, Sichtermann, *AA* 1959, cols. 301-14, and subsequently, P. Mingazzini, *L'insula di Giasone Magno a Cirene*, 1966.
[90] Stucchi, *Cirene 1967-66*, 1967, pp. 113-4.
[91] *AI* 1, 1927, p. 322, fig. 7.
[92] L. Moretti, *Epigraphica*, 31, 1969, pp. 139 sqq., evidently the first recorded man of the name Claudius Jason Magnus, (*OGI* 507 = *IGRP* IV, 576), archon of the Panhellenic Federation in 157.
[93] *AI* 1, p. 335, no. 17; *SEG* 9, 172.
[94] *DAI* II, Cir. ii, p. 266, no. 540; *SEG* 9, 175.
[95] Goodchild, *Kyrene u. Apollonia*, p. 123, n. 25.
[96] *DAI* II, Cir. ii, no. 539; *SEG* 9, 174.
[97] Cf. *TA* p. 94.
[98] Unpublished.

columns with Corinthian capitals resembling those of the frigidarium of the baths in the later 2nd century. Outside and near the
triclinium is a 3rd-century inscription referring to the restoration
of the sacred place (νηό[ν]) by the priest Poplios.

The theatre at the west end of the Sanctuary was probably first
built in the 5th century B.C. in timber, and subsequently rebuilt in
stone not before the 4th.[99] In its present form it is an amphitheatre
with circular arena, but with a rockcut auditorium (cavea) which
encloses less than half the arena on the south. The corniced stone
seats bear letters of 3rd-century A.D. style, but the masons' marks
incised on the eastern entrance building are characteristic of the
2nd century, and it would therefore seem that the structure was
repaired and converted to an amphitheatre after the Jewish revolt,
but not completed before the 3rd century.

The American excavations carried out on the Acropolis hill of
the city south of the Sanctuary found Roman, hellenistic and also
older buildings, but the account [100] does not mention indications
that can be linked with destruction during the revolt. The Roman
tiles then found, however, included one stamped with the letters
'Αλεξ[--.[101] The same stamp also appeared on tiles used to rebuild
the baths at the end of the 2nd century A.D.,[102] hence it becomes
possible that reconstruction was also carried out in the Acropolis
area after the years 115-117.

The Agora. The Temple of Apollo (previously thought to have
been that of Demeter) to the north of the western entrance of the
Agora, where the main street connecting it with the Acropolis
entered, was built in the 4th century B.C. to replace an earlier
archaic temenos. It was prolonged eastward by a pronaos in the
2nd century A.D.[103] The record of the finding of statues of Antoninus
Pius and M. Aurelius in this building [104] would support that this
addition was made not later than in the reign of the former emperor.
Damage during the revolt may therefore be suspected, but is not
proven. The west portico of the Agora to north of the temple, last
rebuilt under Trajan, was again reconstructed after the revolt.[105]

---

[99] C. Anti, *Teatri greci arcaici*, 1947, pp. 122 sqq.
[100] *Bull. American Archaeological Institute*, 2, 1910-11, pp. 141 sqq.
[101] *Ibid.*, p. 152.
[102] *AI* 3, p. 150.
[103] Stucchi, *Cirene*, p. 76.
[104] S. Ferri, *Dix années d'activité archéologique en Libye*, 1924, p. 14.
[105] Stucchi, *op. cit., loc. cit.*

The Augusteium at the north-west corner of the Agora was at this period rebuilt with an internal wall dividing it into pronaos and cella, and the flanking intercolumniations were filled in by walls.[106] The two porticoes composing the northern limit of the Agora,—the larger and more imposing of which, a hellenistic structure,[107] was later dedicated to Zeus Soter, Rome, and Augustus, suffered damage between 115 and 117, and were subsequently rebuilt,[108] the latter's internal portico then receiving new columns. Evidence was also found for the restoration of the balustrades between the columns, and of the strengthening of the west wall of the terrace, where coins indicated that the work was carried out in the reign of Antoninus Pius or a little later. On the east side of the square the Claudian shrine (E5) of Opheles south of the site of what is believed to have been the tomb of Battus the Founder, was also destroyed at this time and subsequently rebuilt.[109] Cover-tiles (καλυπτήρες) found in the structure were stamped with the letter 'A', also found on circular *suspensurae* associated with the Hadrianic restoration of the baths in the Sanctuary.[110] The heroon covering the tomb to north likewise met its end at Jewish hands, and was never rehabilitated.

A series of smaller monuments was ranged along the east-west line dividing the northern from the southern part of the Agora. One of these was a small tetrastyle shrine of the Roman period, which embodied in its lower part a long marble base of hellenistic date. The monument which had stood on this was found serving as the base of the statue group in the Temple of Hadrian and Antoninus Pius on the south edge of the Agora. The Roman tetrastyle shrine from whose site it had come, therefore, suffered heavily in the Jewish revolt.[111]

Along the south side of the Agora extended a row of public buildings, including the city's Prytaneum, and to its west, a shrine with a high podium, formerly called, apparently with insufficient justification, the Capitol.[112] The structure of the Prytaneum was

---

[106] Stucchi, *L'agora*, p. 247.

[107] Stucchi, *op. cit.*, p. 147.

[108] Stucchi, *op. cit.*, p. 241.

[109] Stucchi, *Cirene*, pp. 54-5; *L'agora*, p. 251.

[110] Stucchi, *L'agora*, p. 251.

[111] Stucchi, *Cirene*, pp. 83-4.

[112] Mingazzini disputes the building's identification with the Capitol—see *QAL* 4, 1961, pp. 101 sqq.

partly restored in the Roman period with blocks of yellow limestone of the sort very common in Cyrene in the 2nd and 3rd centuries. Simultaneously its northern façade received Corinthian
columns with capitals characteristic of the post-revolt period.[113]
The shrine to its west (the "Capitol") contains a base upon which
originally stood the statues of Zeus and Hera, which were found
here;[114] it bore a Greek inscription[115] dedicated to the emperors
Hadrian and Antoninus Pius in the year 138, by "the city adorned
by him (i.e. Antoninus) with images".[116] The reconstruction of the
two above buildings after the Jews had destroyed them is confirmed by J. B. Ward-Perkins and M. H. Ballance.[117]

The Nomophylakion was also burnt and destroyed at some date,
and Goodchild[118] ascribed the event to the Jewish rebellion, but it
should be observed that inscriptions of the Augustan period had
been inserted into the building's interior pilasters, which were
erected *after* the conflagration.

An extensive dwelling was built in the second half of the 2nd
century between the Agora and the Caesareum to its east, south
of the monumental portico linking the two areas. It was known
as the House of Jason Magnus on the authority of the name found
inscribed on a mosaic pavement in the Temple of Hermes associated
with the complex.[119] This range consisted originally of two distinct
buildings each occupying its own insula. The more westerly section
included the above mentioned temple of Hermes, first constructed
in the 2nd century before the common era, and thought by Mingazzini to have been part of a gymnasium.[120] After the Jewish revolt
the two insulae were united into one building-complex which embodied a twin temple in its north-east quarter and contained in its
western portion an impressive Rhodian peristyle court forming an
approach to a triclinium on the south.[121] Mingazzini understood the
entire 2nd-century complex as a gymnasium, but Goodchild[122]

---

[113] J. B. Ward Perkins, *PBSR* 26, 1958, pp. 194 sqq.
[114] *SP* p. 75.
[115] *SEG* 9, 136.
[116] Ἡ Κυρηναίων πόλις κοσμεισθεῖσα ὑπ' αὐτοῦ καὶ τοῖς ἀγάλμασιν.
[117] *PBSR* 226, 1958, pp. 194.
[118] Goodchild, *Cyrene and Apollonia*, p. 46.
[119] For the post-war excavation see *AA* 1959, cols. 301 sqq.; P. Mingazzini, *L'insula di Giasone Magno a Cirene*, 1966.
[120] *L'insula*, pp. 16, 95.
[121] Mingazzini, *ibid.*, p. 95; Stucchi, *Cirene*, pp. 110 sq.
[122] *Kyrene und Apollonia*, 1971, p. 79; *Lib. Antica*, 3/4, 1966/7, p. 258.

inclined rather to see it as a public residence, the mansion of the city's gymnasiarch.

The interior of the Temple of Hermes was severely damaged in 115, though its exterior apparently remained intact. The statue-base in its cella, which had preceded the inscribed mosaic dating to the time of Commodus, had been wrenched out of its bearing [123] evidently to displace the image standing on it. The subsequent unified complex of the two insulae included an atrium on the north side whose mosaic resembled the mosaics associated with the initial repair of the Baths in the Sanctuary of Apollo immediately after the revolt. The columns of the atrium, moreover, displayed in their second phase a technique similar to that of the columns in the basilica of the Caesareum in its post-revolt rehabilitation. Minor repairs to the great peristyle were also ascribed to the period after the Jewish revolt.[124]

The Agora was linked with the south-western corner of the Caesareum to east by an ornamental colonnade, which adorned the street forming the north limit of the House of Jason Magnus. The colonnade's south wall was adorned with statues of Hermes and Heracles set against pilasters, which were found lying in the street. The Italian researches of 1957-1961 showed that the colonnade had been built in the hellenistic period and subsequently twice reconditioned, in the 2nd and 3rd centuries A.D. respectively.[125] The first repair took place after the Jewish revolt,[126] when the intervals between the pilasters of the southern wall were blocked up, and the row of columns along the interior of the colonnade renewed. To the north of the colonnade and east of the Agora lay a third-century peristyle house, known from an inscription as "the house of Hesychios"; on the south front of the same insula to westward a hoard of 1,158 bronze and 116 silver coins was found, ending with issues of the Emperor Trajan, and clearly deposited at the time of the *tumultus Iudaicus*.[127]

The Caesareum is the most important public edifice known in the south-east of the city. It is a large rectangular enclosure measuring 96 by 85 metres, entered through monumental propylaea of the

---

[123] Mingazzini, *op. cit.*, p. 14.

[124] Stucchi, *Cirene*, p. 113.

[125] *ASAA* 29/30, p. 663.

[126] *Atti del Settimo Congresso Internazionale del'Archeologia Classica*, I, 1961, pp. 443, 447.

[127] R. G. Goodchild, *Kyrene und Apollonia*, p. 90.

Doric order in the east and south sides, and by a further simple entrance at the south-west angle. The peripheral wall encloses an interior Doric colonnaded peristyle on the west, east and south sides, but the northern is closed by a basilica, with exedra and tribunal at the west end.[128] The present Caesareum is now known to be a secondary structure [129] overlying an earlier hellenistic or Roman enclosure, probably a gymnasium. The present structure dates from the beginning of the 1st century A.D. according to inscriptions on the eastern and southern propylaea.[130] The basilica, on the other hand, is thought to have been built under Trajan.[131]

Part of the most important inscription evidencing the destruction of the Caesareum during the Jewish revolt was found incorporated in the inner southern anta of the eastern entrance. Another lies in the south-east of the enclosure, and a third fragment has also been recognized. Although the fragments are small, what remains of the inscription suffices to show that it was a lengthy bilingual text which probably adorned the architrave of one of the internal colonnades of the building. It can be restored as follows :"The Emperor Hadrian (his official titles and functions follow) ordered the restoration, on behalf of the city of Cyrene, of the Caesareum which was destroyed (and burnt ?) in the Jewish revolt (ἐν πολέμωι— tumultu Iudaica)." [132] The date given is in Hadrian's second term of tribunician power and in his second consulship (A.D. 118).[133]

Another inscription was cut contemporarily in the architrave of the southern interior colonnade of the basilica, recording the structures repaired by (or in the reign of) Hadrian at the beginning of 119.[134]

The apse of the basilica contained a podium with a dedication to Hadrian made in 118.[135] A fragment of slab also bearing a dedica-

---

[128] E. Sjöquist, *Opuscula Romana*, I, 1954, pp. 86-108; J. B. Ward Perkins, M. H. Ballance, *PBSR*, 26, 1958, pp. 137-94; Stucchi, *Cirene*, pp. 96 sqq.; Goodchild, *Kyrene und Apollonia*, pp. 71 sqq.; Gasperino, *QAL*, 6, 1971, pp. 3 sqq.

[129] Stucchi, *Cirene*, pp. 96 sqq.

[130] Gasperini, *QAL* 6, 1971, pp. 3 sqq.

[131] Goodchild, *ibid.*, Stucchi, *ibid.* (n. 128); *JRS* 42, 1952, p. 37, pl. viii; Gasperino, *loc. cit.*, p. 15.

[132] *JRS* 40, 1950, pp. 89-91, E1; *PBSR* 26, pp. 161-2.

[133] *QAL* 6, pp. 10-11, C5.

[134] *SEG* 17, 804; *JRS* 40, p. 89, D1; 42, 1952, p. 37; *PBSR* 26, p. 162; *QAL* 6, pp. 10-11, B4.

[135] *AI* 1, p. 318; *AE* 1964, no. 177; *PBSR* 26, p. 163.

tion to the Emperor lies in the south colonnade of the enclosure.[136] A fifth inscription, discovered near the Caesareum, was published in its entirety in 1958,[137] being dedicated to Hadrian in his thirteenth tribunician power and third consulate (A.D. 128/129). The Emperor is here termed "founder, nurse and law-giver" (κτίσταν καὶ τροφ[έα καὶ] νομο [θέταν]).

Three fragments of an inscription are to be seen outside the south-eastern corner of the enclosure. The first mentions the *tumultus Iudaicus*, the second [*co*]*mmilitonum*, and the third the words customarily commemorating a work of building or reconstruction, to wit: [*fa*] *ciendum c*[*uravit*].[138] Gasperini has further published a fragmentary inscription found in the insula of the so-called "house of Jason Magnus", with the words [--*Caes*] *ar*[*eu*]*m tumultu I*[*udaico dirutum*].[139]

Ward-Perkins summed up a detailed study of the Caesareum in the following words: [140] "It was certainly in existence at the beginning of the second century, and was restored by Hadrian after the Jewish revolt." As to the Temple of Dionysus which is situated in the centre of the enclosure, and was a later addition after the erection of the Caesareum, he writes: "There does not seem any particular reason to doubt that the statue of Dionysus found within the ruins is the original second-century cult statue.".[141] He dates the temple to the 2nd century, "probably earlier in the second century A.D. rather than later." [142]

The Temple of Zeus, the largest of the city's places of worship, which stands on the eastern hill, has yielded impressive evidence of destruction by the Jewish insurgents. It was partially exposed in 1861,[143] but its systematic investigation began only in 1927,[144] and was renewed between 1939 and 1942,[145] further exploration

---

[136] *JRS* 40, 1950, p. 89, D2.
[137] *JRS* 40, p. 88, A3; *PBSR* 26, p. 164; *SEG* 9, 54; a completion of the restoration by J. Robert, *REG* 73, 1960, pp. 207-8; *SEG* 17, 809; Gasperini, *QAL* 6, B5.
[138] *JRS* 40, 1950, p. 89, 3 A-C.
[139] *QAL* 6, C9.
[140] *PBSR* 26, p. 167.
[141] *Ibid.*, p. 158.
[142] *Ibid.*, p. 167, cf. p. 194.
[143] *SP*, ch. xi, pp. 71 sqq.
[144] *AI* 1, pp. 3 sqq.
[145] *BCH* 71-72, 1947-8, pp. 307-58; *BSAA* 39, 1951, pp. 83 sqq.

being carried out in 1954 and subsequently from 1967 onward.[146]

Pesce, who dug the temple in the years 1939-1942, came to the conclusion [147] that the edifice had been damaged in the Jewish revolt, as the head of an image of Zeus found in the naos was dated to the Antonine period. He established, however, that the building had been rebuilt again in the last years of the 2nd century, on the evidence of several inscriptions found there; [148] he attributed the need for this restoration to an earthquake which in his view had overthrown the columns of the peristasis, their column-drums being still visible around the Temple.

Examination of the building by British archaeologists in 1958 produced somewhat different conclusions.[149] The inscriptions proved clearly that the Temple had been rebuilt under the Antonine dynasty, the work being completed in the last years of the 2nd century. The most important fragmentary inscription was found in the pronaos, being dedicated to M. Aurelius between the years 172-175 (according to Miss Reynolds' restoration) with the words: "the metropolis of Cyrene set up the temple in honour of Zeus, after it had been overthrown in the Jewish revolt" (τοῖ 'Ιουδ [αϊκοϊ ταράχοι]).[150] This inscription extended over several Doric capitals whose echini had been removed in order to create rectangular blocks, and had apparently belonged to the inner colonnades of the naos dismantled during the revolt or during the Antonine rehabilitation.

The inscription cut round the podium of the image within the naos was dedicated to the Emperor Commodus between 185 and 192, in a formula restored as follows: "the image of Zeus ... was donated and set up by - - - at his own expense on behalf of his sweet country." [151] This dedication was probably followed by a list of further subscribers to the renewal of the statue. The Antonine podium upon which the new image sat was underpinned by a number of column-capitals derived from the edifice of the pre-revolt period.

---

[146] *PBSR* 26, 1958, pp. 30 sqq.; Stucchi, *Lib. Ant.*, 5, 1966-7, pp. 199-201; Goodchild, *Kyrene und Apollonia*, pp. 154-5; *QAL* 6, 1971, pp. 116-21.

[147] *BCH* 71-2, p. 353 n.

[148] *BCH loc. cit.*, pp. 349 sq.

[149] R. G. Goodchild, J. M. Reynolds, C. J. Herington, *PBSR*, *ibid.*; Goodchild, *Kyrene und Apollonia*, pp. 151 sqq.

[150] *AE* 1954, no. 41; *BSAA* 39, p. 91, no. 5; *PBSR* 26, pp. 31-3.

[151] *AE* 1954, no. 42; *BSAA ibid.*, p. 92, no. 6; *PBSR ibid.*, pp. 34-5.

The architrave of the pronaos exhibited a third inscription of which three fragments were found. These are insufficient for a reasonable restoration, but it is clear that we have here a dedication of the Antonine period in Greek and Latin, commemorating the restoration of this part of the temple.[152] As early as 1927 a Greek and Latin inscription of the architect Rufus Aurelius found in the naos, and dedicated to Zeus Olympios, was published;[153] Reynolds believed that it alluded to the completion of a new image of the god.[154]

Goodchild established that the columns of the peristasis had been deliberately undermined and overthrown in ancient times, and attributed this work of destruction to the *tumultus Iudaicus*.[155] More recent work on the Temple, however, seems to have disclosed fourth-century buildings beneath the fallen columns of the peristasis, which would mean that their overthrow was due either to earthquake or to the depredations of the city's Christian population.[156] The smashed state of the architecture of the latest naos supports the latter explanation.[157]

Apollonia

In view of the destruction of the road between Cyrene and its port during the rising, it is hard to believe that Apollonia was not damaged or destroyed during the same event, but the actual evidence for such a destruction is not decisive. A dedication by the citizens of Apollonia to Hadrian in 129 or later, which calls the Emperor κτίστης (founder),[158] may be an echo of his activity in restoring the town after the revolt, but the term is very frequent everywhere in the eastern provinces.

During the Second World War remains of ancient buildings and streets were observed by the writer to have been exposed in the area south-east of the Greek and Byzantine city-walls. Skeleton burials with pottery of the late 4th century B.C. and other sherds of the hellenistic period were also found here. It would therefore seem that the city's area was restricted in the late 4th century

---

[152] *AE* 1954, no. 44; *BSAA ibid.* p. 95, no. 8; *PBSR ibid.* pp. 36-7.

[153] *AI*, I, pp. 38-40 sqq.; *SEG* 9, 126.

[154] *PBSR ibid.*

[155] *PBSR ibid.*, pp. 33-4.

[156] My information is from an authoritative correspondent who saw the evidence personally.

[157] Personal observation. Cf. Goodchild, *Kyr. u. Ap.*, p. 152.

[158] *IG¹* II, 3306.

B.C. when the present walls were built.[159] It may therefore transpire
that suburbs outside the enceinte suffered in the Jewish revolt,
but this cannot be regarded as more than a hypothesis.[160]

Balagrae (Zawia-Beida)

This settlement, about 20 kilometres south-west of Cyrene, was
the site of the well-known Temple of Asclepios.[161] Excavation here
was begun by the Italians before 1918,[162] and was renewed in
1965,[163] when a peribolos surrounded by porticoes and containing
three temples was found. The central shrine of the three was the
principal place of worship, that of Asclepios himself. East of the
peribolos lay a theatre. A fragmentary inscription among the
buildings was of 2nd-century date and reused in a later wall; [164]
the principal structures appear to have been erected in the time of
the Antonine emperors.[165] Another fragmentary inscription of
2nd-century date bore ceremonial regulations affecting visitors
to the shrine.[166] It may therefore be supposed that the temple had
been restored or rebuilt in the Antonine period; it is mentioned
by Ptolemy, whose geographical account of Cyrenaica belongs, as
we have seen, to the middle of the 2nd century.

Teucheira

Although the city's earliest strata have been penetrated by
excavation in certain areas [167] nothing appears then to have been
encountered throwing light on the city's history in the earlier 2nd
century A.D. But several items of indirect evidence point to the

---

[159] The date of the walls: J. P. Lauer, *Rev. Arch.*, 1963, pp. 129 sqq.;
Goodchild, *Kyrene und Apollonia*, p. 189; Hopkins, Pedley. White, *Archeology*, 19, 1966, pp. 56-7; 20, 1967, pp. 219-20; *AJA* 70, 1966, pp. 259-63; 71,
1967, pp. 141-7.
[160] To west of the city a number of ancient field-plots are to be seen;
although they are of irregular shape and area, they hinge on a straight
central axis laid from north to south, suggesting that a mathematical,
perhaps Roman, system of survey had been used. I know of no evidence at
present of the date of this division.
[161] Paus. II, 26, 9; *Tab. Peut.*, VIII, 5.
[162] *RAL* 27, 1918, pp. 356 sqq.
[163] *AA* 74, 1959, cols. 325 sq.
[164] *AA* 74, 1959, col. 334.
[165] *Ibid.*
[166] *SEG* 9, 347.
[167] Goodchild, *Lib. Ant.*, I, 1964, p. 144; 2, 1965, pp. 138-9; Boardman,
Hayes, *Excavations at Tocra*, 1963-5—BSA Supplementary Volume IV, 1966.

destruction of the city by the Jews. These are: 1) the size of the Jewish community of Teucheira, and 2) the establishment of the town of Hadrianopolis on the plain to west of Teucheira after the revolt, with the aim of settling and repopulating the area. Notable in this respect is the resemblance of the plan of Teucheira [168] to the colony of Antinoupolis in Egypt, founded by Hadrian.[169] The line of Teucheira's present walls dates from Justinian,[170] but older building material is to be found in them, more especially on the west side, while the Greek and Roman rockcut tombs situated near them on the east, west and south, show that the course of the walls and the town's area have not altered much since the earlier period. The area of Teucheira is about 44 hectares; that of the colony of Augusta Praetoria (Aosta), planned by Augustus for 3,000 praetorian veterans, 40 hectares.[171] It is accordingly very possible that Teucheira was the place of settlement of the 3,000 legionary veterans sent "to settle Cyrene" in the language of the inscription from Attaleia in Turkey (p. 270). It may have been at the same time that the town received the title of "colony".[172]

Teucheira further witnessed building activity under the Antonines, according to a fragmentary inscription which contains the name of the governor Numisius Marcellinus; [173] this is cut on an architrave in the north-eastern church. The city, indeed, is referred to threateningly by the *Sibylline Oracles*.[174]

The Italian colonizing institutions normally allotted 30-70 hectares of unirrigated land per family, and 31 hectares of land where six could be irrigated.[175] The Romans generally allotted 25 hectares to their settlers, hence at least 75,000 hectares would have been needed to settle Trajan's 3,000 veterans. This is very nearly the area of the coastal plain between Teucheira and Bengazi as defined by the line Bengazi-Benina on the south; Hadrianopolis occupies the centre of this tract. Even if this fact had no connection

---

[168] *AI* 4, 1931, p. 242; C. Kraeling, *Ptolemais, City of the Pentapolis*, 1962, p. 45, fig. 7.

[169] E. F. Jomard, *Description de l'Égypte*, 1803, Atlas iv, pl. 54.

[170] Procop., *de Aedif.*, VI, 2, 4.

[171] Strabo, IV, 7 (206); F. Haverfield, *Ancient Town Planning*, 1913, pp. 89-90; cf. *Archaeological Journal*, 103, 1947, pp. 66 sqq.

[172] *Tab. Peut.*, VIII, 4.

[173] *DAI* II, Cir. ii, no. 168.

[174] *Orac. Sib.* V, 195; where instead of Τέντυριν, Τεύχαριν should be read, according to the earlier mss.

[175] Keen, *Agric. Development*, p. 32.

with the supposed settlement of the three-thousand at Teucheira, the latter does suggest that not less than 75,000 hectares of land had been ravaged in some given district by the Jewish insurgents.

Bengazi

We have no precise information on the fate of Berenice in the rebellion. Excavations in the city in the late 'sixties established that the city had been replanned, at least in part, in the late 1st or early 2nd century of the present era, when a regular street-grid and a new drainage system were laid out.[176] It seems very likely that this replanning took place after the Jewish revolt, the more so in the light of the discovery in the town in 1941 of a coin-hoard whose issues terminated in the reign of Trajan, when the hoard had been hidden.[177] But the precise date of the town's reconstruction awaits authentication.

Ptolemais

Nor is there yet clear evidence for the fate of Ptolemais in the years 115-117. There is no lack of epigraphical testimony for the presence of Jews in the city before Trajan's time,[178] but archaeological excavations have not generally reached strata belonging to the earlier Roman period. Two fragmentary inscriptions, however, do reflect Hadrian's activities in connection with the academy and gymnasia of Ptolemais;[179] if it is recalled that an important fragment of a stele from Cyrene,[180] dated to 135, contains a letter from the Emperor concerning gymnasium organization, which constituted part of his activity on behalf of the city, then wrestling with problems of revival after the rebellion,—then it is very likely that the fragmentary texts from Ptolemais possess a similar significance.

The oldest known building of importance at Ptolemais excavated to date (if we except the west gate of the city walls), is a large and splendid hellenistic edifice, known to the Italians as il Palazzo

---

[176] Vickers, *JHS Archaeological Reports*, 1971-2, p. 57.

[177] *AA* 56, 1941, col. 702.

[178] *SB* 5819; *CIG* III, 5328; *CIL* XIV, 2109; *SEG* 9, 399 (?); C. Kraeling, *Ptolemais*, p. 215, nos. 48-51; *NAMC* 1, p. 152, fig. 42. The last inscription belongs, I think, to a Jewish epitaph, although it looks later than the time of the rebellion.

[179] *JRS* 40, 1950, p. 90, Pl, 2.

[180] *Ibid.* pp. 77 sqq. and see below pp. 293 sqq.

dei colonne, which occupies a complete insula in the north of the city.[181] It stands on the foundations of an earlier hellenistic structure. It has two principal parts, namely, a great columned hall built on a terrace, and to its south a fine peristyle. Additional rooms abut on the hall on the east, while to its north-east is a residential wing in the form of a two-storeyed peristyle house. A small bath-range was added onto this in the Roman period, when shops were also annexed to the north of the bath-range. A series of reception rooms and storerooms were built at the south end of the peristyle in Byzantine times.

Both the original blocks and the peristyle house were built, in the view of Pesce, in the second third of the 1st century B.C.[182] The bath-range was dated by him in the 1st or 2nd century A.D. It contained three rooms, a frigidarium on the south and two heated rooms to its north. The jambs of the praefurnium of the easterly heated room were new when abandoned, and had not been used; the same applied to the jambs of the aperture communicating between the hypocausts of the east and west rooms. The floor of the easterly was supported on suspensurae composed of circular tiles of the type also used in the baths at Cyrene in the last decades of the 2nd century, i.e. after the Jewish revolt.[183] The pottery from the Palace ran to the end of the 2nd century A.D., and the bath appears to have been repaired in that century but not reused. This evidence is not sufficient to establish damage in the Jewish revolt, but a find of coins in the westernmost shop north of the bath is more indicative. These consisted of bronze pieces of Cyrene of the 5th and 4th centuries B.C., a gold coin of Domitian, two of Nerva, a third of Trajan dated to 103-112, and a gold piece of Plotina dated 112 or 113. The swimming-pool in the great peristyle contained a number of Roman bronze coins which could not be dated, and two of Trajan.[184] Hence even if it cannot be proved that the building was damaged in the rebellion, the coins point to the alarm and flight of the inhabitants at this time, nor can it be doubted that the coins found in the western shop were lost then.

---

[181] G. Pesce, *Il Palazzo delle Colonne in Tolemaïde di Cirenaica*, 1950.

[182] Pesce, *Il Palazzo*, pp. 104 sqq.; Ward Perkins differs (*PBSR* 26, 1958, p. 194), and suggests that the building was erected in the Flavian period.

[183] Since the above was written *suspensurae* of this type have been found in the baths at Masada, which belong approximately to the first half of the 1st century A.D.

[184] Pesce, *Palazzo*, p. 92.

Repairs or modifications were also made to the *ludus* (an amphitheatre used for the training of gladiators) in the north-west of
Ptolemais in the reign of Commodus, according to an incomplete
inscription found cut into a cornice of the arena-wall south of the
western entrance.[185]

Evidence from Eastern Cyrenaica

Finally evidence can be indicated for damage in the eastern part
of the territory (Marmarica). In this region, 35 kilometres south of
al-Dab'ah, a small temple of the Roman period has been excavated.
A dedication of the 2nd century showed that it had been erected
for Isis and Ammon, while the finds, though preserved by the fall
of the roof, had been smashed deliberately. They included fragments of statues mutilated and broken by human action. This
damage was attributed by the excavator to the Jewish rebels in
the reign of Trajan.[186]

The extent of the damage wrought by the rebellion in Cyrenaica
can therefore be assessed as of considerable scope. Signs of devastation in Cyrene itself have been detected in every area where excavations have been conducted, and it is probable that the city was
destroyed completely. The evidence for damage in the residential
quarters of the city, however, is not sufficiently established, but
the excavations have so far concentrated chiefly on the sacred
areas and the public buildings, hence the matter has not been
investigated to the extent it should. Generally it is hard to believe
that so thorough a work of destruction of sacred buildings was
carried out leaving the dwellings of the gentile population un-
scathed. Evidence of damage is also found at Apollonia, Balagrae,
Teucheira and perhaps Messa, although further enquiry is desirable in all these centres in order to authenticate the indirect evidence. It is at any rate clear that the coastal plain between Teucheira and Berenice was thoroughly devastated, while the appearance of the town of Kainopolis between Cyrene and Barka
points to destruction also in the western Jebel. The fate of Barka
and Berenice is less clear, and the evidence at Ptolemais is not
decisive. On the other hand the evidence for the spread of the
revolt in the east of the country, in Marmarica, and the successive

---

[185] Unpublished.
[186] G. W. Murray, *JEA* 17, 1931, pp. 81 sqq.

transfer of two regions of eastern Cyrenaica to the administration of the province of Egypt in the second half of the 2nd century, hint at the difficulties of reconstruction encountered by the authorities in that period. The evidence for the devastation of the country extends from Berenice to al-Dab'ah, emphasizing the absolute accuracy of Orosius when he writes of the Jews that "per totam Libyam. . . atrocissima bella gesserunt."

Two testimonies drawn from epigraphic sources round off the picture and confirm Orosius' already quoted statement on the ravaging of the country. The first testimony is the language of an inscription from the Caesareum already discussed (p. 281), and more especially its conclusion, which terms Hadrian "founder, nurse and lawgiver." The meaning of "nurse" (τροφέα) appears to allude to the supplying of food to the remnants of the Greek population of Cyrenaica, or to its new colonists, after the end of the rebellion. Another interpretation is proposed by Robert,[187] who believes that the reference is to Hadrian's support of an *alimenta* scheme, i.e., a project for the adoption of orphans.[188]

More graphic is the evidence of an inscription from Cyrene first published in 1963.[189] This is mutilated and its five surviving fragments are not sufficient to complete the entire text. It is a marble stele on which is inscribed a Greek text of which twenty-two lines survive incomplete; these are divided into a preamble and a list of names. It is therefore evident that this is a stele recording thanks for aid or assistance to a number of people. The first line which is to any extent decipherable (no. 3) contains a number (the word "hundred" is visible), and the word "wheat" appears in the second, followed by the word "given as a present". The fifth includes the words "wheat which was not expected" or something similar (σείτων ἀνελπισ [- - -]) the sixth, "Hellenes, save!" Line seven begins with the words "Cyrene the mother" in the accusative. The list of contributors opens with the name of Hadrian himself, but he is entitled "god", meaning that the inscription was cut after his death. The remaining people listed after him possess Greek names, in so far they can be read or restored, and Claudii are prominent among them, in contradistinction to the high proportion

---

[187] *Hellenica* XI-XII, 1960, pp. 569 sqq.

[188] B. W. Henderson, *Five Roman Emperors*, 1927, pp. 214-24; *CAH* XI, 1936, pp. 210 sqq.; *PW* II, 1894, sv. Alimenta, 1484 sqq.; 1488.

[189] *ASAA* 39-40, 1963, pp. 219-76, no. 68; p. 257 [39].

of Aurelii who appear in the inscriptions of gymnasium pupils at
Cyrene after the revolt.[190] Thus there is little doubt that the people
mentioned also include citizens of the old families — as is evidenced
by characteristic names such as Barkaios and Clearchos. Among
the contributors therefore are Greek citizens of Cyrene who had
escaped from the Jewish insurgents and returned to their native
place, or at least, if they had remained in another province, were
in a position to make contributions. The remaining words of the
stele leave no room for doubt that these were consignments of a
not inconsiderable quantity of grain sent to save their native city,
Cyrene, and in the circumstances it is probable that the citizens
concerned were still abroad. The appearance of Hadrian's name
reflects his activity on behalf of the stricken province, and the
erection of the stele after his death in 138, proves that the consignments were despatched a short time after the rising, on a scale that
caused them to be graven deep in the memory of the surviving
inhabitants. But is clear that the inscription itself was executed a
long time after Hadrian's death: the letter style is characteristic
of the 3rd century and even of its second half, to judge from an
epitaph of similar type at Cyrene,[191] in which the year A.D. 262 is
recorded. Generally it may be assumed, that we have here a copy
of the original inscription, which had been damaged or become
illegible and was replaced by the city authorities.

This replacement has a parallel in the Cyrenean stele bearing
fragments of the orders or rescripts of Hadrian to the city some time
(A.D. 135) after the end of the Jewish revolt.[192] The epigraphical
style of this document shows that the stele itself belongs to the 3rd
century, a considerable time after the composition of the original
text, which was copied afresh in order to preserve its contents.[193]
This inscription too dealt, in so far as its text can be restored (see
below), with the city's still unstable plight after the events of 115-
117. Hence it is clear that the stele recording the corn contributions
was thought important enough to be renewed a hundred or even
a hundred and fifty years or more after its first publication. In

---

[190] Eg. *SEG* 9, 128.

[191] A white marble tombstone; the fifth line records: ἔτους σπβ τοῦ καὶ
πρώτου.

[192] P. M. Fraser, *JRS* 40, 1950, pp. 77 sqq., and see below p. 293.

[193] *Ibid.* p. 87: "It will then be a copy of a Hadrianic inscription which
had been damaged in some way, and of which it was felt desirable to make
a copy."

its preamble, despite its defective condition, the echo can be heard
of the despairing cry of the city's surviving inhabitants or of its
new settlers—"save Cyrene, city and mother"; this is an appeal
first and foremost to Greeks, and probably to the cities of Dorian
origin which still saw themselves bound to Cyrene by ties of
history and sentiment,[194] and also to past inhabitants of Cyrene
possessed of means and still resident abroad, probably due to the
great dearth prevailing in the country.[195]

The third inscription, which is the late copy of Hadrian's order
of 135 already mentioned, also reflects the plight of Cyrene in the
years after the end of the revolt. Following the Emperor's name and
titles, the text begins with a short letter by Hadrian directed to the
citizens. This is followed by part of a letter, evidently from the
governor of the province, Salvius Carus, and by extracts from the
imperial order. The stele is incomplete and the stone is broken
obliquely from the righthand upper to the lower lefthand side, so
that nearly half the text is missing, and its restoration involves
numerous difficulties. It is nevertheless clear that the subject of
the contents is Cyrene's membership of the league of Greek cities
known as the Panhellenion,[196] the right of an unnamed community
to join the organization, and the problem of the repopulation of the
city. The last surviving sections speak of the gymnasia of Cyrene,
and Hadrian is probably rebuking the city authorities for the un-
satisfactory condition of these institutions. Oliver [197] has suggested that the inscription deals with some doubt cast upon the
hellenic origin of the Cyreneans, notwithstanding that they are
sending two deputies to the assembly of the Panhellenion. Larsen
has rightly criticized this suggestion,[198] pointing out that if the

---

[194] The most important of these would have been Thera, Rhodes, Samos,
Tenos and the other Aegean cities; also those of Peloponnesos (more particularly Sparta, Elis and Mantinea) and Crete.

[195] Cascellius Aristoteles who as priest (ἱερεὺς καλλιέτης) signed the completion of the restoration of the Temple of Apollo in 181 (SEG 9, 173) was
elected eponymous Patronomos of Sparta in approximately the middle of the
2nd century (BSA 43, 1948, pp. 258-9; IG V¹, 70, 1; 71, col. iii, 2). This
appears to be a case of the migration of a wealthy citizen from overseas to
Cyrene in response to the needs of the country after the Jewish revolt.

[196] This federation or league was established by Hadrian in order to
strengthen the hellenic spirit among the Greeks of the Empire. For its
details, see M. N. Tod, JHS 42, 1922, pp. 173 sq.; P. Graindor, Athènes sous
Hadrien, 1934, pp. 102-11.

[197] Hesperia 20, 1951, pp. 31 sqq.

[198] Classical Philology, 47, 1952, pp. 7 sqq.

derivation of the Cyreneans had been impugned, they would not
have commemorated the fact in their archives, whereas the inscription, as stated, is a late copy made for the records. Larsen
correctly concluded that Cyrene was in fact accepted into the
Panhellenion, since we are informed of the membership of Apollonia, Cyrene's port, in the League.[199] He therefore interprets
the second paragraph of the inscription as a decision taken by
Hadrian in favour of the Cyreneans in the matter concerned, supposing that it was the latter who had expressed doubts on the hellenic origin of some other group of people. These he thinks to have
been the inhabitants of Marmarica in the east of the territory. His
conjecture is reasonable, but there is no absolute proof of it; the
doubts concerning that region may have arisen because of its
pending transfer to Egypt, which was implemented towards the
middle of the century.[200] Whatever the case, it can be deduced
from the text, that the repopulation of Cyrene at the end of Hadrian's reign was creating various problems in the cultural sphere,
and that the Emperor, as an enthusiastic hellenist, was displaying
concern for the new community's cultural level which had declined
due to the mixed composition of the new settlers. This concern
seems to have found expression both in the incorporation of Cyrene
in the Panhellenion and in the fostering of the cities' educational
institutions in order to raise their standards.

ii. *The Revolt in Egypt*

The evidence of Archaeology, Literature and Papyrology

The Jewish revolt in Egypt has been studied by a number of
scholars; our object here is to recapitulate the evidence and to
embody it in the general account. The conclusion has already
been drawn, that the battle which took place between Jews and
Romans in Alexandria before October, 115, was an isolated event.
Disorders began subsequently in the Egyptian countryside during
the autumn, but only when the Jews of Cyrene invaded Egypt at
the beginning of 116, did real fighting break out in the country's
rural areas. The sources relate, that after the Greeks had been
defeated on the countryside, they fled to Alexandria, and there

---

[199] *IG* I, 2, 3407.

[200] Further fragments of this inscription have now been found, which
include a letter from Antoninus Pius whose subject falls beyond the scope
of the present book. (Goodchild, *Kyrene u. Apoll.*, p. 43, n. 58).

attacked the Jews; [201] thereupon, it appears, there broke out the
violent conflict in which not only the city's great synagogue, but
also the Temple of Nemesis and the Serapeium were destroyed.
Meantime the Jews of Cyrene, having "lost the alliance" of the
Alexandrian Jews (τῆς δὲ παρὰ τούτων συμμαχίας ἀποτύχοντες)
ravaged wide areas of the countryside. The scope of the conflict
in Alexandria is indicated by two principal items of evidence,
namely, a) Jerome's statement that "Alexandria was destroyed
by the Romans",[202] which need not be an error, since it is highly
probable that the Roman forces were compelled to demolish
buildings for military reasons, as Alon has conjectured: [203] Eusebius
moreover tells us that Hadrian set about rebuilding the city; [204]
b) we hear of the destruction of the three public buildings already
referred to; that of the great synagogue is described by a talmudic
tradition,[205] and that of the Sanctuary of Nemesis is recorded by
Appian.[206] Evidence for the demolition of the Serapeium was found
when the edifice was excavated in 1943.[207]

Tcherikover and Fuks [208] have surveyed the geographical extent
of the rebellion in the rural areas and provincial towns of Egypt, in
so far as the information is furnished by papyrological and literary
sources, and at present little can be added to their list.

Appian informs us of fighting in Pelusium; he himself escaped
from the rebels who had seized control of the town and held the
roads in the vicinity.[209] According to Appian [210] Hadrian restored
the tomb of Pompey near Pelusium on his visit to Egypt in 130;
its statues had evidently been damaged, and this is fair evidence

---

[201] Eus., *HE*, IV, 2, 3.

[202] Eus. (Hieron.), *Chron.*, (Helm), 97.

[203] *Hist. of the Jews of Eretz Yisrael*, I, p. 246.

[204] Eus., *Chron.* (Hieron.) ad ann. 2133 (*PG* 19, 555).

[205] Jer., *Sukkah*, V, 58b.

[206] *Bell. Civ.* II, 90.

[207] *Ann. Serv. Ant. Alex.*, 2, 1946 (2), pp. 62 sqq.; A. Rowe, *PEQ* 94,
1962, p. 139; also information from Mr A. Rowe. For a criticism of his conclusion, however, see J. Beaujeu, *La religion romaine à l'apogée de l'empire*, I,
1955, pp. 230 sq., but he too admits that the present evidence allows no
final dating.

[208] Tcherikover, *Jews in Egypt*, pp. 161-2; *CPJ* I, p. 88, II, 225; Fuks,
Aegyptus, 23, 1953, pp. 141 sqq.; *JRS* 51, 1961, p. 99; *Zion*, 22, 1957, pp. 4
sqq.

[209] Reinach, *TRJ* no. 77 = Appian, frag. 19.

[210] *SHA Had.* XIV, 4; Appian, *B. Civ.* II, 86; in II, 90 Appian seems to
have confused the tomb with the Nemeseion outside Alexandria.

that the monument had suffered at Jewish hands.[211] We hear of
Jewish lands in the Athribis district which were confiscated after
the revolt.[212] In Memphis a battle was fought between the Jews and
the Romans; [213] in Fayyûm damage to agricultural property
is recorded,[214] and Jewish property was also confiscated in the
district of Heracleopolitis.[215] Buildings burnt by the Jews are
mentioned at Oxyrhinchos, where a festival commemorating a
victory over them was still being celebrated in the year 199-200.[216]
Lands were also confiscated from Jews in the Caenopolite nome; [217]
in the Hermopolitis fighting and damage to property are further
recorded.[218] Orosius, Eusebius and Syncellus all inform us of fighting in the Thebais,[219] and papyri tell of disorders in the nomes of
the Lykeopolitis and Apollinopolitis.[220] We may here add that
payment of the Jewish tax ceased in Apollinopolis Parva (Tell
Edfu) in the year 116, hence we may assume that the rebellion
extended to that town,[221] *PSI* 1063, dated in September 117 shows
that a Roman cohort (see p. 314), had suffered numerous casualties
in the fighting, probably in Upper Egypt. Further, the appearance
of Libya in Eusebius' list enumerating the centres of the rebellion,[222] must be interpreted to mean that the movement manifested itself also in the Western Desert between Egypt and Cyrenaica (see p. 315).

Fuks sums up by saying: [223] "This evidence largely corroborates
Orosius: 'Aegyptum vero totam ... cruentis seditionibus tur-
baverunt' ".

---

[211] Appian. *B. Civ.* II, 86.

[212] *CPJ* no. 448.

[213] *CPJ* nos. 438, 439; *Orac. Sib.*, V, 60-74.

[214] *CPJ* no. 449.

[215] *CPJ* no. 445.

[216] *CPJ* nos. 445, 447, 450.

[217] *CPJ* no. 445.

[218] *CPJ* no. 443.

[219] Eus., *Chron.* II (*PG* 19, 554), ann. 2131; *vers. Arm.*, 164; Oros. VII, 12,
7; Syncellus, 347d; Hieron., *ad Chron. Eus.*, 196 (Helm).

[220] *CPJ* nos. 436, 444.

[221] Tcherikover, *Qedem*, I, 1942, p. 82. Here should also be mentioned a
coin-hoard deposited under Trajan in the area of the Delta, evidently during
the revolt. Out of a total of 267 coins, 66 were of Domitian, 24 of Nerva, and
138 of Trajan. The latest of the latter belonged to the years 114-117. (S. H.
Webster, *Numismatic Notes and Monographs*, 54, 1932; S. Bolin, *State and
Currency in the Roman Empire to 300 A.D.*, 1958, p. 340, Table 3. Cf. *JJS*,
13, 1962, p. 42).

[222] Eus., *Chron.* II (*PG* 19, 554), 164.

[223] *JRS* 51, 1961, p. 99.

iii. *Cyprus*

The chief source for the outbreak in Cyprus is the historian Dio, who writes that the insurgents placed themselves under a leader, Artemion, and slew 240,000 gentiles.[224] Among the cities destroyed by them only Salamis is mentioned,[225] although it is clear from the number of casualties that the movement spread over the entire island, since Dio records 220,000 victims in Cyrenaica, and even if these numbers are exaggerated, the extensive devastation of that territory has been demonstrated.[226]

On the effects of the *tumultus* on the island we may first quote Vessberg,[227] who writes in relation to the rebellion: "It is therefore not merely fortuitous that the archaeological material appears to be meagre for the Hadrianic epoch. The inscriptions are few from that time, and, as far as I am aware, it has not been possible to point to a Cypriote coinage under Hadrian." One inscription, probably from Salamis, dating from the time of Trajan or Hadrian, almost certainly relates to restoration work after 117.[228] It speaks of the rebuilding of the Temple of Zeus by a man who is "in charge of the project" (ἐπιμελητὴν τοῦ ἔργου)—indicating that it was on a considerable scale.

A second inscription from Salamis, a dedication by the city to Hadrian in the year 129-130, apparently also reflects conditions after the revolt:[229] the city here calls the Emperor "its own saviour" (τῶι ἰδίω]ι σωτῆρι), and while the term is not uncommonly applied to Hadrian, we may think that it bore special significance in Cyprus in the years after the devastation of 116-117. The excavations at Salamis have not yet detected many signs of the devastation testified to by Dio, but the reason may be the lack of interest in the event manifested by former investigators. Karageorghis, on the other hand, has now published several suggestive indications furnished by the city's contemporary sculpture. One of them, a statue representing an emperor of the Flavian house, or alternatively Hadrian, was found to have been severely damaged, the

---

[224] Dio LXVIII, 32.

[225] Eus., *Chron.* II (*PG*, 19, 555); Hieron., *ad Eus.*, 196; *vers. Arm.*, 219; Syncellus, 348A.

[226] *JJS* 13, 1962, pp. 41-2; cf. Alon, *Hist. of the Jews*, I, p. 241.

[227] O. Vessberg, A. Westholm, *Swedish Cyprus Expedition*, IV, 1956, Part iii, p. 240.

[228] *Opuscula Archaeologica*, 6, 1950, p. 89, no. 48.

[229] *IGR* III, 989; Mitford, *BSA* 42, 1948, p. 212, n. 47.

figures of the deities on its cuirass having suffered most of the damage.[230] Karageorghis inclines to the view that the statue is a portrait of a Flavian emperor, and that the defacing of the divine figures was Jewish work. Another discovery is part of the head of a male statue repaired in antiquity, the damage being attributable, on Karageorghis' suggestion, to the period of the revolt.[231]

In a Hadrianic inscription found at Carpasia, the Emperor is called—assuming the editor's restoration is correct—"Saviour and benefactor of the entire world" (τὸν σωτῆρα καὶ] εὐεργέτην τοῦ κόσμου).[232] Mitford remarks, with reference to the fate of Salamis, that "There is no reason to suspect that Karpasia shared either these misfortunes or these benefactions". A third inscription, which honours Hadrian with similar epithets, is known at Lapethos,[233] being dedicated by the council and people of the town. The supposition that these terms have no inevitable connection with work of restoration after the revolt is doubtless admissible, but it is going too far to state dogmatically that such a connection was impossible; the possibility is considerable if the numerous casualties caused by the rising are taken into account. It should further be noted that a Greek inscription is known from Lapethos evidencing the existence there of a Jewish synagogue; it cannot be precisely dated, but it was certainly after the rebellion.[234] But in this context it should not be forgotten that there was a tendency to re-establish Jewish settlements on sites where they had formerly existed. (cf. below, the case of Golgoi). Another inscription from Soli, already mentioned (p. 269), is mutilated and incomplete, but seems to have commemorated the erection of a statue to Trajan, together, perhaps, with the dedication of a shrine. The date is the twentieth year of his reign, i.e. between September, 116 and August, 117. Soli was the location of the copper-mines leased by Augustus to Herod in return for half their proceeds,[235] and it is

---

[230] V. Karageorghis, *Sculptures from Salamis*, I, 1961, no. 48, p. 48, pl. xliii.

[231] *Ibid.*, no. 65, p. 48; pl. liv, 5.

[232] *AJA* 65, 1961, p. 123, no. 25.

[233] *AJA ibid.*; *IGR* III, 934: τὸν σωτῆρα καὶ εὐεργέτην τ[οῦ κόσμου].

[234] Εὐχὴ ῾Ραββὶ ᾿Αττικοῦ—*REJ* 48, 1904, pp. 191 sqq. T. Reinach ascribes the column to the 3rd century CE, but the inscription includes an *upsilon* with a cross-bar, which is peculiar to the Severan period; cf. G. Hill, *Hist. of Cyprus*, I, 1940, p. 243, n. 1. This form appears at Cyrene as early as the reign of Hadrian.

[235] Jos., *Ant.*, XVI, 4, 5 (129).

therefore probable that a Jewish population (criminals condemned to work in the mines?) was present here.

It is further possible that the memory survives of a Jewish community in Cyprus which met its end in the revolt. A Greek inscription cut on a column at Golgoi (Athenaiou) in the centre of the island, reads: "Jose son of Synesius, elder (of the community) renewed the worship of the Jewish congregation." [236] It belongs, according to Reifenberg,[237] to the 4th century, and attests the renewal of a Jewish population in Cyprus after the decree prohibiting Jewish settlement had been forgotten; [238] its language makes it clear that there had been Jews at Golgoi before the rising in Trajan's time.

In order to gauge the topographical extent of the rebellion in Cyprus, it were well to consider whether evidence exists pointing to Jewish settlement in the Cypriot ecountryside in the Second Temple period. Josephus relates [239] how Helena of Adiabene imported pressed dates from Cyprus to Jerusalem in time of famine, and it is to be assumed that these came from Jewish plantations.[240] Important in this respect is the discovery of a military inscription at the village of Knodara between Salamis and Leucosia.[241] It is dedicated by the men of Cohors VII Breucorum, which had arrived with other forces to suppress the revolt, and established a fort (*praesidium*) in the vicinity, as the inscription records. The establishment of a permanent garrison in this area shows that fighting had taken place over a considerable area of the island before the insurgents were annihilated, and that it had become necessary to control the road-system for a certain period.

iv. *Mesopotamia*

Very few archaeological or epigraphical traces of the Jewish revolt remain in Mesopotamia, if the movement there can be regarded as part of the contemporary rising within the Empire. Only two known inscriptions there are connected both with the Roman campaigns in the area in the years 115-117 and with the

---

[236] *REJ* 61, 1911, pp. 285 sq.; *JPOS* 12, 1932, p. 212.
[237] *JPOS ibid.*
[238] Dio, LXVIII, 32, 3.
[239] *Ant.* XX, 2, 5 (51).
[240] For Cypriotic produce eaten in Judaea see M. *Nedarim* IX, 8 (onions); Jer .*Demai* II, 22a (cummin).
[241] *CIL* III (1), 215.

Jewish revolt. The first is a stele at Dura Europos on the Euphrates
found near the north-west corner of the city wall; it bears an
inscription of the years 115-117, and records the restoration, after
the Roman retreat (μετὰ δε τὴν αὐτῶν ἔνθεν ἀποχώρησιν) [242] of the
doors of a temple which "had been removed by the Romans".
The second belongs to a triumphal arch erected by the men of the
III Cyrenaican legion near the city in the year 115.[243] It shows
that a considerable engagement took place here during the southward advance of Trajan's army in the same year. Both these
records furnish evidence that the Romans behaved to Dura Europos
as to a captured place, meaning that the inhabitants of the hellenistic cities of Mesopotamia and Babylonia were opposed to the Roman
invasion. The fact is important for a reconstruction of the background of the clash between Rome and the Jews during the revolt.
This evidence is supplemented by archaeological information at
Seleucia-on-Tigris, where evidence was discovered of the burning
of buildings in the years 116-120, and was connected by the excavators with the capture of the city by the Roman forces in 116/
117.[244]

V. *Eretz Yisrael*

The question how far hostilities broke out in Judaea during the
revolt of the Diaspora under Trajan has long been a subject of
controversy among scholars. The evidence bearing on the problem
is mainly literary and epigraphical, and both types of evidence
overlap to a considerable extent. They are now supplemented by
several fragments of archeological evidence which require consideration. The problem has been discussed chiefly by Schlatter,
Schürer, Groag, Alon and Smallwood.

The outstanding fact is that Jewish tradition knows of a "Pulmus
Qitos" or "War of Quietus"[245] which took place between the war
of the destruction (66-73) and the Ben-Kosba rebellion; the cal-

---

[242] *Excavations at Dura-Europos, Preliminary Report, Seventh and Eighth
Seasons of Work, 1933-34 and 1934-35,* Ed. Rostovtzeff, Brown and Welles,
1939, p. 129. no. 868.

[243] *Ibid., Fourth Season,* ed. Baur, Rostovtzeff and Bellinger, 1933, pp. 56
sqq.; *ibid., Sixth Season,* ed. Rostovtzeff, Bellinger, Hopkins, Welles, 1936,
pp. 480 sqq.

[244] M. McDowell, *Coins of Seleucia-on-Tigris,* 1935, p. 233, n. 71; H. C.
Debevoise, *A Political History of Parthia,* 1938, p. 236, n. 115.

[245] M. *Sota* IX, 14; *Seder 'Olam R.,* 30 (Neubauer, *Seder Ḥakhamim,* II,
p. 66).

culations of *Seder 'Olam Rabba* date it in the years 116-117.[246]
Smallwood's argument that the phrase refers to events outside
Judaea is to be rejected on the grounds that such expressions
invariably refer, in talmudic literature, to occurrences in Eretz
Yisrael, which alone interested the Jewish scholars.[247] The appointment by Trajan of Lusius Quietus as governor of Judaea
with consular rank, which indicated the existence of an emergency,
as the normal grade of the Judaean governors was praetorian,[248]
is known to us from Cassius Dio and other historians.[249] The *Historia
Augusta* also writes that Judaea was in a state of rebellion at the
beginning of Hadrian's reign. (117).[250] Alon has summarized a
number of later sources [251] (Moses of Chorene, Malalas, Michael
Syriacus, Ibn Batrik) and shown that all refer to Judaea when they
are listing the centres of the rebellion in Trajan's reign.

The movements of the Roman forces also lend support to the
view that Judaea was in a state of ferment at the time; the inscription at Jerusalem attesting the contemporary presence of a
detachment (vexillatio) of the III Cyrenaica in the city is well
known; [252] the vexillation had come to reinforce the garrison in
the absence of the X legion Fretensis in Parthia.[253] Alon has
added two epigraphical documents to the above evidence.[254] The
first is a dedication to the "African God" in Jerusalem.[255] Its
exact date is unknown, but Alon thought that it was the work of
one of Quietus' Moorish cavalry which composed an important
part of his force.[256] It may indeed be noted that the spelling *geniu*
instead of *genio* in the inscription is characteristic of speakers of
Libyan.[257] The other document which Alon thought to be connected

---

[246] Cf. Yeivin, *The War of Bar Kokhba*[2], pp. 144-7; Alon, *Hist. of the Jews*,
I, p. 256.

[247] Alon, *op. cit.*, p. 255. Smallwood, *Ha*, XI, 1962, p. 502.

[248] *Ibid.* But on the possibility that Judaea became a consular province in
123, Pflaum, *IEJ* 19, 1969, pp. 225 sqq.; M. Avi-Yonah, *IEJ* 23, 1973, pp.
209 sqq. who places the change in 115/6; L. J. F. Keppie, *Latomus*, 32, 1973,
pp. 859 sqq. Cf. also Applebaum, *Prolegomena to the Second Jewish Revolt*,
1976, pp. 19-20.

[249] Dio LXVIII, 30, 3; Euseb., *vers. Arm.*, 219; Call. Niceph. III, 22.

[250] *Vita Had.*, V, 2.

[251] *Ibid.*, pp. 256-7.

[252] *CIL* III, 13587.

[253] *ILS* 2727.

[254] *Hist. of the Jews*, I, p. 258.

[255] *Rev. Bib.*, 1931, pp. 292-4.

[256] *Vita Had.*, V, 5, 8.

[257] Cf. *DAI* II, Cir. ii, nos. 272, 480, 481, and especially *NAMC* II, pp.
173, 177 n.

with Trajan's reign—albeit with some reservation—is the epitaph,
found in Jerusalem, of a soldier who had fought in Armenia,
Parthia and Judaea.[258] Although the accepted view is that the
Jewish war here referred to was the one under Hadrian, Alon
observed that if this was so, the soldier would have served over
twenty-five years, the normal term of auxiliary troops, hence it
is credible that the "Pulmus Qitos" was meant. A third document,
not perhaps noticed in this context, is an inscription [259] found at
Nablus, commemorating a cavalryman of a numerus Maurorum
with a patently Libyan name (Auginda) who died at the age of
thirty, i.e. probably in action. He may have belonged to one of
Lusius Quietus' Moorish troopers, although most attested uses of
the term "numerus" on inscriptions in relation to military units
belong to the later 2nd century or even later.

A number of less direct sources may perhaps be linked with the
reinforcement of the Roman garrison at Jerusalem during the
Diaspora rising. Hippolytus' report that "Trajan-Quietus" erected
an image of Kore in the Temple [260] seems to relate to Lusius
Quietus' activity in Judaea at the time.[261] In the year 116/117,
at any rate, the Roman authorities found need to reinforce the
garrison of Jerusalem, and various traditions, both Jewish and
Christian, indicate the erection of pagan shrines in the city in
Trajan's time, as if to emphasize its non-Jewish character. Talmudic sources also preserve several echoes of persecution, danger
and capital sentences executed upon Jews in the country in Trajan's
reign; these have been collected by Alon.[262]

A time of danger, in which circumcision was prohibited, is indicated by sayings cited in the name of R. Eli'ezer ben Hyrcanus,
who died before Hadrian's reign.[263] *Tosephta Kelim* [264] reports
that four scholars, R. Ḥutzpit, R. Yashabab. R. Ḥalaphta and
R. Yoḥanan ben Nuri, spent some time in hiding at Tzippori
(Sepphoris) in the house of R. Ele'azar ben 'Azariah, who also

---

[258] Alon, *ibid.*; *AE* 1929, p. 45, no. 167.

[259] *QDAP* 12, 1946, pp. 93-4; *AE* 1948, no. 148.

[260] Ap. Bar Saliba, Sedlaede, *Scriptores Syri²*, CI, p. 17; cf. Hieron.,
Comment. Matth. XXIV, 15.

[261] *JJS* 2, 1950, pp. 29 sq.; also Alon, *op. cit.*, pp. 258-9. Cf. further
Eutychius Ibn-Batrik, (*PO* III, 986-7), that "in the days of Trajan the
Jews returned to Jerusalem"; see Alon, *op. cit.*, p. 257.

[262] Alon, *op. cit.*, pp. 261-3.

[263] B. *Shab.* 130a.

[264] *Tos. Kel. BB* II, 2.

died before the Second Revolt (132-135). It is moreover probable
that the tradition concerning the execution of R. Simon and R.
Ishmael by the Roman government, belongs to the time of Trajan,
and does not refer to the deaths of Rabban Simon ben Gamliel
and the high priest Ishmael who were killed in the period of the
Great Rebellion of 66-73; this view gains support from the predic-
tion that they would die by the sword, attributed to Samuel
"the Little", who died some time after the Revolt of 66, in the
time of Gamliel the younger.[265]

Finally a note of religious persecution is sounded by the report [266]
concerning "Lulianus and Pappus, to whom they gave water in a
vessel of painted glass, and they refused it"—i.e. that they refused
to make a show of offering a libation to the Emperor. The problems surrounding these two men are discussed briefly below; but
it is clear from the associated traditions that they were put to
death by Lusius Quietus acting in his capacity of emergency
governor of Judaea.

It is harder to evaluate the information reproduced by very late
sources concerning Lucuas, the leader of the Jews of Cyrenaica.
According to Abu'al Faraj (Bar Hebraeus), a 13th century author,
Lucuas broke through to Judaea and was killed there by the
Romans after a number of small engagements; [267] this report is
repeated by Michael Syriacus,[268] who writes: "At the end of Trajan's
reign the Jews of Egypt rebelled and set up a king called Lump-
saios, who led them to Judaea. Trajan sent Lusius upon them and
he annihilated them in their ten-thousands." [269]

A very complex problem is presented by the various traditions to
be found in talmudic literature concerning the figures of Lulianus
and Pappus. The events related by these sources amount, in brief,
to this. These two Jews, Lulianus and Pappus, were seized at

---

[265] Alon, *op. cit.*, pp. 262-3; *Tos. Sota*, XIII, 4; cf. *Sem.* VIII, 7.

[266] Jer., *Shev.* IV, 35a.

[267] Gregorii Abulfaragii, *Historia Compendiosa Dynastiarum*, 1663
(Pococke), p. 76.

[268] Michaelus Syriacus, Chabot, IV, p. 105.

[269] For the historians Michael Syriacus and Bar Hebraeus (Abulfaraj)
see Baumstark, *Gesch. der Syrischen Literatur*, 1922, pp. 298, 312 sqq.
Michael, who died at the end of the 12th century, wrote an Aramaic history
that went down to the year 1194/5; he is extremely erudite and frequently
cites earlier material now lost, although his model is Eusebius. Bar Hebraeus
(13th century) was author of a Syriac chronography, largely dependent on
Michael, but supplementing him and adding new material.

Laodicea by "Troginus", and put to death by him; but Troginus
was at once put to death himself.[270] According to other traditions [271]
"the day of Tirion" was abolished due to the death of Simon and
ʿAzariah. A tradition cited by *Midrash Genesis Rabba* [272] relates
that "in the days of Joshua ben Ḥananiah the Empire decreed
that the Temple should be [re]built, and Pappus and Lulianus set
up banks from Akko to Antioch to supply pilgrims."

The difficulty in interpreting the events hidden behind these
traditions is to reconcile the information dating the death of
Pappus and Lulianus to Trajan's reign—since clearly "Troginus"
who executed them, and was himself executed, is Lusius Quietus
governor of Judaea, who was put to death by Hadrian shortly
after his accession [273]—with the statement linking the episode of
the banks to the time of Joshua ben Ḥanania, who lived under
Hadrian. The difficulty, however, may have been exaggerated
somewhat, since Quietus was executed by Hadrian in July, 118,[274]
and not by Trajan, hence it may be believed that Lulianus and
Pappus were also put to death after Trajan's decease. The substitution of the name Trajan for Qitos is natural, since Quietus was
Trajan's general. On the other hand Hadrian's alleged decision to
rebuild the Temple, if it was ever taken, is hardly likely to belong
to a period immediately after his accession, when the disturbances
occasioned by the Diaspora revolt had barely died down. The
"Day of Tirion", on the other hand, probably has no connection
at all with Trajan, who is always known as "Trikinios" or "Troginus" in talmudic sources.[275]

The character of Pappus and Lulianus is indicated by other
talmudic passages. They are called "proud men, the strength of
Israel" by Rabbi ʾAqiva,[276] and in *Sifra* [277] are compared to Joab,
David's general. The precise significance of the tradition relating
the imperial decision to rebuild the Temple is problematic, but it
seems clear that Pappus' and Lulianus' project was the organization of infiltration by Jews from outside the country, and their

---

[270] *Siphre Emor*, IX, 5 etc. (Alon, *op. cit.*, I, p. 260, n. 169).
[271] Jer., *Taʾaniot*, II, 66a; Jer., *Meg.* I, 70c.
[272] *Gen. Rab.*, par 64.8 (Theodor Albeck, p. 710).
[273] Dio LXIX, 2; SHA Had., V; VII.
[274] Smallwood, *Ha*, 11, 1962, p. 505.
[275] *Mid. Lam. R.*, I, 16; Baber, p. 80.
[276] *Siphra*, Be-ḥuqotai, V, 2.
[277] *Ibid.*

activity "from Akko to Antioch" can be understood against the
background of the rising in Cyprus and the island's nearness to
the Syrian harbours,—i.e. as the transfer of insurgents from
thence to the coast of Eretz Yisrael. This operation can also be
connected with the policy of Quietus during his governorship,
meant to emphasize the pagan character of Jerusalem by the
setting up of new images. The operations of Pappus and Lulianus
would have been directed to enabling the infiltration of Jews into
the city (the feeding of pilgrims), in order to prevent its conversion into a centre of idolatry, and *Genesis Rabba* [278] is perhaps to be
interpreted as the decision of the Roman power to convert the
Temple into a pagan shrine. The phrase "the Empire decreed"
(מלכות גזרה), at all events, can with difficulty be interpreted
in a favourable sense. This would explain the words of *Siphra*,[279]
which compare the brothers Pappus and Lulianus to Joab, who
captured Jerusalem for David,[280] The date of Quietus' appointment makes it clear that the movement organized by Pappus and
Lulianus began as early as 117 and continued after Trajan's death,
and if our suggestion is correct that the Cyprus rising was suppressed in 117, the movement of entry into Syria and Judaea must
have reached its height not later than the beginning of the same
year.

A tradition in the *Jerusalem Ta'aniot* [281] perhaps preserves a
memory of one centre of insurgency in Judaea in 116-117. This
says that "Bethar lasted fifty-two years after the destruction of
the Temple." As the Temple was destroyed in 70 and the year 122
has no significance (70 + 52 = 122), the calculation here probably
proceeds from the opening of the rebellion in 66, making the fifty-
second year 118, i.e. the end of the disorders that had begun under
Trajan and terminated under Hadrian. It is therefore possible,
according to this text, that Bethar was a centre of unrest in the
years 116-118, as it was to be again in the war of 132-135. While
it must be admitted that the context of the statement is such
as to relate it to the revolt in Hadrian's time,[282] the independent
tradition of *Midrash Rabba* on *Lamentations* [283] of hostility between

---

[278] See n. 272.
[279] XXII, 9.
[280] I *Chron.* 11:6.
[281] Jer., *Ta'an.* IV, 69a.
[282] Cf. Smallwood, *Ha*, ii, 1962, p. 502-3.
[283] *Mid. Lam. R.*, II, 69, Baber, p. 103.

Jerusalem and Bethar before the Destruction is such as to make the present interpretation credible.

The written tradition is now perhaps reinforced by evidence furnished by archaeological research. The fifth campaign of excavation in the ancient tell of Jaffa near the Church of Saint Peter revealed an occupation-stratum belonging to the beginning of the 2nd century A.D. (Stratum V). We cite here the account of the excavator, Dr. Ya'akov Kaplan: [284] "To the fifth occupation stratum, dated in the beginning of the 2nd century C.E., belonged part of the cellar of a building for whose erection the builders had dug deep into the older strata; two of its walls, the southerly and the easterly, were found built in the form of a stout retaining wall. Numerous signs of burning and soot seen on the cellar floor and on the surrounding walls, were apparently the result of the destruction of the building. The floor also yielded much pottery, stone objects, a bronze jug and a hoard of bronze and silver coins. Examination of the finds, including a Greek inscription, leads to the conclusion that the building was destroyed by fire in the time of the Emperor Trajan, and this destruction is perhaps to be connected with the Jewish rebellion in north Africa (115-117 C.E.). As is well known, we possess only hints that the Jews of Palestine joined the rising." Finds in the same stratum included three stone moulds for casting metal weights, stamped in Greek with the name of the agoranomos Judah, who served in this post in the ninth (?) year of Trajan's reign (106/107).[285]

It occasions no surprise that the rising may have affected Jaffa, which was a harbour-city possessing close connections with the Diaspora centres,[286] and the population of which was mixed, including Jews from Egypt and Libya, as the epitaphs of the cemetery at Abbu Kabir evidence. It is enough to mention the inscription of a Jew of the Libyan Pentapolis,[287] of another with

---

[284] Y. Kaplan, *JQR*, 54, 1963, p. 111; cf. *IEJ* 12, 1962, pp. 149-50.

[285] Kaplan, *loc. cit.* But there is now evidence of trouble in Judaea in A.D. 107 (see *AE* 1972 (1975), no. 577)—cf. Applebaum, *Prolegomena to the Study of the Second Jewish Revolt (A.D. 132-135)*, p. 77, n. 149a.

[286] Cf. *SEG* 9, 2, 54, which furnishes evidence for the despatch of grain from Cyrene to 'Akko at the end of the 4th century B.C.E.; further the alleged influence of Jewish currency in Judaea on Cyrenean coinage in the 2nd and 1st centuries B.C.E., which, if genuine, would be the result of the seizure of Jaffa by the Hasmoneans.

[287] *CIJ* II, 1936, 950.

a distinctively Libyan name,[288] and of Jews from Egypt and Alexandria.[289] Jaffa had suffered heavily in the war of the destruction (66-73) and from the subsequent punitive action of the Roman army,[290] yet as early as Trajan's reign the Jaffa Jewish community had its own agoranomos,[291] and a numerous Jewish population had again taken root in the port. Most of its known epitaphs doubtless belong to the later Roman and Byzantine period,[292] but the occupational structure they reflect points to a predominantly proletarian community.[293] It may be assumed that it possessed a similar composition in the early 2nd century and its members doubtless responded readily to extremist influence.

The second item of archaeological evidence that invites consideration is from Gerasa, in Transjordan, the Decapolis city on the border of the province of Arabia. The structure of the triumphal arch of Hadrianic date (A.D. 130) south of the village of Jerash, incorporated fragments of a Doric frieze and a Corinthian capital derived from a demolished building. The frieze fragments bore the carved figures of an amphora and a bird, while between the volutes of the capital appeared the figure of a menorah (candelabrum) with seven branches.[294] The stylistic details of the frieze (the absence of regulae and guttae) were found by Dettweiler, who published the material,[295] to be paralleled mainly among hellenistic Jewish monuments of the 2nd and 1st centuries B.C., also in synagogues of the Severan epoch. The building had been destroyed, in his opinion, when Vespasian's commander L. Annius captured and burned the city in A.D. 68.[296] But as several scholars have remarked, the settlement called Gerasa then attacked by

---

[288] *CIJ* II, 905.

[289] Alexandria—*CIJ* II, 918; *JCPI* 135, 141; Egypt—*ibid.* 137.

[290] Jos., *BJ* II, 18, 10 (507); III, 9, 2-4 (414-430); cf. Kaplan, *JQR* 54, 1963, pp. 112-3.

[291] See ref., n. 284.

[292] With regard to the Libyan Jews buried at Jaffa, it would be logical to assume that in view of the annihilation of Cyrenean Jewry in Trajan's time, they had reached Judaea before the revolt. Yet cf. Benoit et al., *Murabba'at*, 1961, p. 218, no. 90c, 8—Hillel of Cyrene, serving as a soldier in the forces of Ben Kosba.

[293] From the epitaphs we learn of fishermen, linen-weavers, a wool-dresser, a trader in linen, a dealer in cummin, a rag dealer, and a simple labourer. The *Acts of the Apostles* (9:43) informs us of Simon the tanner.

[294] *BASOR* 87, 1942, pp. 10 sqq.

[295] *Ibid., loc. cit.*

[296] Jos., *BJ* IV, 9, 1 (487-8).

the Romans was not Gerasa in Transjordan, since earlier in the war the Jews themselves had attacked the Decapolis town,[297] while Josephus states that the latter's citizens had protected their Jewish inhabitants.[298] These two reports therefore testify that Gerasa of the Decapolis was neither a centre of revolt nor hostile to Rome, hence there is no reason to identify it with the place burnt by L. Annius. If so, we are obliged to seek another occasion when the Jewish public building at Gerasa was destroyed on the evidence of the remains reused in Hadrian's arch. The appropriate setting for the destruction might well have been the rebellious ferment in Judaea in the years 116-118.

4. THE COURSE OF THE REBELLION [299]

Fuks has devoted a brief investigation to the Greek and Latin terms used by ancient documents in relation to the Jewish rebellion.[300] The sources use the following terms: στάσις,[301] θόρυβος,[302] ἔφοδος,[303] τάραχος,[304] *tumultus*[305] and πόλεμος.[306] The first four

---

[297] *BJ* II, 18, 1 (458).

[298] *Ibid.*, II, 18, 5 (480).

[299] Four general studies have been written on the Trajanic revolt. The first comprehensive scholarly account was by K. Friedmann in 1931 (*SAI* ns. 2, ii, 1931, pp. 108 sqq.: Le grande rebellione Giudaica sotto Traiano); a second account, including much material which had accumulated subsequently, was that of G. Alon, *Hist. of the Jews*, I, 1954, pp. 202 sqq. A third, by the present writer, mainly concerning Cyrene, appeared in *Zion* 19, 1954, pp. 25 sqq. The fourth was that of A. Fuks, *JRS* 51, 1961, pp. 98 sqq.: Some aspects of the Jewish revolt in A.D. 115-117. Other general accounts have been written by P. Romanelli, *CR* 1943, pp. 113 sqq. and in *CAH* XI, 1936, pp. 246 sqq. Four studies have been devoted to the revolt in Egypt: A. Tcherikover, *The Jews in Egypt in the Hellenistic Roman Age in the Light of the Papyri*², 1963, Chap. 6, pp. 160 sqq.; V. Tcherikover, A. Fuks, *CPJ* I, 1957, pp. 86-93; II, 1960, Section xi, pp. 228-60; A. Fuks, *Aegyptus*, 33, 1953, pp. 131 sqq.; cf. *Zion*, 22, 1957, pp. 1 sqq.; also H. A. Musurullo, *APM*, 1954, pp. 182 sqq. For a detailed bibliography down to 1954, see the present author, *Zion* 19; down to 1962, *JJS* 1962, pp. 36 sqq. Since then, Vermes, Millar, *The Hist. of the Jewish People in the Age of Jesus Christ*, I, 1973, pp. 529 sqq.: M. Smallwood, *The Jews under Roman Rule from Pompey to Diocletian*, 1976, Ch. XV, pp. 389-427.

[300] *Aegyptus*, 33, 1953, pp. 1955-6.

[301] P. Brem. 11, 30.

[302] *Ibid.*, 25-6.

[303] P. Giss. 41, col. ii, 4-5.

[304] *BGU* 889, 23; cf. *SEG* 9, 168 (restoration).

[305] *SEG* 9, 168, 252; *JRS* 40, 1950, p. 89, D4.

[306] Acta Pauli et Ant., col. ii, 3, 6; App., *frag.* 19; *SEG* 9, 189; P. Oxy. 705, col. ii, 33; Eus., *HE* IV, 2, 2; cf. Artem. Dald., *Oneirokritika*, IV, 24: ὁ πόλεμος ὁ Ἰουδαϊκὸς ἐν Κυρήνῃ.

terms appear in contemporary documents. The word στάσις denotes, of course, any collision between two classes or groups in a given state. The meaning of θόρυβος is any undefined civil disorder, while ἔφοδος simply means an attack. But τάραχος (or ταραχή) was used as a synonym of the Latin word *tumultus*,[307] and the inscriptions at Cyrene show that this term was the official Roman description of the revolt of 115-117. The word πόλεμος, as Fuks has observed, appears once almost contemporarily with the revolt, in Appian; forty years after it, in Artemidorus Daldianus in the 2nd century, also in a Cyrenean inscription at the end of the same century— and it is used by the inhabitants of Oxyrhinchos in the year 199/200.[308] Its absence from Latin sources may not be due to chance, since *tumultus* denotes a graver situation and event than simple war; Cicero writes:[309] "There can be a war without a *tumultus*, but there cannot be a *tumultus* without a war. For this reason our ancestors spoke of a *tumultus Italicus* because it occurred at home, and of a *tumultus Gallicus* because it was very close to Italy. What is more it can be understood that a *tumultus* is graver than a *bellum* (war), because in wartime military furlough is still legal, but in a *tumultus* it is not."[310] Livy says:[311] ". . .The Boii also had set their faces to rebellion. Therefore the Senate proclaimed the existence of a *tumultus*. . ." This situation is defined by Forcellini:[312] "The name *tumultus* was applied by the Romans to any sudden war which seriously alarmed the city due to the magnitude of the danger and the nearness of the enemy." Cagnat wrote of such a situation: "A critical situation caused by an internal rising or a sudden attack by the enemy. When the country was thus endangered, the Senate proclaimed a *tumultus*, and all activities public and private ceased for the time being . . . and every man put on military uniform . . . all citizens were summoned . . . to take up arms."[313]

These definitions enable us to comprehend why both Apollonius, the civil district commissioner of Apollonipolitis,[314] and simple

---

[307] Plut., *Caes.* 33.

[308] *CPJ* II, no. 450.

[309] VIII *Philip.*, I.

[310] Cf. *CIL* II, 5439, 26 sqq.: Lex coloniae Genetivae Iuliae.

[311] XXXIV, 56.

[312] *Totius Latinitatis Lexicon*, 1805, ad voc.

[313] Cf. T. Mommsen, *Röm. Staatsrecht*, 1887, I³, p. 120; *DS* V, 532 sv. Tumultus.

[314] *CPJ* II, no. 436 (= P. Giss. 19).

Egyptian peasants [315] were summoned to take up arms to fight the
Jews in Trajan's time. It also makes clear that the authorities saw
the conflict with the Jews as more serious than a normal war.
Tumultus was not a mere disorder or riot, but a rising or attack
which imperilled the very existence of the state.

We have seen that the collision between the Jews and Romans in
autumn, 115, was, to judge by the atmosphere of the account, an
isolated occurrence. But it is very likely that the revolt had already
broken out in Cyrene in the middle of the year, and by early 116
the insurgents were advancing from Libya and penetrating Egypt.
Two sources survive that may throw some light on the fighting
in Cyrenaica at the outbreak of the revolt. The first is the tomb
stele of Gaius Julius Carus, a military tribune of the III legion
Cyrenaica, who died at Cyrene while in command of a recruiting
party composed of centurions and troops of the same legion
and of the XXII Deiotariana.[316] This party has been despatched
to recruit for the Roman army, presumably for the abovemen-
tioned legions, then stationed in Egypt. Carus had served previously as commander of the Second Cohort of Asturians (Cohors
II Astyrum equitata) and had been decorated in "the British
war". A terminus post quem for his death is provided by the fact
that the Cohors II Astyrum was still in Germany in 89,[317] and
recruiting activities are known in Cyrene in the year 100,[318] when
a milestone was set up three miles from the city inscribed with
Trajan's name and titles and the words "Viam fecit / per tirones
lectos / in provincia Cyrenensi." Carus' tombstone, however,
need not inevitably be associated with such activities in 100,
as there was a similar recruiting drive in the province in 59,[319]
and such drives recurred, it seems, at various times. But the
liberal award of military decorations is more characteristic of
Trajan than of Hadrian,[320] hence the British campaign mentioned
on Carus' monument is more likely to have taken place between
89-115. Serious fighting in North Britain had begun by 100; [321]

---

[315] *CPJ* II, no. 438 (= P. Brem. 1).

[316] *Zion*, 22, 1957, pp. 82 sqq.; E. B. Birley, *Roman Britain and the
Roman Army*, 1953, pp. 23-4.

[317] Diploma XVI, 5; Birley, *op. cit.*, p. 22.

[318] Goodchild, *PBSR*, 18, 1950, pp. 83-91; cf. *Zion*, 22, p. 83.

[319] Tac., *Ann.* XIV, 18, 1.

[320] Cf. Birley, *op. cit.*, p. 23.

[321] S. Frere, *Britannia*, 1967, pp. 120-123.

there was something like a disaster in about 105 and the Roman frontier was subsequently being withdrawn to the Tyne-Solway line; fighting was still going on in 108.[322] Military tribunes were young men at the beginning of their careers, and those of them who were of the equestrian order normally took command of a second auxiliary unit after their term of service in a legion and prior to promotion to the next rung of the equestrian cursus.[323] As Carus was a young man when he died, he may not have died a natural death. Having distinguished himself in Britain, he passed to his legionary tribunate in Egypt and died before reaching his third military post. It is therefore possible that he was killed at the outbreak of the Jewish rising in Cyrene.

But if the connection of Carus' tombstone with the Cyrenean revolt is uncertain, this is not the case concerning a well known passage of the 'Ονειροκριτικά (Dream Book) of Artemidorus Daldianus, who writes:[324] "A camp prefect (στρατοπεδάρχης) (dreamt) he saw the letters I, K, Θ written on his sword. The Jewish war in Cyrene began and the man who dreamt this distinguished himself, and it was as we have related: The I meant "Jews" ('Ιουδαῖοι); the K—"Cyreneans" (Κυρηναῖοι); and the Θ— death (θάνατος). Before the event it was indeterminate, but after the outcome (ἀποβάντων τῶν τελεσμάτων) the interpretation presented no difficulties". The identity of the camp prefect concerned may be conjectured.[325] In Trajan's time the two Egyptian legions (the XXII Deiotariana and the III Cyrenaica) were commanded by a *prefectus castrorum*;[326] thus there is little doubt that in the event of serious trouble in Cyrene which the garrison stationed there could not control, it would have been the duty of the prefect of Egypt to intervene by despatching a detachment (*vexillatio*) of troops, which might well have been commanded by the camp prefect, or by proceeding personally at their head to the scene of action.[327] It may therefore be supposed that when the rising broke

---

[322] Frere, *loc. cit.*; Birley, *op. cit.*, p. 24; R. G. Collingwood, J. N. L. Myres, *Roman Britain and the English Settlements*, 1937, p. 128.

[323] H. M. Parker, *The Roman Legions*, 1958, p. 189.

[324] IV, 24 (Hercher).

[325] See also *Zion*, 22, 1957, pp. 82-4.

[326] J. Lesquier, *L'armée rom. d'Égypte, d'Auguste à Dioclétien*, 1918, pp. 120-132.

[327] The acting commander of the Egyptian legions, serving under the *Praefectus Aegypti*, his commander-in-chief, was the *praefectus castrorum*, but the former might actually take command, and did so on various occasions

out, troops of the Egyptian legionary garrison proceeded by sea to Cyrene under the command of their camp prefect. Nor can it be doubted that Artemidorus' story belongs to the beginning of the rebellion rather than to its end, for few Jews requiring suppression by strong forces can have remained at the end of the *tumultus*; the devastation of Cyrenaica which is so clearly revealed by the evidence points to the intention of the insurgents to evacuate the country utterly. The fate of the camp prefect in the fighting, on the other hand, is problematic. I think that Artemidorus' narrative is to be interpreted to mean that he was killed in action, otherwise there seems no way of understanding the third letter—Θ.

It is possible to adduce grounds for this view. Writing of Origen's work on the Old Testament, Rufinus [328] says: "(Origen) noted Jewish additions or omissions ... by marks at the beginning of the line ... in a manner used by one who, having received a nominal roll of troops, attempts to ascertain from it how many ranks are still alive, and how many have fallen in battle; and having been sent to ascertain, searches and, instead of a word, sets the customary appropriate mark, "Θ", against the name of each man deceased, and marks each survivor with the appropriate sign."

This information is repeated more briefly by Isidore of Seville [329] who states that the letter 'tau' (T) was placed at the beginning of a line indicating a survivor, and "theta" (Θ) against the name of a dead man. "For this reason it has a cross-line (*telum*) through it, a sign of death." [330] The correctness of Rufinus' information is confirmed by at least one papyrus, to be described below (p. 314), dated latest to a few years (A.D. 96-127) after the revolt; this is a roster of men of the III legion Cyrenaica, in which the names of men deceased are marked with the letter "theta". [331]

The derivation of the use of the letter theta in Artemidorus'

(*DS* IV, 1878-, p. 615), In a situation demanding a division of the forces on account of disorder in several different localities, the *praefectus castrorum* would have taken command of part of the available legionary force.

[328] *Adv. Hieron.*, 2:36 (Migne, *PL* 21, 392, col. 614); see G. R. Watson, *JRS* 42, 1952, pp. 56 sqq.: Theta nigrum.

[329] *Etymologiae*, I, 24.

[330] *Ibid*.

[331] R. O. Fink, *Roman Military Records on Papyrus*, 1971, pp. 160 sqq., no. 34. For other examples of the use of θ to denote casualties in military lists, see Daris, *Documenti per il essercito Romano in Egitto*, 1964, p. 66 nn. Cf. also *ILS* II, 2, 7228, where the deceased members of the collegium of marble-workers at Luna (Carrara) are distinguished by the same letter.

account is such as to suggest that the events described really took
place, or at least that the original source of the narrative was
familiar with army life. It might also suggest that nominal lists of
casualties who had met their deaths in the *tumultus*, including also
Cyreneans and Jews, were drawn up by the Roman authorities
at the time.

If the tombstone of Carus related to the revolt, the legions XXII
Deiotariana and III Cyrenaica were in Egypt when it broke out
in 115, but the inscription from Dura Europus already mentioned
shows that the III Cyrenaica was in that city, on the Euphrates
frontier, in the first or second year of Trajan's Parthian expedition,
i.e. in 114 or 115 [332] The excavators of Dura believed that the
whole legion was operating there, but a vexillation derived from
it appears at Jerusalem in 116,[333] and it is very possible that it was
identical with the unit recorded at Dura. There is however evidence
that units of both legions remained in Egypt during the revolt;
probably one legion at least, was at full strength. A papyrus usually
dated to the period between 116 and 117 speaks of "Rutilius'
(Lupus) other legion which has come to Memphis." [334] It is therefore clear that one complete legion was present in Egypt at that
time, i.e. XXII Deiotariana, with part of III Cyrenaica. The
presence of at least some troops of the latter seems to be confirmed
by an unexpected quarter, namely by the *Sibylline Oracles* (XII),[335]
where we read: "and the third great ram of Cyrene, which fled,
as I have said before, from the battle by the dykes of the Nile." [336]
The ram is the symbol of the God Ammon,[337] and accordingly of
Cyrene; there can be no doubt that by "the third great ram of
Cyrene" we must understand the legion III Cyrenaica, or part of it,
which appears to have suffered a reverse near the Nile, and it is
difficult to find any occasion for such an event except the revolt
of 115-117. Most of Book XII of the *Sibylline Oracles* belongs to

---

[332] As Trajan was "Imperator X" in December, 114, and his twentieth
tribunicia potestas fell in January 115, the inscription belongs to 115 at latest.

[333] *CIL* III, 13587.

[334] *CPJ* II, no. 438 (= P. Bremen 1), 15-18.

[335] *Orac. Sib.* XII, 326-8.

[336] καὶ τρίτατος αὐτοῖσι κριὸς μέγας ἐκ Κυρήνης ὅν πρίν ἔλεξα φύγοντα μάχης
παρὰ χεύμασι Νείλου. For further details and discussion on legions in Egypt
during the revolt and casualties suffered by Roman military units at the
time, see A. Kasher, *Zion*, 42, 1976, pp. 127 sqq. and here *Summing Up*,
pp. 339, n. 457.

[337] Herod. II, 42, 4; Lucan. IX, 545; Ovid., *Met.* V, 328 etc.

the 3rd century, but the phrase ὁ πρὶν ἔλεξα indicates an interpolation, and we seem to have here an ancient tradition, the more so
as the book contains much material older than its final redaction.

The defeat of III Cyrenaica, moreover, may be confirmed by
papyrology. Pap. Vindobonensis L2 is a list of soldiers of that
legion drawn up not later than A.D. 127. It is certainly not earlier
than the reign of Nerva (96-98). It contains a record of nine men
deceased out of the 28 recorded, while two or even three of the nine
centuries named are without centurions.[338] There can be little
hesitation, therefore, in ascribing this high casualty list to the
Jewish revolt, thus confirming the tradition preserved in the Jewish
source. In this list the letter "theta" is used, moreover, to distinguish
the names of deceased soldiers.

It may therefore be concluded: a) that at the outbreak of the
rising in 115, two legions were in Egypt, but part of one had left
the province to take part in Trajan's Parthian War; b) that a
detachment from one of the two, or both, set out for Cyrene by
sea at the outbreak of the fighting, and was either defeated or
retreated, having lost its commanding officer; c) that in the course
of the rebellion in Egypt itself, the III Cyrenaica, or that part
that had remained there, was severely handled. Evidence further
exists that at least one auxiliary unit in Egypt, the Cohors I
Lusitanorum, also suffered heavy casualties in the fighting of
115-117. This is in the form of a papyrus, *PSI*, 1063 [339] dated to
September, 117. This record indicates that the cohort then received
an exceptionally high percentage of recruits, amounting to a third
or more of its strength. The first and third centuries now received
20 men each, the fourth, 22, the sixth, 23, and the fifth, 24. As
there is only restricted evidence of the participation of Egyptian
auxilia in Trajan's Parthian campaign,[340] this heavy scale of
replacements can safely be ascribed to casualties inflicted in the
Jewish revolt. The cohort did not know of Trajan's death (Aug.
117), and was therefore probably deep in Upper Egypt in that
year,[341] showing that the fighting in that region must have been
exceptionally severe. Additionally one auxiliary unit is known

---

[338] R. O. Fink, *Roman Military Records* (n. 331) pp. 160 sqq., no. 34.
[339] *Op. cit.*, pp. 277 sqq., no. 74.
[340] J. F. Gilliam, *Antiquitas*, 4, Bd. 3, p. 96. For what evidence there is, see
Kasher's article, n. 36.
[341] *Ibid.*

which was moved from Europe to reinforce the Egyptian garrison; this was the Cohors I Hispana, diverted to Egypt, on papyrological evidence,[342] from its march through Macedonia.

Eusebius [343] in his account of the rising mentions Libya first among the centres of the movement, then Cyrenaica. He may have been influenced by the administrative division prevalent in his own time, in the 4th century, when Cyrenaica was divided into Libya Superior (the Pentapolis) and Libya Inferior (Libya Sicca, Marmarica).[344] Even if this was the case, he seems to have preserved a distinct tradition of disorders in the eastern region. This impression is strengthened by his mention of the Thebais at the end of the same list, whereby he designates that Egyptian nome as a particular centre of disorder at the time. We already know that Marmarica had a Jewish population and that signs of destruction dating to the time of the revolt have been found there. The province of Inferior extended to the frontier of the Nile Delta, and took its origin in the "Libyan Nome" of the Ptolemaic period.[345] Accordingly it is possible to see in Eusebius' report confirmation of the location of Cyrenean Jews on the fringes of the province, and groups of activists may have occupied the desert borders in the frontier regions between Egypt and Marmarica.

The appearance of the Thebais as a special centre of fighting in Upper Egypt may further be interpreted to mean that groups of Jewish insurgents reached the area by crossing the desert from Libya, using the chain of oases known as Ḥargijeh, Daḥliyeh, Farafa, Siwa and Jarabub, which together constitute a well known caravan route.[346]

According to Pap. Giessen 19,[347] there was trouble and even fighting in the Egyptian countryside as early as August-September, 115; at the beginning of 116, on Eusebius' testimony,[348] the Cyrenean Jews broke into Egypt, and the trouble assumed the scale of a full war. The correspondence of Apollonius, strategos of the

---

[342] W. Wagner, *Die Dislokation der römischen Auxiliarformationen in der Provinzen Norikum, Pannonien, Moesien u. Dakien, von Augustus bis Gallienus*, 1938, pp. 150, 230.

[343] *Chron.* II, 164 (Migne, *PL* 19, 554 (346-7)).

[344] *Not. Dig. Oriens* (Seeck), pp. 6, 51; *Laterculus Veronensis* (Seeck, *Not. Dig.*, p. 247), 3-4; Romanelli, *CR*, p. 135.

[345] Ptol. IV, 5, 5; cf. Jones, *CERP*, pp. 300, 344.

[346] See here Chap. V, n. 106, and cf. Kraeling, *Ptolemais*, p. 15, n. 16.

[347] *CPJ* II, no. 436.

[348] *HE* IV, 2.

Apollinopolite nome, indeed witnesses to sharp fighting at a time
placed by Tcherikover and Fuks at the end of June of the year
116.[349] Between June and January of the following year, belongs,
in their view, the letter in Apollonius' archives which speaks of a
severe defeat suffered by the Egyptian villagers at the hands of
the Jews, apparently in the vicinity of Memphis, and of the approach of "Rutilius (Lupus') other legion which has come to Memphis" (above)—Rutilius Lupus being the Roman prefect then
governing Egypt. The defeat referred to was possibly identical,
or contemporary with, the defeat of the legion III Cyrenaica
referred to by the *Sibylline Oracles*.

This was the high point of Jewish success. Now, if not previously,
the Greeks who had fled from the rural areas attacked the Jews of
Alexandria, according to Eusebius, and there flared up in the city
the long and fierce conflict in which a considerable part of its
buildings was laid in ruins and the Great Synagogue, the Temple of
Nemesis and the Sanctuary of Serapis were damaged or destroyed.
Appian writes of the Temple of Nemesis that "it was destroyed by
necessity of war",[350] which seems to mean that it was destroyed by
the Greeks, to prevent the Jews using it as a position, as it lies
close to the Jewish quarter in the east of the city. A similar picture
is revealed by the discoveries in the Serapeium: the excavations
of 1943 showed that the building had been utterly destroyed in
the rebellion and rebuilt under Hadrian.[351] The building's later
history perhaps throws some light on the events under Trajan.
The Serapeium continued to be the stronghold of the pagans in
Alexandria, and although it was closed in 325, evidently by order of
the Emperor Constantine, continued to discharge this function
till it was taken by storm by the Christians in 391, in the time of
the Patriarch Theophilos.[352] It is therefore more than possible that
the building was used as a citadel in Trajan's reign, and one archaeological detail would suggest that it may have been seized by
the Jews. The excavations of 1943 found here amphora-handles
stamped with Hebrew letters,[353] and Tertullian writes that the
manuscripts of the Septuagintal rendering of the Bible were kept

---

[349] *CPJ* II, no. 437 = P. Giss. 24.

[350] *Bell. Civ.* II, 90: εἰς τὰς τοῦ πολέμου χρείας.

[351] A. Rowe, *PEQ* 94, 1962, p. 139; cf. *Bull. John Rylands Library,
Manchester*, 39, 1957, p. 496.

[352] Rowe, *PEQ* 94, p. 139.

[353] *Ibid.*

in the Serapeium.[354] This fact, though not positive proof, may be taken as an indication and measure of the place's importance in the eyes of the Jews of Alexandria, hence its defenders at this time may have been the Jews and not the Greeks. The Serapeium is situated at the opposite end of the city to the Temple of Nemesis, in its south-west corner, and if it was not seized by the Jews, it was attacked by them. Whether we accept the first version or the second, it emerges that the fighting raged at both ends of the city, and that the Jews must have attacked with considerable violence.

Pap. Giessen 27,[355] written by a member of the strategos Apollonius' entourage in the first months of 117, in Fuks' view, announces an important victory over the Jews in the vicinity of Memphis, although its exact location has not been determined. Fuks notes that there is no certainty that this was a decisive victory, in view of Eusebius' statement that the revolt was suppressed by Marcius Turbo "in many battles and over a long period." [356] But it may be supposed that Memphis was situated near the strategic focus of the war,[357] since in its vicinity the Nile divides into several arms which fan out northward to form the Delta. Marcius Turbo, who had been despatched by Trajan to suppress the Jewish movement in Egypt,[358] may have been appointed commander in the province in 116 or in early summer of the succeeding year, not long before the accession of Hadrian to the imperial throne.[359] According to Eusebius he commanded both land and sea forces,[360] and if so probably his advance southward was made with the accompani-

---

[354] Tertullianus, *Apol.*, 18: Hoc quoque a Iudaeis Ptolemaeo subscriptum est septuaginta et duobus interpretibus indultis. . . hodie apud Serapaeum Ptolemaei bibliothecae cum ipsis Hebraicis litteris exhibentur.

[355] *CPJ* II, no. 439.

[356] *HE* IV, 2, 4.

[357] Cf. *Orac. Sib.* V, 60-74, which threatens the city because it "had encouraged evil in the hearts of the good".

[358] Eus., *ibid.* IV, 2, 4.

[359] A. Stein, *Die Präfekten von Ägypten in der römischen Kaiserzeit*, 1950, pp. 59 sqq., considered Turbo was appointed Prefect of Egypt; cf. Fuks, *Aegyptus*, 33, 1953, pp. 151-2. But Syme (*JRS* 52, 1962, pp. 87 sqq.) has shown that the well-known inscription from Caesarea in Mauretania, *AE* 1946, no. 113 = *CRAI* 1945, pp. 144 sqq., does not concern the Marcius Turbo who suppressed the Jewish rising in Egypt and Cyrene, nor does he consider the latter's appointment as prefect of Egypt probable, but thinks he was appointed to the Egyptian command in 116.

[360] IV, 2, 4. In 114 Turbo commanded the *classis praetoria* which took Trajan to the east—*CIL* XVI, 60; *AJA* 1926, pp. 418 sq.

ment of the fleet sailing up the Nile.[361] The importance of control-
ling the crossroads at Memphis was emphasized by the location in
its proximity of the strong fortress of Babylon.[362] The bastions of
this formidable stronghold are paralleled in forts of the 2nd century
on the Syrian and Transjordanian frontiers; [363] it was reconditioned
by Turbo according to a Byzantine source,[364] and constituted the
departure point of the *Traiani Amnis* [365] a transport canal that
linked the Nile with the Mediterranean, and whose use was renewed
by Trajan. It entered the sea by the Pelusiac arm of the Nile, and
command of it would have given the Jews rapid access to Sinai
and to Judaea. Appian's story [366] that the Jews had seized a ship
at Pelusium during the revolt, and that he himself was rescued by
a Roman trireme (i.e. a warship) in the same district—may possess a similar significance. Pelusium had been the seat, in Ptolemaic times, of a Jewish military settlement which was in a position
to hold any army advancing from Judaea and Sinai.[367] The contemporary incidents at Pelusium are therefore to be understood in
the light of the Jewish aim of seizing control of the route from
Babylon to the Red Sea and the approaches to Sinai and Judaea.

The dates of Apollonius' two applications for leave from his
military service have been placed by Fuks between September and
November 117,[368] and according to the *Historia Augusta's* life of
Hadrian, Turbo was appointed to the Mauretanian command in

---

[361] As suggested by C. G. Starr, *The Roman Imperial Navy*, 1960, p. 112.

[362] On the fortress, *JEA* 4, 1917, pp. 174 sqq.; *Antiq.* 4, 1930, pp. 483 sqq.

[363] The fortress generally resembles the fortresses of Odruh, el-Lejjun
(Beth Horon) and e-Dumeh in Transjordan and Syria, which differ from the
Diocletianic forts and those of the subsequent period in the number of their
gateways and their internal arrangements. Ed-Dumeh has yielded an
inscription of the time of L. Verus (AD 162) (R. E. Brunnow, A.von Domas-
zewski, *Die Provincia Arabia*, 1904-1909, III, p. 197); the Roman fort at
'Avdat appears to belong to the same type (plan, *Rev. bib*, 1904, pp. 404,
414), but Professor Negev believed that it was not later than the early 2nd
century AD, and recent excavation seems to have confirmed his opinion.

[364] Johannes Nikiu (Zotenberg), LXXVII.

[365] J. Ball, *Egypt in the Classical Geographers*, 1942, pp. 117, 130; Ptol.
IV, 5, 23.

[366] App., *frag.* 19 (Reinach, *TRJ*, no. 77).

[367] Jos., *BJ*, I, 8, 7, (175): "(Antipater) persuaded the Jewish garrison
guarding the estuaries at Pelusium to let Gabinius pass." (55 BC). It is to
be noted that in the year 48 BC, when invading Egypt, Mithridates of
Pergamum and Antipater capture Pelusium and seize Leontopolis (the
military territory of the Jew Onias) and Memphis (*BJ* I, 9, 3-4 (189-91).
The decisive battle for the Delta takes place at the Ἰουδαίων Στρατόπεδον.

[368] *CPJ* II. no. 443 = P. Giss. 41; *Aegyptus* 33, 1953, p. 150.

the first period of Hadrian's rule.[369] He therefore left Egypt shortly after August, 117, when Hadrian acceded; the following Egyptian prefect, Rammius Martialis, took up his duties between the 11th and the 28th of August in the same year.[370] It is therefore clear that the revolt in Egypt had been put down, for the most part, by August of 117.

The revolt in Cyprus had terminated, as we have seen from epigraphical evidence, at the end of 116 or the beginning of 117.[371] Hadrian must have visited the island personally at the time, for he was governor of Syria in 117,[372] and had been so earlier,[373] and a vexillatio of the VII legion Claudia had been sent to Cyprus from his province, while an inscription proves his personal presence in August, 117 (p. 268); during the same month, however, he was again in Antioch.[374] The VII Cohort of Breuci is known to have taken part in the suppression of the rising [375] together with the detachment from the VII legion Claudia.

In 115, having overrun Armenia, Trajan invaded the country of Adiabene, then Mesopotamia (Aram-Naharayyim). In the winter of that year and in the succeeding year, 116, he turned south, took the Parthian capital of Ctesiphon and reached the Persian Gulf. But at this point a violent and widespread rebellion broke out in the conquered areas in his rear, and Trajan was compelled to retire northward. The three centres of the rising were Seleucia on the Tigris, Nisibis and Edessa in Aram-Naharayyim. His marshal Lusius Quietus reconquered Nisibis; S. Arucius Clarus and Tiberius Julius Alexander subdued Seleucia. The rebellion was put down, but had so weakened the Roman effort that the conquest of Parthia could not be completed, and the Emperor died on his way back to Rome, in August, 117.

Scholars are divided on the question whether the Jewish movement of the years 115-117 also found expression in Mesopotamia, and if it did, whether this was a separate Jewish operation, or one carried out as part and parcel of the rising of the entire population

---

[369] *SHA Had,.* V, 8; VI, 7.
[370] P. Oxy. 1023; Syme. *JRS*, 52, 1962, p. 87.
[371] See p. 269.
[372] *SHA Had.*, IV, 6; Dio. LXVIII, 33 (2, 1).
[373] Dio, LXIX, 1, 2; cf. *JJS* 2, 1950, p. 28.
[374] Dio, LXIX, 2.
[375] *CIL* III (i), 215.

against Rome.[376] Groag [377] thought that there was no connection
between the rebellion of the Mesopotamian population and the
order given by Trajan to Lusius Quietus, according to several
sources one of whom is Dio Cassius,[378] to exterminate the Jews; in
his view this action followed the suppression of the rising. Jerome,
however,[379] explains Quietus' attack by the assumption that the
Jews were already in revolt, an allegation repeated by Pseudo-
Dionysius Tel-Marensis.[380] Alon appears to share Groag's view.[381]
As to the Roman apprehension that the Jews might attack the rest
of the population—this is Eusebius' justification of the Roman
action—it would have been unfounded because the Greek population appears to have been ranged with the Jews in their resistance
to Rome (as Alon saw), as is shown by the rebellion of Seleucia and
the desecration of the temple at Dura, which was treated by the
Roman forces as a hostile town. Alon does however argue, that the
powerful participation of the Jewish population in the fighting
against Rome in Mesopotamia, would have imparted to the insurrection of 116 an outstandingly Jewish appearance, and we
might add that the circumstances of the time would have converted
that community into the spearhead of the resistance movement.[382]

---

[376] For the political position of the Jews of Parthia see J. Neusner,
Iranica Antiqua, III, 1963, pp. 51-6. Neusner sees in the internal political
structure of Parthia factors inducing her rulers to accord a large measure
of autonomy to the Jewish community. If this is correct, it might be reasonable to suppose that the Jews acted as a distinct and separate body in the
rebellion of 116.

[377] *PW* XXVI, 1927, col. 1881, sv. Lusius Quietus (9).

[378] Dio LXVIII, 32, 3; Eus. *HE*, IV, 2, 5; cf. *Suda* (*Suidas*), Adler, I,
p. 400, sv. Ἀτασθαλία; IV, p. 53, sv. παρείκοι; Niceph. Call., *PG* 145, p. 941.

[379] ad Eus., *Chron.* (Helm), XXIX, p. 196. (*PG*, 19, p. 554 ad ann. 2130).

[380] Chabot, I, p. 123.

[381] *Hist. of the Jews*, I, p. 254.

[382] Various views have been expressed on the problems of the relation of
the Diaspora rising with the Mesopotamian rebellion and the relation between
the latter and Lusius Quietus' suppression of the Jews. A few may be cited.
Mommsen (*The Provinces of the Rom. Emp.*, II, (Eng. trans.) 1909, p. 221),
thought that the Jewish movement in Mesopotamia was an integral part of
the general Jewish insurrection. Schürer (*GVJ*[5] I, p. 666) wrote: "The Jews
of Mesopotamia in his (Trajan's) rear also became restive. Trajan commanded... Lusius Quietus... to sweep the insurrectionists out of the
province." Juster (*Les Juifs dans l'Empire romain*, II, 1914, p. 89 nn.) saw
the Mesopotamian movement as part of the entire Diaspora revolt. Graetz
(*Hist. of the Jews*, JPS edn., 1949, p. 397), shared his view, but apparently
believed that Quietus' repressive massacre was a consequence of the rising.
Longden (*CAH* XI, 1936, pp. 249-50) distinguishes between the general
rebellion of the population of Mesopotamia, and the fear of a renewed rising

It were well here to emphasize that history has preserved reports which indicate a very ancient military tradition among the Jews of Mesopotamia and Babylonia. At the end of the 3rd century B.C. Seleucus III transferred 2,000 Jewish families from Babylonia to settlements in Lydia and Phrygia as military settlers, to hold down the rebellious elements of those countries.[383] It was probably in the same years that a force of Jews played an honourable and successful part in an action between Seleucid troops and a force of Gallic mercenaries in Babylonia.[384] Later, in 9-6 B.C.. the Babylonian Jew Zamaris passed at the head of a force of Jewish mounted archers from Babylonia to Syria, and settled near Antioch with the permission of the Roman governor Saturninus. These troops were later transferred by Herod to Golan and Bashan as military colonists in order to reduce to peaceful settlement the predatory inhabitants of Trachonitis (a-Lejja).[385] In the 1st century of the current era (A.D. 10-30), two Jewish brothers of the city of Nehardea on the Euphrates, Hanilai and Hasinai, established a short-lived independent principality in the area, which held out as long as it did by force of arms.[386] It seems possible, moreover, to deduce from Josephus, that the fortified towns of Babylonian Nehardea and Nisibis [387] were held by Jews on their own military responsibility.[388]

It would therefore be natural to suppose that Quietus' exterminatory action, whether carried out before or after the suppression of the rising, was impelled by the success of the insurrection in Egypt in 116, by the intensification of ferment in contemporary Judaea and, not least, by the considerable military potential of Babylonian Jewry.

---

on the part of the Jews, which led to Quietus' repressive action. Abel (*Hist. de la Palestine*, II, 1952, p. 62) connects the action of the Mesopotamian Jews with the revolt of Edessa and Nisibis. Fuks (*JRS* 51, 1961, p. 99) accepts the view that the Mesopotamian Jewish rebellion was part and parcel of the general rising of the whole country. Important as a factor influencing the Jewish attitude to Rome may have been Trajan's plans for reorganizing the caravan trade (in the year 116)—Fronto, *Princ. Hist.*, 1—referred to by Smallwood, *The Jews under Rom. Rule*, p. 411, n. 91.

[383] Jos. *Ant.* XII, 3, 4 (148-53), and see Schalit, *JQR* 50, 1960, pp. 289 sqq.

[384] II *Macc.* 8, 20; for the battle concerned, see B. Bar Kokhba, *Pr. Cambridge Philological Soc.²*, 19, 1960, pp. 289 sqq.

[385] Jos., *Ant.*, XVII, 2, 1-3 (23-31).

[386] *Ant.* XVIII, 9 (310-79).

[387] *Ibid.*

[388] The reference is to Nisibis in Babylonia, not to the Mesopotamian town of the same name.

There are no proofs that any link existed between the Jews of Cyrene and Egypt and those of Mesopotamia during the rebellion or before it. But it may be remarked that the timing of the revolt in the latter country (A. D. 116) coincides, at least where the year is concerned, with the widest spread of the war in Egypt. Yet we may have more tangible evidence that the ideas and aims of the Jewish war in Cyrene, Cyprus and Egypt left their mark and memory on the Jews of the Euphrates valley. I refer to certain elements visible in the wall-paintings of the synagogue at Dura-Europos. We have seen (p. 299) that the Roman forces treated Dura as a conquered city, and the Roman triumphal arch nearby bears witness that a battle took place here during Trajan's advance. The synagogue's third-century wall-paintings embody four general themes, namely, the achieving of independence, the exodus to freedom, the destruction of idolatry, and national rebirth. The upper frieze of the west wall shows the Exodus, and more especially the departure of the Israelites as warriors in array in full hellenistic panoply.[389] The central frieze of the same wall exhibits, among other themes, the episode of the capture of the Ark of the Covenant by the Philistines and its restoration to Beth Shemesh. In one of the pictures [390] is seen the temple of the Philistine god and his shattered image, while fragments of the idols lie scattered over the entire area before the building. These two elements, the departure from exile "with a high hand" as an armed force, and the smashing of the idols, figure so prominently in the rebellion of Trajan's time, that their prominence on the Dura murals is not likely to be a coincidence. In the Diaspora rising of 115-117 the consciousness of these aims as part of the aspiration to national independence, had struck so deep, that their influence was still alive over a century later, and found expression in the mural paintings of the synagogue of Dura Europus.[391]

The epigraphical and literary evidence for the situation in Judaea at the time of the revolt has been surveyed, and they point, in sum, to tension and even to bloodshed, although not to a genuine military outbreak. Some words, however, must be added on certain

---

[389] C. H. Kraeling, *Excavs. at Dura-Europos, Final Report*, VIII, *Part i*, *The Synagogue*, 1956, Plates LII, LIII.

[390] *Ibid.*, Pl. LVI.

[391] Kahrstedt seems to have interpreted the Dura murals in much the same spirit—see his *Kulturgeschichte der röm. Zeit*, 1958, p. 390.

social factors which may have intensified a readiness for revolt among the Jews of Judaea.

The two relevant factors demanding consideration are the absorption of the kingdom of Agrippa II into direct imperial administration, and the general agrarian position. Smallwood [392] has rejected the possibility that the first event influenced the attitude of the Jews of the country, observing that the greater part of Agrippa's kingdom lay outside the areas of dense Jewish population. Recent archaeological surveys may not bear out her assessment,[393] which in any case does not take into account the royal estates in Judaea which Agrippa II would have inherited indirectly from the last Hasmonean rulers.[394] These estates, which corresponded technically to the χώρα βασιλική of the hellenistic kings, were identical in my opinion with the "King's Mountain" (Har ha-Melekh) [395] of talmudic sources, which extended over the entire western area of the mountains of Samaria and Judaea as far as the Darom.[396] These contained several centres which had been foci of the Great Rebellion,[397] and it may be supposed that at the end of it, when Vespasian confiscated considerable areas in Judaea,[398] some tracts in Har Ha-Melekh passed into imperial hands. The change doubtless induced Vespasian to inaugurate various innovations in tenurial procedures, although Agrippa II had remained loyal to Rome. It is very probable that the "King's Mountain" means simply χώρα βασιλική, and when Josephus wrote [399] that Vespasian "kept the χώρα for himself" (to lease out), that the same region was meant. The Mishnah and the Midrashim

---

[392] *Ha* 11, 1962, p. 508, n. 34.

[393] Fifteen ancient synagogues have been identified on the Golan plateau since 1967.—See the *Archaeological News* of the Dept. of Antiquities of Israel, nos. 26, 30, 33, 37, 41, 42, 45 etc. (1968-73). Some of these villages appear to have originated in the 2nd and 3rd centuries AD, but Josephus' evidence of Jewish settlement under Herod (*Ant.* XVII, 2, 2-26 sqq.) indicates a considerable Jewish population from the end of the 1st century B.C. at least.

[394] Cf. Jos., *Vita*, 24 (119); *Ant.* XIV, 10, 6 (207).

[395] A. Büchler, *JQR* XVI, 1904/5, pp. 187-8; Applebaum, *Eretz Yisrael*, VIII, 1967, p. 284 (Heb.).

[396] S. Klein, *Tarbiz*, I, 1930, pp. 136 sqq.; Büchler, *loc. cit.*, pp. 180-8; Z. H. Horowitz, *Eretz Yisrael and her Neighbours* (Heb.), 1923, p. 240; R. Benoit, J. T. Milik, R. de Vaux, *Les Grottes de Murabba'at*, 1961, p. 126; B-Tz. Luria, *King Yannai*, (Heb.), 1961, pp. 39 sqq.

[397] S. Yeivin, *The War of Bar Kokhba*[2] (Heb.), 1952, p. 25 and Map 1.

[398] Jos., *BJ* VII, 6, 6 (217).

[399] *BJ* VII, *loc. cit.*

leave very little doubt that much of the confiscated land was taken
by the so-called *matziqim*, whose precise status may be controversial but whose social and economic impact is clear, for they harassed and oppressed the Jewish peasants who, in so far as they were
allowed to remain, became their tenants. The contemporary
Jewish sources make it clear that they held land from Galilee to
the borders of Nabataea.[400] The tradition that R. Eliezer ben
Harsum, who lived after 70, "had ten-thousand villages in the
King's Mountain and a thousand ships on the sea",[401] though
doubtless hyperbole, nevertheless suggests that the region so
named survived the destruction as an administrative unit. It may
also be supposed that on the transfer of Agrippa II's kingdom to
the Empire on his death (c. A.D. 100), his administration of such
land as remained in royal possession was dissolved, and its work
transferred to non-Jewish officials, a change which may well have
caused a further deterioration in the position of the Jewish subtenants.[402]

If this was the case, the annexation of the kingdom to the Empire
at the beginning of Trajan's reign may have been a factor in the
sharpening of the agrarian situation, nor were the confiscation of
lands, the expansion of imperial estate and the increase of oppressive new landowners (the *matziqim*) restricted to the King's Mountain. The catalogue of the distribution of the *matziqim* occurs in
a document datable on internal evidence at latest to Trajan's

---

[400] *Mid. Siphre, ad Deut.*, Friedmann, p. 357, para. 149. The opinion that
the *matziqim* were *conductores* on imperial domain (Alon, *Hist. of the Jews*,
I, p. 37; Applebaum, *Eretz Yisrael*, VIII, pp. 283-7) cannot be sustained,
since it is evident from rabbinical literature that they had free disposal of
their lands, which they were able to alienate. The midrashim must be
interpreted to mean that they were mainly ex-soldiers and the agents of
Romans who had received grants of land from the Emperor (Cf. *Mid.
Siphre ad Deut.*, Friedmann, para. 317; *Mid. Tannaim ad Deut.*, Hoffmann,
13, p. 193). For a new discussion of the problem, see now Applebaum,
Prolegomena to the Study of the Second Jewish Revolt, (*A.D.* 132-135), 1976,
pp. 10-12.

[401] Jer., *Ta'aniot*, IV, 69a.

[402] Momigliano was certainly right in believing (*Ricerche sull'organizza-
zione della Giudea sotto il Dominio Romano*, pp. 392-3—Annuali della R.
Scuola Normale Superiore di Pisa, ser. ii, II, 1934) that the confiscation of
land did not apply to entire Judaea, and that not all the Jews lost their
holdings. But if our interpretation of the term χώρα is right, in relation to
Josephus' statement that Vespasian kept it all for himself, the confiscated
tracts would have been more than enough to constitute an economic and
social factor of considerable importance.

time but probably of the 1st century, since the reference to Tzoar,
outside the Empire until 106, is likely to be an interpolation.[403]
A comparison of these sources with the distribution of imperial
estates in the country as known from other evidence,[404] confirms
their presence in all the regions mentioned in the Midrashim—in
Galilee, the Plain of Jezreel, Ephraim, western Judaea, Yavneh,
Jericho, 'Ein Geddi, in the Beer Sheba district and in Transjordan.
In addition areas round Jerusalem were confiscated for the use
of the Tenth Legion, and thus became, legally, imperial land.[405]

The agrarian situation created by the confiscations at the end of
the war of 66-73 continued into the reign of Trajan, and is indirectly
reflected in the documents of Ben Kosba's administration found
in the caves of Murabba'at [406] and Naḥal Ḥever.[407] These include
a number of lease-contracts signed between the officials of the
Nasi's administration and various Jews in the time of the restored
Jewish commonwealth (132-135), their subject being the leasing
of plots of land by the Nasi to assignants who thus became lessees
of the government. This evidence makes it clear that Ben Kosba
as secular ruler had taken over considerable tracts when the Roman
yoke was thrown off; these would have consisted of Roman state-
land not till then inhabited by Jews, lands of gentiles who had
fled or been killed, and also Jewish lands whose previous owners
had died without heirs. And although it is clear from other contemporary documents that land existed held by Jews in private
possession, state-domain must have been an important economic
and social factor when the revolt broke out in 132. This, indeed,
can be demonstrated by the centres associated with the outbreak.[408]

Notable events already observed with reference to Judaea
between 115 and 118, therefore, were the reinforcement of the
Roman forces in Jerusalem, the appointment of Lusius Quietus as
governor of the province, and the erection of pagan shrines in the
holy city. On the Jewish side, we hear remote echoes of the pres-

---

[403] *Mid. Tannaim*, Hoffmann, p. 193, 317; *Mid. Siphre de Bei-Rav*,
Friedmann, pp. 317, 354; cf. *Zion*, 22, 1957, p. 81. (Heb.).

[404] *Zion, loc. cit.*, pp. 81-2.

[405] For a summary, Applebaum, *Eretz Yisrael* VIII, 1967, pp. 283 sqq.:
The agrarian question and the Revolt of Bar Kokhba.

[406] P. Benoit, et al., *Murabba'at*, pp. 122 sqq.

[407] Yadin, *BIES*, 26, 1962, pp. 227, 228, 232, 233; *IEJ* 12, 1962, pp. 249
sqq., nos. 43, 44, 45, 46.

[408] B. *Gittin*, 57a.

ence of the Cyrenean leader, Lucuas, in the country, and of the
operations of Lulianus and Pappus, directed, apparently, to the
infiltration of Jews from outside Judaea. Archaeology has further
revealed signs of disorder at Jaffa and Gerasa.

The tradition of *Seder ʿOlam Rabba* [409] places the beginning of
"Pulmus Qitos" in 116, but according to the chronology of the
Parthian War as restored by Longden and others,[410] Lusius Quietus,
after his military successes in Mesopotamia, was appointed to
govern Judaea at the end of 116 or at the beginning of 117. His
consular rank,[411] unusual in a praetorian province, if not the result
of a previous administrative change, hints at the gravity of the situation in Judaea, and perhaps at the presence of more than one legion
stationed in the country to hold down the Jewish population.[412]
A detachment of III Cyrenaica, at any rate, set up an inscription
at Jerusalem not earlier than 116. On the other hand, on the assumption that the revolt had come to a final end in Egypt in August
117, it is to be supposed that Lucuas penetrated Judaea at the
head of the remnants of his warriors latest by summer of that
year. But as the Jewish movement in Cyprus had been liquidated
not later than early 117, we have to place the beginning of the
activities of Lulianus and Pappus in organizing entry into the country and to Jerusalem from Cyprus, in 116. Their capture by Quietus
belongs to the beginning of Hadrian's reign (which began in July,
117) before the execution of the Judaean governor,[413] and the
prolongation of seditious activity in the country after Trajan's
death is confirmed by the *Historia Augusta* [414] and by the tradition
of *Seder ʿOlam Rabba* which sets the end of the "Pulmus Qitos"
in 118.[415]

Among the centres of ferment and revolt may be noted, beside
Bethar and Jaffa, also Darom, the southern region between Eleuthe-

---

[409] Rattner, 30, pp. 145-6.

[410] *JRS* 21, 1931, pp. 2-6; *CAH* XI, 1936, pp. 858-9; Alon, *Hist. of the Jews*, I, p. 251 sqq.

[411] Eus. *HE* IV, 2 etc.; Dio LXVIII, 32, 5; *Groag, PW* XXVI, 1927, col. 1883.

[412] For discussion of the status and forces of Judaea after 70, see n. 248 to p. 300. (Ch. VIII, § v).

[413] Abel, *Hist. de la Palestine*, II, 1952, p. 64; M. Smallwood, *Hᵃ* 11, 1962, p. 504.

[414] *SHA Had.*, V, 2; Libya denique ac Palaestina rebelles animos effere-bant.

[415] Rattner, 30 (see n. 409).

ropolis (Beth Govrin) and the Nabataean frontier. Schlatter [416] and Alon [417] have demonstrated, against the view of Bacher and others, that the killing of R. Ishmael preceded the Ben Kosba war, and both scholars associate the event with the "Pulmus Qitos". If R. Ishmael, who lived at Kefar ʿAziz in the Darom on the Idumaean frontier, was the R. Ishmael put to death with R. Simeʾon, as Schlatter and apparently Alon think, then it is evident that the south of the country was also in revolt or near to it. This is hardly surprising if we recall what Appian relates [418] concerning his flight to the desert near Pelusium, namely, that numerous Jewish rebels were at large in the neighbourhood—i.e. in the Sinai desert.

In summing up, we may propose the following chronological order for events in Judaea in the years 115-118. Ferment began in the country as early as 116, evidently due to the agrarian situation and under the influence of events abroad. Not earlier than the same year, Roman reinforcements were sent to Jerusalem, and active erection of pagan shrines is perceptible. In early 117, if not before, had begun the activity of Lulianus and Pappus, directed to the infiltration of Jews into Judaea and Jerusalem, and at the end of 116 or in early 117 Quietus was appointed governor of Judaea to suppress the rising which had broken out or was likely to break out. We have to place the incursion and death of Lucuas not later than mid-summer, 117, but Lulianus and Pappus do not appear to have been executed before July, 118. We are not in a position to date the supposed outbreak at Jaffa, but it would be natural to see it as the result of the capture of Pelusium by the Egyptian Jews, probably before the Roman victory near Memphis in the first months of 117, which closed the sea-route as a way of access to the coast of Judaea. If our chronological reconstruction is anywhere near the truth, the conclusion becomes reasonable that Quietus was not despatched to Judaea to prevent a rising, but because it had already begun, so that the operations of the Roman commander were directed to restricting its scope and putting it down. The critical moment seems to have been in the earlier half of 117, with the outbreak of disorders at Jaffa and the arrival of Lucuas, if such a break-in ever did take place.

---

[416] *Die Tage Trajans*, 1897, pp. 96-99.
[417] *Hist. of the Jews*, I, p. 262.
[418] App. *frag.* 19; see p. 318.

5. SUMMING UP

An examination of the physiography of Cyrenaica and the factors which moulded her settlement and economy, has shown that the seasonal cycle and the two forms of economy inherent in the conditions of the country have exercized a decisive influence on her history, causing a constant tension and a repeated oscillation between mixed farming and the raising of livestock, between settled agriculture and nomadic pastoralism. The concentration of the Jewish peasantry on the state lands, which were more sensitive than any other category to the results of the above alternation, as most of them were on the desert fringes, open to political vicissitudes and the arbitrary character of the rulers—caused the Jews to suffer to a greater degree than other elements from a reaction in favour of pastoralism and extensive agriculture at the end of Ptolemaic rule and at the beginning of Roman domination.

The process of the restoration of the intensive economy took place in a period of growing conflict between Rome and the Jewish people. Nero's decision concerning tenant rights on the state domain was directed to the advantage of the population which had not suffered in this way, namely, the private landowners, which meant the Greek citizens of Cyrene. The penetration of extremist influence during the Great Rebellion of 66-73 therefore found a fertile field of activity among the multitude of landless and impoverished Jews in the country.

An analysis of the events of 73 at Cyrene has proved important in that it has revealed the close connection between them and activist revolutionary trends that fostered the messianic movement in Judaea; the same events led to the annihilation of the hellenizing class of Cyrenaican Jewry, and thereby prepared the way for the rising of 115, since it left no buffer element between the Jewish masses and activist influence. The points of contact between the acts of Jonathan the Weaver and the ideology of Ḥirbet Qumran, chiefly as it is expressed in the scroll of "The War of the Sons of Light with the Sons of Darkness", prove, with other features of the rebellion under Trajan, the Sicarian content of the movement; Eusebius' reports on the movement's activity in the Western Desert and in the Thebais point to concentrations of insurgents on the desert fringes and to their penetration into Egypt along the desert routes.

But if we are permitted to trace the roots of the revolt in Cyrene to a combination of the Sicarian activist current and economic, chiefly agrarian, conditions implicit in the country itself, does this explanation hold good for all the centres of the movement in Trajan's time? If this is not the case, we are faced with the alternative: either the agrarian situation in Cyrenaica possessed no real importance for the historical episode under discussion, or Cyrene stood at the head of the movement and played the leading rôle in igniting the conflagration. Historical data are in favour of collusion between the Jews of Cyrene and Egypt, more especially in the rural areas outside Alexandria, at least from the time of Lucuas' incursion into the Nile valley. The Alexandrine Jews are referred to explicitly as "the allies" of the Jews of Cyrenaica, although both the historical and the papyrological evidence suggest that the Jews of the city in 116 were not the attackers but the attacked; nor did the Roman authorities treat their remnants as rebels.[419] But this evidence should not mislead us in our assessment of events in Alexandria; the widespread damage shows beyond all doubt that the broad strata of Alexandrian Jewry were drawn into the defensive war against the Roman power by their own violent reaction, and at a certain point of time the initiative passed into their hands (the capture of the Serapeium); we may be sure that the activist element was also present. The Romans, for their part, could permit themselves some clemency at the end of the struggle, or at least a show of compassion towards the miserable remnant.

It is equally erroneous to see in the struggle waged by the Jews of Alexandria with the Greeks of the city for equality of rights between πολίτευμα and πόλις, a factor in the war of 116. It was certainly not a struggle for Greek citizenship. The striving for such citizenship belonged logically to the hellenizing group in Alexandrine Jewry, meaning the wealthy and the well-to-do among them, and was bound up with an attitude that harmonious co-existence with Greek neighbours must be sought by all possible means. The sharp antagonisms between the Jewish masses of Alexandria and their Greek neighbours originated elsewhere and their sources were more complex; the most prominent were the radiation of national influence from Eretz Yisrael, differences of religion and custom,

[419] Alon, *Hist. of the Jews*, I, p. 248; cf. Tcherikover, *The Jews in Egypt*, pp. 163-6.

relations with Rome as a ruling power, and above all, the ethnic-intellectual compactness of the Jews themselves.

The aggressive Jewish movement in Egypt seems to have originated chiefly in the rural districts, hence it may be possible to perceive among its causes an agrarian economic factor. The situation of the Egyptian fellah had always been difficult, and had been in a state of crisis throughout the later period of Ptolemaic rule. Roman administration had not modified his situation in any fundamental fashion. Milne has surveyed the economy of Egypt in the 1st century A.D.[420] in a way which can be summarized as a condemnation of the régime. He observed that the Romans transferred to themselves those lands previously granted to private proprietors, imposed the poll-tax on the majority of the population (especially the peasants), and subjected the merchant-class to an inexorable system of licensing. They confiscated the temple estates in return for an annual grant-in-aid, and thrust the greater number of administrative functions upon Egyptian citizens, who had to discharge them without remuneration. The system of currency introduced by Rome into Egypt was valid only within the province's frontiers, thus affecting adversely its export and import trade. Although the economic position improved temporarily at the beginning of the Roman occupation, thanks to improved conditions of security and order and the restoration of the irrigation system, most of Egypt's production—chiefly her grain—was exported to Rome for her own benefit without requital, while the export trade as a whole was mainly in Roman hands.[421] Milne concludes that "before the end of the first century, the pauperization of the middle classes must have been fairly complete: . . . and, as there was no more to be squeezed out of them, the pressure was transferred to the actual cultivators of the soil."

Bell [422] does not contradict Milne's assessment, and thinks that in the 1st century A.D., after the initial period of prosperity, the members of the Egyptian middle class already faced a burden of taxation beyond their capacity to bear, and that economic diffi-

---

[420] *JRS* 17, 1927, pp. 1 sqq.: The ruin of Egypt by Roman mismanagement.

[421] Also in Jewish hands, according to Milne, but I am doubtful whether the evidence is sufficient to confirm his opinion. It is that of Josephus, *C. Ap.*, II, 64 (Nam amministratio tritici nihilo minus ab eis quam ab aliis Alexandrinis translata est), which hardly favours Milne's statement.

[422] *CAH* X, 1934, pp. 314-5.

culties were now perceptible. Villages which had been evacuated
and abandoned by the flight of their inhabitants are known as
early as 55-60.[423] These data would therefore suggest that in Trajan's day the economic conditions of Egypt were such as to foster
a rebellious mood among certain elements of the population.
Milne explains the clash between Jews and Greeks in Alexandria
partly in terms of the economic situation described. But these
factors applied more especially to the rural areas, and if we cannot
yet point to a real agrarian crisis, growing poverty is perceptible
in the steadily increasing difficulty in finding candidates to fill
honorary official positions in the provincial centres. The elements
of the Egyptian situation, therefore, do not contradict the explanation given for Cyrene, and were equally likely to act as one insurrectionary factor among several.

In Judaea, on the other hand, the agrarian factors are prominent,
and the evidence for them reaches us through the sayings of the
talmudic scholars and the documents of Ben Kosba in a clearer
form than in any other province except Egypt.

Cyprus constitutes a weak link in the approach which sees the
agrarian factor as one of the factors in the Jewish rebellion. Here
the Jewish outbreak assumed no less violent and murderous a
form than in Cyrenaica, yet the proofs of an agrarian element are
slender and almost non-existent. All that can be said is, that the
use of the island's agricultural produce by the Jews of Judaea in
Second Temple times encourages a belief that a Jewish rural population existed in Cyprus, and the little that is known of the extent
of the revolt and the distribution of Jewish archaeological finds,
suggests the presence of Jews throughout the island and that they
were not confined to the cities.

We are therefore forced to conclude, that the agrarian factor
was common to two centres of the rising—Cyrene and Egypt—
(the movement in Judaea did not attain the dimensions of a war,
being faced by an overwhelming Roman force) but the degree of
decisiveness of the factor cannot be proved in Egypt, while the
position in Cyprus is obscure. The decisive universal factor was
psychological—the messianic aspiration derived from the destruc-

---

[423] Thus also Rostovtzeff, *SEHRE* p. 295, and especially *op. cit.* pp. 298,
677, on the situation of the fellaheen. But concerning the deteriorating
position of the middle classes in this period, Milne and Bell do not agree with
Rostovtzeff.

tion of the Temple, and the activist ideology of which the Sicarian is an example, intensified to no small degree by the economic situation. It is to the peculiarity of the conditions of Cyrenaica, however, that we may ascribe specific features of the revolt. In Mesopotamia, on the other hand, the Jewish struggle originated as an organic part of the entire population's reaction to the Roman invasion, although doubtless the influence of events within the Roman Empire was also considerable.

Having examined the impulses at work in the rising, we must consider the nature of its manifestations. These can be divided into three heads: a) the massacre of the gentiles; b) the destruction of gentile temples and images; c) the destruction of the enemy's habitation-centres. The visible traces of the second and third phenomenon are most prominent in Cyrenaica, but are also to be found in Alexandria and Salamis of Cyprus. Allusions to them are preserved with reference to the rural areas of Egypt. The slaughter of gentiles is described by the non-Jewish historians, but chiefly in the *Roman History* of Dio. Xiphilinus, in his abbreviation of Dio, tells how the Jews devoured the flesh of the slain, made girdles from their intestines, and forced their prisoners to fight one another in the amphitheatres.[424] Critics have noted Xiphilinus' general anti-Semitic outlook,[425] and Joel justifiably observed [426] that no account of such atrocities is to be found in any other source, even in Eusebius, who states explicitly that he had drawn on Greek authors writing at a time much closer to the events described, including, very probably, Dio Cassius himself.[427] The mother of the strategos Apollonius nevertheless believed (according to her letter) that the Jews roasted (ὀπτήσουσι) their foes,[428] and the belief may have been influenced by the tendencies of the Egyptians themselves. Polybius,[429] describes the atrocities committed by them upon

---

[424] Xiph., *Epit.* Dio, LXVIII, 32.

[425] K. Friedmann, *Miscellanea di studi Ebraici in memoria di H. Chajes*, 1930: Le fonte per la storia degli Ebrei di Cirenaica nel'Antichità, pp. 52-3; U. Wilcken, *Hermes*, 28, 1892, p. 479; Juster suggests that Xiphilinus' statements are derived from Alexandrian anti-Semitic literature; he thus rejects Joel's view that Xiphilinus' allegations are entirely his own invention.

[426] M. Joel, *Blicke in die Religionsgeschichte*, 1893, II, pp. 153 sq.; 165 sqq.

[427] *HE* IV, 2, 4: "The Greeks who lived at that time reported these things in writing and related them in the same words."

[428] *CPJ* II, no. 437 = P. Giss. 24.

[429] XIV, 12.

their antagonists in times of revolt, from the 3rd century B.C. onward, and the poet Juvenal testifies [430] that they ate the flesh of their enemies. During the rebellion of the Bucoli in the reign of M. Aurelius, their leader Isidorus shared out among the insurgents the flesh of a captured Roman officer.[431] Milne comments on this incident,[432] "that it was an act of ceremonial cannibalism which was typically Egyptian". It is not impossible that some Jews of the Egyptian χώρα had been influenced in the same direction after centuries of residence among Egyptians. But the authenticity even of the above incidents is difficult to assess: we have only to recall Josephus' insinuation [433] (the charge is not directly levelled) that Simon bar Giora *nearly* ate the flesh of his victims, a feature so entirely inappropriate to what we know of that leader, as to be utterly incredible. Only one fact can be stated with certainty on the entire question: the two sides fought savagely and slew without mercy.

The aim of the destruction of pagan cults and images does not constitute a problem if the general objects of the movement are considered. The Maccabees [434] and the activists of 66-70 [435] behaved in much the same fashion. The educated pagan was doubtless equal to doubting whether his cult-images were more than symbols of the deities he worshipped, but the written testimony must be interpreted to mean that the simple Greek and Roman saw in the image the god himself. Plato writes: [436] "We behold the laws of the gods clearly and honour them, setting up images and statues in their honour, and although they are not alive when we worship them, we consider them to be the living gods themselves, who extend to us abundant good will and grace on that account." In case we should think that Plato's words applied only to the 4th century B.C., but not to the 2nd century of the current era, we have the words of Plutarch, priest of Delphi (A.D. 120-146):

---

[430] Juvenal, *Sat.* XV, 93-115; cf. G. Highet, *Juvenal the Satirist*, 1954, pp. 149 sq.

[431] J. G. Milne, *Hist. of Egypt under Roman Rule*, 1898, p. 63.

[432] *Ibid.*

[433] Jos., *BJ* IV, 9, 8 (541).

[434] I *Macc.* 2, 45; 5, 63. For a hellenistic statue at Beth Shean (Beisan) decapitated, probably by the Jews in the reign on John Hyrcanus, (135-104 BC) see *The Ancient Historian and his Materials*, Essays in honour of C. E. Stevens (ed. B. Levick), 1976, pp. 66-7.

[435] Jos., *Vita*, 12 (65).

[436] Plato, *Leg.* XI, 931A.

"As philosophers claim, those who do not learn to understand names correctly misuse things also; like those Greeks who, not having studied, are in the habit of calling bronze objects, paintings and things of stone, not statues or offerings to the gods, but 'gods', and even dare to say that Lachares clothed Athena, and that Dionysius trimmed the golden curls of Apollo." [437]

Even after the middle of the 2nd century A.D., when the Jewish scholars had begun to take a more lenient view of statues, distinguishing between those used for idolatrous worship and those designed for mere ornament—since they no longer feared that Jews would be led astray by images—they nevertheless persisted in their austere attitude to all images of the emperors and all actions associated with their cult. [438] But in the earlier 2nd century they had not yet reached leniency even in spheres outside the imperial cult, and, clearly, the revolutionary activists even less so. Even subsequently, we hear of R. Nahum ben Samai at the end of the 2nd century, who refused to look upon a coin because it bore the image of Caesar. [439] The degree of courage and hostility vis-à-vis the alien power involved in the smashing of the idols is made clear by the testimony of John of Ephesus, [440] who relates that as late as the year 572 the statues of Trajan were still standing in Persia, and the Persians feared to pass by them. But we should not think that iconoclastic actions were confined to the Jews. Occasionally im-

---

[437] *Moralia*, de Is. et Os., 71. E. Bevan (*Holy Images*, 1940, pp. 20 sq.), although stating that there were few people who saw the image as the god himself, adds (*ibid.* p. 23): "Yet it is quite plain that these people did think of the god as in some sense animating the image—animating all the many consecrated images in different places." In proof he cites the custom of clothing the images, and the various stories describing how divine statues moved and gave signs.—Cf. the tale in the "Acts of the Pagan Martyrs" (*CPJ* no. 157 = P. Oxy. 1242) relating to the actual period of the rebellion. On the mechanical animation of statues for magical purposes, a very widespread practice in Egypt, see E. R. Dodds, *The Greeks and the Irrational*, 1963, pp. 292-4.

[438] E. Urbach, Rulings on Idolatry and the Archaeological and Historical Reality, *Eretz Yisrael*, V, 1958, pp. 199 sqq. On this theme see also Saul Liebermann, *Greek and Hellenism in Eretz Yisrael*, 1963, pp. 236 sqq. But Liebermann's discussion is mainly restricted to the outlook of the country's scholars, and does not touch upon the attitude of Diaspora Jewry. He observes (p. 237) that the scholars entirely refrained from attacking the Greek pagan gods; such attacks were engaged in only by the Jews of the Diaspora; see also H. A. Wolfson, *Philo*, 1948, I, pp. 14 sqq.

[439] Jer., *AZ* VII, 42c.

[440] Johannes Ephesi, (Schönfelder), 251-3.

perial statues became the targets of other rebels in times of revolt. Thus we find at Bath in Britain an inscription of the 2nd or 3rd century, which reads: Locum religiosum per insolentiam dirutum virtuti et n(umini) Aug(usti) repurgatum reddidit C. Severius Emeritus centurio reg(ionarius).[441] Plutarch too, after the extract already quoted, proceeds to refer to "the statue of Zeus Capitolinus which was burnt and destroyed in the civil war." [442] The *Res gestae Divi Augusti* tell us that M. Antony plundered numerous dedications, including statues, from the temples of Asia, although this desecration did not reach the point of destroying the images themselves.[443]

The destruction of gentile settlements becomes increasingly clear as the excavation of the city of Cyrene progresses, and details amounting to a comprehensive picture of what occurred in the province have been assembled above. The work of destruction embraces most of the country, despite the defectiveness of our information on various settlements. The picture at Alexandria and Salamis is similar. It is hard not to see in this destruction, more especially in Cyrene and Cyprus, judging by the number of casualties which occurred there, the result of a premeditated plan, and the systematic character of the demolition at Cyrene (e.g. the felling of the internal columns of the Temple of Zeus and of the peristasis of the Temple of Apollo) does not dispel the impression. Both this writer and Professor Fuks [444] have put forward a reason for this work of destruction: it was a corollary of the determination to abandon the lands of the Diaspora and to concentrate in Eretz Yisrael. But it was also directed against certain factors, and the question is, against which?—The Greeks, the Romans, or all idolators indiscriminately? Many scholars tend, relying on ancient sources, to see the Jewish effort as directed first and foremost against the Greeks.[445] Their view finds support in the texts of

---

[441] R. G. Collingwood, R. P. Wright, *The Roman Inscriptions of Britain*, I, 1965, no. 152; *CIL* VII, 45.

[442] *Moralia*, De Is. et Os., 71; cf. Tac., *Hist.*, III, 71, 19-20.

[443] E. G. Hardy, *Monumentum Ancyranum*, 1923, pp. 108-9, ch. xxiv (IV, 49-51); cf. Dio LI, 17; Strabo, XIII, 30 (595); XIV, 13 (637).

[444] *JRS* 51, 1961, p. 104.

[445] Cf. J. M. Jost, *Gesch. der Israeliten*, III, 1822, pp. 221-5; Tcherikover, (*The Jews in Egypt*, p. 178) sees the movement as directed primarily against the Greeks; Fuks too sees its beginning in Alexandria and Cyprus as a clash of Jews and Greeks (*JRS* 51, p. 102); cf. Lepper, *Trajan's Parthian War*, p. 92. But Xiphilinus, *Epit.* Dio, LXVIII, 68 says explicitly: "The Jews from the vicinity of Cyrene . . . exterminated the Romans and the Greeks."

Eusebius,[446] Orosius,[417] and Syncellus.[448] There is no doubt, of
course, that a great proportion of the victims of the events in
Cyrenaica, Cyprus and Alexandria, were Greek-speakers, because
they were the inhabitants of the urban centres where the revolt
raged most violently. But the revolt blazed up also in the Egyptian
countryside, and in two places at least we hear of collisions between
the Egyptian villagers and the Jewish insurgents.[449] In Alexandria
the rising appears as a continuation of the constant clashes between
Greeks and Jews which were a recurrent phenomenon during the
1st century A.D., but this does not prove that only the Greeks were
the objects of Jewish hostility. We do not hear, for instance, of
the spread of the movement to Greek Asia Minor, where anti-
Semitism had manifested itself in the early days of the Empire,[450]
and an anti-Jewish literature existed much like that in Egypt.[451]
In Babylonia, as emerges from the revolt of Seleucia against Trajan,
Jews and Greeks shared a common front against Rome. We must
therefore conclude that only in the Hellenic-Roman cities was the
Jewish onslaught directed against the Greeks, as they were the
majority, and because the Jewish urban communities were concentrated in the hellenized cities of the eastern Empire. But the
leaders of the insurgents must have known perfectly well that they
had no prospect of defeating the Greeks, or any other community,
without colliding with the Roman power. The very scope of the
rebellion shows that the movement made no distinction between
Greek and Roman, hence its purpose was to destroy not only the
pagan cults, but also the Roman government. It is hard to think,
however, that the insurgents hoped to overthrow the entire Roman
Empire at one blow; their immediate objective seems to have been
Eretz Yisrael. This is the meaning of the Cyrenean Jewish advance
upon Egypt, their struggle for the Delta junction at Memphis,
Lukuas' break-in to Eretz Yisrael, and Lulianus' and Pappus'
organization of Jewish infiltration from Cyprus to Syria and Judaea.
It may indeed be supposed, on the evidence of the Apocalyptic

---

[446] *HE* IV, 2, 3; *Chron.* II, 164 (*PL* II, 554 (346-7); *vers. Arm.*, p. 219.
[447] VII, 12, 6.
[448] I, 657.
[449] *CPJ* nos. 438, 450.
[450] Jos., *Ant.*, XVI, 6, 4 (167-8); 6, 6 (171); XIV, 10,8 (214); 10, 16
(234); 10, 21 (244).
[451] The anti-Jewish writer Apollonius Molon, born at Alabanda in Caria,
was active in Rhodes.

literature, that the ingathering of the exiles to Eretz Yisrael was regarded as a precondition of the messianic kingdom. This aim, inspired by expectation of the Messiah, is expressed in its clearest form in an Egyptian-Jewish source—in the writings of Philo Judaeus,[452] who says: "And even if (the Jews) are slaves at the ends of the world under the enemies who have led them captive—at one signal and in one day all of them shall be freed, and their unanimous conversion to virtue will strike their masters with amazement . . . and when this unexpected liberation comes, they, who were originally scattered over Greece and the barbarian lands, over islands and continents, shall arise with one impulse, hastening from all quarters to the destination shown to them, with a divine insight beyond the power of human nature, invisible to others and visible only to them, as they pass from exile to their mother-land . . . and as they go, the ruins shall become cities again and the ravaged land shall become fruitful."

The reasons for the failure of the rebellion remain to be examined. The rebel forces were doubtless far inferior to the Roman in military qualities, training and discipline. But their ability should not be underestimated: the evidence already summarized indicates that the Cyrenean insurgents probably underwent a period of physical and military training in the desert regions for a number of years, and the possibility should not be discounted that a number of Egyptian Jews received similar training. Nor should it be forgotten that no small part of the Jews of Egypt and Libya were cultivators whose forefathers had served for generations in the Ptolemaic armies and had earned their livelihood as military settlers under the same dynsties. The Libyan Jews' march across the desert from Cyrenaica to Egypt itself testifies to physical endurance and organized morale. The route had been traversed in ancient times by the armies of Egypt (Apries) and Persia—twice in the reign of Arkesilaos II (see pp. 26-7), —also by the forces of Magas and Euergetes II. In that period the coastal plain was better settled than it is today; the winter rain collects in rock-basins, and ancient cisterns are to be found in considerable numbers along the coastal belt.[453] The season would also have facilitated the march, for Lucuas' men moved on Egypt in the rainy season of the early months of 116. In 1805 an American force 600 strong under the

---

[452] Philo, *de poenis et praemiis*, XXVIII-XXIX (165-6).
[453] O. Bates, *The Eastern Libyans*, 1914, pp. 6 sqq.

command of Captain William Eaton made the march from Alexandria to Bomba in eastern Cyrenaica, albeit with much privation, in thirty days.[454] The overthrowing of the inner columns of the Temple of Zeus and of the outer peristasis of the Temple of Apollo in the Sanctuary of Cyrene, required technical skill,[455] and implies a degree of organized effort exerted on a considerable scale. The general impression is, indeed, that the Jews of Libya acted as the spearhead of the entire movement. Unlike them or the Jews of the Egyptian countryside, on the other hand, the Jews of Alexandria lacked a military tradition and probably had received no moral preparation for the struggle; they were the attacked, not the attackers, and their combat methods were probably those of men experienced in rioting and street-fighting.

In the light of the events we have portrayed, therefore, we may conclude that it was the Jews of Cyrene and the Egyptian countryside who acted in a coordinated fashion according to a prepared plan; the same is perhaps to be assumed with regard to the Jews of Cyprus, but we know nothing of their military conditions. It is still more difficult to determine whether some sort of coordination developed between the Jews of Cyrene and Egypt on the one hand, and those of Cyprus on the other.[456]

---

[454] Bates, op. cit., p. 13; for a bibliography of the journey, Dictionary of American Biography, 5, 1930, sv. Eaton, William, p. 613.

[455] The columns of the peristasis of the Temple of Zeus at Cyrene are now known to have been overthrown in the Christian period (see p. 352), but the inner columns of the naos suffered in 115-117. For the Temple of Apollo, whose outer columns were overthrown in 115-117, see p. 275.

[456] The question arises whether the naval monument in the agora of Cyrene which takes the form of a warship's prow surmounted by a female figure, commonly thought to be Nike, has any connection with the Jewish revolt. The monument was found in 1929, but its base was located only during the excavations conducted after the Second World War (Stucchi, Cirene 1957-66, p. 87). The figure surmounting it was discovered by the American expedition of 1910, and the location of the base established that the figure belonged to the same monument. Unfortunately authorities have differed greatly as regards the statue's date and identity; dates vary from the hellenistic period to the 1st century A.D. (For the references, see Stucchi, op. cit., pp. 87 sqq.). Opinions on the identity of the figure range between Nike, an Aura, Athene and Athene-Nike. Since Stucchi wrote, Caputo (PP 23, 1966, pp. 232 sqq.) has suggested that this is an Augustan monument commemorating Actium. The following however may be stated: 1) Structurally the warship's prow is not pre-hellenistic, and could well be Roman. 2) Its structure bears a considerable resemblance to the ancient clay models of ships' prows common in prehistoric Cyprus. (L. P. di Cesnola, Cyprus, 1877, p. 259). A possibility therefore exists that the naval victory commemo-

If we endeavour to formulate the strategic object of the Jews of Cyrene and Egypt, then, it was directed to achieving two aims: first, the liquidation of lesser resistance at the enemy's weakest point, Cyrene, and the establishment of contact with the strongest Jewish centre outside Judaea, that is, Egypt, which was also a vital crossroads and the base of Rome's corn supply. The aim of the second stage was to annihilate with united forces the Roman garrison of Egypt, which had been weakened in 115-116 by the despatch of a detachment of the III legion Cyrenaica to Mesopotamia and Judaea.[457]

The second stage of the Jewish plan was the most crucial, as on its success depended the insurgents' ability to capture Alexandria and to seize control of the sea, in order to pass on swiftly to Eretz Yisrael. The Jewish victory in Cyrenaica may have given the Jews control of the adjacent sea, if Apollonia was taken, while, as we have noted, the revolt perhaps affected Jaffa, and Jews seem to have crossed from Cyprus to Syria and Judaea. But such control of the sea would have been far from complete, as witness the fact that most of the insurgents reached Egypt from Cyrenaica by land across the desert.

It may be supposed that the inhibiting factor was the Roman fleet—the classis Alexandrina, stationed at Alexandria.[458] The capture of the city would have enabled the Jews to close the sea-ways and cut off the corn supply, so starving the capital of the Empire. The fighting may indeed have affected this supply adversely for a period, since an inscription [459] commemorates *T. Flavius Macer, curator frumenti comparandi urbis factus a divi Traiano*

---

rated was connected with Cyprus and was won in the Roman period. A connection with the Jewish revolt is not therefore beyond the bounds of credibility, but further evidence is needed.

[457] See A. Kasher, *Zion* 41, 1976, pp. 127 sqq., (Heb.), on the question of the despatch of Roman forces from Egypt to the Parthian campaign (especially pp. 130-32). The evidence is not impressive, concerning chiefly the whole or part of III Cyrenaica and the Ala Augusta. It is difficult to estimate the Roman garrison's strength at the time of the rebellion; in 83 it included two legions, three alae of cavalry and eight cohorts of infantry, four of which were *equitatae*, (Lesquier, *L'armée rom. d'Égypte*, pp. 103 sqq.), totalling some 17,500 men. Under Hadrian, after the removal of the two former legions and their replacement by one legion only, the garrison consisted, according to Cheesman's estimate (*The Auxilia of the Roman Army*, 1914, pp. 163-4) of 2,500 cavalry, 750 mounted infantry and 10,950 infantry.

[458] *CIL* II, 1970 etc.

[459] *ILS* 1435; *CAH* XI, 1936, p. 213, n. 2.

Augusto, which may reflect a corn shortage in Egypt known to have existed in 99, but might equally have been the result of measures taken due to the war situation between the years 115-118. But the Jewish plan to capture the city of Alexandria, if it existed, was frustrated, and this was the vital failure of the rising.

The Jews of Alexandria did not seize the initiative when the moment was ripe, perhaps due to the opposition of their comfortable classes; doubtless they were also influenced by the proximity of the Roman garrison and by memory of past failures.

The failure in Alexandria produced two grave consequences: the Jewish advance upon Judaea was stopped, and the Roman forces in Syria were able to mount a counter-attack by sea at a time chosen by themselves. The rebels' plan required the swift liquidation of the imperial forces in Egypt—in order to concentrate as large as possible a force in Eretz Yisrael for the decisive struggle with the principal Roman armies. This aim explains the consistent Jewish policy of annihilation carried out towards the Greeks and Romans equally, and the method of "scorched earth" followed in Cyrenaica and Egypt, the object of which was to leave no effective opposition in the rear. A sea-crossing would have ensured the success of this operation, but Alexandria remained untaken and the battle for the Delta crossroads near Memphis ended with defeat. Further, the resistance in the remaining districts of Egypt exceeded what was anticipated. Fighting continued along the entire Nile valley in the form of local engagements, and it would seem that the insurgents failed, due to the great distances over which the struggle was waged, to concentrate enough force at one point to bring the contest to a decision before the legions advanced to join the battle. Characteristic of this situation was the far-flung fighting between the two remote poles of Memphis and the Thebais, —if the latter theatre may be regarded as the outcome of an attack by activists who had crossed from Cyrenaica by the oases of the western desert. This division and dispersion of the rebel forces must be counted among the factors of the Jewish failure.

The movement in Trajan's reign reveals, where inner class-relationships are concerned, certain common features with processes in Judaea in the years 66-70. To judge by the premature outbreak in Alexandria in October, 115, and by the passive attitude of the Jewish population of the city till it was attacked by the Greeks in 116, most of the wealthier class stood aside from the revolt, whereas in Cyrene, the elimination of the hellenizing upper group in 73 had opened the way for the radicalization of the Jewish masses and their adherence to the revolutionary movement. While the Jewish upper class in Jerusalem and Judaea did revolt in 66, it did so because it was swept away by the more powerful current of the social revolution—which was intimately connected with the extremist and Zealot trends—and was destroyed as a result. At that time the wealthy of the Diaspora in Alexandria and Cyrene recoiled from rebellion; in Egypt they collaborated with Rome to bring the extremists to book. In the Diaspora revolt in Trajan's time, they stood aside, but were nevertheless overwhelmed and destroyed.

It may be doubted whether there ever arose in the early Roman Empire any movement which so imperilled Roman authority as did the Jewish Diaspora revolt in the reign of Trajan. No one of Rome's subject peoples had risen in active rebellion on this scale, and none was both located within and without the imperial frontiers and distributed over several important provinces of the Empire itself. Nor do we know of any instance of so extensive a degree of cooperation between various communities which were both within the Empire and hostile to it. The aid given by the tribes of southern Britain to the peoples of northern Gaul in Julius Caesar's time preceded the principate,[460] and if the Dacian king Decebalus was in correspondence with the king of Parthia in order to strengthen his position against Rome,[461] he did not succeed in forming an effective military alliance.[462] Tacitus, writing not long before the Jewish rebellion, could express his satisfaction at the disunion and fratricidal strife of the Germans, and pray "that this mutual hatred persist and continue among the peoples if they cannot love us, since ... fate can grant no greater boon than the quarrels of our enemies." [463] It remains but to add that the Parthian kingdom, for all its internal weaknesses, was the only power within reach of the Roman Empire capable of measuring up to her, and therefore constituted a constant threat to Rome; scanty as is our knowledge of the relations between the Jews of the Empire and Parthia during

---

[460] Caes, *BG*, IV, 20.

[461] Plin., *Ep.* X, 74.

[462] Debevoise (*A Political History of Parthia*, 1938, p. 217), thinks that the mailed cavalrymen seen on Trajan's Column may be Parthians, in which case Pacorus aided Decebalus by actually sending military assistance.

[463] Tac., *Germ.*, 33.

the period of 115-117 or immediately before, it is hard to refrain from supposing that the Jews saw in Parthia a potential ally, and that the Parthian rulers were ready to exploit Jewish hostility to Rome in the event of a military confrontation.

Jewish tradition saw the rebellion of Ben Kosba as a continuation of the Diaspora rising,[464] and even if this is incorrect, it is clear that the events of 115-117 influenced the outlook of Hadrian, who ascended the imperial throne a short time after the *tumultus* had passed its height, and had previously taken part in its suppression in Cyprus. From Trajan he doubtless derived his estimate of the Jewish people as an important factor and a grave problem bearing on the safety of the eastern frontier. This attitude was also affected by his sympathy for hellenism, which inclined him to see the Jews of Eretz Yisrael as an element which marred the integrity of hellenism in the east. The *tumultus*, the last great collision between Jews and Greeks in the hellenistic and Roman periods, must have made a deep impression upon him, and may have decisively influenced his decision, fifteen years later, to transform Jerusalem into a citadel of Graeco-Roman civilization.

The revolt's failure led directly to the destruction of the three important Jewish centres of Cyrene, Egypt and Cyprus. The archaeological evidence in Cyrenaica can be interpreted to indicate the renewal there of Jewish settlement as early as the 3rd century, but the supposition needs further confirmation.[465] Jewish communities existed in Cyprus, according to inscriptions, by the 4th century, when the decree prohibiting Jewish entry appears to have been forgotten. Papyrological material in Egypt conveys that "Jewish life in the country was completely paralysed"; [466] only in the 3rd century do we hear again of evidence for the existence of

---

[464] Yeivin, *Bar Kokhba*[2], pp. 42, 66; *Seder 'Olam R.*, Rattner, 30.

[465] An epitaph from Ptolemais, the style of whose letters seems to belong to the 3rd century, is Jewish (*NAMC* I, 1915, p. 152, fig. 52). It is also possible that Jewish influence went to the making of the heresy of Sabellius, who lived at Ptolemais. (Cf. Bonaiuti, *Nuova Antologia*, II, 1950, p. 183). In the 4th century Jewish ships were plying between Alexandria and Cyrene (Synes. *Epp.* 4). Cf. also Antiochi monachi, *de insomniis*, (*PG*, 89, col. 1692): ἔρχεται εἰς Παλαιστίνην καὶ ἀπῆλθεν εἰς Νοάρα καὶ Λιβύαδα, τὰ ὁρμητήρια τῶν Ἰουδαίων. I am indebted for this reference to Drs. B. Jones and P. Llewelyn of the University College of North Wales, also to Professor Anthony Birley, who sent it to me.

[466] *CPJ* I, p. 94 (Prolegomena): "The general impression is that of a complete breakdown of Jewish life in Egypt."

a Jewish population consisting of more than scattered individuals.[467]
The annihilation of these three large communities may well have
intensified national feeling in Eretz Yisrael—one case at least is
known of a Cyrenean Jew who fought among Ben Kosba's warriors [468]—but had not these Diaspora centres met their end under
Trajan, they might have furnished vital assistance to Judaea's
war against Hadrian; their ruin doomed the second revolt to failure
before it had begun.

As a result of the rising (Pulmus Qitos) the scholars of Eretz
Yisrael prohibited the teaching of Greek to the younger generation.[469] The prohibition, indeed, did not last, if it was ever rigor-
ously applied—and some recent scholars have ascribed to it no more
than qualified application—for the family of Rabban Gamliel
"permitted the teaching of Greek to (its) sons because they were
associated with the Roman government"; [470] by the early 3rd
century many epitaphs were being written in Greek in the great
cemetery of Beth Shea'rim. But this did not mean that the Kultur-
kampf of Judaism and hellenism was at an end; it merely died
down, and revived in different form in the struggle between Judaism and Christianity in the 4th century.

The failure of the rising also terminated the period of the active
onslaught of Judaism as a missionary religion proselytizing among
gentiles outside Eretz Yisrael. The collision symbolized by the confrontation of the God of Israel and the god Serapis,[471] no longer
takes political form, except perhaps when imperial statues are
smashed at Tiberias in the following century.[472] On the other hand,
it is not impossible that the defeat under Trajan caused the expansion of Jewish influence over the African continent. The report
of the judaization of Libyan tribes in the Aurez Mountains of
Algeria lacks, apparently, reliable evidence, and it is not easy to
prove that Jewish influence in western Africa originated in the
flight of Jews from Cyrenaica westward before and after the revolt.
Yet archaeology permits no doubt that reciprocal influences were
at work between Libyan Jewry and Libyan-speakers in the 1st

---

[467] *Ibid.*
[468] Yadin, *IEJ* 11, 1961, p. 46, no. 11 (Naḥal Ḥever).
[469] M. *Sota,* IX, 12; cf. S. Liebermann, *Hellenism in Jewish Palestine,* 1950,
pp. 100-101.
[470] *Tos. Sotah,* XV, 5
[471] P. Oxy. 1242; cf. Musurillo, *APM* pp. 162 sqq.
[472] Jer., *AZ,* IV, 43.

century of the current era, and the conclusion to be drawn from
Jonathan the Weaver's departure to the desert, which hints at the
dispersal of extremist elements on the fringes of the Sahara, and
derives confirmation from the instructive analogies of Ḥirbet
Qumran and the work of the Sanusi order in Cyrenaica in the
present century—assists the credibility of an influence exerted
by the insurgents upon the nomadic Libyan tribes and even of
active cooperation between them. The result of such influence is
likely to have been the spread of Judaism over north and central
Africa after the rebellion's failure.[473]

The Jewish activist movement found its last expression in the
rebellion of Ben Kosba. But where the Diaspora was concerned,
R. Simeon bar Yoḥai's words on the massacre of the Jews of Egypt
by Marcius Turbo sum up the situation: "In that hour the horn of
Israel was torn out, and will not return to its place till the son of
David comes." [474]

---

[473] J. Basnage, *Hist. des Juifs*, 1716, VII, p. 185; Marcier, *Hist. de l'Afrique
Septentrionale*, 1888, I, p. 137; for a criticism of these views, Hirschberg,
Jour. of African Hist., IV, pp. 313 sqq.

[474] Jer., *Sukk.* V, 55b.

APPENDIX

A Brief Bibliography of the Archaeology of the Pentapolis Cities

For an exhaustive bibliography of Cyrenaican archaeology 1962-1972, see M. Vickers, *JHS Archaeological Reports* 1972-3.

The periodicals *Quaderni dell'archeologia Libica*, Rome, 1962-7, and *Libya Antiqua*, Tripoli 1964- should also be consulted.

Cyrene

AI 1-7, 1927-40 passim.

Enciclopedia dell'Arte antica, I, 1958, sv. Cirene.

R. G. Goodchild, *Cyrene and Apollonia, a Historical Guide*, Tripoli, 1959.

——, *Kyrene und Apollonia*, Zürich, 1971.

R. Mingazzini, *L'insula di Giasone Magno a Cirene*, Rome, 1966.

L. Pernier, *Il tempio e altare di Apollo a Cirene*, Bergamo, 1935.

E. Pesce, *BCH* 71-2, 1948/8, pp. 307 sqq.

A. Rowe, D. Buttle, J. Gray, *The Cyrenean Expedition of the Manchester University*, 1952. I, Manchester, 1956; II, 1959.

R. M. Smith, E. A. Porcher, *A History of the Recent Discoveries at Cyrene*, London, 1864.

S. Stucci, *L'agora di Cirene*, Rome, 1965.

——, *Cirene 1957-66*, Tripoli, 1967.

Apollonia

R. G. Goodchild, *Cyrene and Apollonia.*

— —, *Kyrene und Apollonia.*

Encip. dell'Arte antica, I, 1958, pp. 482 sq. sv. Apollonia.

AA 1962, pp. 431-2.

AJA 70, 1966; 71, 1967.

Berenice (Euesperitae)

R. G. Goodchild, *Benghazi, the story of a city*, Shahat, 1962.

Antiq. 26, 1952, p. 210.

Libya Antiqua, 3, 1965, pp. 91 sqq.

NAMC I, 1915, pp. 74 sq.

Barka

NAMC I, 1915, pp. 110 sq.

Ptolemais

F. H., H. W. Beachey, *Proceedings of the Expedition to Explore the North Coast of Africa*, London, 1828.

C. H. Kraeling, *Ptolemais, City of the Libyan Pentapolis*, Chicago, 1962.

G. Pesce, *Il palazzo delle colonne in Tolemaide di Cirenaica*, 1950.

Teucheira

AJA 1913, pp. 191 sqq.

DAI, II, Cir. ii, 1936, pp. 39 sqq.

Boardman, Hayes, *Excavations at Tocra* 1963-5. BSA Supplementary Volume IV, 1966.

Libya Antiqua, I, 2. 1964, 1965.

PEJ 1963, pp. 22 sqq.

SH 7, 1961, pp. 27 sqq.

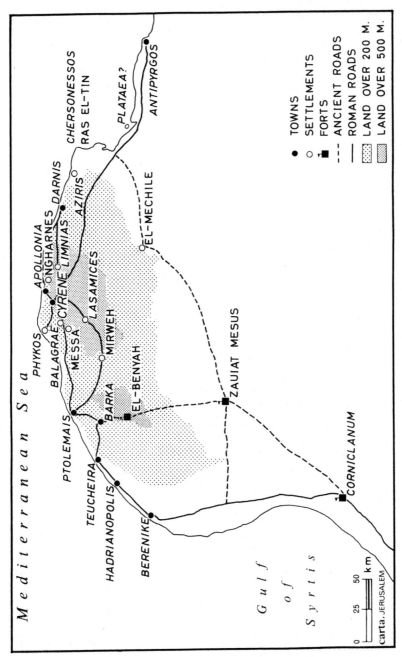

Map 1. The cities and settlements of ancient Cyrene.

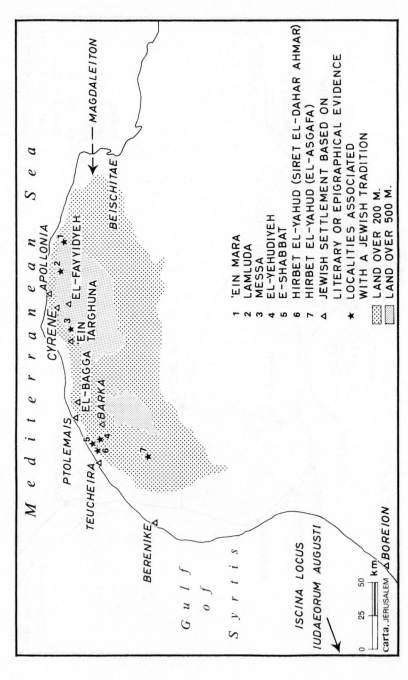

Map 2. Jewish settlement in ancient Cyrene.

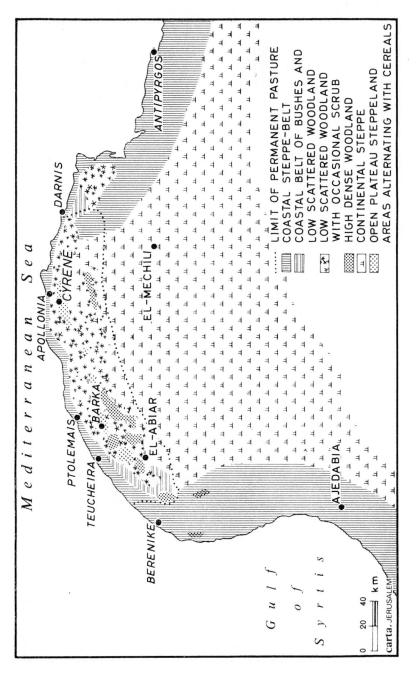

Map 3. Cyrenaica—natural vegetation.

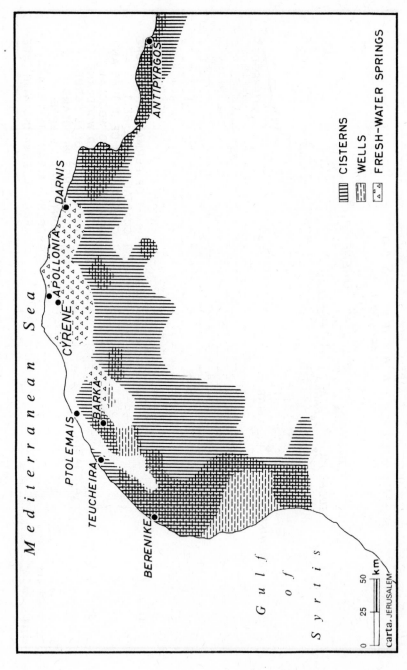

Map 4. Cyrenaica—the Water Supply.

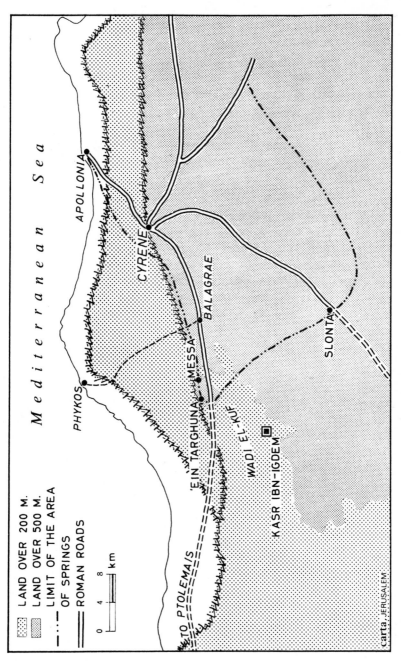

Map 5. The geographical setting of ʿEin Targhuna.

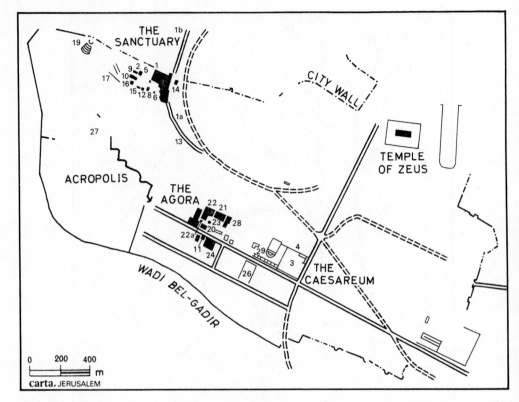

Map 6. The city of Cyrene. Structures damaged in the Jewish Revolt.

Key to Map 6

1. Baths.	15. Temple of Apollo Nymphagetes.
1a. Roman milestone.	16. Temple of Isis.
1b. Road to Apollonia.	17. Fountain of Apollo.
3. Caesareum.	19. Theatre.
4. Basilica.	20. Temple of Apollo (Agora).
5. Temple of Hecate.	21. Stoa of Zeus.
6. Prothura.	22. Augusteum.
7. Temple of Dioscuri.	23. Tomb of Onymastos.
8. Temple of Pluto.	24. Prytaneum.
9. Temple of Artemis.	26. The House of Jason Magnus.
10. Temple of Apollo.	27. Roman Buildings in Acropolis.
12. Temple of Apollo Ktistes.	28. Shrine over the Tomb of Battus.
13. Sacred Way.	29. Monumental Portico.
14. North Gate of City.	

INDEX